The New Wedmore Chronicles

Hazel Hudson

Best wishes

Hazel

Published by Hazel Hudson 2002

Published in 2002 by
Hazel Hudson
Bempstone Hundred
Wedmore
Somerset BS28 4DU

ISBN 0-9543983-0-0

Designed, printed and bound by
Direct Offset, 27c High Street, Glastonbury, Somerset BA6 9DR

© Hazel Hudson, 2002

Hazel Hudson asserts the moral right to be identified as the author of this work.

All rights reserved. No part of this publication may be reproduced, stored in a retrieval system or transmitted, in any form or by any means, electronic, mechanical, photocopying, recording or otherwise, without the prior permission of the publisher.

Front Cover:
R Morden, Map of Somersetshire, for W Camden's Britannia (1695/1715);
Wedmore Church from the southeast, Wedmore Chronicle *vol I (1887)*
Wedmore Board School Class, 1893; William Eyre's letter 1801.

For my Grandchildren
Georgina and Laurence

Acknowledgements

Many people have helped me over the years, but I would specially like to thank Mick Aston, Michael Costen, Vince Russett, Steven Minnitt, David Bromwich, archivists at Somerset Record Office, especially Steven Hobbs, who formerly worked there. Thanks also are due to the people who have provided and/or taken photographs, my husband Bill and daughter Ruth Lucy, Richard Neale and Kathleen Curtin. Illustrations nos 14, 36, 37, 46, 49, 65, 67, and 79 are reproduced by permission of Somerset Archive and Record Service; documents from the Wells Cathedral Archives are reproduced by permission of the Chapter: and drawings 64 and 66 by kind permission of Roy Millward. A debt of gratitude to the many more people who have also lent me photographs and documents, shared reminiscences, and allowed me to poke around their private property!

Finally, but most importantly, a heartfelt thank you to Frances Neale, colleague and friend. Without Frances I would never have started on my quest to find out more about the place where I live. Together, we have trudged over fields, pored over documents, written articles and given talks. Her advice and editorial skills has made it so much easier putting together this book. After 25 years we still get a thrill in making new discoveries and piecing together the time jigsaws of Wedmore's history.

Hazel Hudson
2002

Contents

	page
Acknowledgements	4
List of illustrations	7
Location map	9
Map of the Isle of Wedmore, after S.H.A. Hervey (1887)	10–11
Introduction	13
The Reverend S.H.A. Hervey	

1 **Villages Old and New** 15
    Place names in the Parish
    New villages
    Lost settlements
    Two vanished Tudor villages

2 **Parish Road Names** 28
    Wedmore
    Road names around the Parish

3 **Wedmore Manor and its Manor House** 47

4 **St. Mary's Parish Church, Wedmore** 57
    A busy day in Wedmore Church, 1350
    In Wedmore churchyard

5 **Wedmore Borough** 63
    Markets and Fairs

6 **Wedmore Houses** 69
    People and houses in The Borough
    Two house plots in The Borough: Jobs & Drakeshay
    Minstrels Gallery and Lloyds Chemist
    The Old Vicarage and Buoys Cottage, Wedmore

7 **Ancient Landscapes** 88
    The search for King Alfred's Palace at Mudgley
    Alexander of Mudgley's farm 1220
    Theale landscape: The Battle of Kyppmerwalle

8 **Ancient Landmarks** 100
    Ancient stone crosses
    The manorial pounds
    Holy wells and other springs
    Crossroad elms and boundary trees

9 **The Mills of Wedmore Parish** 109
    Watermills
    Windmills
    A miller's diary

10 **Local Industries and Transport** 126
    The Wedmore Gas Company Ltd.

Wedmore Electric Light and Power Company
Wedmore Brick and Tile Works
A Wedmore Tannery
The Highbridge, Wedmore & Cheddar Light Railway
Wedmore's first bus service
The Wedmore Cheddar Cheese School

11 Schools **147**
Early Schools in Wedmore
Hannah More at Wedmore
Early schools in Blackford and Theale
Wedmore Board School
Theale and Bagley Close Board School
Blackford Board School
Hugh Sexey and Sexey's School, Blackford

12 Chapels **171**
Wedmore Methodist Chapel
The Mission Chapels of Wedmore
Church v Chapel, 1891

13 People **181**
Jeremy Horler and Ann Hodges: a Civil War love story?
Wedmore and the Monmouth Rebellion, 1685
John Tucker of Blackford, 1770-1779
The story of Mary Hardwick, 1752-1813
Joseph Stickland, 1773-1824: an apprentice and his descendants
The Reverend William White, 1793-1867
Richard Lyde Stott, 1816-1899: the Bard of Wedmore

14 The Wrong Side of the Law **207**
The Wedmore Riot, 1885
A village burglary in 1909
The Tin-Pot Band

15 Wedmore in Wartime, 1939–1945 .... **219**

16 A Field Name Alphabet: A–Z **229**

17 Lost and Found **250**
The Wedmore coin hoard
Stray finds
The lost letter
Another lost letter

18 The Vicar and the Dinosaurs **259**

Postscript **261**

Notes and References **262**

Abbreviations **274**

Bibliography **275**

Measures **276**

Index **277**

Illustrations

R Morden, Map of Somersetshire, for W Camden's Britannia (1695/1715);
Wedmore Church from the southeast, Wedmore Chronicle vol I (1887)
Wedmore Board School Class, 1893; William Eyre's letter 1801. .... front cover
Location map of the Isle of Wedmore 9
The Isle of Wedmore after the Revd S.H.A.Hervey 10–11
The Reverend Sydenham Henry Augustus Hervey 12
View of central Wedmore, looking north, c1960 15
A pair of cottages in Clewer, c1900 16
The Panborough Inn, c1930 17
Centre of Blackford, looking east, c1910 17
Latcham Farm, 1998 20
Looking down Church Street, Wedmore, c1960 30
Grants Lane, c1930 30
Cottages in Guildhall Lane or Guilo, c1950 34
Wedmore Manor House from the church tower, 1880 47
Wedmore Manor House west front, 1900 49
Memorial brass of George Hodges, 1634. 51
Signature of Jane Strachey, Lady of the Manor, 1675 52
Memorial to John Barrow, Lord of the Manor (d 1853) 56
St Mary's parish church, Wedmore, c 1900 57
Interior of St Mary's 1880, before restoration 59
Tombs in St Mary's churchyard 61
Aerial view of The Borough, Wedmore, 1953 64
The Portreeves, Arthur Duckett and Harry Godfrey, c1953 66
The Borough, Wedmore: Medieval Burgage plots 70
The Borough Court of Wedmore 1717, from a lantern slide 71
The Borough, Wedmore: later development 72
The Borough, Wedmore, looking north, c1960 74
Holdenhurst, c1900 76
The shop and house built by John Tonkin, now Lloyds Chemist and Minstrels Gallery, c1900 78
John Tonkin the younger, c1885 79
The Old Vicarage, Wedmore 81
Buoys Cottage 85
Plan of excavations at Court Garden, Mudgley, 1878 89
Original photograph of part of the excavations of the Dean's House, Mudgley, 1878 91
Wedmore Market Cross from C Pooley 100
Wedmore Churchyard Cross from C Pooley 101
Stoughton Cross from C Pooley 102
Wedmore manorial pound, 1953 103
Days Mill, Enclosure Map, 1791 112
Signature of John Westover junior (1645-1706) 113
Heath House Mill with William Tucker miller 117
William Tucker, miller (c1859-1902) 118

Entries from William Tucker's diary, 1886 123
James and Mary Batten at the Gasworks, c1910 126
Plan of Wedmore Gasworks, 1918 127
Gas receipt from Wedmore's Gasworks, 1894 128
William George Burrough (1876-1940) 130
Stamps on Wedmore bricks (1901-6) 138
Map of the proposed Highbridge, Wedmore and Cheddar Light Railway, 1899 141
Inaugural trip of the G.W.R. steam omnibus, April 6th 1905 144
Hannah More (1745-1833) 148
Part of the resolutions of 1799, opposing Hannah More's school in Wedmore. 150
Blackford Old School, built 1832 152
Theale National School, built 1864 153
Wedmore Board School, c1900 154
Wedmore Board School class, 1893 155
Bagley Close Board School, c1900 159
Sexey's School, Blackford, 1899 169
The Farm School, 1913 170
Wedmore Methodist Chapel, built 1817 172
Richard Drake baker, 1889 174
The Reverend James Goudie, 1889 175
Floods in Tealham Moor, 2000 175
James Cavil, blacksmith, 1889 175
Turf worker's cottage, c1900 176
Blakeway Methodist Chapel, now a barn. 177
The Hodges memorial, St Mary's, Wedmore 181
Signature of Jeremy Horler, 1685 183
Chandelier in St Mary's, Wedmore 187
Signature of Mary Hardwick, 1787 192
The Sticklands' work book, October 5th 1899 196
George Stickland and family outside their house in Grants Lane, 1897 197
Theale Church, c1900 200
Richard Lyde Stott, the Bard of Wedmore, (1816-1899). 204
Barnards in The Borough, Wedmore, with Victor son of Sidney Redman, c1936 208
The New Inn, Combe Batch, Wedmore 209
William Parker, blacksmith, c1908 214
The Cheddar Times February 27th 1909 215
Wedmore Patrol 203 Battalion, Home Guard Auxiliary Unit, 1944 221
Keith Puddy off to Wedmore School 223
Wedmore W.V.S. Netting Team, 1944 227
Wedmore field names in a Highway Rate book, 1818 230
Silver penny of Cnut (1016-35), found in Wedmore Churchyard 1853. 250
Bronze Age torcs found at Heath House 1846. 253
Saxon ring found in Wedmore 253
Wedmore public house tokens, 19th century. 254
William Eyre's letter, 1801 255
Solomon Wall at Stonesteps, c1930 257
A Wedmore dinosaur as visualised by Dr Bracey 260

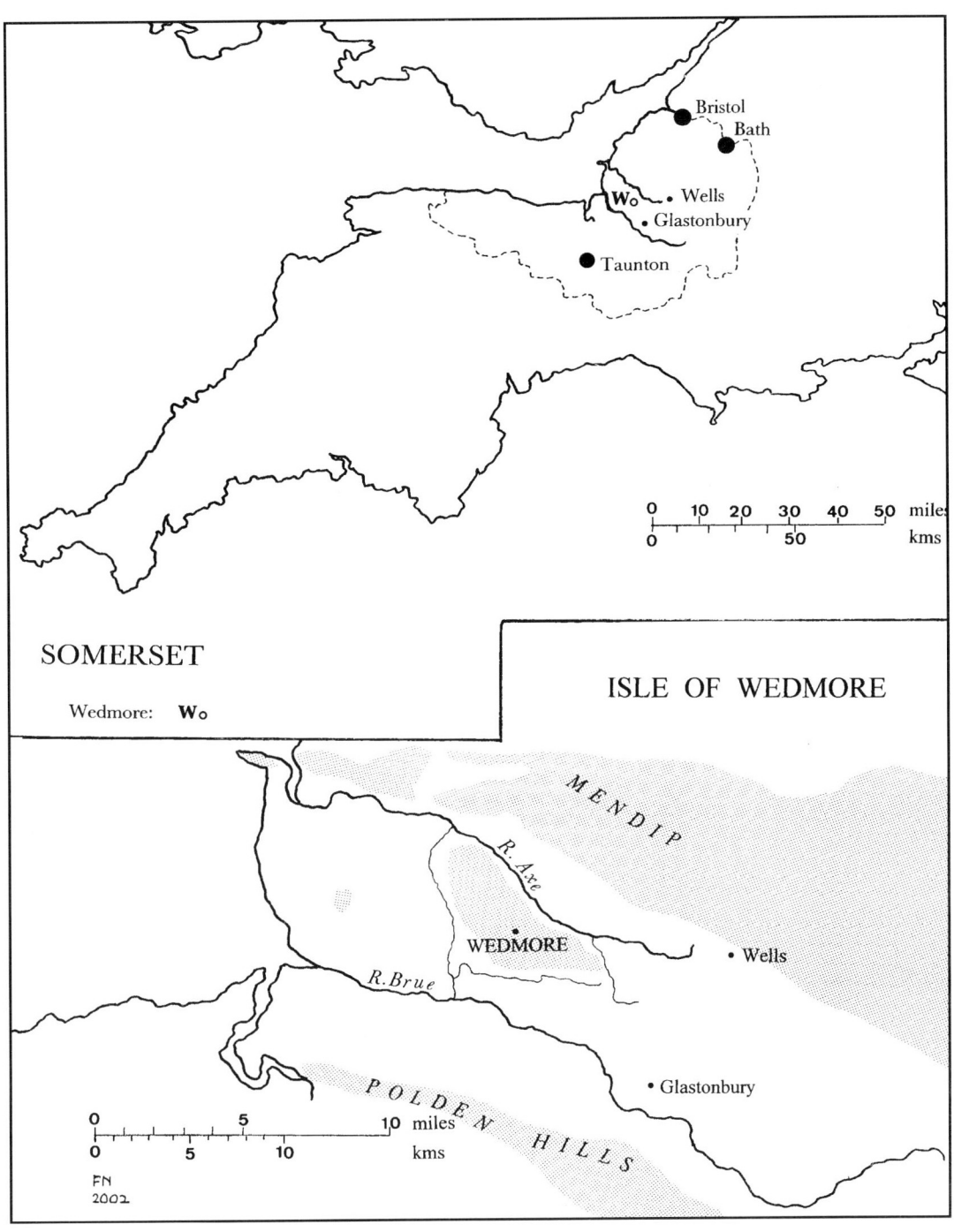

Location map of the Isle of Wedmore

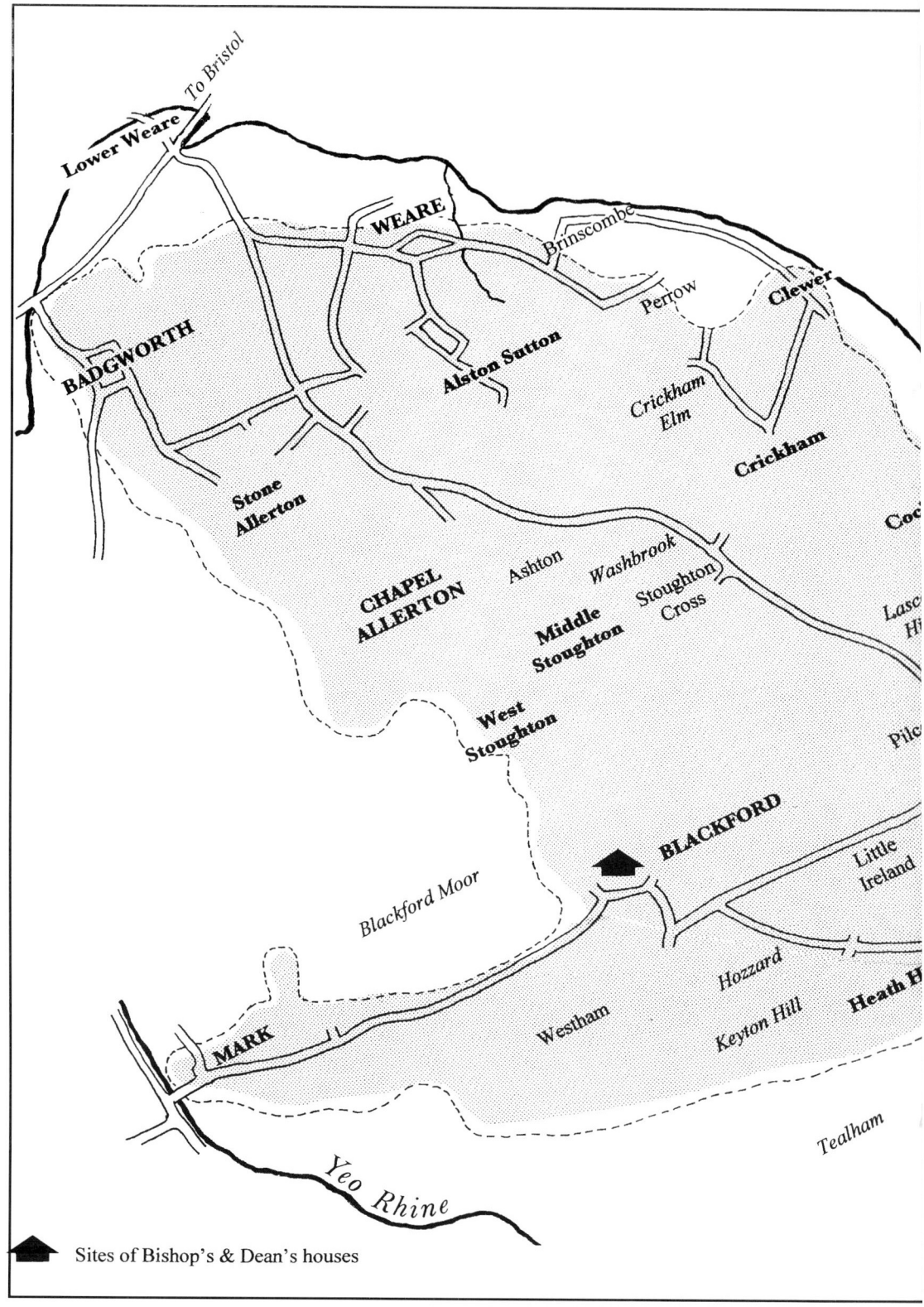

The Isle of Wedmore after the Revd S.H.A.Hervey,

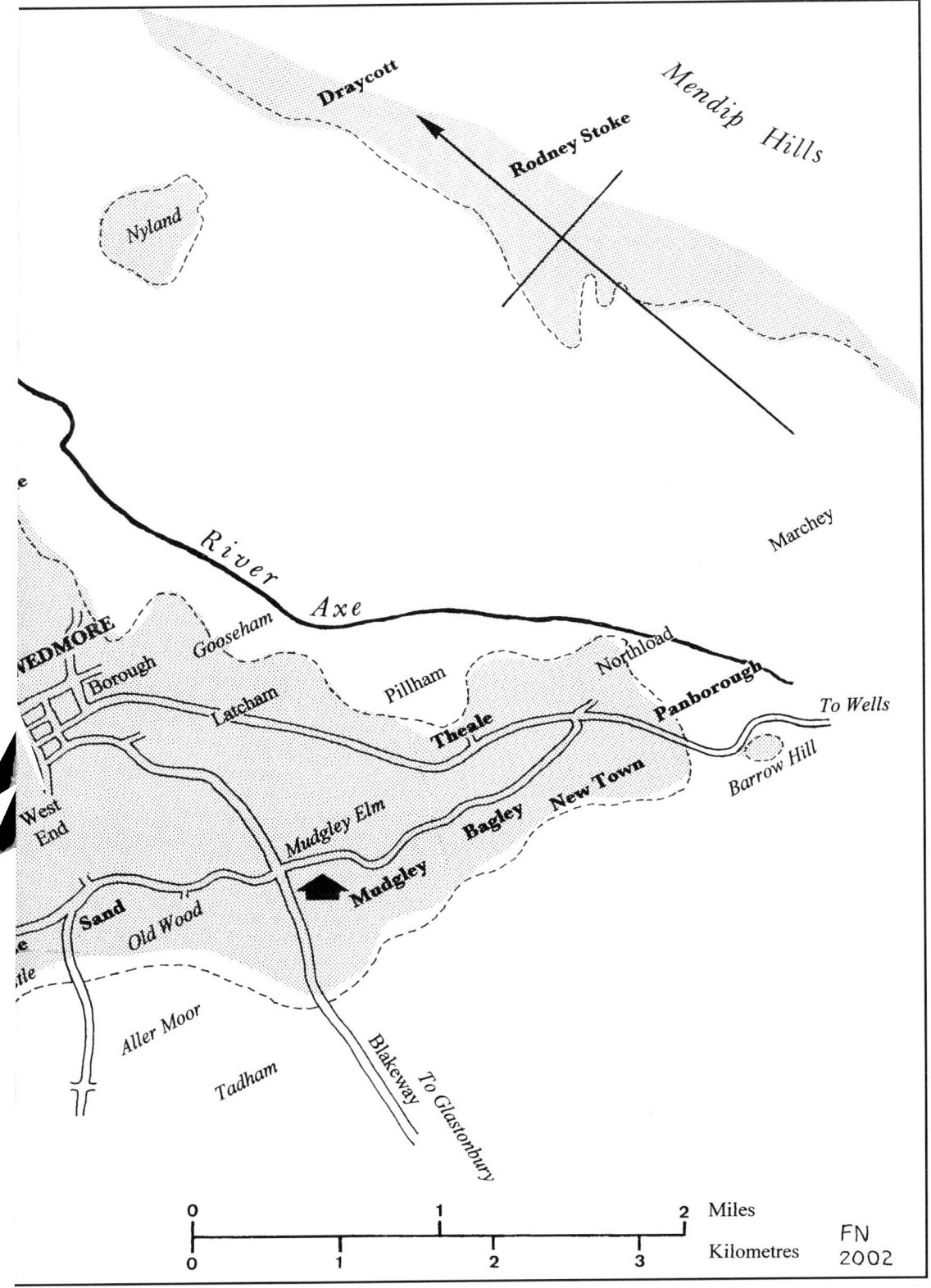

Wedmore Chronicle *vol I (1887) facing page 360*

The Reverend Sydenham Henry Augustus Hervey
Vicar of Wedmore 1876-1898
Author of the original Wedmore Chronicles *(1880-1898)*
The cover of this book echoes the familiar red of Hervey's books.

Introduction

In 1989 I was asked to write something with an historical flavour for the *Isle of Wedmore News*, the monthly parish magazine. These articles, called 'The New Wedmore Chronicles', eventually reached one hundred by 1997, and reflected various aspects of my interest and research; a few were written by request. They were not written as a complete history of the parish.

The Reverend S.H.A. Hervey

My inspiration in writing these articles was to continue the work of the Revd S.H.A. Hervey, Vicar of Wedmore 1876-1898. He produced the *Wedmore Chronicles* between 1880 and 1898. The original idea was to publish them every two months as a parish church magazine. Each issue was to be divided into two parts. The first part was to include parish and church business; marriages and deaths; political meetings and cricket matches. The second part was to contain articles on the history of Wedmore and its inhabitants, plus two pictures or photographs. The first issue was an opportunity for Hervey to describe his excavation of the Dean's house at Mudgley in 1878. The magazine soon became sporadic; the original paper-back copies are quite rare, as many were bound into the two red hardback volumes, familiar to and still highly prized by Wedmorians. They have proved a mine of information for everyone who has since studied the history of Wedmore. The articles, and now this book, follow in his footsteps, and describe some more recent discoveries and ideas.

The Revd S.H.A. Hervey was a bachelor, the third son of the Bishop of Bath and Wells, who was himself a younger son of the Marquis of Bristol. He was born in 1846, educated at Eton and Cambridge, ordained in 1869, and after acting as curate in several parishes, he was presented with the living of Wedmore by his father the Bishop in 1876. He had other interests besides history, including bell-ringing, music, choral singing and cricket. He appears in many of the formal group photographs of these and other village organisations, mostly taken outside the Vicarage (now the Old Vicarage) or in the Church porch (see *Wedmore Past* and *More Wedmore Past*). He organised the restoration of the church in 1880/81, and encouraged his wealthier parishioners to contribute the present stained glass windows, made by the leading manufacturers of the day; his mother gave the window in what is now the vestry. His strong Liberal views did not, however, endear him to most of the parish. His Vicarage windows were deliberately smashed in the riot of 1896. He retired from the parish in 1898, aged only 52, after his father had died. Harvey had been an obedient son but perhaps a reluctant cleryman, as his private and unpublished diary seems to indicate.[1] He spent the rest of his life in Suffolk, pursuing his antiquarian and historical interests. He always maintained an interest in Wedmore, keeping in touch with Mrs Joan Connelly, daughter of his favourite churchwarden Arthur Wall. He died in his 100th year, in 1946 - a remarkable link between our historic past and the present.

Much of Hervey's historical work has lasting value, such as his practice of copying out many of the documents which were kept in St Mary's Church in those days. He also published, as separate volumes, the Baptism (1560-1810), Marriage (1564-1810) and Burial (1854-1860) Registers of Wedmore. Hervey looked at Wedmore wills kept at the Probate Registry in Wells in the 1880s. These were moved to Exeter Probate Registry in the early

1900s - only to be destroyed during a bombing raid in World War II, so Hervey's notes are all the more valuable as they are all we now have of those Wedmore wills of long ago. Hervey also collected local gossip and reminiscences, along with local folk tales; some of these he kept in his private papers - perhaps too sensitive to publish at the time! Some of his ideas are, however, outdated today and we can now, over a hundred years later, reassess and correct the historical record with the results of more recent researches.

'The New Wedmore Chronicles' as published in the *Isle of Wedmore News* had no footnotes; these have now been added to make the sources of my research more available. Some editing has been done to bring a few articles up to date, and to put together groups of articles which had originally been published many months apart.

Much of this research would have been impossible without the help and interest of my fellow Wedmorians. Sadly many of these have since died, but their memories will live on through this book.

Chapter 1
Villages Old and New

Place names in the Parish

First of all we will look at some of the place names in the parish, and their meanings. Wedmore is a large parish with three main villages, Wedmore, Theale and Blackford; and fifteen hamlets. The meaning of a name may give an insight into its origins, although people have been living in many of the settlements long before the name by which we know them today came into being.

WEDMORE is first mentioned in a 12th century reference to a lost Saxon Charter[1] which was dated between about 676 and 685 AD. In this charter Centwine, King of Wessex, gave Bishop Wilfred (a famous Saxon missionary bishop) a sizeable estate on the *'insulam de Wethmor'* - so it was the 'island of Wedmore' from earliest recorded times. The 'island' rising out of the moors is still completely ringed by rivers and streams, but it was rarely an actual island surrounded by water. Flooding could be sudden but was infrequent, for the low-lying moors were farmed even in Roman times.[2] The moors have been drained since the late 18th century, but the name 'The Isle of Wedmore' survives as a general term for the whole hill area of the parish and the villages on it - as in the *Isle of Wedmore News* and The Isle of Wedmore Society.

View of central Wedmore, looking north, c1960

The Saxons gave Wedmore its name. *'Wethmor'* is Old English, meaning 'the hunting moor'.[3] There were prehistoric and Romano-British people living on the island long before the Saxons arrived, but what they called it we shall never know.

Wedmore belonged to the Saxon kings and was part of their great estate, which included the Royal Forest of Mendip. 'Forest' in this context means a hunting area, not necessarily densely wooded. Wedmore was on the southern edge of the Forest. Perhaps this good hunting ground was one reason why King Alfred brought the defeated Danes to Wedmore in 878 AD for twelve days of celebrations, to mark the Peace of Wedmore.[4] There was a plentiful supply of deer, wild boar, and other animals to be hunted, for their amusement and their feasts.

Two other places in the parish are also mentioned in Saxon charters, Clewer and Panborough.

CLEWER is first mentioned when King Centwine, between about 676 and 685 AD, also gave Bishop Wilfred a small estate at Cliwere.[5] In Domesday Book, written in 1086 AD, it appears as 'Cliveware'. This name in Old English means 'the dwellers at the cliff'. Viewed from the north-west the cliff rises dramatically from the low lying moors, and one can see why the Saxons gave it this name. The usual spelling of Clewer from the 16th to 19th centuries was Cluer, but the modern spelling first occurs in 1550.[6]

A pair of cottages in Clewer, c1900, now demolished

PANBOROUGH first appears in a Saxon charter of 956 AD when King Eadwig confirms that Glastonbury Abbey holds land at Patheneberg.[7] This estate was part of what is now Panborough.[8] In the 10th century Panborough included the distinctive hill now called Barrow Hill, which was moved into the adjoining parish of Meare a century later. The Old English 'Patheneberg' is thought to mean 'the wayfarer's hill', from *patha* - a wayfarer, and *bergh* or 'barrow' - hill. 'Barrow Hill' thus means 'hill-hill'. Coming across the moors from Glastonbury, Barrow Hill was a prominent landmark for which the traveller would look out. So far I have collected over forty different spellings of Panborough, all ending with variants of 'berg' or 'barrow'. It seems that it was the local surveyor and map-maker William White, in 1779, who first spelt it 'Panborough', giving the name the appearance of an entirely different and mistaken meaning.[9]

Villages Old and New

The Panborough Inn, c1930

With some place names their meaning is obvious - they are words we still use today. Others are surprisingly tricky to understand, and even the experts cannot be sure of their meaning.

BLACKFORD makes its first appearance in Domesday Book, 1086 AD - or does it? Glastonbury's estates are listed and include a 'Blacheford' or Blackford. But there are two villages in Somerset called Blackford; the other one is near Wincanton. Both were held by Glastonbury Abbey about this time. Experts disagree over which Blackford is meant in Domesday Book. However, in a survey of Glastonbury lands made in 1189 'Blakeford' in Wedmore appears as a large and thriving settlement of over fifty families.[10]

The name Blackford is Old English, using words we still use, so that the meaning is instantly clear - the crossing or ford which is black. When the Saxons named Blackford, they noticed that the usual brown soil was black around the ford. The soil had become black from the rubbish and humus of earlier settlers. Some of these were Romano-British people, as I have found pieces of pottery from this period at Blackford. There were at least four fords crossing Blackford Brook in the village, in medieval times. The ford in the centre of Blackford was

Centre of Blackford, looking east, c1910

finally bridged over in the 1980s, so that the meaning of its name is now part of its past history.

SAND is another Old English word still meaning just that - sand. It takes its name from the sand outcrop about 2 metres thick on the brow of the hill and extending almost to Blackford. The northern edge of this sandy soil used to be visible at the Wedmore end of Madwomans Lane. The earliest mention of Sand occurs in a document dated about 1219 when Alexander of Mudgley and David, a peasant, both had land 'in Sonde' (see Chapter 7).[11]

HEATH HOUSE is also a place name made up of words we still use and understand. Before about 1500 the usual description of the unenclosed, uncultivated moor with its vegetation of gorse, ling, rough grasses and light brushwood, was 'the Hethe'. By about 1219 Robert Malherbe is cultivating land next to 'La Hethe'.[12] From 1543 onwards the little settlement on the dry hill slope just above the moor becomes known as 'Heath House' - the house(s) by the heath or moor.[13]

In contrast to these straightforward place names, Westham, Crickham and Latcham all end in the word 'ham'. In fact, there are two different Old English words: *hamm* meaning low lying, enclosed meadow land, usually by a river or stream; and, more rarely in this area, *ham* meaning village or homestead, which became our present-day 'home'. A detailed knowledge of the place and its history is needed to distinguish between the two, and even then one cannot always be certain of the truth.

WESTHAM is first mentioned by name as late as 1555,[14] although from other evidence we know it has much earlier origins. In 1555 'Westham' is spelt as it is today, so there is no clue in the spelling as to whether it is a *hamm* or a *ham*. Westham is a settlement on the edge of the moor, so it could well be a *hamm*, referring to the important hay-meadows along the edge of the moor. On the other hand, it is the westernmost of the line of small settlements and farmsteads along the southern slope of the hill. In particular, it lay west of the oldest and most important settlement of Mudgley. The Manor of Mudgley in fact extended through Sand and Heath House, to include Westham Farm at its western limit. The rest of the settlement took its name from this, probably the oldest, farmstead - so it might be the western ham or homestead. Although most of Westham was part of the adjoining Manor of Blackford, it lies south not west of that village. Mudgley thus seems to have been the dominant influence in its naming and its early history.

CRICKHAM is first written down in 1562 as 'Creckham'.[15] Its shape, and the fact that it is up on the hill away from any river or stream, suggests that this might be a *ham*, meaning a village. But what does 'Crick' - or 'Creck'- mean? It may well be *cruc* from the Old Welsh or Celtic, meaning a prominent hilltop (as in Crook Peak), so that Crickham might be simply 'hilltop-village'; but it hardly looks a very prominent hill! It could possibly be a distortion of Old English *cirice*, a church. In medieval times Crickham was the centre of the Manor of Churchland - but there is no evidence of any church ever existing there; the church in question was Wells Cathedral, to which it belonged. It could well be the *ham* or farmstead of a Saxon called something like 'Creck', of whom we shall never know anything because there are no surviving early records. One tantalising clue to the existence of a much earlier settlement there, is the fact that in 1609 part of the open field was called 'Blackland'.[16] This was near the present village and 'Blackland' is a name which always excites the archaeologists as it usually indicates the dark soil resulting from the rubbish and debris of early human habitation, often Romano-British or even Iron Age.

LATCHAM first appears in the 12th century, when in 1176 Pope Alexander III confirmed that the Dean of Wells held 'Lecham' along with several other places on the Isle of Wedmore.[17] In 1378 the house at 'Lacheham' was in need of repairs.[18] This ancient farmstead may have occupied a site farmed since Roman times, to judge from the quantities of Romano-British pottery that have been found nearby. It was probably on the same site as present-day Latcham Farm, just off the main road. The 1791 parish map of Wedmore shows Latcham Farm and two wayside cottages, probably farm cottages, either side of the farm entrance.[19] Both the cottages have now disappeared. The rest of Latcham as we know it today, stretching along the road, did not exist before the early 1800s.

What does Latcham or 'Lecham' mean? The setting makes it very difficult to decide whether the -ham part of the name is *hamm*: an enclosed meadow lying next to the moor; or *ham*: homestead. The antiquity of the farm suggests that *ham* is perhaps slightly the more probable. 'Lech' or 'Lach', now Latch-, might be from Old English *lacu*, meaning a small stream. Streams were usually called lakes (as in Cocklake, to be discussed later); and what we now call a lake was in Somerset called a pool or mere. Although there is little sign of any stream today, a stream did bubble down the hill slope and across the road near Ratcliffe Bros Garage, formerly Dunnicks Mead Garage, before meandering through the moor to meet the River Axe. Where the main road at Latcham crossed this stream, a nearby field was called 'Stenning Bridge' as far back as 1543.[20] This means a 'stenning' or 'stoning', a cobbled fording-place, with a narrow bridge alongside for foot-travellers.

Latcham could, alternatively, be derived from a personal name: Lec's homestead (or meadow). Latcham, in turn, certainly gave its name to the Latcham family, which had many branches living in the parish until recently. The favourite family name, over three hundred years, was William. There are so many William Latchams living at the same time that it is difficult to disentangle the family tree. Most of the Latchams were upright, honest yeomen and artisans, taking prominent positions in village life. I have however, found a William Latcham who was not such a pillar of society.

At the beginning of the 19th century William Latcham was born, one of three children of Philip and Hannah Latcham. They lived at Blakeway, and were one of the poorer branches of the family. On 18th August 1827 at the age of 26, William was arrested for burglary and taken to Ilchester Gaol.[21] In the register of felons, he is described as 5 foot 6 inches height, with dark complexion, grey eyes and sandy hair. William was sent for trial at the Lammas Assizes, and was found guilty of burgling a dwelling house in West Pennard. The sentence was pronounced - death.

Looking through the Ilchester prison records one sees that it was very unusual at this time for the death sentence to be passed for burglary. However, at this particular assizes the judges were Sir WD Best and Sir J Burrough. Lord Chief Justice Best stated that: 'the prevalence of the crime of burglary had at length rendered an awful example necessary and that example he was determined to give in all cases where the guilt was clearly established.'[22]

Although the prosecutor recommended mercy, the death sentence was passed for theft of coins, plate and even for stealing a pair of boots. What William stole is not reported, and there are no details to suggest he committed an 'aggravated' burglary. Most of the prisoners sentenced to death were later reprieved. Their sentences were commuted to transportation, for life or for between seven and twelve years. Transportation here would not have been to Australia or the West Indies. For most it meant transportation to rotting captivity hulks, old warships beached, mostly after the Napoleonic wars, and used as prisons in Devonport or Woolwich - a fate probably worse than death.

Not so William Latcham, who was hung on 12th September as an example, along with three other burglars.[23] His body was buried the same day in Ilchester churchyard. His mother Hannah lived on at Blakeway to the age of ninety-nine - a long time to suffer such disgrace and sadness to the family name of Latcham.[24]

So three Wedmore places with names which appear rather similar, have quite different meanings; and even an insoluble puzzle can raise interesting questions about the early history of our villages.

Latcham Farm, 1998

The Saxon estate of Panborough later became the Manor of Northload. The place name **NORTHLOAD** now only exists in Northload Farm, which was the 'manor house' of the estate. The actual Lord of the Manor was the Abbot of Glastonbury, and Northload Farm was occupied by a tenant. The 'load' in Northload comes from Old English *lad* or lode, usually meaning the way to a river crossing. So Northload could be the way north from Panborough and Bleadney, to cross the River Axe. The earliest reference to it by name occurs in 1189 when 'Ralph of Northilade' lived there and paid 30 salmon as rent.[25] Northload remained a farmstead on the lane going down towards the river.

THEALE first appears in a document of 1176 when it is written as 'Thela'.[26]

As Theale developed it spread along the road from Wells to Wedmore. The part in the

Northload estate was called East Theale and belonged to Glastonbury Abbey, and the part that lay in adjoining Wedmore was called West Theale, and belonged to the Dean of Wells. The boundary between Northload and Wedmore crossed the road at the junction with West Well Lane. In medieval times West Well was called Theale Well, an important water source which until this century bubbled out and ran down West Well Lane. The name Theale is from Old English *thelu*, meaning plank or planks. This well could have made the road muddy or slippery, and traffic might have polluted the drinking water, so perhaps planks were put down as a simple causeway giving Theale its name.

COCKLAKE is written as 'Coklak' in 1310.[27] The -lake ending comes from the Old English *lacu*, a stream as in Latcham. The stream must be the one which formed the road called The Dungeon, now only a trickle of its former self except in times of flood. The first part of the name is a puzzle. It could be from Old English *cocc*, a cock bird; or *cocc* meaning a heap or hillock, as in haycock. Finally, it could be from a personal name 'Cocca', meaning Cocca's stream.

Whatever the true meaning, this 'stream village' nestles on the edge of the hillslope above the River Axe into which the stream eventually flows. It overlooks the moors abounding in remains of Romano-British fields and canals. Without earlier documentary reference and finds of pottery in Cocklake, it is impossible to say when the village was first settled. With so many Romano-British remains nearby, it seems highly likely that the Romans were living at Cocklake, as in every other moor-edge settlement in the parish. But we need hard evidence of this - literally, in the form of pottery fragments.

STOUGHTON consists of three separate settlements, spread out along the road for over a mile. West Stoughton first appears by name in 1675,[28] Stoughton Cross in 1747[29] and Middle Stoughton was not so called until 1847.[30] Before that they were called, collectively, Stoughton or 'Stocton', as it is first written in 1315.[31]

Why do these three different settlements with medieval origins all have the same name? All other distinct villages in the parish have different names, even when very close together. The answer to this puzzle may lie in the meaning of the word 'Stocton'. The ending *-ton* or *tun* is Old English or Saxon for a fenced, enclosed homestead or village. *Stoc* is an early Old English word with several meanings; it might mean a trunk of a tree or log, or it can mean a cattle or dairy farm, which seems more likely for our Stoughton. So 'Stoc-tun' perhaps began as a fenced cattle or dairy farm or homestead. It could be that the big open hilltop area of Stoughton was where the early Saxons ranched their cattle. This would explain why, when villages developed in place of the cattle ranch, the name Stoughton was shared between all three settlements.

From the 900s the huge Royal Saxon estate of Wedmore was being split up into separate manors. The hilltops became large ploughed open fields, and cattle were pastured instead for much of the year out on the moors. The later ownership of the Stoughtons shows that they were divided up mostly between the manors of Blackford and Wedmore, with the manor of Mudgley and one of the Cheddar manors holding just one farmstead each. It seems as if everyone was claiming a share in this former cattle range, perhaps reflecting ancient rights they had held under the earlier farming system when they all turned their 'stock' out in this area.

Bagley and Mudgley are two place names which both end in the Old English word *leah*, meaning a glade or clearing in a wood.

In the Panborough Saxon Charter of 956 there is a reference to a *leah* in a wood on the top of the hill where old Bagley School now stands.[32] It was called 'Oslakeslegh', Oslak's clearing. This place name has disappeared, but fields nearby were called 'Lygh' in 1517,[33] and one is still 'Leigh' today. Clearings, then, were being made in the wood in the 900s, but great stretches of woodland survived for centuries.

BAGLEY did not exist as a village until the late 1500s. It was really the name of the great wood spreading over the hilltop. The earliest reference to Bagley itself comes from a document in Wells Cathedral archives dated 1248.[34] It seems that William de Hoyland, one of the Vicars Choral, had been seen misbehaving in the 'Wood of Baggelegh' with Isobel, the daughter of Josceus or Josce. On a previous occasion he had been caught 'carrying his shoes in his hands next morning'. I will leave that incident to your imagination.

William was charged with the offence of being 'incontinent' with Isobel, and also with being violent towards her father Josce. The ecclesiastical court decided that, because of the public scandal, William should 'take his place with the boys on their bench' for the next three months, and should be made to resign his position as Vicar Choral if the offence was repeated. So William's public disgrace was to sit in the front row with the little choirboys, in the Cathedral. This humiliation did not work, however; for in November William again appeared before the court, accused of 'backsliding' with Isobel, and resigned. William de Hoyland's misdemeanours show us that the wood of Bagley was a well-known feature in 1248. This should serve as a warning to be careful, as you never know what documents a local historian will use to illustrate a point in future!

What does the 'Bag' of Bagley mean? It is a fairly common place name which is usually associated with woodland. Some experts consider it might be derived from a lost word for a fox or badger, which would live in a woodland clearing. I prefer to think that it is more probably a personal name, from a Saxon called 'Bacga', so that Bagley is Bagg's clearing. The Bagg family of Wedmore can be traced back to the 1500s, indeed one of my great-grandmothers was a Bagg!

MUDGLEY is first written as 'Mudesley' in 1136, when it was given to the Dean of Wells as one of his holdings on the Isle of Wedmore.[35] This 'mud'-*leah* could be just that, a Saxon muddy clearing; or more probably a personal name, 'Mudd's clearing'. Mudgley may not be the most romantic of place names, but it certainly has a romantic past.

Until recently it was thought that Mudgley was first settled in Saxon times. Later, in the 1100s the Dean of Wells chose to build one of his country houses on the sunny, south-facing slope. The complex included a chapel, a garden, a fishpond and associated farm buildings. It was the site of this medieval house which was excavated by the Revd S.H.A. Hervey in 1878, in a quest to discover whether the remains were those of the royal palace used by King Alfred in 878, a thousand years before.[36] No trace of anything of Alfred's time was discovered. Around the Dean's house, the medieval village of Mudgley grew up.

However, since 1988 exciting finds in the centre of Mudgley have shown that there were people living there long before the Saxons or the Dean arrived. Fragments of Romano-

British pottery have been picked up in several places, which prove that at least one or more Roman farmsteads existed at Mudgley, pushing back the age of the settlement by several hundred years.[37] These may not have been the first settlers. Just a short distance away, near the turnpike toll cottage at Blakeway, traces of two prehistoric wooden trackways have been discovered.[38] These trackways lead straight from Westhay to Mudgley. One track is dated about 500 BC; the other is much older, about 2500 BC. The earlier trackway was made of similarly sized woven hazel sticks and this is said to be the first evidence of man coppicing trees in the world! So almost 4,500 years ago prehistoric man walked along the trackway in the moor to and from Mudgley. He certainly hunted in Mudgley, as I have picked up flints dropped in the chase, and he probably lived there on the hill slope growing hazel to coppice for the construction of his trackways.

New villages

Not all our villages or place names are Old English in origin. Some are surprisingly recent, and no less interesting for that. Two 'new' hamlets are Little Ireland and New Town.

LITTLE IRELAND is a tiny settlement which grew up at the roadside in the 19th century around one older farmstead. It consisted of a few wayside cottages, only one of which survives today. The name 'Little Ireland' is first mentioned in the 1880s and was a mystery until I discovered, near Wellington, another hamlet which was nicknamed 'Little Ireland' from the Irish tinkers who settled there.[39] Perhaps it was the tinkers who built our Little Ireland and earned it a derogatory name.

Many of these tiny cottages were built in the late 1700s and 1800s on waste land, usually road verges. This coincided with the time when many of the unsurfaced mud roads were first being made up in stone. The hard surface could be narrower, leaving wide verges unused at the sides. The road verge was part of the manorial 'waste' or rough grazing, and it was illegal to build on it without permission; but the tradition was that if someone could (with the help of friends) build a cottage in a day, and get the roof on and a fire burning in the hearth before sundown, then they could claim it and the land on which it stood. In Wedmore's records such squatters' cottages are always referred to as 'waste cottages', but elsewhere they often acquired romantic names such as 'sundowners'. The cottages, usually one up and one down, were built of whatever material was to hand: cob (compacted mud), stone, wood and mixtures of all three, often reusing old materials. The builders were usually poor labourers who otherwise had no chance of acquiring a house or land of their own, the starter homes problem of yesteryear! Such tiny cottages are often set in gardens, also taken out of the verge, which can still be easily recognised by their long narrow shape, tapering at one or both ends.

NEW TOWN is precisely what it says: a little new settlement created in the 1830s in an area of former woodland. No houses are shown there on the 1791 map.[40] This scrubby area belonged to several landowners, who decided to lay out a deliberately planned new estate at a time when the population of the parish was growing rapidly. Sometime, probably about 1830, a new road was put in, and about seventeen house plots laid out, six on either side of the road, with a few others behind. There were two sizes of property to choose; the plots on the south side of the road were twice as large as those on the north.

The Tithe Map of 1838 shows this new village just completed, and the Tithe Schedule tells us who owned each house.[41] The houses were 'self-build', put up by ordinary working men, mostly agricultural labourers and stonemasons. Possible the village was developed as a response to expansion of local quarries, with the spread of stoned roads and 19th century house-building. One house later became the Alma Inn. Several of the houses have now gone, spoiling the symmetry of the original plan, but their plots can still be traced.

New Town was created at a time when the landless labourer was desperate for housing. Wedmore's New Town invites comparison with the experimental Chartist villages of the late 1840s, such as Corse Lawn in Oxfordshire and Snigs End in Gloucestershire; but New Town is slightly earlier. Not enough is yet known about the background to this local example of a deliberately planned village for the working man. We do not know who decided to build New Town, or who gave it its name; nor whether it was entirely self-supporting, or if there was an element of philanthropy. Our first reference to it is on 12th March 1831, when John the son of James Bunn, stonemason, and Ann his wife, was baptised in Theale Chapel.[42] The new village had its newest resident.

By 1841, three-quarters of the inhabitants of the village were agricultural labourers, together with two retired 'independent' householders and a 'pensioner, one with a servant'.[43] There were also three paupers who lived in households where they too were probably servants; one elderly pauper, Ann Warr, in a cottage on her own looking after 3 year old Sydney Court; and the Bunn families: three households, all stonemasons by trade.

One inhabitant of New Town loved it so much that he had no wish ever to leave it. In April 1920 Mr Charles Catley died. Charles and Mary Ann Catley appear in the baptismal registers of St. Mary's, when their five children were christened, between 1861 and 1868.[44] On each occasion, Charles Catley is listed as 'Wedmore policeman'. He must have been one of our earliest village policemen. Eventually he retired to New Town. Many years later, in fulfillment of his dying wish, he was buried in his own orchard at New Town. His grave is still there, overlooking the view he loved.

Lost settlements

Villages seem to be very permanent, but sometimes even comparatively recent settlements can completely disappear. In the 1800s several small new settlements were created in the parish; now all that we can find are just humps and bumps in the ground, and a little documentary evidence to show that they once existed.

Before the 18th century Enclosure Acts drained and enclosed the moors, it was illegal to build there because they were common land for pasturing cattle. When the moors were finally drained in the late 1700s, small houses began to appear, dotting the moorland landscape, particularly in Tadham and Allermoor. Greenwood's map of 1822[45] shows a scattering of houses where none existed before the Enclosure Acts. In the censuses of 1841 and 1851, this settlement was called The Heath.

By the time of the first census in 1841, almost fifty little cottages had been built in Tadham and Allermoor, not including those along Blakeway. Most of these houses were fairly short-lived and have since disappeared completely, although one or two are left in picturesque decay.

There were, however, two groups of houses which might qualify as small villages. One cluster of about five houses survives today as Allermoor Farm. The other group was built along Sand Drove, and in 1841 consisted of five houses; however, the layout of plots shows that originally it could have been a settlement of about ten houses. The main house in this group became Sand Drove Farm, and it survived many years longer than its surrounding cottages. Nonetheless, all that can be traced today is the outline of the main house and its farmyard. In 1841 Joseph Roper lived there with his family. He is listed as a publican in 1841, and a cider-seller in 1851, so that the moor dwellers had their own 'local'.

The 1841 census shows that every other moor house in The Heath was occupied by agricultural labourers and their families. These labourers were mostly rhyne workers, employed to cut, clean and maintain the network of rhynes (or drainage ditches), newly created after the Enclosure Acts. The census of 1851 shows that decline was already setting in, with five houses uninhabited - and this was just the beginning.

Why did no-one maintain or rebuild these homes? There were three main reasons. The demand for labourers to work out on the moors inevitably fell off, once the major work of laying out the newly enclosed and drained landscape was completed; fewer were needed for routine maintenance. Secondly, despite enclosure, the moors were still subject to flooding, which could make life rather uncomfortable. In the winter, families usually lived upstairs. They boated over to the Isle of Wedmore for supplies. One of my grandmothers, who lived on The Heath for a while as a child, sometimes went to school by boat, mooring at Jacks Drove and walking the remainder of the way. Going to school by boat was in fact much quicker than walking all the way. Dr Bracey, Wedmore GP from 1898-1948, often used a turf boat to reach his marooned patients. It was common practice for expectant mothers to stay with relatives on higher land to await the birth, rather than risk being trapped by floods. The third reason why these houses on the moor were abandoned was that many people emigrated to America or Australia, in search of a better life than a damp cottage on the moors. By 1886 only about 25 houses remained.[46]

The exception to this decline was the community along Blakeway which has continued to survive to the present day, probably because it was edging an important route across the moors. In its heyday, Blakeway had its own chapel and two cider-sellers. By the census of 1851 these are proper inns: The Traveller's Rest, and The Sportsman's Arms.

Another lost settlement is **GOOSEHAM,** just off the Latcham road. In the 1830s, a group of four cottages was built at the end of Gooseham Lane. These tiny cottages were built of stone, each with its garden. In the census of 1851 three of these cottages were still inhabited. In one lived widow Hannah Harding, her seven children and three grandchildren. In another were George and Sarah Leigh and their six children. The third cottage was occupied by George and Maria Bagg and their two adult children: quite a population. The cottages have disappeared almost without trace. The name Gooseham first appears in writing in 1558, as 'Goosehame'.[47] It takes its name from the *hamm* or enclosed meadow where geese were pastured on the edge of the village, probably since at least early medieval times.

If these scattered 19th century settlements had not decayed and disappeared, the landscape around Wedmore would look very different today.

Two vanished Tudor villages

At **OLDWOOD**, near Sand, there is one house. This is the only remaining house of what was once a thriving hamlet. Oldwood took its name from the wood which once formed part of the medieval deer park of the manor of Mudgley, first documented in 1220.[48] This was just called 'Olde Parke'. In the 1500s, when it was sold, the name changed to 'Olde Woode'. It was acquired by the trustees of the Old Almshouses in Wells.[49]

The first mention of Oldwood as a settlement, rather than a wood, is in 1587 when Thomas Webb, husbandman, Brigett his wife, and Judyth their daughter lease a 'cottage at Olde Woode' from the Wells Almshouses trustees, for 3s 4d a year.[50] It seems as if the trustees had decided that income from houses would bring in more money than income from land, at least from woodland. A little, deliberately planned settlement was created in the 'old wood' in the 1580s - a piece of speculative Tudor housing development. The estate consisted of about seven cottages laid out in regular plots on the north and west side of the Oldwood track. By 1700 there were ten houses; but 150 years later the number had declined to seven once again. In the 1881 census there were only four dwellings; now there is just the one.

The little community at Oldwood was involved in a case of theft in 1675, for which vivid details survive.[51] Hester Edwards lived with her brother Richard in Mudgley, probably at Court Farm. On 18th March 1675 she complained that some of her clothes had been stolen. She reported to the Justice of the Peace:

> *'that she had lost severall thinges lately*
> *About 6 dressings for the head lased [i.e. decorated with lace]*
> *4 handkerchiefs for the necke plaine*
> *2 pairs of ruffled sleeves*
> *4 linen hoods*
> *1 pair of worked shoes with red work*
> *2 new petticoats, red, one shag, the other searge*
> *1 pair of red worsted stockings'*

The headscarves were subsequently found in the home of Gabriel Boulgin, of Oldwood, in Wedmore.

On 1st April, two local girls, Welthian Savidge (aged 21) and Diana Venne (22) made statements to the magistrate[52]. They were probably close neighbours, also living in Oldwood. Welthian said: 'about Christmas last Margery Pridy brought two dressings for a womans head and a hood, to her father in law Gabriel Bulgen's house in the sight of her [Welthian]' and said that 'she could fetch two more better than those from Mr Edward's his house either by day or by night.' Diana's evidence also condemned Margery. She said, 'that about Christmas last Margery Pridy came to her house having on her head a dressing of her master Edwards' sister, and a red whitell [woollen shawl] upon her back, and a pair of red worsted stockings upon her legges of the same person, which Margery confessed she had brought from Mr Edwards' house'.

Margery Pridy was 21 and a servant of the Edwards family at Mudgley. She had stolen the fine clothes of Hester Edwards, and had dressed herself up in the cheerful scarlet finery to show off to her friends, boasting that she could get more 'by day or by night'. There is an amusing tailpiece to the story.

On May 3rd 1675 the Bishop of Bath and Wells heard an allegation by Thomas Cole the tithingman of Wedmore, and John Merevill of Wedmore.[53] They both swore that Richard Edwards, Hester's brother, said that John Baylie Esq., Justice of the Peace, 'was so puffed up with glasses of wine by Mr Urch that he, Richard Edwards, could have no justice in a case concerning Margery Pridy and his witnesses could not be heard'. Mr Urch, also of Mudgley, and the judge had imbibed so much wine that, clearly, the judge was too drunk to hear the case. We do not know if Margery was ever punished; no further records exist.

This Tudor planned settlement in Oldwood was unusual, but not unique. A similar development was undertaken by the same Wells Almshouses trustees in another area of ancient woodland which they had acquired at the same time, at **BAGLEY WOOD**. Here again, the old woodland was cleared and a completely new small estate of about seven dwellings was laid out, but only one survives today. This Bagley Wood estate virtually disappeared as the settlement moved to develop instead along the road and around Bagley Green from the 18th century onwards, becoming the present village of Bagley.

Chapter 2
Parish Road Names

Wedmore

The network of streets and roads in and linking up our villages all have names. Several names can be traced back hundreds of years; others are fairly recent. How did our street and road names in the parish acquire their names and what are the stories behind them? Some road names have changed over the years, sometimes more than once, and I have turned up some surprises. Two main factors have influenced the fixing of road names as they are today. One was the naming of roads on Ordnance Survey maps. The second was the setting up of road nameplates in the parish. Even this last simple exercise caused a few arguments over whether a spelling or even a name was correct. We will start by looking at the names in and around Wedmore village.

The four roads which today make up 'The Square' in Wedmore are The Borough, Church Street, Grants Lane and Glanville Road.

THE BOROUGH needs the longest explanation. The Borough today is just one street, from the bottom of Church Street to the corner of Combe Batch. It used, however, to extend further, up Church Street as far as the George Hotel, and along the Cheddar Road as far as the corner; and it continued in the other direction up Combe Batch to the beginning of Mutton Lane.

Wedmore village belonged to the Dean of Wells Cathedral. About the late 1100s, it would seem that the Dean decided to lay out a new street, to accommodate markets and fairs. He probably hoped to bring more trade and prosperity to the village, and more revenue to himself as owner.

Much of this deliberately planned medieval street can still be seen today, 800 years later. It was designed to funnel through traffic, and potential customers, on a dog-leg route from the Church and the pre-existing village to the Wells road, past all the shops and market stalls. The Borough roadway was originally three times as wide as it is today, and cigar-shaped, narrowing at each end. This shape is characteristic of early medieval planned market-streets, and was designed to accommodate market stalls and stock pens. Some of the older house-fronts set back from the road still mark the original width of the street as shown on the 1791 parish map. At the end of the 1700s householders started to take in the roadway in front of their houses, creating front gardens and narrowing the street. Some houses, such as The Borough Venture and Providence House were actually built on this spare frontage land. By this time the market had waned and less space was needed for it, although fairs were still thriving at the beginning of the 20th century.

The layout of the new Borough must have had quite an impact on the villagers of that time. There may have been existing roads and houses which fitted into the new plan; or it may have been a completely new layout. Any existing houses may or may not have been swept away. Who laid it out and how houses on the new street were allotted, we just do not know. Its name, however, reflects the stir its development must have caused in the medieval village. 'Borough' is an urban term, and the name suggests that the Dean may have hoped to make Wedmore into a town. The village of Montacute also has a 'Borough', of very similar layout, which was in existence by 1240.[1] Although there is no evidence that Wedmore ever applied for town or borough status, the name has stuck. Wedmore was granted its market, held in the specially-designed new street, in 1255.[2] The earliest dateable reference to The Borough is in 1325, when one Bartholomew is described as living in the 'Bourgh'; but it almost certainly existed long before the name was first written down.[3]

The Borough was also called the New-port. *Portus* is Latin for a town market-place (nothing to do with *porta*, a harbour). This is the 'new market-place' of Wedmore. Furthermore, the village and its market was managed for the Dean not by a plain reeve, a country 'farm manager', but by a port-reeve, a market official associated with towns. Wedmore still has its portreeves.

In 1342 Adam atte Breche left his daughter Crispina 'one burgage, with one half of a burgage and a fourth part of a burgage lying in La Nuport of Wedmore' - probably in that part of The Borough now known as lower Church Street.[4] It is still being called the 'New' market-place more than a century after it was set out. A 'burgage' is, once again, a term more usually met in medieval towns, and means a long, narrow town property packed with others along a street frontage. Adam atte Breche's will shows that by 1342 there were a number of burgages in The Borough, sufficiently well established and sought-after to be subdivided: suggesting a thriving community with urban aspirations in the Borough.

By looking at the existing layout, we can see clues to the size of these medieval house-plots or burgages. The Borough, between Church Street and Combe Batch, was built on an artifical bank across the lower, marshy end of the village. This bank accommodated the roadway, and the houses on the east side. The ground falls away behind these houses, down their gardens to the continuous line of their back garden boundaries, marking the precisely planned eastern edge of this new layout. The house plots were measured out to a set size, still preserved in some property boundaries today, and several can be reconstructed from the 1791 map.[5] The plots were 3 ropes wide and 15 ropes long. A rope (as used by the medieval surveyor for a handy, portable measure) was 20 feet; so the plots measured 60 x 300 feet. The best surviving plots are those from Stones to Barnards on the east side of The Borough. Plots were subsequently subdivided (as was already happening in Adam atte Breche's will of 1342) or amalgamated, always lengthwise so as to keep a road frontage. The width of later plots may thus be fractions or multiples of the original 60 feet. Cross Farm now takes up two plots. Many of the other medieval house plots in the village seem to be the same measurements as those of The Borough; but whether this means they are also part of an early planned layout or whether these are simply standard medieval sizes is uncertain (see Chapter 6).

CHURCH STREET is a surprisingly late name. It does not seem to appear until the middle of the 19th century, although this is probably the oldest part of the present village. It is first written down in the census of 1861. Before that, the lower half of Church Street was part of The Borough, and the top half needed no name. People simply lived near or 'atte Church'.[6]

GRANTS LANE on the other hand, is one of our older street names. A Grant family are living in the centre of the village in 1638; and Thomas Andrews married Ann Grant in 1681.[7] The earliest reference to this lane is to be found in Dr John Westover's journal. In

Looking down Church Street, Wedmore, c1960

Grants Lane, c1930

1698 Dr Westover gives 'an electuary of marmalade of quinses [quinces] to John Andus [Andrews] in Grants Lane his daughter'.[8] Grant is probably a personal name.

GLANVILLE ROAD takes its name from the Glanville family who built Elmsett Hall in the late 1700s. The Glanvilles were doctors for several generations; and a Dr William Glanville, retired surgeon, was living there in 1871. However according to the census of 1871 Dr Glanville was living in Elmsett Hall in Silver Street; while in the census of 1881 Elmsett Hall is in Victoria Street! This was the first time I had ever come across either name. Victoria Street presumably commemorated the 40th anniversary, in 1877, of the accession of Queen Victoria, but went out of use not long afterwards, as the name Glanville Road is being used in the mid 1880s. Silver Street could be a much older name.

Silver Street occurs in many villages and towns: including Cheddar, Wrington, Congresbury, Wells and Glastonbury in this area. We do not know its meaning, but it does always seem to be associated with a stream - and Glanville Road does bridge the Lerburne. The name also seems to have a curious association with Roman settlement sites. Did our Silver Street have such a link? During the last century the Revd S.H.A. Hervey, Vicar of Wedmore, dug up several fragments of Romano-British pottery, including some imported Samian ware, in the garden of his Vicarage (now the Old Vicarage) abutting on Glanville Road opposite the Church, and Romano-British pottery is still found in the garden. This shows that there was a Roman settlement somewhere nearby. Perhaps Silver Street is the original name for Glanville Road, and takes us back to our Roman past.

The road now called **THE LERBURNE** was originally part of The Borough but is known to older Wedmore residents as Gasworks Lane, from the gasworks built there in 1870. The Lerburne, properly, is not a road but the name of the brook which flows through Wedmore, under The Borough, and runs out through the moor to join the River Axe. *Burna* in Saxon or Old English means a stream or brook. In Porlock there is an area called Lowerbourne, locally pronounced 'Lurban' as is ours; so perhaps our Lerburne is 'the lower stream'. In the 1800s it was spelt Lurban. There was a stream in Wells called Ludborne or Lurteburne, which may well be the same name.

A drawing of The Borough in Wedmore on a deed of 1805 shows a very narrow bridge across the Lerburne, with a circular shape on its east side. This is probably a pond with a ford, alongside the bridge.[9] Wagons and horses went through the water, while pedestrians kept dry on the little footbridge. This little bridge was taken down about the 1820s, and replaced by a wider bridge more suitable for carriages. Gradually all signs of the stream disappeared into a tunnel under the road.

The road now called **COMBE BATCH** has had several names. The lower section from the end of The Borough to Mutton Lane was originally a part of The Borough. Later it became Wells Road. Combe Batch officially started beyond Mutton Lane. A sketch map on the deed of 1805 shows that Mary Chambers had just sold her cottage with a garden at 'Coombe Batch'.[10] This is the cottage now called Hillside. The road below the cottage is clearly marked 'Wedmore Borough'.

The word 'combe' is Old English *cumb*, meaning a narrow valley, presumably the valley of the Lerburne which it overlooks. It was borrowed from the still older Ancient British *cumbo*, which in Welsh has become *cwm*. Batch, in Somerset, usually means a slight hill, often used as a settlement site because it is rather drier than the surrounding area. The original Combe Batch was probably just around the hilltop. Combe Batch as a road name does not seem to exist before the 1800s, but there are 'Combe' field names below the hill, the earliest of which occurs in 1554.[11]

THE DRANG will be known to a few old Wedmorians. It was the narrow alleyway which once existed by the side of Honeybourne in The Borough, and is now incorporated into that property. It led to six tiny cottages, built between 1820 and 1840, edging the brook. In 1887 it is called Martin's Drang after the Martin family who lived there.[12] In the census of 1871 there is a little community somewhere within The Borough called The Rookery. In No.1 lives Frederick Martin, while Charles Latcham, Henry Andrews and Benjamin Stone live in Nos. 2, 3 and 4. This is the only occasion, before the development of modern housing estates, that I have found house numbers being used in Wedmore. It seems probable that The Rookery was an alternative name for The Drang, most likely a good-humoured local nickname for the huddle of tiny cottages. It has been preserved in the formal census return, although both names have subsequently disappeared from the village itself.

The name **LASCOT HILL** is a mystery, and many variations in spelling have occurred over the centuries. It has been written as Laskers, Lashcott, Laycock and Laccotts Hill. The earliest reference I have discovered so far is in 1678 when it is actually spelt Lascotts Hill.[13] The second part of the word is probably Old English *cot*, that is, a cottage or more often a shelter or hut, especially for sheep. 'Las' could be a personal name. Lascot Hill is the old main route out of Wedmore towards the west and north. Although the modern road nameplate gives Lascot, most older references spell it as Lascott.

BILLINGS HILL was just one of several tracks leading out of Wedmore towards Mudgley. It was chosen as the route for the turnpike road from Shipham through Wedmore to Pedwell in 1827.[14] It has taken its name from John Billing who was living in the early 1800s, in a house that once stood in Grants Lane at the foot of the hill, where he kept a general store.[15] South Bank and other houses now stand on the site of his house and shop, facing up the hill which took his name. Deeds prove that the earlier name for Billings Hill was Clay Hill, the general name for that part of the hillside above Grants Lane. As those who live there can testify, Clay Hill was a good name for it.

DANDOS LANE is an example of how often a road name can change. The name does not appear until this century. The Dando family lived in an old thatched farmhouse which stood at the corner of the lane and Sand Road. The house burnt down in 1897, and Westover House now stands on the site.[16] The Revd S.H.A. Hervey writing in the 1880s, did not give the lane any name at all, so that presumably at that time it was nameless! At that time, according to the 25" OS map of 1886, there was just one wayside cottage in the lane; that has long since disappeared under the lay-bys of the modern bungalows. Hervey, however, did say that he had discovered some deeds which called it Haines Lane, which is, presumably, an earlier name, perhaps from an occupant of the cottage.[17] Earlier still, in the census of 1841, there is a mysterious lane called 'Cooks Lane'. Analysis of households, by a process of elimination, shows that Cooks Lane of 1841 must be present-day Dandos Lane. There were three households living in Cooks Lane in 1841, but none of them were called Cook. Just three years earlier, in 1838, the tithe map shows no houses there at all.

SHORTLAND LANE forms a right angle between Dandos Lane and Sand Road. It cuts off a section of Maltfield, within the great Wedmore East Field which was one of the arable open fields on the hilltop. The medieval cultivation strips at this end were arranged in groups that were shorter than those elsewhere in the field, where groups could and did extend in long blocks, called furlongs, for half a mile or more.

PLUD STREET is one of our oldest unaltered road names. *Pludde* or *plodde* is an early medieval word meaning a small pool or puddle. The earliest reference to Plud Street is in 1653, when 'Richard sonn of John Wall of Plud Streete' is baptised.[18] The unusual thing about Plud Street is that 'Street' is actually part of its official name as far back as the 1600s, although it was outside the main village. It is the only early example of such a 'Street' name

Parish Road Names

in the village (the Street added to Pilcorn came much later). The word street comes from Old English *straet*, a Roman or stone surfaced road. Was it a surfaced road? Is it significant that it is on a line between a known Roman site at West End, and a possible Roman site at Castle in Heath House?

The name was distorted, or misunderstood, and appears as Flood Street in the censuses of 1861, 1871 and 1881, and on the 25" OS map of 1886. Those who remember how the stream used to bubble down the side of the road to join The Brook, spilling over the road in time of flood, can well understand how the misunderstanding arose. Now the name is restored to the original spelling of 'Plud', recalling the stream, even though that has now been forced underground.

KELSONS LANE is named after the Kelson family who once lived in nearby Kelsons Farm. The Kelsons were a very small family, with just two branches in Wedmore between the 1590s and 1650s.[19] In the late 1500s William and John Kelson both held properties in Wedmore. William was probably John's father, and he seems to have been living in Kelsons Farm, while John was living at Crickham. In 1653 Wedmore church registers record the burial of Nicholas, son of Nicholas Kelson of Theale. This is the last reference to any Kelson in the registers. In 1687 Dr John Westover was sending potions 'for Mellencholey' to Mrs Elinor Kelson, then living in Bristol; since Dr Westover was treating her she presumably came from Wedmore originally.[20]

Kelsons Lane therefore seems to have acquired its name in the early 1600s; and although the family was not there for long, the people or their farm were sufficiently well known for the name to have stuck ever since - unlike several other 'personalised' road names which, like Dandos Lane have changed with confusing frequency.

GUILDHALL was, originally, the name of an area between the two roads leading west out of the village. Now the name is used for the T-shaped Guildhall Lane. Few people born in Wedmore ever say Guildhall. It has always been 'Guilo', pronounced 'guy-low'. Why two names for the same area?

The earliest appearance of Guildhall so far discovered, is in 1814.[21] It would seem to be a comparatively recent form of the name. If we trace references to it back in time, we can unravel the subtle changes in pronounciation, because earlier people wrote a word as they spoke it. In a deed dated 1609 there is mention of an area of pasture in Guildhole.[22] Then in a lease of 1546 I found a description of 'a lane that dothe leade into Gylle Hoole'.[23] This discovery throws a new light on the meaning of the name and suggests how, perhaps, the discrepancy arose. The original Gylle Hoole was corrupted into Guilo, as it is still pronounced after 400 years. Perhaps it was Giles's Hole, or Gilly's Hole or even 'gully' Hole. The origin of Gylle Hoole, and who was Giles or Gilly, if he existed, is lost in time. The Hole or hollow of the upper part of The Brook, below The Close but above Glanville Road, is still a distinctive feature of this little area tucked away between the two main roads westwards out of the village. The Guildhall name might have arisen because someone misread old writing, or it might be an example of wishful thinking. It certainly seems to coincide with the time that Ordnance Survey surveyors were preparing the first maps of the area, and trying to clarify and define names - not always accurately.

Cottages in Guildhall Lane or Guilo, c1950

There is no evidence for the existence of any guildhall building in Guildhall Lane, as suggested by the Revd S.H.A. Hervey in the 1880s.[24] There was a 'Fraternity or Guild' of the Blessed Mary of Wedmore, founded in 1449, to which all parishioners might belong.[25] This was a kind of forerunner of the later friendly societies. The guild met in the parish church after which it was named; but had no known connection at all with this area of the village. Hervey did not know of the 1546 'Gylle Hoole' document.

The maps show that several tiny wayside cottages were built in the hollow of 'Guilo' during the late 1700s and early 1800s, of which only one now, precariously, survives. This made quite a population of poorer folk. In 1885 the headmaster of Wedmore School wrote, 'Questioned Richard Fisher and Henry Tincknell as to their absence from school yesterday afternoon. They are two of the bad lot from Guildhall Street'.[26] Perhaps this adds weight to my theory that the reason for the enormous wall built around The Hall was to keep out the hordes of children who lived in Guilo and who may have been tempted by the exotic fruits which once grew in the garden and orangery.

PILCORN STREET was the area to the west of the church. The 'Street' was added only at the end of the last century. Pilcorn has nothing to do with a *pill* or creek, as has been suggested in the past. Pilcorn was an alternative name for 'pilled oats', a type of oats in which the husks did not adhere tightly to the grains, making it easier to separate the two by winnowing. The road ran out of the village along the southern edge of one of the great open fields which stretched across the hilltop. Presumably pilled oats were remembered as one of the main crops in this particular field, introduced no doubt by innovative farmers.

Pilcorn Street originally ran behind the former Police Station and adjacent houses, to join Quab Lane on the bend above the present road junction. In 1814 it was straightened and widened to its present course, leaving a depression in back gardens which marks the old road.[27]

QUAB LANE is another old name, as old as the equally expressive *plud* (see Plud Street). Quab comes from the Old English or Saxon word *cwabba*, meaning a marsh or bog. It describes the boggy area which gives rise to Blackford Brook, flowing west, and the tributaries of Wedmore Brook, flowing east. Quab Lane is one of the old tracks leading through the medieval open fields, across an area which is still remarkably wet through most of its length, all the way to Stoughton. It is first mentioned in 1559 as 'Quabbe'.[28]

The Wedmore end of Quab Lane was renamed Coronation Road to commemorate the coronation of George V in 1911, but few people used or even liked the change of name.[29] When the street signs were erected, it was decided to revert back to the original name.

In 1909 there was a public enquiry about responsibility for repairing certain roads in Wedmore. Witness John Leigh, who lived in Quab Lane and was 'going 70', said he knew Quab Lane well and remembered it as a boy. 'Whenever there had been heavy weather the lane had always been deep in mud' but that it 'was used, when it was fine, by a great many farmers, inasmuch as it was a better way than Lascots Hill.' Joseph Larder, 78, who had been 'born and bred' in the lane, said 'Hundreds of people had asked him if they could go through the lane, and he had told them they couldn't, as they would go so far and get stuck. It was good at both ends, but the middle was bad'.[30] The Axbridge Rural District Council accepted responsibility for Quab Lane as a public road, as a result of this enquiry, since it still exists today.

The **WEST END** of Wedmore has been a separate settlement to the west of the village for hundreds of years. In 1554 we have our first written record of the name, when it is called 'a Streate in the Weste Towne'.[31] Its shape, turning through several right angles between Quab Lane and Sand Road, probably reflects its origin as a track round blocks of medieval strips in the open fields.

MADWOMANS LANE leads from Kelsons Lane to Sand. It is completely different, in name and appearance, from the roads described so far. It has no name-plate, and is a green lane; no modern road surface has ever been put on it. It is however a direct route to Sand.

So who was the mad woman who has this permanent memorial, and when did she live? The evidence suggests that she may be older than we might expect. The Revd S.H.A. Hervey was told, in the 1870s, that it was called Madwomans Lane because a mad woman once lived there in a tree house.[32] I have now found a deed of 1758 in which the field adjoining the lane is called Madwomans Lane.[33] The local story, therefore, was current over a century before it was told to Hervey; it must have been around some time before the name became attached to the lane, and then, by 1758, to the adjacent field. The madwoman herself, therefore, could have been living in her tree in the 1750s or even earlier. This road name shows how folk tales can be much older than we sometimes realise.

MUTTON LANE is another, more recent, local folk tale name. The original name of Mutton Lane was Shutters or Shooters Hill or Lane. *Shute* or *scyte* is Old English for a steep hill or watershed, as in Shute Shelve, above Axbridge. Although the name Shutters Hill was sometimes still being used in the 1950s, the road acquired its nickname of Mutton Lane during the 1800s, and it is this name that has now stuck. The tradition, passed down in my family, was that one of the cottagers stole a sheep and hid it up the chimney. Perhaps other stories were told about the origin of the name. So far I have been unable to trace the truth behind this tale. However, 'one of a gang of notorious thieves who infest the neighbourhood' was caught by Police Sergeant Bowler of Wedmore in 1857, and brought to trial for stealing and killing two sheep, the property of William Reeve the younger, on Blackford Moor. His name was William Leigh.[34]

Leigh was a common name in the parish at this period, and in the 1841 census there is a lane called Leighs Lane. My research shows that this lane is in fact Shutters Hill, now Mutton Lane. In 1841 there were eleven tiny cottages there. In one of them lived Sarah Leigh, washerwoman, with her seven children and grandchildren; and it seems likely that it is her family that gave the lane its name. In 1851 she was still living there. Although no son or grandson called William is listed, it may be that there was some family link, and perhaps it was in Sarah Leigh's cottage that William Leigh hid the sheep's carcase in 1857. William himself, according to Shepton Mallet Jail remand list, was a labourer, aged 34, who could read and write. He was committed for trial by Joseph Wollen the local magistrate, who lived in The Hall at Wedmore, on 7th January 1857.[35] The case was heard on 13th January, and he was sentenced to four years penal servitude.[36]

The late Mr Leslie Cook told me that in the 1920s-30s Mutton Lane and other steep lanes were used for local hill climbs as practice runs for the famous London to Lands End motorcycle trials, which were held every Easter. A good number of local riders entered, including the late Mr Leslie Harding who once owned Latcham Garage, now Ratcliffe Brothers of Dunnicks Mead Garage. Leslie Harding, who won a gold medal in these trials, is remembered as riding his motorcycle up Mutton Lane to show how it should be done. Mutton Lane, then just a rough stone track, was ideal for this type of practice. Mr Cook recalled how he and the late Mr William Tucker, who lived down Combe Lane, were the only two lads to climb the lane on pedal cycles, with special low gears fitted to the rear wheels. When the rough stones were steam-rollered in the 1930s, and later resurfaced in tarmac, their fun was spoiled.

MILL LANE ran past Wedmore's East Mill, situated on the brow of the hill near the top of Mutton Lane. A bungalow is now built on the mill site. The mill was there at least from 1554,[37] but the lane itself is probably considerable older. It goes all the way to Townsend Lane, and is a fine example of an access track to the medieval open fields, running along between two of the furlongs or subdivisions of Wedmore East Field. These huge arable open fields were probably laid out about the 1000s; and the lane may be of much the same age.

PILLMEAD LANE runs down by the side of Wedmore Cemetery into Wedmore Moor. The name Pillmead has survived through many centuries and is now attached to this little dead-end lane. In medieval times Pillmead was the name of a large area, the part of Wedmore Moor which lies below the village around the mouth of the valley where the Lerburne flows down to the River Axe. It was called 'Pulmedmore alias Wedmore More' in 1579[38] and there is a reference to land 'in Pulmede' in 1343.[39] Pillmead Lane marks the northwest limit of Pillmead Moor. The earliest documentary reference to Pillmead so far found, is in about 1280, when there is mention of a ditch there, called Pulmedesdych.[40]

So what does the name mean? 'Mead' or 'medes' refer to the haymeadows and best quality pasture which edge the moor. These are a very ancient and important part of the historical landscape. The first part of the name, 'Pill', always appears as 'Pul' in older spellings. This is probably derived from the Old English or Saxon *pol*, meaning a pool: so that Pillmead could be the 'meadow by the pool'. That part of the area below Pillmead Lane is known as The Lowgrounds, and is still the first to go under water in time of flood. Before it was drained, was there a permanent pool? I have never found any evidence of a pool in this area, but it could have gone by the 1200s. The reference to Pulmedesdych Ditch c1280 may indicate that drainage had already taken place. Alternatively, 'Pill' could be derived from the Old English *pyll* a stream or creek, referring, presumably, to the meadows beside the Lerburne; although this does not agree with the earlier spellings.

CLUB LANE was the name of a lane which ran straight up Lascot Hill from Manor Lane towards Crickham. Most of this track has totally disappeared, although part of it can be traced as a hollow-way along the hedge line to the west of the former Vicarage. The Revd S.H.A. Hervey, in the 1880s,[41] suggests that the lane was called after one George Club who held land in the area about 1730. Club Lane formed a direct route used by parishioners to walk from Crickham to church at Wedmore.

Some road names are obvious. They are the main routes to adjacent places, from which they take their names, such as Sand Road, Cheddar Road and Blackford Road. There are, however, some fairly recent road names which do perhaps need explanation, especially to newer residents. Some new names have good reasons behind their choice; others, such as Birch Close, have no real relevance to Wedmore.

GOGS ORCHARD was built on the orchard which belonged to Gog's House opposite. I cannot be certain how or when Gog's House acquired its name, but there are some fields called Gogsham, not far away towards Sand. The Old English or Saxon word *gog* was similar to *cwabba* (as in Quab Lane, see above), suggesting a boggy meadow.

THE ORCHARD is a very plain name given to one of the newest roads; it could be one of the many old cider apple orchards in Wedmore which have been built on. This orchard, however, is something different in that it is the site where evidence was found of people who have lived on this spot through the ages from prehistoric times. Archaeologists, excavating downwards and back in time, found traces of a medieval farmstead, a Saxon farm, some Roman occupation and an Iron Age farm. There were even remains of a Bronze Age rubbish tip! [42]

SPRINGFIELD DRIVE is named after the farmstead near Wedmore Brook which was destroyed in the 1960s when the estate was built. The ancient farm only acquired its name in the 20th century.

The biggest problem in recent years has been the naming of the various roads which make up the large estate off Pilcorn Street. Most of the houses are built on a field of twelve acres which was called just that, Twelve Acres, in 1820.[43] In 1814, just for a while, it became Parsons Twelve Acres, called after Mr Jeremiah Dewdney Parsons who owned it at that time.[44] Twelve Acres was not considered a sufficiently exciting road name for Wedmore, so we have **SAXON WAY, KING ALFREDS WAY** and **DANES LEA** to remind us of Wedmore's moment of national fame when the Peace of Wedmore was made in 878 AD between Saxon King Alfred and the Danes.

ST MARYS CLOSE is called after Wedmore's parish church of St Mary, although it is some distance away. I have met drivers searching for the road, assuming it to be around the church. **ST MEDARD ROAD** is of course named after our twin town Saint-Médard de Guizières in France.

DUNNS CLOSE was the actual name of the small field adjoining Twelve Acres, so at least that field name has survived intact as the road name on the spot.[45] Dunn is probably a personal name, although I have only been able to find two Dunns in the parish registers, both in the early 1700s - and one of those came from Mark, to be married in Wedmore church, and so hardly counts!

HERVEY CLOSE was named after the Revd Sydenham Henry Augustus Hervey (pronounced Harvey), who became Vicar of Wedmore in 1876. He was a keen local historian and amateur archaeologist. His enthusiasm for Wedmore's past along with his other passions of cricket, bell ringing and music endeared him to many. Being a staunch Liberal, however, he did not always see eye to eye with the extreme Toryism of Wedmore. He retired at 52 in 1898, and devoted the rest of his 99 years to historical research (see Introduction).

Another road, **CONNELLY DRIVE**, is called after Joan Connelly (to rhyme with jelly). Joan was born Joan Wall, a member of one of Wedmore's oldest families. Her father was a churchwarden and friend of the Vicar, the Revd S.H.A.Hervey, and this friendship stimulated her lifelong interest in the history of Wedmore. She married three times, becoming Mrs Reakes, then Mrs Mathews, and later Mrs Connelly. Among her many interests she was keen on local government and became Chairman of Wedmore Parish Council and an Axbridge Rural District Councillor. Joan had a great love of Wedmore, and she gave generously to the parish before and after her death in March 1978. She provided Wedmore with parish council rooms, and left thousands of pounds to the various village churches of all denominations.

Finally we come to two personal names, Gardiners Orchard and Worthington Close. **GARDINERS ORCHARD** adjoining Elmsett Hall takes its name from John Gardiner who lived in a cottage fronting Glanville Road with his orchard behind the house. In 1766 John was paying rates for his 'tanhouse' which was by the side of the brook, behind his cottage.[46] This must have been a particularly smelly area of Wedmore; the tannery is first recorded in 1640 (see Chapter 10).[47]

WORTHINGTON CLOSE is the name for the new estate off the Lerburne. It has been called after Worthington or 'Worthy' Cousins, the former owner of the land. Unless its origins are recorded now, this could become a modern example of how the meaning of a road name can so easily be forgotten. If one did not know why Worthington Close was so called, it would be very difficult in the future to explain its meaning accurately, especially as the name Worthington has a perfectly good Saxon meaning, the settlement of Worth's people. Worthington Close, a new road name, shows how careful one has to be in interpreting the true meaning of some of our road names, whether they are very old or fairly recent.

These road names, which we use every day, have ranged from Saxon times to the present, and provide us with a great variety of meanings. Some are reminders of almost-forgotten folk tales; others have lost their origins. Together, all these road names give us an insight into many aspects of our history.

Road names around the Parish

Blackford

The other settlements in the parish have equally interesting names. The largest village after Wedmore is Blackford. Curiously, although Blackford has a very long and distinguished history dating back to Roman times, some of the road names in the centre of the village are fairly recent. If there were early names these have not been recorded in the surviving documents.

The main road through Blackford village, now the **HIGH STREET,** is called 'The Streete of Blackford' in 1636.[48] **CHURCH STREET** and **CHURCH LANE** seem to be extremely recent, appearing long after Blackford Church was built in 1823. Before that, Church Lane was nameless and Church Street was part of High Street.

The name **REDMANS HILL** has puzzled me as it is clearly called after the Redman family who lived out at Westham from the 1680s.[49] However, none of the records searched so far show any Redman living in this road, although there are Redmans living elsewhere around Blackford in the 19th century. It may well be a very recent naming, as people recall a Redman family living there in the 20th century.

CHOLWELL or **CHARLEWELL LANE** is the little lane, first recorded by name in 1637, which runs west of Redmans Hill past Sunnydale.[50] It led to the holy well of Charlewell. This lane was once one of Blackford's main streets. Part of the way now is only a footpath, but the worn hollow way of the lane can still be seen. The name, however, has not been used for many years.

OLD FARM COURT is one of the newest road names of the 1980s, taken from Old Farm which once stood there. The name 'old farm' could apply equally well to any one of Blackford's farmsteads, as they all stand on sites dating from at least early medieval times.

Another new name is **TRINITY CLOSE** which takes its name from Blackford's Holy Trinity Church. This small estate is on the site of a factory. The first use of the building was as a milk factory or collection point for milk; it later became a depot for Reckitt and Colman, before Grove Industries took it over.

POOLBRIDGE ROAD links Blackford with the settlement of Poolbridge on the Blackford/Mark boundary. Poolbridge means just that: the bridge over the pool. There must originally have been quite a large pool there, long since disappeared. The water now runs through Shipham Rhine to the Brue, and was formerly crossed by a 'bow' bridge, a single-arched bridge which gave its name to Bow Farm nearby. In 1189 Norman and Richard de Pola (of the pool) lived at Poolbridge.[51]

On the Ordnance Survey maps **NEW ROAD** refers to the road past Hugh Sexey's school. Only part of this road is 'new'. The road originally went round a sharp corner, which still runs behind Blackford's former primary school, Blackford Board School. This angle was cut off in 1838 when the Turnpike Trust from Highbridge to Wells was set up, and the short length of 'new road' linked the two ends more smoothly.[52] The primary school was built on the leftover triangle of waste ground.

WELLS WAY is the oldest recorded road name in Blackford. It is the way to Wells across the hill-tops, avoiding Wedmore. In 1558 the road is described as 'Welles Weye ... the highwaie beinge a hard gravell way'.[53] At the end of the last century and until fairly recently it was often called Cotton Street. The earliest reference found so far to Cotton Street is in 1881 when the headmaster at Blackford School wrote in his log book, 'cautioned children against throwing stones in Cotton Street.'[54] I have found no clue as to why 'Cotton Street' was so called. Eric Wride, who lives there, suggested it might have had something to do with women taking in sewing. This suggestion was strengthened when the 1881 census showed that Sarah Wilkins, 26, shirt-maker, Emma Crease, 26, and Mary Urch, 17, both plain sewers, all lived there. It is a pity that we do not know who might have given it the nickname Cotton Street after this local cottage industry.

Leading out of the village to the open arable fields were numerous green lanes. Often these were named to help farm labourers get to the right field. As the fields became enclosed, some lanes were stoned, other became droves and some totally disappeared. In some areas, the Wedmore parish map of 1791 shows quite a different road pattern from that of today.[55]

SNIPEFIELD LANE links Blackford to Snipefield, which was part of the great open East Field and could also be reached from West Stoughton along **EASTFIELD LANE**. Snipefield takes its name from the bird, the snipe. The Blackford end of Snipefield Lane is an ancient track, while the rest of it was built after enclosure, in the 1800s, striking straight across East Field to meet Eastfield Lane and Quab Lane at the present crossroads.

The original medieval Snipefield Lane from Blackford twisted eastwards through the East Field, to arrive halfway along Quab Lane. Part of this old lane can still be traced. It was called **DAMSES LANE** in 1661,[56] or **DAMSELLS LANE** in 1739.[57] This part of East Field was called Damseland, perhaps the place where damsons grew. Nearby was another track called **GALLINGALE WAY** in 1661.[58] Galingale is a type of sedge, with an aromatic root, formerly used in cookery and medicine.[59] This lane has now totally disappeared, as has the other end of the original lane called **GOLLEDGE WAY** where it joined Quab Lane. Golledge Way, first mentioned in 1772,[60] no doubt takes its name from the Golledge family who lived in the parish in the 1500s and 1600s. The road between Blackford and Stoughton, now apparently nameless, was called **ROGERS LANE** in 1747, likewise probably from the Rogers family living there at some earlier time.[61]

The road name **PERRY LANE** does not exist now, but the beginning of this lane is still there. Perry Lane led from the High Street past the site of the Bishop's Palace. The name Perry Lane is first recorded in 1744,[62] and 'perry' probably comes from Old English *pirige*, a pear tree. Perhaps it was the way through the pear orchards. Just outside the village, Perry Lane became the **GREEN WAY**, which is a field track running all the way to the Ashton Road. This is first recorded as Greene Wey in 1635.[63] Most of Perry Lane is now footpath, but Green Way has become a drove.

Another lane which still exists today has also lost its very ancient name. This lane is the continuation of the road through Middle Stoughton, which swings west and eventually comes out on the Ashton-West Stoughton road. It was called **SULLINGWAY**, spelt Sullenway or Zullingway in 1609.[64] *Sulh* is the Old English or Saxon for a plough, so Sullingway was the ploughway along which the Saxons walked their plough-teams of oxen

Parish Road Names

to the great open fields. This same lane continues across the Ashton-West Stoughton road, southwest and then south all the way to Blackford where it becomes Green Way and Perry Lane (see above).

Another green lane, **RUSH HILL LANE** leads from Wells Way past Poplar Farm to the Wedmore Road. It is first called Rush Lane in 1769.[65] Rush Hill seems to be a corruption of Rush Well, as this is the name recorded much earlier, in 1557.[66] This is an example of how a 'nonsense' name can develop – it is not going uphill, it is probably the result of slovenly speech by running the two words together making 'Rushell Lane'. The early name means the well or spring where the rushes grew.

HOZZARD LANE opposite Rush Hill Lane was a field track leading to Hozzard, another area of medieval open arable field. It is not until the mid-1700s that Hozzard is spelt with a double 'z'. Before that, working backwards towards the oldest and more original spelling, it was Hosarde (1657)[67] and Hossett (1635).[68] In 1542 it is written as Horesette.[69] This name could have several meanings. 'Sett' is probably from the Old English word for a dwelling-place or a fold where animals were kept. The first part of the name could be Old English *hore* for 'dirt' or 'mud', but is more likely to be 'horse'. Horesette is thus possibly the place where Saxon or medieval horses were kept. In Domesday Book (1086) there were nine unbroken mares on the lord's demesne at Blackford; so horses have long been a feature of this manor.

FOSS LANE between Blackford and Westham is a name which always excites interest as it can have links with Roman roads. The *fossa* (in Latin) was the ditch that ran alongside the road. Foss Lane does lead from Poolbridge Road to Westham and the moor beyond, in which are Roman salt-works. However, its seems that this Foss is a corruption of something totally different. In 1635 the tenants of Blackford manor are ordered to dig and scour the ditch along 'the road called Vorsway'.[70] 'Vors' or 'vorse' is probably derived from the Old English or Saxon *fyrs*, furze or gorse, in a broad Somerset accent, spelt as it was sounded. Adjoining fields are called Voss in 1642,[71] Fors in 1652[72] and so the name gradually changed to Foss by the 1700s.

Heath House, Sand and Mudgley

The roads around Heath House, Sand and Mudgley may seem today little narrow country lanes just giving access to those settlements. Some of these lanes, however, were main routes and streets in medieval times. They probably carried much more traffic than they do today, although at a more leisurely pace.

Heath House

KEYTON HILL, pronounced Ky - (to rhyme with pie) - ton, is the road between Heath House and Westham; it also gave the medieval farmers access to the great open arable fields on the hill top. In 1559 the name is spelt Kydon,[73] in 1554 Kyden or Kyten.[74] In 1608 it is Kiton Hill.[75] The name probably means cow hill, from the Old English or Saxon *cu* or *cy*, cow(s) and *dun*, hill. Interestingly, it adjoins Horesett, now Hozzard, the horse-fold.

JACKS DROVE is the drove from the bottom of Heath House hill south across the moor. It is so called because it is a continuation of the lane down from Heath House which was originally Jackes Lane. The earliest reference to Jackes Lane is in 1557.[76] The name 'Jack' is a mystery; it may be a personal name from someone who once lived nearby - possibly long ago, for the farmsteads at the foot of the hill have very ancient origins. It is a pity that the road name Jacks Lane is not used any more. The drove which preserves the memory of Jack is in its present form a creation of the late 1700s enclosures.

CASTLE LANE is a route leading east from Heath House to Sand. It is still partly a green lane. The lane takes its name from an area of the medieval open field called Castle. The first reference to this field name is Castell, in 1558.[77] Was there once a castle there? Certainly not a medieval castle with knights and ladies, nor a Norman motte and bailey; but perhaps there was a structure of some sort. The name 'castle' can be derived from Old English or Saxon *ceaster* meaning old fortifications or remains of the still earlier Roman or Iron Age periods. It can also be a corruption of Old English or Saxon *chessel*, small stones - often used as a name where a medieval peasant had turned up the distinctive stones of the mosaic floor of a buried Roman villa, during his ploughing. In the 1800s, along Castle Lane, several skeletons were discovered when stone was being quarried from a field.[78] These skeletons were thought to be of the Romano-British period, so perhaps there was a Roman building or fortification there. The eastern end of this lane near Sand seems to have been called **PIG LANE** in the 1600s.[79] In the census of 1881 the Heath House end of Castle Lane is referred to as **BATTENS LANE**. George Batten is recorded as living in one of the little cottages there in the 1851 census.

Sand

The main road through Sand is nameless and in the 16th century was often referred to as the 'waye to Welles'.[80] The lanes leading off the main road did have names. We have already discussed **MADWOMANS LANE** which is the direct link with West End in Wedmore.

SAND HILL is a green lane which leads down past Sand Hall, to become Sand Drove, running out across Aller Moor. It used to be a straighter track called **SAND** or **MOOR LANE**, but was diverted further from the house in 1778, when the grounds of Sand Hall were extended westwards.[81] In the 1500s there was a lane making a crossroads with the Wedmore/Sand Road at Townsend Farm. This lane went down the hill to the meadows beyond the houses. It was called **CHITTERLEYS LANE** in 1557 because it led to the meadows called Chitterley.[82] Just a trace of the lane can be seen as a hollow way today.

OLDWOOD LANE was originally **OLD PARKE LANE** in 1558.[83] The lane originally went straight down through the medieval deer park to Aller Moor where it became **ALLERMOOR LANE**. When the little cottages of Old Wood were built in the mid-1500s the lane turned westwards to provide their access.

Mudgley

The main road through the centre of Mudgley village does not nowadays seem to have a name but in 1559 it was the **TOWNE WEYE**. Heading off Towne Weye was **STYCHEN WEYE**, the **STITCHING LANE** of today.[84] A 'stitch' was a very small piece of land, smaller than the usual 'strip' of ploughland in a medieval open field.

The lower end of **MUDGLEY HILL** is a fairly new stretch of road, built c1827 by the

Turnpike Trust.[85] Before that the road went down the hill in a great westwards curve. This road was called **HANGARY LANE** in 1546.[86] It can still be seen as a bank around the field west of the present road. The name Hangary comes from the Old English *hangra*, meaning a slope. The lane westwards from Mudgley Hill Farm was called **LADY MEAD** or **LADIE MEDE LANE** in 1544,[87] because it led to the field called Ladie Mede. The part of Towne Weye east of Mudgley Hill ran past the Court, the great house built by the Dean of Wells in the 1100s. This section of lane was called **COURTE WEYE** in 1554, but by then the ancient house was just a ruin.[88] The name **COURT LANE** continued until this century, when it seems to have fallen out of use. Memory of the court house is preserved in the name of nearby Court Farm.

BLAKEWAY is the latest in a series of roads that cross the moor from Mudgley to Westhay. On a map of 1779, New Blake Way is shown as the road we use today.[89] Old Blake Way is also marked a little further east. It is not known when New Blake Way took over from Old Blake Way, or how old Old Blake Way was. In 1947 the remains of a wooden trackway were discovered buried in the peat; it ran parallel to Blakeway but east of the line of Old Blake Way. This wooden trackway was given the name the Tollgate Track, and was dated as being built about 500 BC.[90] Three years earlier, another trackway, named the Blakeway Track, had been discovered, almost in line with the Tollgate Track.[91] It was at first thought that the two were parts of one and the same trackway. Radio-carbon dating, however, has proved that the Blakeway Track was constructed much earlier, about 2,500 B.C. Early man was thus making roads across the moor below Mudgley over 4,500 years ago. There may well be more earlier 'Blakeways' waiting to be discovered. The name Blakeway is first recorded as Blake Weye in 1558.[92] It must mean the 'black road', from the Old English or Saxon *blaec*, meaning black! It refers, of course, to the black peaty soil.

Theale and Bagley

The main road through Theale has never had a proper name, and is generally known just as the Wells Road; but the roads and lanes running off the main road have names which often turn out to be quite old.

WEST WELL LANE takes its name from the well which once bubbled out at its junction with the main road. The well was originally Theale Well (see Chapter 8). Why the name changed to West Well is not known, but it was West Well in the eighteenth century. The lane leads directly down into **SKITMORE DROVE**. Together, these form the boundary between the ancient estates of Panborough (later Northload) and Wedmore - a boundary which goes back to Saxon times.[93]

The correct name of Skitmore Drove should be **KITMORE DROVE**, which can be traced back to the name Kippmere in 1494.[94] At the time of the enclosure of the moor in 1778, the name Kitmore suddenly became Skitmore, and this error has stayed ever since. How did the intrusive 's' come about? I remember I once had a six-year-old pupil who insisted that the word morning was spelt 'smorning', because that is what everyone said, 'Smorning!' - if you listen to us locals, she was right! No doubt the same thing happened with Skitmore. Some official came to check up on the names for the Enclosure Act in 1778 and was told, 'O ah, tha's Kitmore' - and S-kitmore it became. The Ordnance Survey mapmakers have endorsed this version in print ever since.

BROWNS LANE, I can only assume, takes it name from a Brown family who once lived there. The road name does not seem to occur in any records until fairly recently. Before that, the lane was nameless. Perhaps someone in Theale knows the answer.

SNAKE LANE is in a very deep cutting as it runs down from Bagley to Theale. The name must refer to snakes seen there, as the lane itself is not twisty like a snake. In 1517 a field by the lane is called 'Snakehegge ende', suggesting that this dark deep lane was a haven for adders or grassnakes at least as far back as the 1500s.[95] It is an early example of how placenames can provide a record not only of people, landscapes and farm animals, but also of past wildlife.

DAGGS LANE at Bagley forms part of the ancient Saxon boundary line between Northload and Wedmore.[96] It may be a very old route down onto the moor. Daggs are dirty pieces of fleece which would make this an unusual road name. It is more likely to be the name, perhaps long ago a rude nickname, of a family who once lived there. In 1636 Wedmore registers record the baptism of Elizabeth daughter of John and Alice Dagg of Bagley. They seem to have belonged to the family variously called Dagg or Daggle *alias* Cutler, prominent in the 1600s.

The part of Bagley now called **THE SQUARE** was the western end of the area of open land known as Bagley Green, where a scattering of late 18th century cottages appeared on the road verges.

COLDNOSE is just a part of the main Bagley Road on the eastern tip of the hill. This area on the ridge, exposed to all the elements, is very aptly named as no doubt the people who live there now can testify. It is not an old settlement, and the name first appears in the census of 1861. Perhaps it was the first inhabitants, in the 1800s, who gave Coldnose its name.

TOWNSEND LANE seems a curious name for a lane right out in the country. The 'town' to which it refers, from the Saxon or Old English *tun*, a settlement, is Theale. It marks, in effect, the boundary between West Theale and Latcham. In the 1500s there were two other 'townsends', at either end of Sand. Townsend Farm at Sand survives to remind us of one of these placenames. Townsend Lane at Theale is called 'the weane way' in 1543, when a tenant of Mudgley Manor has to pay ½d a year to use this way for his waggons (or 'waines').[97] It was obviously a quick way from the hilltop fields and the top road, down to the main road, which he had to pay to use; the idea of toll roads is not new!

NORTHLOAD LANE leads to Northload Farm, the ancient 'principle court house' or manor house of the estate of Northload.[98] The meaning of the name Northload has already been described, and was probably the way north over the River Axe.

WHITE HORSE LANE, so called in 1779, is the green lane that links Bagley with the east end of Mudgley.[99] Nowadays it tends to become so overgrown that it is difficult to walk along it; but in the census of 1841 there were five cottages in White Horse Lane. A few tumbled remains can still be seen. The name conjures up images of a phantom white horse galloping up and down, as the Revd S.H.A. Hervey, writing in the 1880s, believed.[100] It could, however, have nothing to do with folk tales and ghosts. It might be a memory of a real white horse kept there for some long time; or it could be something even more down to earth. White Horse Lane was the western boundary of Bagley Wood. In 1544 there was a boundary stone there called the Leaping Stone.[101] This name certainly suggests scenes of youngsters leap-frogging over the stone marker as a way of remembering its position and purpose, as was done with parish boundary marks on Rogation Day when beating the bounds. As such, it could well be medieval in origin. There is still a stone standing in the hedgebank of the lane. Whether it is the Leaping Stone I cannot be sure, but it is old and whiteish. Ancient boundary stones are often called 'Hoar' or 'Hore', from the Old English or Saxon word *har*, meaning grey-white and/or old (whence our modern words hoary, and hoar frost). Could it be that the white stones or white hoars, of which one now survives, gave the lane its name? There may, of course, be a totally different explanation.

In addition, there are two lost lanes, one called **GOATWAY** in 1782, which ran across the tip of the hill from Russells Hill above Panborough Inn, south to Old Rhyne (now Panborough Drain).[102] The other was called **SOUTH HORSE WEY** in 1517 and was one of the field access tracks running westward from Panborough along the hill spur.[103]

Cocklake

The road leading down into Cocklake is called **THE DUNGEON**. I have not yet found out when and why this name came into being. It does appear to be fairly recent. No 'Dungeon' has been found in any of the many old documents studied so far. By the time the name first appears in print in the *Wedmore Chronicles* of the 1880s, it must have been in common use by villagers. Unless earlier references with different spellings are found, we must presume it was the nickname for the dark and creepy lane worn deep over the centuries by water and the passage of traffic.

NEW LANE, linking The Dungeon with the Cheddar Road, is only partly new. For most of its route, it was an old track leading to fields, until the new turnpike road was cut through in 1827.[104] At this time the track was linked up with the turnpike road and named New Lane.

SOUTH MEAD LANE in the centre of Cocklake starts as one of the old village streets which led to what was then a field track to the fields called South Mead. It is first recorded in 1605.[105]

RUGHILL, before the turnpike road was cut from Cocklake's former Post Office towards Clewer in 1827,[106] was the main road from Wedmore to Clewer and Cheddar. It seems to be a corruption of Rugwell, and can be compared with Rush Hill/Rush Well Lane at Blackford. In 1820 it is also spelt Rughill and Rugell.[107] In 1756 Ruggwell is recorded,[108] and back in 1678 it is spelt Rugwell.[109] This well was probably the spring which bubbles out from the hillside behind the former Post Office. Rugwell may mean the well on the ridge, from the Old English or Saxon *hrycg*, a ridge. Local people always pronounce it as 'ruggle' today.

Crickham

The **LONG HILL** is the promontory between Crickham and Clewer with the road running along its spine. The earliest reference to Long Hill so far discovered is in 1822.[110]

CRIB HOUSE LANE is the other road running roughly parallel to Long Hill, linking Crickham and Clewer. It takes its name from a cow shed; but where this particular cow shed or crib house stood or when it first gave its name to the lane is not known.

WALLS LANE is the lane opposite South View Farm at Crickham. It was once one of the main streets of the village and originally turned to join up with Crib House Lane. The end of the lane now is just a hollow way, a slight dent in the fields. Walls Lane might sound as if it was named afer the local Wall family, but in 1674 there is Woole Lane in Crickham.[111] This is an earlier and less altered spelling of our present Walls Lane. It is written as Whool or Wool Lane in 1743.[112] Wool Lane could have taken its name from wool, but many 'wool' place names in fact come from personal names, or from Old English or Saxon *wella*, a stream. Our Walls/Wool Lane is probably such a corruption of *wella*, as the lane still crosses the stream that flows through Crickham today.

PERROW LANE is a dead end leading to, and taking its name from, Perrow Farm, one of the series of ancient farmsteads along the moor edge. Perrow Lane is first written down in 1605 as Pirwaye or Perwaye, perhaps itself a corruption of Per[row] Way.[113] Pir- or Per- could be from the Old English or Saxon *peru*, for pear; perhaps there were pear orchards round the farmhouse. More cautiously, it might be derived from the Norman-French *pierre*, referring to some paved way leading down to the ancient farmstead and the nearby River Axe.

Clewer

Clewer does not seem to have any surviving road names today. **CLEWER LANE**, first mentioned in 1762, is now just a track off the main turnpike road near Nethercote Nursery.[114] It never was more than a field track, as until the turnpike road was built in 1827 there was no direct link along the foot of the hill between Cocklake and Clewer.[115]

In 1816 a boundary description refers to **MEAD LANE** in Clewer, when the boundary is described as going 'round by The Ivy House and down Mead Lane'.[116] As I cannot find where Ivy House was, it is impossible to say if Mead Lane was the main street running past Manor Farm, the lane to Ragwood Farm, or a zigzag track between the two which is shown on maps but now apparently vanished.

THE BATCH was probably the top of the hill at Clewer. In 1578 John, son of Elizabeth and John Thurston junior was baptised in the parish church. The Thurstons were described as being 'de [of] Batche' in Clewer.[117]

Some lost and forgotton names

Some lost lanes and forgotten names have already been looked at, but here are a few more strays. There are three lost lanes called after people. On the hilltop between Sand, Mudgley and Wedmore was **WHITES LANE**, mentioned only in 1711.[118] There were also two lanes, both called **TUCKERS LANE**, one in Wedmore in 1814[119] and one in Blackford in 1751.[120] The whereabouts of all three are now unknown. In 1554 there was a lane called **EXETTER LANE**.[121] It was somewhere on the western outskirts of Wedmore. Perhaps Exetter Lane was an earlier name for Kelsons Lane or Madwomans Lane, before the Kelson family or the mad woman left their mark on the landscape. The meaning of Exetter is unknown, probably nothing to do with Exeter in Devon. Nearby was **THE CHURCH WAY**, recorded in 1705, which led from Heath House to the parish church in Wedmore; but whether this was an alternative name for the main road, or whether it was another track which has now disappeared, I cannot find out.[122]

Chapter 3
Wedmore Manor and its Manor House

The origins of Wedmore as a village must be sought in the history of the Manor and its manor house. The Manor House stands next to Wedmore Church. The present house is probably on the site of a building which stood in King Alfred's time. Wedmore belonged to the Saxon king, and he had his *villa regia* or royal house here. It may have been a simple hunting lodge or a hall like the one found at Cheddar.[1] In 878, Alfred moved from his headquarters at Athelney to defeat Guthrum and the Danish army at the battle of Ethandune (Edington, in Wiltshire).[2] After this decisive battle, Alfred brought the defeated Danish leader Guthrum and his entourage back, first to Aller near Athelney, where Alfred stood sponsor at the baptism of Guthrum, and then to his estate at Wedmore. During the twelve days they stayed at Wedmore, amid much lavish demonstration of Saxon royal power and hospitality, the second half of the christening ceremony - the 'chrism-loosing'- took place and the famous agreement called the Peace of Wedmore was made between the Saxons and the Danes.[3]

Wedmore Manor House from the church tower, 1880

The religious ceremony probably took place in a Saxon church standing on the site of the present church, and the great company of Saxons and Danes were accommodated in Alfred's *villa regia* nearby. So far no trace of any Saxon building has been found in this spot; both church and house have been in use continuously, and rebuilt many times since 878.

Wedmore belonged to the Saxon kings until 1062, when King Edward gave it to Giso, Bishop of Wells.[4] The great Saxon estate of Wedmore had by then been subdivided into separate units of more manageable size, which the King could bestow on favoured subjects. Part of Wedmore had been granted to Glastonbury Abbey. In the Domesday Survey of

1086, Bishop Giso, who was a royal chaplain to both Edward the Confessor and William the Conqueror, was still holding the Manor of Wedmore. By this time we know there was a church of some importance at Wedmore, probably a 10th or 11th century stone church replacing that of Alfred's time; and the early village would have been developing around it and the manor house.

In 1136 the Bishop gave Wedmore to the Dean of Wells, along with other estates on and around the Isle of Wedmore.[5] At one of these, Mudgley, the Dean built a grand house. We do not know why the Dean preferred Mudgley, other than perhaps for its south-facing aspect and fine views. The ancient manor house at Wedmore was probably left for the Dean's steward to live in. He ran the manorial courts and supervised the management of the manor.

The first documentary evidence of this manor house occurs in 1334 when Dean John de Godelee dies.[6] His manor houses at Wedmore, Mudgley and Totney are all in need of repairs, totalling £15 10s 0d. Among the goods left at Wedmore for the next dean are two tables in the hall with trestles. This would be the main hall of the medieval Wedmore Manor House. In 1378, when a later Dean died, repairs are needed to 'chambers' (upstairs rooms in the Manor House), along with granges, bovaries, and garners (storage barns, oxhouses, and granaries for the threshed grain) which may have been part of the manor compound.[7] In 1452 the Dean issued a land-use agreement at Wedmore, in a three-part document; one copy was kept at Wells by the Dean, the second by the tenant, and the third was to remain 'in the Manor at Wedmore' probably kept in a locked chest in the Manor House.[8] There is no other reference to Wedmore Manor House during this century. By contrast, the many references to the Dean's house at Mudgley suggest that it overshadowed Wedmore Manor House, which may have been left gently decaying.

In 1501 the churchwardens of Wedmore are granted permission from the Dean to build a church house on some vacant land 'south of the steps of the western churchyard'.[9] In 1508 there is a curious reference to this church house, as it appears to have been built partly on 'a certain part of a tower'.[10] This tower, standing outside the churchyard, was certainly not the church tower. It may have been the remains of a former medieval gatehouse leading to the church and manor house. This in turn raises the possibility that the early medieval manor house and church were inside a walled compound, like that at the Saxon Cheddar palace, which had fallen into ruin by the early 1500s.

When King Henry VIII had all church property assessed in 1535, Wedmore manor was valued at £51 8s 4½d.[11] The estate was taken away from the Dean and reverted back to the Crown. When King Henry died, his son the boy-king Edward VI gave Wedmore to his cousin and regent, the Duke of Somerset. Four years later in 1551 the Duke was beheaded and his estate including Wedmore again reverted to the Crown.

Five years after this, in the time of Queen Mary I, on 28th July 1557, plans were in hand for Sir Henry Jernegan to buy Wedmore.[12] The estate was valued at £44 22¾d, which included the 'Farm of the Capital Mansion'. This means the income from letting the demesne, the land belonging to the Manor House itself. This income came to 17s 4d a year, and the steward or reeve who looked after the estate had outgoings of 9s 2d a year. However, Sir Henry Jernegan never actually bought Wedmore, as three months later we find Queen

Mary granting it to John Elyott, citizen of London. To Elyott, Wedmore was just another business transaction. He sold it on again to another Londoner, Sir Thomas Gresham, on 8th January 1559, in the first year of the reign of Queen Elizabeth I.[13]

Wedmore Manor House west front, 1900

The deed of sale to Sir Thomas Gresham records that the estate consisted of 150 messuages and 50 tofts (smallholdings), 200 gardens, 10 dovecots, 10 mills, 2000 acres of ploughland, 300 acres of meadow, 2000 acres of pasture, 200 acres of wood and 1000 acres of gorse and heath. The total acreage was 5,500 acres, about half of the area of the parish today. These figures look suspiciously rounded and are, one presumes, approximate. It not known if Sir Thomas Gresham, the famous Elizabethan financier, ever visited Wedmore; probably not, as to him it was, again, just another investment. After seventeen years Gresham sold off the Manor of Wedmore in bits, breaking up the ancient estate and making its later history very complicated. Few documents about this break-up survive, but some of them do concern the actual manor house. On 1st October 1576 Gresham sold the capital messuage (that is, the Manor House) with two other tenements, two cottages, three barns, one dovecote, three gardens and three orchards to Thomas Hodges.[14] Thomas Hodges also acquired 40 acres of ploughland, 15 acres of meadow, 15 acres of pasture, 3 acres of wood and 100 acres of heath, just a tiny part the original large manorial estate.

The Hodges family had originated in the Somerton area, but had for some time been living in Allerton. At last, in 1576, the Manor House was occupied - for the very first time in its history - by a local gentry family, as Lords of the Manor. Thomas and Margaret Hodges had four children, Agnes and John who died as babies, and Thomas II and Isobel. Thomas II grew up in Wedmore and married a local heiress, Agatha Rodney, daughter of George Rodney of Rodney Stoke. They in turn had three children, George (born in 1581), Suzanna (born 1583) and Hannibal (born 1584).[15]

Thomas II was a soldier, and went off to fight in one of the Elizabethan campaigns in the Netherlands. He was killed at the siege of Antwerp, fighting the Spanish. The brass plaque in St Mary's Church commemorating his death has on it the date of the siege as 'about

1583', but this is an error. Perhaps the brass was only made some time later. The siege actually took place in 1585, and baby Hannibal had been born the previous year in 1584. The brass, with a heart at the top and the inscription between two furled flags, reads:

> **Wounded**
> **not**
> **Vanquisht**
> **SACRED**
> **To the memorie of Captaine**
> **THOMAS HODGES**
> **In the county of Somerset Esq.**
> **who at the Seige of ANTWERPE about 1583**
> **with vnconquerd courage wonne two**
> **Ensignes from the ENEMY where**
> **receiuing his last wound, he gaue**
> **three legacyes; his soule, to his LORD**
> **IESVS; his body to be lodgd in Flemish**
> **earth; his heart to be sent to his deare**
> **wife in England.**
>
> **HERE LYES HIS WOVNDED HEART FOR WHOME**
> **ONE KINGDOME WAS TWO SMALL A ROOME**
> **TWO KINGDOMS THEREFORE HAVE THOVGHT GOOD TO PART**
> **SO STOVT A BODY AND SO BRAVE A HEART**

Imagine the scene: Agatha with George (4) and Suzanna (2) awaiting news of her dashing husband; baby Hannibal had died soon after his birth. There is a knock at the Manor House door and the bearer of bad tidings is ushered in, carrying her dear husband's heart pickled in a casket. That heart is buried somewhere in the chancel of Wedmore Church.

A few years later Agatha married Sir George Young, and went to live on another of the family estates. Thomas's father and mother, Thomas I and Margaret, were however still alive and living in the Manor House. It is not known whether Agatha's two small children George and Suzanna went with their mother, or stayed behind in Wedmore with their grandparents, but George, some time during the next few years, was made the ward of one John Rosse of Shepton Beauchamp.[16] Perhaps his mother had died and the grandparents were too old to look after him. John Rosse was a relation, being married to Mary Hodges, who was probably first cousin of George's father Thomas II. George grew up in Shepton Beauchamp and at the age of eighteen in 1598/99 married Eleanor Rosse,[17] daughter of his guardians John and Mary. His grandfather Thomas Hodges I died in Wedmore in 1601, and his grandmother Margaret in 1617, 'very aged'.[18]

George and Eleanor Hodges lived in Shepton Beauchamp for the first few years of their marriage. Their first four children were born there, Hannibal (in 1599), Mary (1600), Henry (1601) and Thomas (1603).[19] The rest of their thirteen children were born in Wedmore: Jane (in 1609), George (1611), Ann (1612), Jane 1613), Agatha (1614), Margaret (1615), Elizabeth (1616), Barbara (1617) and finally Penelope (1618).[20] They were, therefore, living in Wedmore Manor House by 1609; but there is a gap of six years between the births at Shepton Beauchamp and those at Wedmore. Maybe George was away soldiering, or they

Memorial brass of George Hodges, 1634, in Wedmore Church. This is one of the latest examples of a military brass

lived somewhere else during those years; but there is no trace of any other children born during this time, so the former is perhaps more likely.

George Hodges died in 1634 aged 53,[21] and only two of his children are of interest to Wedmore: Thomas Hodges III and George Hodges II. Thomas III, who never married, became Member of Parliament for Ilchester. He was able to live in Wedmore most of the time, as Parliament rarely met in those days of Charles I. Thomas III was certainly living in Wedmore in 1643, as the parish register records that Ann Worten, servant to Thomas Hodges gentleman, was buried on 25th May 1643. Thomas III, as the oldest surviving son, had inherited the family estates. He died, a bachelor, in Wedmore in May 1649, and was buried in Wedmore Church just five days after his mother Eleanor. His brother George II then inherited the estate; but Thomas III left all his goods 'within and without his dwelling house in Wedmore' to his sisters, Jane, Agatha, Margaret and Barbara.[22] George was not living at Wedmore at the time of Thomas III's death. He had married Ann Mansell from Monmouthshire, and they had two daughters, neither of whom were born in Wedmore: Mary, born 1641, and Jane, a few years younger. These were troubled times. During the Civil War, George was away fighting, but it is not known whether he was on the Royalist or the Parliamentarian side. King Charles I was beheaded in 1649, the year of brother Thomas III's death. Only then did George II and Ann move into Wedmore Manor House.

In 1654 during the Commonwealth when the living had been left vacant for four years, a new vicar was appointed to Wedmore. His name was Jeremy Horler.[23] George Hodges II died in March 1655, and within three months his widow Ann was married again - to Jeremy Horler (see Chapter 13). Jeremy and Ann lived in the Manor House until 1660. Jeremy was then appointed Rector of Yate in Gloucestershire,[24] and the family moved to Yate. When Ann Horler died in 1684, her body was brought back to Wedmore to be buried in her family tomb in the parish church.

Ann's daughter Jane Hodges married John Strachey in 1662.[25] She appears to have been a bright, intelligent girl. Her husband John was an intellectual. His greatest friend was John Locke, the philosopher, who was born in Wrington. John and Jane Strachey lived at Sutton Court, near Chew Magna. Jane's elder sister Mary had married, been widowed, and married again, but she did not come back to the Wedmore area. What was happening to the Manor House during all this time? There were probably just a few staff looking after it, and someone to attend to manorial business, and to collect rents and dues. The family may have returned to Wedmore on occasional visits.

Tragedy struck the Stracheys in 1674. John Strachey's mother died; and before John had sorted out all her business affairs, he too suddenly died. Young Jane was left with three children, two daughters Elizabeth and Jane,[26] and her son and heir John, aged only three, and with the immense task of sorting out and running the various family estates. There was their Strachey estate at Sutton Court, property in London and Gloucester; her own Hodges estates, held jointly with sister Mary, in Wedmore, Elm and Buckland near Frome; and there was also land in Mark, South Brent (now Brent Knoll) and Weare. John Strachey seems not to have been a very practical man, more concerned with his discussions with John Locke, and with two deaths coming so close together the estate was in some disarray. Jane had the task of getting everything onto a sound footing for her son John to inherit in due course. Mary, although married twice, died childless in 1709, without making a will, so that Jane was left as her heiress. Jane, since the death of her own husband in 1674, had been living at Sutton Court near Chew Magna, but still ran the estate at Wedmore.

Fortunately for Wedmore, we know a little of how she did this. An account book of the day-to-day running of the Manor House and estate has survived.[27] The book is written in two different hands, and has been turned upside-down several times so that entries do not

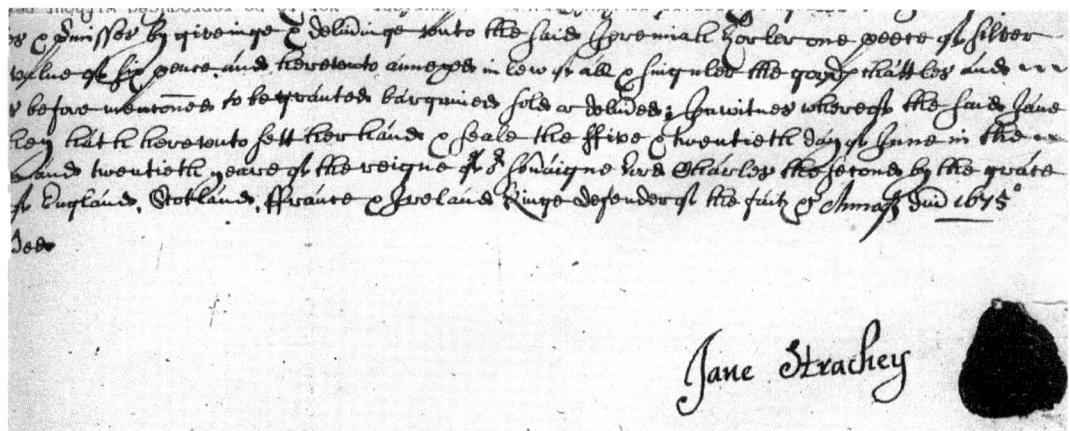

Signature of Jane Strachey, Lady of the Manor, 1675

always run in sequence. Eleven pages, covering 1677 and 1678, are in a neat clerical hand. The later pages are written by someone else in a different, more fluid hand. The 1677-78 accounts are kept by William Hodges of Wedmore. He was probably a cousin of Jane Strachey. The later accounts are clearly kept by Jane herself.

William Hodges was in charge of running the estate on behalf of the two sisters, Mary and Jane. He was responsible for bringing in the 'parsonage corn'. The Dean of Wells in the 1600s still held the 'parsonage' tithes; these were the 'great' tithes of corn and other cereals, hay, herbage, wool and lambs. The vicar of Wedmore, appointed by the Dean and Chapter, received the 'small' or 'lesser' tithes, of honey, calves, geese, eggs etc. Tithes, originally a church levy of one-tenth of all these farming yields each year, were gradually being changed or commuted into money payments. The Dean received some tithes in money, but still got his corn straight from the field. The Lord of the Manor of Wedmore was responsible for collecting the Dean's tithes. As there was no family resident at the Manor House to do this, Mary and Jane appointed William Hodges as their agent. His accounts show how it was done: 'Paid Edward Syms for one weeks crooking 5s... Paid John Quick for two weeks crooking 12s'. He also paid Francis Cutler, William Deane and George Warman for crooking. Crooking has nothing to do with sheep. A crook in Somerset dialect is a metal pole, about five feet long and curved. It is joined to another one with struts, making it something like a curved ladder. A pair of crooks were stuck into the pack saddle of a horse, making a large open framework into which corn or hay could be packed. A great amount of corn could be crammed into the crooks. It is recorded that men even jumped up and down on the corn to press it down. These men were called 'crookers'. Crookers went out with their horses, and filled up their crooks with the parsonage corn. They collected one tenth of each tenants' crop; and the packhorses with their capacious crooks would be much more convenient than a cart as they went from field to field, collecting one tenth from each place.

Some men were paid for plough work. Joseph Tutton was paid 6s for one day's work with his plough. John Churchouse did the same but was only paid 5s. John Lacham earned £1 2s for four days' work. Edward Stone was paid 1s 6d for carriage of one load of corn, probably in his cart. People were being paid good money for their work at this time. One hundred and twenty years later a labourer was paid just 1s or 1s 4d a day.[28]

William Hodges paid Joseph Tutton 8s 6d. for making the mows in the barton and thatching them. The barton was the yard belonging to the Manor House, and the mows were the haystacks. Stephen Miceter was paid 16s for three weeks 'riding in the field', and another 4s for having 'lent' his mare for two weeks. He had probably been appointed to supervise the collection of the tithes. Seven shillings was also spent by William Hodges on beer 'in tyme of having in the parsonage corn', for the workers during their thirsty job of getting in the Dean's tithe-share of the Wedmore harvest.

The account book kept by Jane Strachey and William Hodges also gives an insight into the Manor House and estate. By 1677 the Manor House had, it seems, fallen into disrepair, while the Hodges heiresses were living elsewhere. William's accounts at the beginning of the book show he bought 'nailes 2s 11d', '3 sacks of lyme 3s' (for lime-washing), '600 tiles 10s', and paying 11s 6d for making the gate. The tilers were paid 16s for seven days work and they used 2,000 tile pins. Perhaps the manor house was being stripped of its thatch and the roof newly tiled. The masons were paid 2s 4d for repairing the walls. Jane was still at Sutton Court, as William sent off a load of wheat to Sutton, cost 5s.

The Manor House garden was being cared for. 'Paid for carrying soil into the garden 2s 6d.', 'Grass 10s' (presumably this was for cutting the grass during the summer). The walls of the court and garden were repaired for 15s. Plants and seeds for the garden cost 1s 6d. Six young elms cost 1s 6d. These were probably planted as a windbreak. Gardening cost 1s 8d (he does not say for how long), and 1s was paid for digging the garden to 'sett petates' (potatoes), still a relatively novel crop in the south west at that time. It was usual for the Lord of the Manor to be responsible for the upkeep of the chancel of the parish church. Since the Hodges bought the Lordship from the Dean of Wells, this was their responsibility as well. Jane Strachey paid £2 18s for glazing the chancel windows and 18s for tiling the church roof.

Out of the many close-written pages of entries, just a few examples are selected to show details of daily life at Wedmore Manor House: shoeing horses 2s 6d, a new sack 3s 4d, mending the baker's saddle 1s. Threshing the corn cost anything from 1s to 2s a day. Winnowing was more expensive, at 3s to 3s 6d a day, as it was harder work. William paid out 7s for two weeks' 'diet', paying for food for the servants or workers in the Manor House. It cost 6d to wash thirteen sheep, and 1s to shear them, including the provision of beer to quench the shearer's thirst. A sheep pen at Wedmore's July Fair cost 6d. During the summer, little jobs were being done around the house: bedcords, 2 pans and 2 dishes cost 1s 7d; lamp black and colouring 1s; 'nailes and sope 9d'; 'Glassing the windows' 8s 6d - suggesting that quite a number must have been broken - and 2 locks were bought for the inner doors at 1s 8d. It would seem that the house was being rescued from neglect.

Many of the goods which William bought, such as nails, pitch and candles, came from Widow Petheram's shop in the village. William Hodges' account finishes in August 1678, and from then on Jane keeps the accounts herself. Her writing begins on August 31st, and, with items being entered nearly every day, it is clear that she is staying in Wedmore. This is why the Manor House and its garden had been done up. During September the corn is being harvested, and lattice is bought for the corn chamber windows at 4s. Symes is paid 5s for a week's threshing, standing of horses at Wells, and mending saddles. The horses had taken the tithe corn to Wells for the Dean. The accounts finish on October 5th as Jane has clearly returned to Sutton Court. She receives monies from William. The 'corne and mead tythes' for 1678 came to £319 4s 6d, and involved disbursements of £70 16s 11d 'Received clear £248 - 7- 7', quite a profit out of the tithes. The rent paid to the Dean was £70 a year, and Jane has to pay her sister and co-heir Mary half of the income from the estate. She also has to pay, each year, various national and local taxes.

The accounts recommence in August 1679 when Jane again stays at Wedmore to see in the harvest and to make sure the Dean's tithes are being collected. The first thing she does is to spend £1 to pay the carpenter for fourteen days work about the house. Jane paid for the usual crooking and plough works. On August 21 a load of reed, bringing home a load of peas, and candles, together cost 11s 5d. In September William Wall is paid 1s for gathering briars. At the end of September Jane pays Thomas Hill for 'a meshing vate, garten stauff & huckmuck, £1.' Jane is busy brewing, for a huckmuck is a strainer used in brewing. It consisted of a bundle of twigs which was placed in the bottom of the mashing vat, to prevent the grains running out when the wort was drawn off; wort is the fermenting malt. The 'garden stuff' may or may not have been needed for the work of brewing. On November 4th Jane 'paid A Rate for whiping Some corne Stealers.' George Lye, William Wall, Edward Syms and Simon Thorn are busy threshing the corn. Afterwards, Jane returns again to Sutton Court and William Hodges continues as steward.

Jane arrives back in Wedmore on 10th August 1680. She pays Goody Cornish and her maid 2s 9d for 'weeding the cawseys' (the paths) and 3s for 'showing (shoeing) the horses and things at Shop.' The only occasion that cider is mentioned is on September 27th when Mistress Westover is paid ls 3d 'for grinding 15 bushels of appels' and Richard Addams gets 1s 'for making Syder.' The chancel windows have been broken again, and were repaired by the glaziers for l9s. Half a year's chimney-sweeping costs 7s. Jane returns home on October 30th. From then on there are just scattered accounts taken on shorter visits. In November 1681 she pays William 'for John Sweets polishing my fathers toumb 4s', and 'For A mat for the toumb from Spirrin' 2s. John Sweet was the parish clerk, and earned this extra money for keeping such church monuments in good order. Part of the tomb still survives in the church. William Hodges now seems to be living in the Manor House, as the accounts show him paying out rent for it. His name disappears in 1691, when one John Smith sends monies off to Jane.

In 1691 Jane's son John Strachey came of age and inherited the family estates. The last account entry is on 18th May 1694, when Jane wrote, 'Richard Hardy brought from Wedmore for tyth lambs to my son & me' £3 8s 6d.

Jane Strachey died in 1727; her son John married twice, and had eighteen children by his first wife, and one by his second wife.[29] The manor of Wedmore was let to tenants, but who was living there is not known. The Strachey family held onto the Wedmore estate until the 1770s and perhaps a little longer. Three generations after Jane Strachey, however, successive large families had so reduced the family fortunes that in 1757 several estates were mortgaged, including Wedmore. Wedmore is described as 'All that messuage with garden and pigeon house commonly known as the Court or Manor House with eight acres of land.'[30] In the mid-1700s a John Barrow leased the house for £190 a year. The Barrow family had been in the parish since at least the l600s. In 1798 it was John Barrow of the Manor House who was described by Martha More, when she and her sister Hannah came to Wedmore to start a school for the poor children, as 'an ill-looking, coarse man'.[31] His son John, a magistrate, bought the manor and the Lordship on 7th October 1808, for the sum of £15,600.[32]

Charles Augustus Homfray bought the manor from the Barrows in 1871, including a close of 25 acres, part pasture and part plantation; this is Lascot Hill Copse.[33] It is said to be he who modernised the house, adding the north wing with library and smoking room; he possibly also carried out the reconstruction of the south wing to form a dining room and 'ballroom'. He also built the stables which are still there (2002), constructed of Wedmore stone and brick, with original cast iron partitions, mangers and water bowls. In 1878, Homfray sold out to Bailey, a solicitor;[34] from the Baileys the house passed to the Smiths, also solicitors, and ultimately to Mrs Pitcairn, who will be remembered by some as the last 'Lady of the Manor of Wedmore'. The house was sold in the l960s, and divided into three. The barn was converted into another house.

Wedmore Manor House has had a long and chequered history, and has been rebuilt many times since King Alfred's day. It has never been lived in continuously for more than a

Memorial to John Barrow, Lord of the Manor (d 1853), in Wedmore Church

hundred years at a time. Often it remained empty for many years, but it has always been at the centre of the village and, as with any ancient building, if only its stones could talk, how much more we could learn of our Wedmore history.

Chapter 4
St. Mary's Parish Church, Wedmore

The parish church of St Mary overlooks the village of Wedmore. In 878 AD Saxon King Alfred owned Wedmore, and it was to Wedmore that he brought the defeated Danes and their leader Guthrum. During twelve days of feasting two important ceremonies; the 'chrism-loosing' and making of the 'Peace of Wedmore', took place probably in a Saxon church on the site of St Mary's. No trace of any Saxon church has yet been found.

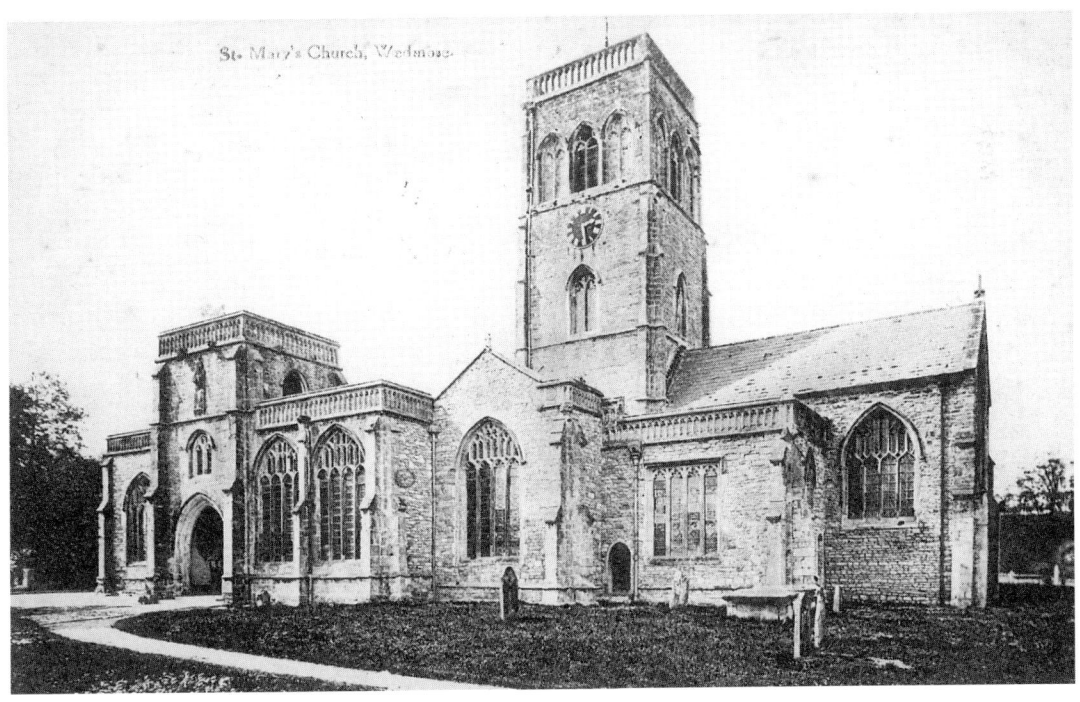

St Mary's parish church, Wedmore, c 1900

However, there was certainly a Saxon church of some importance here by 1066-68, when Queen Matilda, wife of William the Conqueror, granted it to Bishop Giso of Wells. The church had formerly belonged to the Bishop of Exeter, which might well indicate that it existed before the creation of the Wells Bishopric in 909 AD. Later on Bishop Robert (1136-1166) transferred Wedmore to the Dean and Chapter of Wells Cathedral.

The present church, with its central tower, is probably founded upon an earlier one of the 12-1300s of which traces remain. The tower piers and arches date from the early 1200s. Between the late 1300s and early 1500s the church was almost entirely rebuilt in the Perpendicular style. The simple cross shape was extended in all directions, and aisles, three chapels, and a two-storey porch were added. The Decorated east window (1300s) of the Lady Chapel is earlier than the chapel itself and may have been saved from the earlier church, perhaps from the chancel, and reused. The beautiful Early English doorway (1200s) in the porch has likewise been saved and reused.[1]

The Revd J Byrchmore, Vicar in the early 1900s, wrote a short note in *Somerset & Dorset Notes & Queries*, that muffled bells were rung 'from the tower of St Mary Magdalene' in Wedmore.[2] This was immediately refuted by James Coleman, citing a will dated 1528 of Thomas Cras, who wished to be buried 'in the church of the Blessed Mary the Virgin of Wedmore'.[3] How did this erroneous idea about St Mary Magdalene arise? It was later suggested by Marston Acres in his *Brief History of Wedmore*, in 1954, that because Wedmore Fair was held over the feast of St Mary Magdalene, the church could have been dedicated to her. While some medieval fairs took place on the saint's day to which the parish church was dedicated it was not so in every case.

However, this mistaken idea was perpetuated by N Pevsner in *South & West Somerset* (1958), and even on official county web sites Wedmore church is referred to as St Mary Magdalene. It is abundantly clear from other documents besides the will of Thomas Cras in 1528, that Wedmore church is dedicated to St Mary the Virgin. John Retford's will in 1503 states that he wishes to be buried in 'the church of Our Lady of Wedmore'[4]; likewise, William Wichfilde in 1555/6 wishes to be buried in 'the churchyard of Our Blessid Ladie of Wedmore'.[5] Wedmore Fair's date was probably set on the most convenient saint's day in July, and had nothing to do with the dedication of the church.

A busy day in Wedmore Church, 1350

An early document which gives vivid details of just one day in 1350 shows how important the church was in village life.

On Monday 10th May 1372 several local men travelled from Wedmore to Bridgwater to attend the court there. They went to give evidence to show that William Modesley was now 21 years old and the rightful heir to his property in Modesley, now Mudgley in Wedmore.[6]

William was the eldest son of the late John of Modesley and Joan his wife. John had died when William was a baby, and he had been made a ward. The Mudgley estate was administered during his minority by John Rothwell. Before William could claim his inheritance, proof was needed of his exact age. This was in the days before church registers, and the men went as witnesses to help prove William's age.

William was baptised on Sunday 15th August 1350. The events which the men recollected to pinpoint the exact day 21 years before give us an insight into what went on that particular Sunday.

William Porter (aged 53), Richard Wely (48) and James Coker (44 or more) remembered that they had seen baby William lifted from the font by his godfathers William Colne and Simon Michell, and Beatrice Bradreney his godmother. They rememberd that James Coker made a lease that same day, granting property in Pawlett to William Porter for 30 years. Perhaps a copy of this lease was produced, showing it was dated and witnessed on that day.

Ralph Barwe (45) remembered that day well as it was his wedding day. He had married Joan de Chiplegh, and many friends and neighbours, including William Athelard (46), had attended the wedding at the church, where they all saw the baby being baptised. Ralph Barwe was probably one of the Barrow family from Barrow House Farm near Panborough. Joan de Chiplegh was a girl from Sand. There is a large field at Sand which has been called

St. Mary's Parish Church, Wedmore

Interior of St Mary's 1880, before restoration

Chitterley at least since the 16th century; before that it had various spellings. In 1332 the Dean of Wells leased land in the Manor of Mudgley, of which Sand was part, to John de Chudderlegh.[7] One of the witnesses of this lease was William de Modeslee, who was baby William's grandfather. Chitterley, Chiplegh and Chudderlegh are all variations of the same word.

On that same Sunday 15th August 1350 a new chaplain, John Palmere, was celebrating his first mass in the church. William Athelard (60), probably father of the other younger William Athelard, John Rakesworth (52), Nicholas Tournour (48), John Payn (60) and others attended the service 'for kindness sake' to the new chaplain. These witnesses all remembered the baby at the church door waiting to be baptised.

To us it would have seemed very busy inside the church, with a wedding, a baptism, a first mass and a document being witnessed; but outside, still more was going on. John Hugyn, the steward of the Dean and Chapter of Wells, Lords of the Manor of Wedmore, was holding a manorial court in the churchyard. Several villagers had been summoned to attend the court, including Henry Pareys (70), William Newcomb (52) and Phillip Taillour (63). They all recalled seeing Alice Modesley carrying the baby in her arms after his baptism.

All this evidence gathered together proved that William was the rightful heir and had attained the age of 21 by 15th August 1371. The local witnesses ranged in age from 23 to 49, when the baptism took place 21 years before. William duly came into his property at Mudgley. He was a member of an important local family which had held land there since the 1200s.[8]

The Wedmore church of today would not be recognised by William Modesley and his friends. It was almost completely rebuilt in the 15th century. The present font bowl may have been the one in which little William was baptised, but it is now set on a later shaft. The font was often retained, in a rebuilt church, because it was an important symbol of the antiquity of the pastoral authority of the church.

We rely so much on the written word nowadays, and it seems as if every moment of our lives is documented by someone, somewhere. This episode on a Sunday in Wedmore church in 1350 shows how they did it before reading and writing were widespread. I wonder how good our memories would be if we had to recall a particular day 21 years earlier? [9]

In Wedmore churchyard

When Wedmore churchyard was being tidied in March 1991 a small gravestone was noticed, lying in the corner close under the Manor House wall, opposite the northwest corner of the church. Engraved on the little cross was the name 'Francis Homfray, born Jan. 30th, died May 23rd 1873'. The Wedmore parish registers show that baby Francis, baptised on 6th April, was the youngest son of surgeon Charles Augustus Homfray MRCS and JP and Anna Marie Homfray. The Homfrays were living in the Manor House. They had three other children who are recorded as being born in Wedmore: Augustus Leo in 1868, Florence in 1870 and Hugh in 1872. Before becoming 'lord of the manor' Charles Homfray lived at The Poplars, now Mulberry House, at West End. The Homfrays did not stay long in Wedmore.

The quest to find out about baby Francis prompted me to look again at some of the other tombstones in our churchyard.

One tomb on the far northern side is always of interest to boys, small and large! This cross has a bi-plane carved on it. It is the tombstone of Victor Charles Edelsten Bracey. Victor was the only child of Dr and Mrs Bracey of Uplands, Grants Lane. Victor was a second lieutenant in the Royal Flying Corps. He was killed, aged 19 years, at Beaulieu on 22nd September 1917. He had been recently appointed as flying instructor to his squadron. While he was making a trial flight in a new aeroplane, the engine failed and it stalled, crashing from a height of 300 feet. Victor died within half an hour. He had, shortly before, told a friend that when his time came he wanted 'it to be in a sudden crash with no lingering pain'.[10] Sadly the crash came all too soon, ending a daring and gallant life. His mother Florence was so distraught that she mourned for many years, sitting by her window looking out over the village where she could just glimpse her son's grave. His father William Bracey was our village doctor for over fifty years. He died in 1952. Both parents are interred with their beloved son.

To the southeast of the church are three chest tombs, which are listed as monuments of historic quality and interest. On the central one can be seen the names of Gabriel Ivyleafe, who died 1727, and his son Gabriel who died 1732. They were members of the Ivyleafe

Tombs in St Mary's churchyard

family of Blackford. The Ivyleafes were great benefactors to the community, several leaving money to the parish poor. The tomb to the north of Gabriel's has no remaining epitaph. The southern one of the group commemorates the family of an earlier Gabriel Ivyleafe. Its inscription is now very eroded, but the names 'Edith wife of Gabriel Ivyleafe Deceased Dec. 30th' and a 'daughter' can be traced with difficulty.

A search of the parish registers shows that Edith and Gabriel Iveleafe were married in 1636. They had ten children: Gertrude in 1637, Mary in 1638 (died 1659), Anna in 1640 (died 1661), Richard in 1643, Gabriel in 1645, Edith in 1647, Hannah in 1648, William in 1653, Robert in 1655 and another Mary in 1659. Mother Edith, who according to the surviving inscription died on 30th December 1659, was buried on 5th January 1660. Her baby daughter Mary, four months old, was buried ten days later on 17th January, and is probably the 'daughter' on the worn inscription. She had been named after her elder sister Mary who had died shortly before, aged 21 years.[11]

There is one other listed table tomb, near the northeast corner of the church. This commemorates another important Blackford family, the Savidges. George Savidge died 30th January 1768 aged 47 years. He and his wife Betty had a baby daughter Jane who died on 3rd April 1758 aged 10 months. Their two sons George and Simon died within two days of each other in 1773: George aged 13, on 20th October and Simon aged 10 on 22nd October. The registers show them to have been buried together on 29th October 1773, 'Mr George and Mr Simon sons of Mrs Savage of Blackford'; unfortunately it does not record the cause of death.

Adjoining the Savidge tomb are three marble tombstones in an enclosure. These stones commemorate the White family who lived in Sand House. The southern one records the burials of the Revd William White, first vicar of Theale Church, who died in 1867, and of his family. The northern one is of Benjamin Tyley White, died 1891, his wife Elizabeth Catharine, and his daughter Clara Jane White who died in 1937. Miss Clara White gave the sports field to the village. The central stone is to the memory of William White who died aged 67 in 1816, and of his widow Ann who died in 1834; she was the daughter of

George and Betty Savidge. This William White, uncle of the Revd William White, was a well known surveyor and mapmaker. He drew the Wedmore Parish Map of 1791,[12] and many others including most of the enclosure maps of this area and the plans for Bristol Docks.

The burial registers show that between 1561 and 1812 there were over 10,500 recorded burials in Wedmore Churchyard. The total can never be known because no records of burials were kept in the middle ages; but Wedmore people have been buried there from Saxon times until fairly recently. Before the 1600s it was not the usual practice to have individual tombstones or memorials over graves: one churchyard cross served as a memorial to all. Wedmore's medieval churchyard cross originally stood near the west door of the Church. Hence, there are many more graves in the churchyard than might appear today. Probably well over 30,000 interments have been made there. The monuments there today are a valuable record of Wedmore's past.

> *'I would rather sleep in the southern corner of a little country church-yard, than in the tomb of the Capulets.'*
>
> Edmund Burke (1729-1797)

Chapter 5
Wedmore Borough

Markets and Fairs

Wedmore was first officially granted a market in 1255 by King Henry III.[1] This market was to be held weekly on Tuesdays, and the fair for three days in July, on the eve, the day and the morrow of the feast day of St Mary Magdalene: that is, 21st, 22nd and 23rd July.

Until recently no early documents describing how these markets and fairs were run had been discovered. Most of the documents of Wedmore Manor are thought to have been destroyed in a fire in the 1800s. Some did survive, only to end up in the Huntington Museum Library in America. Now one document has been found in the Library of Lambeth Palace, in London. It is a parchment roll recording the manorial court of Wedmore Borough in the year 1528-29 and in the reign of Henry VIII.[2]

Before we look at the court record, we must set the scene of the market street, The Borough. Originally The Borough was an area which comprised Church Street below The George, included the Cheddar Road as far as the corner, the street called The Borough itself, and Combe Batch as far as Mutton Lane. The main Borough roadway was three times wider than it is today, each end narrowing to give a cigar shape, wide enough at the centre for market stalls and stock pens. The market cross stood near the junction of The Borough and present day Church Street.

Every Tuesday from 1255, for hundreds of years, The Borough was filled with market stalls and with traders busy selling their wares. The fair was largely a cattle fair, and the annual fair days would have brought dealers from all over the country.

The Borough court roll of 1528-29 gives us a glimpse of what went on at these busy market days in Wedmore. The document is written in Latin, which is frequently abbreviated, while the handwriting is often cramped, faded and difficult to read. The courts were held every six months, and this court was held on 16th September 1528. The roll lists the people who are fined for various offences against the rules of the market and fair. The Bailiff of The Borough presented the cases. The Bailiff was an annual appointment, William Alger being in office in 1528.

John Mareys and Thomas Culbury were both fined 4d each for brewing. They must have been brewing ale and selling it without a licence. John Mareys was a baker. He and another baker called Nicholas Petherham made and sold bread at less than the official weight; they were fined 3d each. John Mareys was probably making enough money from his illegal brewing and underweight bread to pay the fines without difficulty, because he is again fined six months later, at the next court, for the same offences! Brewing was often a side-line of a bakery, as the yeast was readily available with which to brew a few gallons of ale on the quiet.

Thomas Culbury was one of Wedmore's butchers, and he was fined 1½d for selling offal, but the document does not say what he was doing wrong. Thomas Culbury together with John Coke, a tapster, was also fined for selling ale without a licence on St Mary Magdalene's

Aerial view of The Borough, Wedmore, 1953

Day; they were both fined for breaking the Assize - the trading regulations. A tapster was the term for a barman. Another tapster, Peter Willyampus [or Williams] was fined much more for breaking the Assize; he had to pay 12d. St Mary Magdalene's Day was the middle day of the fair, and no doubt the drink was flowing fast; so what were their crimes: short measure, watered ale or serving out of hours?

The Bailiff collects 1d from each stall holder for 'Keveragium'; this was 'coverage', the charge for putting awnings over the stalls - our only clue to what the market scene actually looked like. At the same court twelve freemen of Wedmore Borough were sworn in. They were William Stone, Roger Kynge, Robert Frempton, Nicholas Petherham, John Mareys, Thomas Corell, John Courteys, John Benet, Richard Kyrkeby (or Kerby), John Richards, Richard Harys and Thomas Borde - all from established local families, of whom Benet (Bennet) and Harris are still around. The two bakers fined for underweight bread are nonetheless members of the jury.

Richard Harys and Richard Kerby are to supervise the repair of a hedge lying within The Borough which had been 'broken and open' since the last court, and they are to find the people responsible for the damage.

New officers were elected. The reeve or portreeve of The Borough was John Mareys. Clearly his catalogue of minor offences and regular court appearances was no bar to his election to this office. The reeve or portreeve was in charge of the market. Robert Frempton and Nicholas Petherham were re-elected to the office of constables, despite Nicholas's misdemeanour of selling underweight bread. William Alger was re-elected bailiff and John Benet re-elected ale-taster.

Six months later another court was held on 13th April 1529. Little has changed. John Mareys the reeve is still brewing illegally, this time with John Benet, and they are fined 4d each. John Mareys is still baking underweight bread and is fined 3d, while Thomas Culbury is again fined 1½d for selling offal. It may be that these regular fines are regarded almost as a licence to trade. The same twelve men are again sworn in as jury.

The complaints brought before the court this time are that the footpaths and the King's highway within the precinct of The Borough are worn down and broken up, and a public danger. Some things never change! John Mareys and the burgesses are to repair the roads and paths before the 24th June; if this is not done the fine will be 10s: a very substantial threat, to produce results.

The burgesses were the people who held burgages within The Borough or 'Burgh'. A burgage was a house and its plot. This term usually refers to a house-plot in a town. It is particularly interesting to find these urban terms in use in Wedmore, for a street name, it house-plots and their occupants. The term burgage first appears in a will of the 1300s. Does it indicate that the village at one time had aspirations to develop into a town?

The court also directed the burgesses to make one hanging gate at Spekehegge before the 14th September. The former Victorian Vicarage (now Whitfield House) is built in a field called Speke Close. Spekehegge was presumably the hedge around this field, separating it from the most northerly end of the medieval Borough. It is not clear from the court record whether the gate was across the Cheddar Road at this point, marking the end of The Borough, or a field gate into Speke Close; nor whether it was a new one or a replacement.

These few snippets are all we can find out about the workings of the market in The Borough in the 1500s. One other rare survivor of Wedmore Manorial Court is a copy of proceedings at a Court Leet in 1879, which gives the only detailed account we have of the election procedures of the officers of this manorial court. The original document is now lost, but we are most fortunate that the Revd S.H.A. Hervey made a copy of it in the 1895 in a little exercise book of notes and jottings which was found among the parish records. He probably borrowed the original document from the Lord of the Manor, John Frederick Bailey.[3]

This Manorial Court Leet was held on 10th November 1879 in the George Hotel at 7 pm. Hervey's copy gives some of the oaths used at the swearing-in, in a form which had obviously been in use over a very long time. The court was summoned in the following words:

> 'All manner of persons that do owe suit and service to the Court Leet of [the name of the Lord of Wedmore Manor, John Barrow Esq., has been crossed through and replaced by Charles Augustus Homfray Esq., in turn succeeded by John Frederick Bailey] now to be holden in and for The Borough of Wedmore, draw near and give your attendance and answer to your names.'

The Portreeves, Arthur Duckett and Harry Godfrey, c1953

The portreeves of the previous court, William Gibbs and Robert Redman, were to collect the rents from The Borough and pay them to Mr Bailey, Lord of the Manor. The court officials for the year were appointed. Their job was to see that the market and fair rules were kept. The weekly market had by now ceased to exist, having finished sometime in the 1700s; but the fairs were still held. Only people who lived in the original ancient Borough (the area including lower Church Street, the beginning of Cheddar Road, and lower Combe Batch) would be appointed.

At the court on 10th November the new portreeves appointed were George Redman and Samuel Cozens. Thomas Ridge and Joseph Nichols were appointed water bailiffs. Robert Redman and William Gibbs were the new ale comers [sic: probably Hervey's error for ale conners, the ale-tasters]. Frederick Martin and Harry Green became the bread weighers, and Isaac Hembry was to serve in the office of swineherd or hayward. The ancient office of constable was not filled, because there was now the official police force. The foreman was sworn in as follows:

> 'You, as foreman of this jury, shall enquire and true presentment make of all such things as shall be given you in charge. The Queen's Council [sic], your own and your fellows you shall well and truly keep. You shall present nothing out of hatred or malice, nor shall conceal anything out of love, fear or affection; but in all things you shall well and truly present as the same shall come to your knowledge.' The foreman then swore, 'So help me God.'

Each man was sworn in under the penalty of 20s, and then the jury was sworn. This consisted of twelve men: the foreman Edwin Henderson, Samuel Couzens, Thomas Ridge, Harry Green, Robert Redman, George Redman, William Gibbs, Hugh Howell, Joseph Nicholls, Isaac Hembry, John Young and Frederick Martin. Edwin Henderson the foreman was landlord of The George Hotel. Joseph Nicholls and Isaac Hembry could not sign their names, and made their marks instead. The jury was sworn in, using a similar form of oath to that of the foreman. The hayward's oath followed:

> *'You shall well and truly serve in the office of Hayward for the year ensuing. You shall truly execute all such process as shall be directed to you from this court. You shall from time to time signify and present all such pound breaches as shall happen to be made during your continuance in yoir office and in everthing well and truly behave yourself in the said office.'*

The hayward's job was to impound any stray animals in the manorial pound, which is still in Combe Batch (2002) (see Chapter 8). The owner paid a fine to the hayward before the animal was released. In 1879 the court seems to have imposed a new or increased fine of 1s for a horse impounded from the road, but the list of other penalties has not survived. At the end, the court was closed with the following proclamation:

> *'Oyes. Oyes. All manner of persons that have appeared this day in this Court Leet may hence depart and keep their day and hour again upon a new summons.'*

The Borough Court Leet ceased to exist when the Parish Council came into being in 1895.

A second document now lost but also copied out by Hervey tells us of another aspect of the running of The Borough Fairs. It is a deed of 1719 between Harry Bridges of Keynsham, who was then Lord of the Manor of Wedmore, and John Lawrence of Wedmore, yeoman.[4] Bridges, in return for 10 guineas paid to him by Lawrence, leased to him all the profits arising from the yearly fair at Wedmore held in The Borough, or from 'any of the standing pens or other things to be by him there erected.' Lawrence is authorised to erect a tolzey - a toll booth for the collection of rents and dues from stall holders, which was presumably a temporary structure set up when the fair took place and where he could act as supervisor and agent. He was to 'keep account of all sales and bargains and take all other sums of money and enjoy all liberties and customs belonging to the said fair.' For all this, Laurence was to pay 1s a year. John Laurence lived in what is now Allington House Dress Shop and its adjoining house. This must have been quite a good financial arrangement, for any receipts taken by Lawrence over and above 10 guineas to recoup his original down-payment and the further shilling a year, could be kept by him as clear profit. Unfortunately John Lawrence mortgaged these rights, handing them over on 15th June 1726 to John Edwards of Mudgley. Was the money too slow coming in, or were his financial problems too pressing to wait?

During the 1800s there were two fairs in The Borough: the July fair and one held on the last Monday in September. They were both cattle fairs, famed for their fat stock. A newspaper report of July 26th 1879, however, records that the July fair was 'one of the worst fairs ever known.' This was due to the bad weather and scarcity of grass. There was 'a large supply of stock but the dealers were few, the prices low and little business done. Much stock went away unsold.'[5] In 1896 there was a drought and 'good fat stock were scarce ... There were a few pens of sheep, scarcely any young stock, no pigs, no horses. On the whole the fair was unusually small.'[6]

Two years later in 1898 the parish council decided to move the date of the July Fair to the last Monday in July, as it clashed with Highbridge Market.[7] For a long time this fair had been called St James's Fair, as the holy day of St Mary Magdalene ceased to be observed. The July fair finished in the early 1900s, but the September fair struggled on for a few more years. It finally came to an end during the First World War. Mr Geoffrey Pavey remembered one of the last fair days held in 1915. There were only three stalls: two gingerbread stalls, one run by Mrs Betty and the other by Mrs Barnstaple, both of Bridgwater, and a shooting gallery. This was positioned outside The George, and the object was to hit the ball which was bouncing up and down on a jet of water.

So after 660 years, Wedmore Fair ceased to exist. The fair day which was revived in 1978 to commemorate the 1100th anniversary of the Peace of Wedmore between King Alfred and the Danes has hopefully become an annual event. Although the fair today bears little resemblance to the cattle fairs of the middle ages, it is still a focal point for villagers to meet and enjoy themselves out in the ancient street of The Borough.

Chapter 6
Wedmore Houses

People and houses in The Borough

The layout and shape of The Borough itself can, however, be used to reconstruct the development of this part of Wedmore in quite precise detail. With some detective work among the documents, we can place some of the past inhabitants in their actual houses.

The Borough was a new market street originally laid out in the 1100s or early 1200s: a tidily planned shape added on to the older settlement up by the church. On the modern map of Wedmore certain plot boundary lines can be seen, which show up more obviously on the earlier 1791 parish map.[1] They indicate a pattern of regular plot shapes around The Borough, marking boundaries of the surrounding properties which also, therefore, trace their origins back to the 1100s-early 1200s. This pattern suggests that the burgage plots originally measured 60 feet wide and 300 feet long. The plots were probably measured in 'ropes', each rope being 20 feet. We can imagine the medieval surveyors walking around with their knotted measuring-ropes marking out neat rows of plots 3 x 15 ropes. There seem to have been about 40 of these plots, laid out with their narrow end to the street so as to give a street frontage to the maximum number of properties (see p71). The deliberate dog-leg shape of the streets similarly contrive to pack the greatest number of properties along a tidily defined main route through Wedmore. The whole layout is, like its terminology, mysteriously urban in nature. By the 1400s several plots had been subdivided, and some were later amalgamated; but enough outlines can still be traced today, especially on the eastern side of the present Borough, to reconstruct the early planned development of this part of Wedmore.

A parchment roll which is a rental of The Borough showing rent due to the Lord of The Borough Court or Court Leet at Michaelmas (29th September) 1717 lists the tenants of the burgages in The Borough. Moreover, it lists them in order, along the street. We only know of this vital document because in the early 1900s Dr William Bracey made a glass lantern slide of the first part of the roll; the rest, as can be seen on the slide, is rolled up and hidden from us.[2] There is no clue as to where Dr Bracey found this rent roll. Does it still survive in Wedmore, rolled up among someone's house deeds?

By linking up the part of the rent roll visible in the slide with various other later documents, it is possible not only to reconstruct the original plots, but to say who lived where in 1717. The list starts with John Mannyman. I am sure that he lived in Barnards at the south end of The Borough; and the part of the list that can be seen in Dr Bracey's lantern slide continues from Barnards northwards along the eastern side of The Borough.

1717 Rental	Rent	House in 2002
John Mannyman	7½d	Barnards
Widow Starr	1s 1½d	Old Bakery
Mr John Adams	1s 3d	Lerburne House
William Bunn	1s	Cross Farm
John Lansdowne Esq.	1s 2d	ditto
Henry Mapson	1s 0d	Honeysuckle Cottage

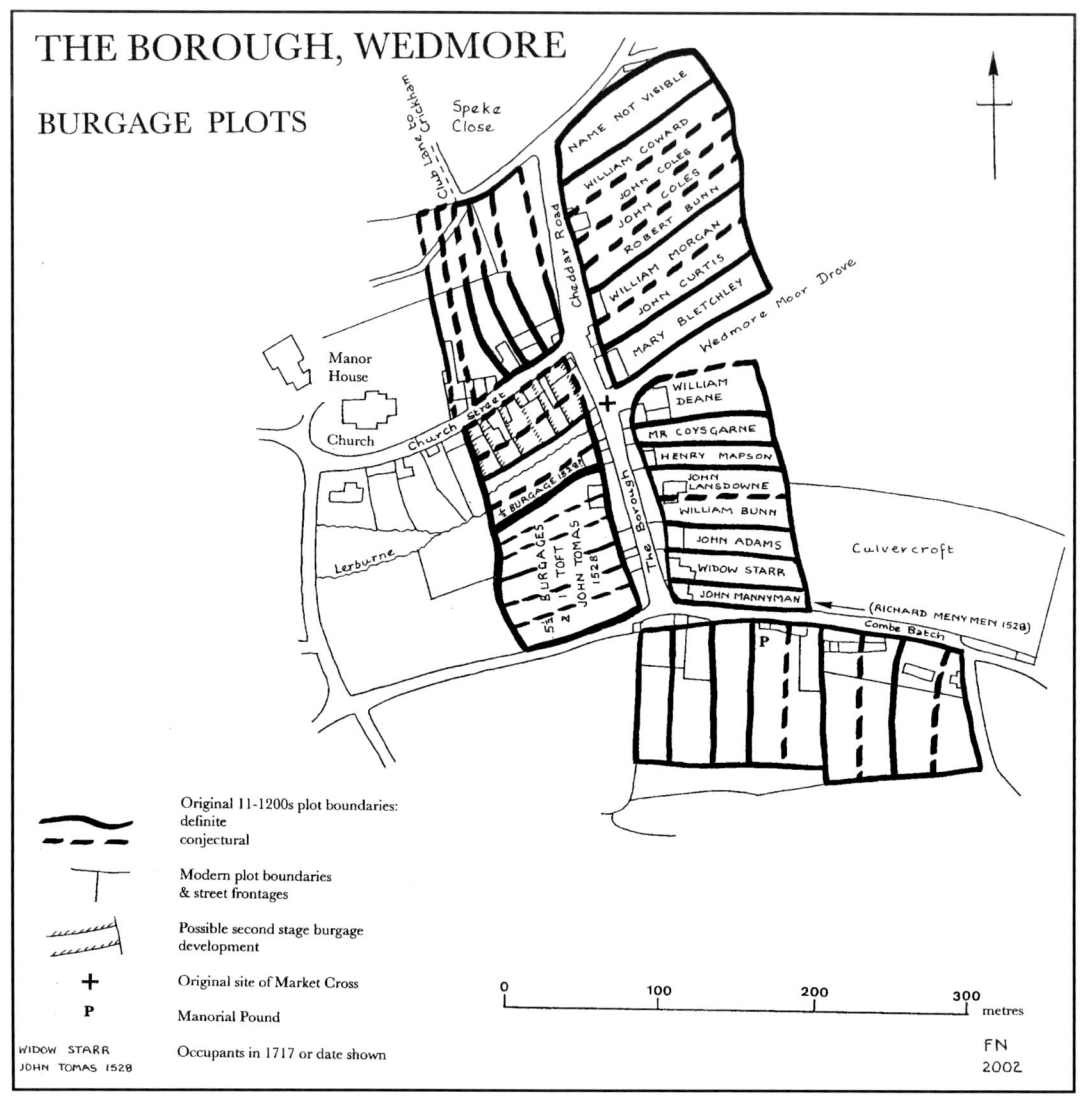

The Borough, Wedmore: Medieval Burgage plots

1717 Rental	Rent	House in 2002
Mr Coysgarne	1s 0d	Borough Mall
William Deane	1s 3d	Stone's Bakery
Mary Bletchly	1s 6d	formerly Cousin's Garage
John Curtis	1s 6d	Providence House
William Morgan	1s 0d	Swan Hotel
Robert Bunn	1s 0d	Holdenhurst
John Coles	2s 2d	ditto
William Coward Esq	1s 9d	ditto

The rent roll went on to list all the rest of the 40-odd burgages in The Borough: but the remainder are tantalisingly hidden within the rolled-up parchment. By 1717 some of the

The Borough Court of Wedmore 1717, from a lantern slide

burgages had been subdivided, and others amalgamated. Holdenhurst, for example, was the site of three or perhaps four ancient burgage properties.

The enclosure awards of the 1700s give each property a name, and using the 1785 award for Wedmore Moor we can make some deductions.[3] Some names changed from time to time, with new occupants, but others remained constant. When this happens, a link can sometimes be made from 1717 and beyond, forward to the present, to pinpoint the property on the ground today.

In 1785, Honeysuckle Cottage is called Mapstones, although no Mapstone family was living there then: it was actually the home of my great-great-great-grandparents, the Comers. In 1717, however, Henry Mapson or Mapstone was living there, his family giving their name to the property. In 1785 Stone's Bakery was tenanted by James Pickford, a tallow chandler or candlemaker. It was called Tutton's or Dean's: and in 1717 William Deane is living there.

Phoebe Tyley, living in a house on the site of Holdenhurst in 1785, claimed that her property was called Andrews, Coles and Cowards, suggesting that this big property was an amalgamation of at least three, and in fact probably four or five former burgages. Two of these three names, John Coles and William Coward, are on the list in 1717, with Robert Bunn as the third. John Coles, from his rent, may be holding what were formerly two burgages. There is no clue as to when someone called Andrews held his plot. The whole group ultimately coalesced to form the large, single Holdenhurst.

Occasionally we can go back even earlier. Barnards, where John Mannyman is living in 1717, was probably the family home of Richard Menymen who was living in The Borough in 1528.[4] It gets its present name in this case from a later occupant, John Barnard, in 1760.[5]

When, on 10th November 1879, The Borough Court was held in Wedmore, (see Chapter 5)[6] the port reeves William Gibbs and Robert Redman were ordered to collect the rents and to pay them into the court. The resulting list of all owners and their rents is then given. I have only listed the first few, to correspond with the part of the earlier rental of 1717 of which we have knowledge (see overleaf).

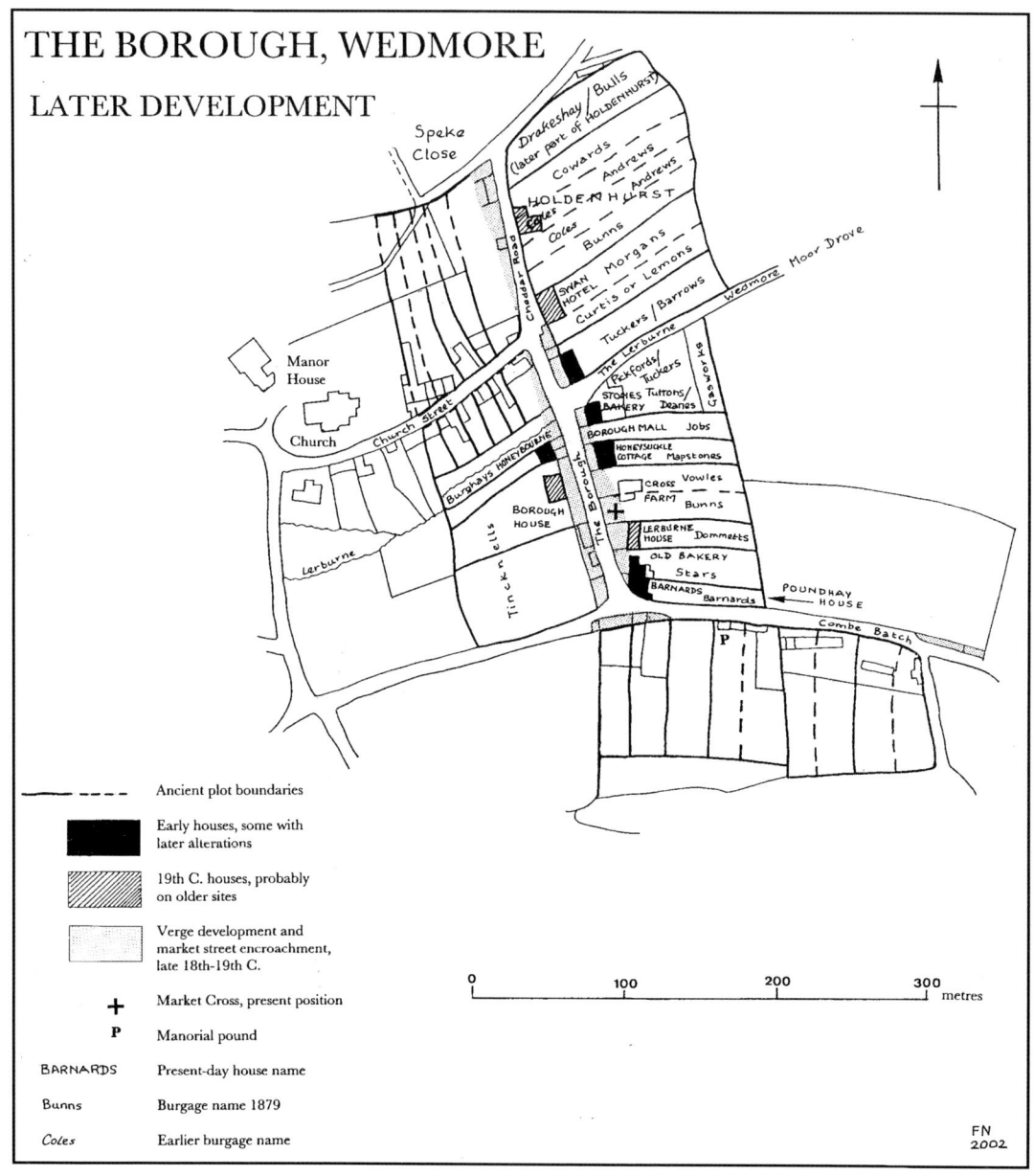

The Borough, Wedmore: later development

1879 Proprietor	Name of property	Rent	House 2002
George Millard (tenant William Millard)	Part of Barnards	2½d	Poundhay House
Edmund Hole (tenant Samuel Couzens)	Part of Barnards	2½d	Barnards
Robert Redman	Part of Barnards	2½d	Cottage
Edmund Hole (tenant RL Stott)	Stars	1s 1½d	Old Bakery

Wedmore Houses

1879 Proprietor	Name of property	Rent	House 2002
Miss Hancock	Dommetts	1s 3d	Lerburne House
Charles Frost (for Arthur Phippen's trustees)	Bunns	1s 0d	Cross Farm
Charles Frost (for ditto)	Vowles	1s 3d	ditto
George Watts	Mapstones	1s 0d	Honeysuckle Cottage
Frederick Tyley (for Ben. Tyley's trustees)	Jobs	1s 0d	Borough Mall
Richard Morgan	Pickfords late Tuckers	1s 0d	Stone's Bakery
Gas Works	ditto	3d	Old Gasworks
Robert Millard	Tuckers late Barrows	1s 6d	Former Garage site
Mrs Knowles, for Jeremiah Wall's representatives	Morgans	1s 0d	Swan
ditto	Curtis or Lemons	1s 6½d	Providence House & Swan
Mary Jane Norman (tenant Henry Banwell)	Bunns	1s 0d	Holdenhurst
ditto	Andrews	2s 2d	ditto
ditto	Cowards	1s 9d	ditto
ditto	Bulls	1s 6d	ditto

Holdenhurst, as can be seen from this 1879 list, actually took up five old burgages: Bunns, Andrews double plot (Coles in 1717), Cowards and Bulls; but the last property, 'Bulls', was hidden in the photograph of the rolled-up 1717 rental. Phoebe Tyley, back in 1785, confused the issue, because she omitted Bunns, and it is clear that Coles and Andrews are the same double plot, at the same double rent. Bulls plot, last in the list of this side of The Borough, is the corner plot on the bend opposite the car-park. It belonged to the Bull family of Shapwick in 1671, when it was called Drakeshay (see below).

It is interesting to compare the rents in 1879 with those of 1717. Many remain the same! Unchanged rents can often provide a vital link in identifying a property. The standard rent for one original burgage would seem to have been about 1s 0d, give or take a few pence for reasons now unknown. Honeysuckle Cottage and Borough Mall, at 1s each, are original sized, unaltered medieval plots of the 1100s. Barnards, paying 7½d in 1717, has by 1879 been subdivided into three holdings, each paying 2½d: Barnards itself, the old shop, and Poundhay House which was built in the former back garden. Similarly, the Gas Works, a recent development and paying only 3d, was built on the end of the original Stone's Bakery plot. Cross Farm on the other hand, built in 1880, takes up two standard plots listed in 1717 and 1879. Holdenhurst can be seen from the 1879 list to be made up of four named plots; but one of these pays 2s 2d, suggesting that Andrews is itself an amalgamation of two plots and so a double-sized rent. There were thus, perhaps, five original burgage plots on the Holdenhurst site; and this, in terms of the medieval measurements in 'ropes', in fact fits better the actual size of Holdenhurst on the ground.

There is another interesting block of plots on the west side of The Borough. Back in 1528 at the Wedmore Borough Court, John Tomas 'holds of the Lord 5½ burgages and one toft of land within this Borough'.[7] His rent each year is 5s 8d, made up of 1s for each burgage, 6d for the half-burgage, and 2d for the toft, which is obviously some very small plot of land. This is our one and only definite indication that the basic going rate for 1 burgage plot was 1s a year. In 1879 there is one property paying a noticeably bigger rent than all the others. Frederick Tyley pays 5s 6d for Tincknells. From the census returns I know that Frederick Tyley was living in the Borough House, and owned the block of land formed by all the former plots on that side, from Bay Tree Cottage south to Grants Lane. All maps since 1791 show this block divided into two unequal parts. Their measurements suggest that they comprised 3 original burgage plots in one part, and 2½ in the other - that is, the 5½ burgages held by John Tomas in 1528.[8] The toft has disappeared from the 1879 list and cannot now be precisely located; but so has its 2d rent - making the total rent for the 5½ burgages 5s 6d through more than three centuries from 1528 to 1879.

Another remarkable example of plot-survival is now The Borough Mall (see below).

The Borough, Wedmore, looking north, c1960

The cigar shape of the original market street can still be seen on the east side of The Borough, where the former edge is preserved in the line of house-fronts. Their later front gardens have encroached on the market area. The old plan is less clear on the west side of the street, where later houses, such as those between the Borough Venture and Allington House, have been built on the actual verge; but the line can be deduced (see plan p73).

Two house plots in The Borough: Jobs and Drakeshay

During my research on The Borough, I found two of the old burgage plots which had behind them stories of special interest. One is the plot called **JOBS** which is now The Borough Mall. Before the Borough Mall was built in the 1980s, this site was a derelict factory known as the Milk Factory. It was originally built in the First World War (1914-1918) as a depot for collecting and distributing all the local milk. After the Milk Factory closed in the 1960s, the building was used as a perfume factory for a few years.

Until the Milk Factory was built on it, this plot of land had been an orchard, with no house on it, for hundreds of years. It was called Jobs in the 1785 and 1791 Enclosure Awards; but who Job was, is not known. Working back in time, in 1717 a Mr Coysgarne held this plot.[9] He was a London merchant. A deed of 1693 shows John Coysgarne leasing to Robert Bunn of The Borough, tailor, two acres of land which were part of a house and cottage situated in The Borough 'called our Lady Chauntry Lands'.[10] This two acre plot, with its house and cottage, had been part of the land belonging to the medieval Chantry of Our Lady, or St Mary's Chantry, in Wedmore parish church.

A chantry was an endowment of money or land for a priest to say prayers for the souls of the donor or donors at an altar in a church, or in a specially built chantry chapel within it. The Chantry of Our Lady or St Mary's Chantry was one of at least three chantries in our parish church, and was probably the present Lady Chapel, on the south side of the chancel.

The rent from the chantry lands supported a chantry priest, quite distinct from the vicar of the parish. The priest of St Mary's Chantry when it was closed down in 1547-48 was William London. He had a house and garden in Wedmore worth 4s a year.[11]

Chantries were abolished in 1547 under the Chantries Act, as part of the Tudor Reformation of the church in England. Chantry lands were taken over by the Crown, and gradually sold off to the highest bidders. St Mary's Chantry lands, valued at £8. 17s. 6d. in 1548, and leased out to Thomas Willet in 1549, were finally sold in 1563 to William Revette and Thomas Bright, two London merchants.[12]

A list of the lands of St Mary's Chantry had been made in 1548.[13] Apart from William London the priest, there were fifty tenants holding chantry property within the parish. Alice Longe holds a house called St Mary's House, paying 3s 8d a year, and Katerine Feoffer holds a shop for 20d a year. This is one of the earliest references to a shop in Wedmore so far found. Thomas Corell, one of the jury in the Borough Court of 1528,[14] holds a tenement and an acre of land for 3s 4d a year. Richard Kirkeby was another juror; he held land for 8d a year rent. Peter Williams, the tapster who was fined for breaking the Assize at that same court, is another chantry tenant, holding a tenement at 4s p.a. Unfortunately the list does not say precisely where these chantry lands were, so we cannot identify exactly which property on the 1548 list was the house and cottage remembered as 'our Lady Chauntry Lands' in The Borough in 1693. It would be nice to think it was Alice Longe's St Mary's House and the little shop; but this cannot be proven.

In 1759 John Benwell of Wells held the plot, described as a messuage or burgage - that ancient term for all the Borough plots - with an orchard, about one acre.[15] This is the orchard, lacking any building, which later became known as Jobs. The shopping area of the village seems to have shifted to what is now Church Street, leaving some former burgage plots such as Jobs empty of houses. By the 1730s the antiquarian John Strachey, whose mother Jane was brought up in the Manor House, could, in his unpublished history of Somerset, write that 'At Wedmore is a Spatious street called the Borow which tho' at present a poor ragged place, yet the name shews it was once of better Accoumpt & a Cross remaining in it as well.'[16]

The revival of The Borough as the prime shopping area of Wedmore started with the construction, in the early 1800s, of shops in front of the original house sites, on the verges of the ancient market street. The 20th century saw The Borough flourish again as a shopping street, with the Borough Mall opening off it. Its shape, remarkably, is still that of a typical original burgage unit in the medieval Borough of Wedmore. It brings us full circle to the kind of prosperous village commerce that the medieval planners must have hoped for when they first laid out their 'borough' burgage plots in the 1200s.

The second burgage plot of particular interest was called **DRAKESHAY** and was part of Holdenhurst. The house and grounds of Holdenhurst, plus the new house in its former grounds, now take up an area originally laid out as five burgages or house plots. Of these, the northernmost corner plot on the Cheddar Road has a curious and perhaps exciting history.

Holdenhurst, c1900

In the 1500s the Sydenhams were one of the wealthiest families in England. One of their country seats was Combe Sydenham, near Minehead, and another was at Brympton d'Evercy near Yeovil. One of the family, Henry Sydenham, held part of the Manor of Wedmore in the mid-1600s, and this was still in the hands of the Sydenham family in 1718.[17] It is not known when the Sydenham family first acquired this interest in Wedmore, but it was perhaps some time in the late 1500s, when they were also holding property in nearby Mark.

In 1591, according to a Mark manorial court book, Sir George Sydenham and his wife Elizabeth held a tenement in Mark which had been in Elizabeth's family[18]. There is also an incidental mention of Sir George's daughter, also Elizabeth, who is described as 'now wife of Francis Drake'. In 1585, Elizabeth Sydenham had married Sir Francis Drake, the heroic Elizabethan sea-captain, as his second wife. Still to be seen at Combe Sydenham is the cannonball which tradition associates with this marriage. The story is that Elizabeth, having waited long for the return of her suitor Francis Drake from across the seas, was on the point of marrying someone else. As the bridal procession moved towards the church, a 'cannonball' (probably a meteorite) dropped at her feet, fired half across the world by Francis Drake. The wedding was abruptly abandoned, and Francis Drake promptly came home and married her. The 'cannon ball' can still be seen at Combe Sydenham.

In 1671, when Henry Bull of Shapwick took a lease of an acre plot in the Borough of Wedmore, it was occupied at the time by Henry Sydenham, gentleman, a descendant of Elizabeth Sydenham.[19] The name of this plot was Drakeshay: Drake's enclosure. The adjacent plot was also on occasion called Drakeshay until as late as 1820.[20] This suggests that Drakeshay was originally the name of a double burgage; and that this earlier name was superseded by those of later tenants. By 1820, the Drakeshay acquired by Henry Bull was called Bulls after him; the adjacent plot was usually known as Cowards from 1717 onwards.[21] In the 1879 Borough rental the plot called Bulls is clearly shown to be the most northerly plot of Holdenhurst's land, edging the Cheddar Road.[22] Back in 1671, therefore, Bulls plot was still occupied by a member of the Sydenham family, into which Sir Francis Drake had married in 1585 - and this plot has the name Drakeshay. What are we to make of this extraordinary coincidence?

Sir George Sydenham, Sir Francis Drake's father-in-law, served with Drake at sea in 1594 and may have taken part in the rout of the Spanish Armada in 1588. Did George Sydenham acquire an interest in this Wedmore burgage in the 1580s-1590s, at the time when he was holding property in Mark? Was there still a medieval house standing on it? Could Sir Francis Drake and his new wife have come to Wedmore and could the name of the greatest hero of his time have become attached to the plot of land as a result?

Before we get too excited, further investigation, as so often happens in local history, brings us back to earth with a bump. By chance, while looking through the parish registers for something else, I came across a marriage between two Wedmore people. They were Joan Lussher and John Drake, who married in 1567. So there was a Drake family living in the village before Sir Francis Drake became associated with the Sydenhams in 1585. Was it the famous seadog, or was it the unknown John and Joan Drake, or one of their children, whose name became attached to this corner of the Borough of Wedmore?

Minstrels Gallery and Lloyds Chemist

Standing on the corner at the junction of Church Street with The Borough and Cheddar Road is an imposing building. This corner of Wedmore, and the buildings which have stood there, have an interesting story to tell.

In 1819 John Tonkin bought a house and shop on this corner from Abraham Dyer and ran the business already established there, which seems to have been an ironmongers.[23] Later

The shop and house built by John Tonkin, later Owens emporium and now Lloyds Chemist and Minstrels Gallery, c1900

he knocked down the old house and shop and erected the premises we see today. The property has now been divided into two. The Minstrels Gallery was the house John Tonkin built for himself, and Lloyds Chemist was his new shop.

John and Elizabeth Tonkin came to Wedmore from St Ives in Cornwall.[24] He was a businessman and an ardent Methodist. After a few years in Wedmore he started the brickworks on the outskirts of the village down Wedmore Moor Drove, at what is now Brickyard Farm. When John had become more prosperous he bought the site in Church Street, or The Borough as it was then still called. He, along with his son John, built the house and the three-storeyed shop using his bricks, stamped with the name TONKIN, and his own tiles. These tiles were a special fish-scale design produced exclusively for this building, but TONKIN bricks do still occasionally turn up around the village. The name Tonkin can still be made out, stamped on the brass sills below the shop windows.

This house and shop were built in the 1830-40s, in flamboyant Italianate style with elegant ironwork and decorative bargeboards. The interiors were lavishly decorated with plasterwork and more wrought ironwork. It seems as if no expense was spared in creating a lovely home and an equally attractive shop. The impact of this big building on the village at that time must have been considerable; its fame as an 'emporium' soon extended far beyond Wedmore.

In 1841 son John and his family were living in the house with their staff of servants. Several live-in shop staff had rooms on the top floor of the shop. Old Wedmorians will remember, on the ground floor of the shop, the long mahogany counters for cutting out the silks, satins and woollens for crinolines and capes. The walls were lined with many drawers and shelves for materials and haberdashery items. There were also grocery and hardware departments, and a savings bank. Upstairs were fashions, linens, fitting rooms and a millinery department with a resident milliner. Almost anything could be bought at Tonkins. The phrase 'from the cradle to the grave' might be truly appropriate, as baby goods and even tombstones could be supplied.

John Tonkin the younger, c1885

The shop continued to be run by John and Elizabeth, with their son John and his wife Sarah taking more responsibility as the years went by. In its heyday this store was the largest in rural Somerset. Sarah Tonkin would travel to London to acquire the latest fashion ideas and the newest materials. A team of dressmakers and seamstresses in the village made up the clothes and dresses. Ladies would arrive in their carriages from all over the county to visit the shop. There were stables, and an ostler to look after the horses and their drivers. A two-seated lavatory was provided for the customers' convenience. Whilst materials were being cut and fittings adjusted, the ladies could partake of tea or other refreshment in the small, ornate tower which topped the building. This tower was demolished in the 1960s. On fine days, good views of the village or the Mendips could be seen, and Wells Cathedral could be glimpsed eight miles away.

In 1856 John senior, who had retired to Bristol, finally handed over the business completely to his son and daughter-in-law, John and Sarah. The date of John senior's death is not known. John and Sarah Tonkin continued to run the business themselves, keeping up a very high standard of service until their deaths in 1888. They were both 73 years old. John died, according to his tombstone in Wedmore churchyard, after 'an active day in the business'. Their son William had moved to Bath and was running his own draper's shop there. Having no wish to return to Wedmore, he leased the shop to William and Isabella Owen. They eventually bought the business in 1895. William Owen was also a Methodist, and his family ran the shop for many years, later taking in Mr and Mrs Stribling as partners. About 1948 the remaining members of the families retired, and Mr Wilson took over, marking the end of the long run of Methodist involvement in this important village 'emporium'.

The nonconformist connection may, in fact, be even more longstanding. Before John Tonkin first bought the site in 1819, it had descended through the Combe family to William Thompson in 1767, then to Richard Colston, a woolcomber, in 1774. It then passed to Thomas Tyley in 1783. He sold out to John Duckett, stocking maker, in 1797. Abraham Dyer, shopkeeper, who in the 1790s ran a business opposite, bought the old shop and house from John Duckett in 1801, and it was he who sold them to John Tonkin.

Abraham Dyer, along with John Tonkin, was instrumental in raising money to build a new Wesleyan Methodist Church on Sand Road in 1817. The old Wesleyan Church had been built in 1795 on the former roadside verge behind and adjacent to the corner property, then held by Thomas Tyley. It stood where the village hall stands today. It was Abraham Dyer, no less, who in 1795 obtained a certificate for this building, which stated that 'his new dwelling house is designed and set apart as a place of worship for protestant dissenters'.[25] It would seem that Abraham Dyer built a small house on the verge, not really for living in but specifically as a nonconformist chapel. Abraham Dyer, Wedmore shopkeeper and owner of the corner premises, thus had a longstanding involvement with nonconformity in Wedmore, well before the Tonkins arrived to take over the shop from him.

At about the same time, another small piece of this same verge, right on the corner, had been incorporated into the old house/shop site. John Tonkin subsequently built part of his house, now the Minstrels Gallery, over it. These acquisitions might perhaps represent the last stages of an even older link between occupiers of this property, and nonconformity in Wedmore. There are documentary clues to support such a link. In 1676 the first deed of the entire site shows that Edith Combe, widow, is transferring her tenancy to her son William. Just a few years later, in 1680, the owners of this burgage plot, part of the manor of Wedmore, were Sir Nicholas Pelham and his wife Jane. They leased the property to eleven men, some from widely scattered distant places. They were Andrew Innys of Bristol, gentleman; Robert Locke of Clements Inn, London, gentleman; Robert Coles of Weare, husbandman; William Deane of Wedmore, husbandman; Edward Combe of Wedmore; William Councell of Westham, yeoman; Matthew Locke of Wedmore, husbandman; Robert Stevens of Sturminster Newton, clothier; Richard Latcham of Stoughton, yeoman; John Baker of Wedmore, carpenter; and Stephen Champion of Sand, yeoman.

Who were these people, so varied in rank and place of origin; and why were they all involved with this one property in the ancient Borough, in Wedmore? The lease does not tell us, but other documentary sources provide clues. Wedmore is known to have been an active early centre for nonconformity in Somerset. In 1675, five years before the mysterious eleven leased the corner site in Church Street, one of them, Richard Latcham of Stoughton, had been fined for holding an illegal religious meeting in his house.[26] Richard Latcham was a 'dissenter': a nonconformist breaking away from the established Church of England. Stephen Champion of Sand was also a nonconformist; in 1689, nine years after the Pelham lease, he applied for his house at Sand to be used as a place of worship. Methodism did not exist at that time, and there is no clue as to which branch of nonconformity Richard Latcham and Stephen Champion followed - but both of them appear on the 1680 list of eleven lessees of this property adjoining the spare patch of roadside verge on which the first Wesleyan Church was subsequently built. Edward Combe of Wedmore also appears on the 1680 list. Was he a connection of Edith and William Combe who held this property in 1676? He does not appear in the parish registers, so a connection cannot be proven; but his very absence from the registers could be because he was a nonconformist. There were certainly members of a Combe family who were fined for nonconformity at Stoke St Gregory, near Taunton, in 1670 and 1683 although, again, no Wedmore connection has been established.[27] Was this corner of Wedmore a meeting place for nonconformists as early as 1680, and are the eleven lessees in fact trustees for an early nonconformist chapel? If so, the 1680 lease marked the start of a tradition of nonconformity associated with this property that lasted until about 1948. Whatever the religious persuasion of the occupiers of this site, we have a legacy of local business entrepreneurs, and a spectacular building, in the centre of Wedmore.

The Old Vicarage and Buoys Cottage, Wedmore

Many histories of houses all over the parish have been compiled over the years, including Northload Farm, Pilham Farm, Fernhall Farm, Horsepool Farm, The Hall, Court Cottage, Waterdale House and Allington House. I have however, chosen two from the centre of Wedmore and although they are next door to each other they have very differing histories.

For hundreds of years, the big house at the top of Church Street, opposite the steps up to the Church, was home to the Vicars of Wedmore of this parish - 37 whom we know by name, and many more whose names have not been recorded. **THE OLD VICARAGE** as it stands now is an amalgamation of several periods of building. The central core is probably 1600s, but there have been several earlier buildings on the site, although few traces remain above ground. From just a few documents, broken sherds of pottery and other items found in the garden, however, we can piece together a little of the story of the house and some of the people who have lived there.

The Old Vicarage, Wedmore

This spot beside Wedmore Brook has been inhabited since at least Roman times. We know this largely because of the Reverend S.H.A Hervey who lived there from 1876-1898. He was a keen local historian and amateur archaeologist. One day he decided to lower the Vicarage garden, and it was while this was being done that he discovered fragments of pottery and other objects.[28] He found sherds of Roman pottery which show that people were living there in the 3rd and 4th centuries AD. As no trace of a Roman building has yet been found in the vicinity, we have no evidence to show whether this settlement was just a simple farmstead, or something more substantial. Some of the pottery was imported Samian ware, and one piece bore a stamp with the potter's name, 'Abbo'. Glossy red Samian tableware suggests a fairly prosperous household, perhaps living in a small villa. We now know that there were several other Roman sites nearby. No evidence of any Saxon building or pottery has been found on this site, although no doubt there was some building of about the 800s-1000s, so close to the Saxon church and King Alfred's *villa regia*, his royal house.

In the 1100s the Dean and Chapter of Wells Cathedral were granted Wedmore Church along with the Manor, and they appointed a vicar to look after the parish. No records remain to tell who these first vicars were. The only traces of early medieval times to be found by Hervey in the Old Vicarage garden, were pieces of broken encaustic (decorated) floor tiles of the 1200s. Harvey found similar tiles in the church in the 1880s, and at his excavation of the Dean's house at Mudgley in 1878.[29]

The earliest vicar whose name we know was Thomas de Harptre, appointed in 1311, during the reign of Edward II. One of the exciting finds that Hervey made was part of a jug of the late 1200s or early 1300s. The jug is decorated with bearded faces, moulded around the rim.[30] The grey clay has been brightly coloured with yellow-green glaze and the decorations stuck on. There were originally five of these heads, one forming part of the spout. Darker clay was used for the eyes and holes pierced for the pupils. The main body of the jug is patterned with spirals and rosettes. Most of the base and the strap handle has broken off. Several other face jugs have been found in the Somerset and Bristol areas. Hervey himself found other tiny pieces of clay human heads, probably from other such jugs but of a much cruder design. While the other jugs that have been found are thought now to have come from medieval potteries in Bristol, the Wedmore jug is of a different and finer design, and was probably made at a Somerset pottery which is so far untraced. Perhaps this jug could have belonged to Thomas de Harptre (Vicar 1311-1317), and he amused his friends by pouring ale for them from his special jug. Whoever owned it must have been dismayed when it was broken and tossed out onto the Vicarage rubbish heap. The jug used to be on display in Wells Museum, along with a medieval cresset lamp - a small stone block with two cups to hold burning oil, which presumably also came from the Vicarage garden. The jug and other Wedmore finds are currently in store at Wells Museum.[31]

Another of Hervey's finds in the Vicarage garden was a medieval circular brooch or cloak-pin,[32] in the shape of a flattened circle with a long transverse pin as fastener. Around the face of the circle were inscribed the words JESUS NAZARENUS. Hervey thought it dated from the mid-1500s, but it might be considerably earlier, of the 12-1300s.[33] It is particularly interesting that a cloak-pin with an obviously religious inscription should be found on this particular spot. Did it belong to a vicar of Wedmore? There is no clue as to who owned it, and we shall probably never know.

In 1492, after the death of the vicar Roger Jannys, it appears that, perhaps because he had been long sick, dues had not been collected, either for the Vicar or for the Dean and Chapter of Wells. A trustee was appointed, and half the Dean and Chapter's share was set aside 'for the use of the future vicar towards sustaining the burden of the vicarage'.[34] The next vicar to be appointed was John Retford, and this money would have provided a small capital fund for the new incumbent, perhaps to restore a neglected vicarage, or perhaps to be used in other ways to re-establish an orderly parish. The new vicar, however, was instructed to repay any expenses incurred during the time that the living was vacant.

During the 1600s one vicar, Mathew Law (1627-1647) baptised eight of his children in the church between 1629 and 1641: Eleanor (who died aged 11), Joyce, George, John, Thomas, Ann, Mary and another Eleanor. In 1632 Mathew Law wrote in the Baptismal Register on March 10, 'Whereas upon my owne certaine knowledge my wife lying now in childbed is very weake and sick, and by eating fishe she may very much if not altogither endanger her life; I, Mathew Law, being vicar of the said parish of Wedmore, doe, as much as in me lyeth, lycence and authorise her to eat flesh according to the forme and effect of the statute in that case provided; in witness whearof I have hear but set my hand the day and year above written. Mathew Law, Vicar ibidem. This lycence was copied out …in the presence of us, - Mathew Law, vicar. Robert Cole X churchwarden, and John Petherham'. Robert Cole, one of the churchwardens, could not sign his name and just put an X as his mark. It was the season of Lent, and Mathew was perhaps conscious that he and his family should be setting an example to the parish by avoiding meat; anxious that villagers should not think he was failing to practise what he preached, he wrote this detailed explanation, fully signed and witnessed, in the parish register. The meat must have done Mathew's wife Eleanor good, as a few days later on the 14th March little George was born.

Family happiness, however, was not to last. During 1640 and 1641 three of his girls died, Eleanor, Ann and Eleanor junior; in 1642 his wife Eleanor died. In 1645 plague seems to have visited Wedmore, and among the many victims were Mathew Law's eldest son Mathew (about 20), Thomas (9) and Joyce (16), and two of his servants Mary Tucker and Henry Barrett, all dying within the four months between September and December 1645. In November alone, 24 people were buried, rather than the usual three or four.[35] Death struck families, especially in The Borough, and affected all ages. Endemic plague seems the most likely explanation.

In 1633 and again in 1635 a survey was made of the Vicarage house, its glebe lands and the small tithes which were due to the Vicar.[36] The survey was taken by Mathew Law, the two churchwardens and several parishioners. The two documents of 1633 and 1635 are identical in content, but signed by different parishioners. They contain a description of the house: 'The Vicaridge howse, contayninge a porch, a hall, a parlour, a Chamber ouer the parlour, a kithin [sic], a chamber ouer the kitchin, a buttery, a Chamber ouer the buttery, a milkhowse, a barne, a stable, a stall, a Orchard, a garden, a court on the north side of the howse, a mow barton a backside; contayning in all by estimacion one acre'. Then follows a list of all the glebe land and details of the small tithes, which the vicar received as part of his income.

The description of the house shows it to have been quite large in the 1630s, big enough to accommodate Mathew Law and his growing young family in happier times. The porch would have led into an open hall, with two-storeyed bays at either end: the parlour with its bedroom above at one end, and the kitchen and buttery with bedrooms above each at the other end. The parlour end may have been to the south, the kitchen end to the north, nearest Church Street. This typical 16-17th century layout was thus of a long, fairly narrow house end-on to Church Street. Some of the 1630s Vicarage probably forms part of the old core of the present house. The walls of this central part are substantial, and at least 2 feet thick; they rest in part on much wider foundations, which may be part of the medieval building. The fragmentary remains of an early roof have been identified, and may be of about this same date.[37] Most of the rest of the house, and all the outbuildings, have however been swept away by later building. Subsequent additions and alterations shortened the earlier house and turned it around onto its present east-west axis.

Reverend S.H.A Hervey thought that the dining room at the east end of the present house was added by the Revd Francis Taylor (Vicar 1742-1779) and the adjoining drawing room by John Richards (Vicar 1811-1825).[38] Between these two vicars were William Bishop (1779-1802) and John Lewis Warren (1802-1811). Neither of them actually lived in the Vicarage, but just stayed there occasionally to collect their dues. They appointed curates to do all their work, while they preferred to live in Wells and elsewhere. John Richards, on his appointment, was put to 'considerable expense [on] the repairs of the Vicarage house'.[39] He also was a non-resident vicar, and appointed a curate, as he held another living in Bath, although he did come to preach quite often in Wedmore.

In 1876 when the Reverend S.H.A. Hervey was appointed Vicar of Wedmore, an extra west wing was built on to the Vicarage. There were already five bedrooms, but two more were added, together with a closet [a lavatory] and a downstairs scullery, coal shed, larder, servants' closet and garden closet. The building was done with Wedmore stone 'from a quarry in the immediate neighbourhood'. The Vicar's closet was to have 'a deal seat and riser with hinged cover' but the servants' closet was to have 'an elm seat, back riser and moveable cover'. The alterations and building works cost £295.[40] Hervey was a bachelor, but had three live-in staff: a cook/housekeeper, maid and boy.

When the Reverend S.H.A. Hervey resigned in 1898, the Reverend Joseph Byrchmore was appointed (1898-1902). In 1900 the Wedmore builder Solomon Wall erected a garden wall around the orchard newly purchased from neighbouring Buoys Cottage. The cost of the wall, built of Wedmore stone, 92 feet long and 10ft 3 ins. high, was £32 10s. 0d.[41]

In 1902 the next new Vicar, the Reverend Robert Augustus May, was said to dislike the Vicarage. He made an exchange with Doctor Tyley, who had built himself a new house in Speke Close on the Cheddar Road in 1879. Dr Tyley moved into what became The Old Vicarage, and the Reverend Robert May moved into Speke Close, (now Whitfield House) which became The Vicarage, and remained so until 1996.

The Old Vicarage is one of the most important house sites in the parish of Wedmore. The chance finds in the garden of a few sherds, broken tiles, a rare jug and other oddments, can be linked together with a few legal documents to help give us a glimpse of some of the people who have lived there over many centuries.

BUOYS COTTAGE in Glanville Road adjoins the south garden of The Old Vicarage. It is a narrow house, one room deep, probably dating from the 1600s and lies below the road level and beside Wedmore Brook as it bubbles down through the village. There has probably been a cottage on this site since the 1200s.

An opportunity to examine the deeds of the cottage has shown just how useful these documents can be to the local historian - not always in the way one would anticipate. The deeds of the cottage reveal some intriguing information on its ownership, which has in turn led on to further research, making what seemed the straightforward history of a little cottage into a more interesting story, part of the social history of Wedmore.

The name itself, 'Buoys Cottage' or 'Buoys' as it is called in the first deed dated 1766, has led to much speculation, situated as it is beside the brook. However, it has nothing to do with the water. It simply means that this was the home of the Boys family, who lived in the village in the mid-1700s. The parish registers show that Elizabeth Boys died in 1731, and

Buoys Cottage

her husband Richard in 1760. Although there is no documentary proof that Richard and Elizabeth Boys lived in this cottage, they are the only people called Boys in the parish, so it seems likely that this was their house. In 1788 the deeds refer to it as 'late Boys' - Richard and Elizabeth have died, and their surname is, in the 1780s, in the process of becoming transformed into a house-name.

In 1766 Buoys Cottage belonged to the Reverend Francis Taylor, who held it on a lease from the Duke of Chandos. The Duke owned many properties in the parish, because he had bought up part of two manors, Wedmore and Churchlands. The Reverend Francis Taylor's lease was for 99 years or the duration of three lives, whichever was the longer (a very usual form of lease in this part of the southwest, valued for ensuring continuity of farmsteads); the lives were those of himself, his daughter Maria Doolan and his young grandson Francis Taylor Doolan, aged 4 years. The rent was 1s 6d a year, and a heriot or death duty of 10 shillings was to be paid to the Duke of Chandos on the death of any of the 'lives'.

There seems to have been a long tradition of Buoys being held by Vicars of Wedmore. Perhaps this was because it was conveniently adjacent to the Old Vicarage and could provide housing for a curate or other staff. In 1683 a survey of the Vicarage itself describes not just the Vicarage (now the Old Vicarage in Church Street) but also 'a messuage and backside adjoining'. In 1683 the Vicar was Thomas Davis, and he held the cottage.[42] When he died he left to his 'dear wife Mary…a messuage and backside adjoining to the Vicaridge House of Wedmore' and three acres of arable lying in the Eastfield of Wedmore. He obviously held it on a sufficiently long lease from the Lord of the Manor, to treat it as his own property. His widow Mary married the new Vicar, Richard Downton, in 1688. Buoys Cottage passed down through several more vicars to the Reverend Francis Taylor. There was, it would seem, some arrangement with the Duke of Chandos and his predecessors as Lords of the Manor.

In 1786, according to the next surviving deed, John Millard innholder rents the cottage. John Millard and family were landlords of the Bell Inn, which is now the Post Office. John Millard died shortly afterwards, and just two years later, in 1788, Francis Taylor Doolan, the grandson of Reverend Francis Taylor and now a surgeon in Wells, the only surviving Taylor 'life', sold his interest in the cottage called 'Boys' for 25 guineas to 'George Millard otherwise Taylor'. A year later, George Millard otherwise Taylor took full possession of the cottage from trustees of his dead father. Who was this George Millard otherwise Taylor? Was he a relation of both John Millard and Francis Taylor Doolan?

The parish registers helped to solve some of the mystery. George Millard or Taylor was born in 1760. He was the illegitimate son of Grace Taylor. Grace was a local girl, Grace Leakey, who at the age of 19, in 1748, married a John Taylor, also of Wedmore. John and Grace had three children, Grace (baptised 1753), Hester (1755) and William (1758). Some time after 1758, Grace's husband John Taylor vanishes from the scene. In 1760, Grace has baby George Millard/Taylor, the son of John Millard the innholder. Sarah Millard/Taylor follows in 1761 and Hannah Millard/Taylor in 1764, both born to Grace Taylor. Soon after Hannah's birth, Grace Taylor married John Millard. This can only mean that John Taylor had disappeared but not died, c.1758-9; and that by 1764 Grace was a widow, and free to marry the man with whom she had already had her second family.

There is no trace of the burial of her first husband John Taylor in the Wedmore parish records. It has been impossible, so far, to find out where he had been from 1758 until Grace's marriage proves that he is dead in 1764. Was he some relation of the Reverend Francis Taylor who owned Buoys Cottage in 1766; or of his grandson Francis Taylor Doolan who was later to sell it to Grace Taylor's and John Millard's eldest son, George Millard/Taylor? The evidence of the names certainly suggests some connection. The Reverend Francis Taylor was born in Winscombe, where both his father and his brother were vicars, and there was a large extended family of Taylors in that parish. John Taylor of Wedmore may have belonged to this branch - but, tantalisingly, it has not been possible to establish any connection. Were the respected Taylor family covering up some unfortunate episode? Or was it just a coincidence of surnames? What happened to John Taylor, who disappeared in 1758-9, yet leaves Grace not a widow? Divorce, of course, was not a practical possibility in the 1750s, except by a special, individual Act of Parliament: something only a very few wealthy aristocracy could contemplate. Did John Taylor merely abandon his wife Grace? Did he go off to join the army, and die elsewhere sometime later? Was there some family tragedy of physical or mental illness, with John incapacitated and 'put away' somewhere else, but leaving Grace with a young family to bring up on no means, and a local suitor, whom she was not free to marry until four or five years later when they had already had three children? It remains a mystery. Whatever the reason, after his death Grace and John Millard brought up their family, latterly at least as tenants of Buoys Cottage, and their son George Millard otherwise Taylor inherited Buoys Cottage in 1788 after his father's death.

The Wedmore Vestry meeting minutes record that in October 1802 the Overseers of the Poor are looking for another cottage in which to house some of the poor.[43] One of the two existing Poor Houses, which stood at the west end of the churchyard facing the Vicarage, was 'nearly in ruins'. Someone suggested that they should ask George Millard if they could purchase 'his house and garden late Buoys adjoining the vicarage for the reception of the poor', and take down the ruinous Poor House, and remove the materials to George Millard's house, presumably to be reused on alterations or improvements there. George Millard was presumably not living in the cottage at this time. This did not in fact come about; no doubt George Millard objected to his family home being used for this purpose.

A few years later, in 1818, George Millard is appointed Vestry Clerk, and is 'to teach the Poor children for the ensuing year and that the School be kept at his own house'.[44] So, from his ignominious birth, George is now an educated man, respected enough to become the vestry clerk and schoolmaster. It is not recorded how long the school was kept in Buoys Cottage.

George Millard/Taylor married Catherine Tucker in 1814. He died in 1844 aged 84. His relations George Henry Millard of Wells, draper, and John Burrel Millard of Huddersfield, accountant, inherited the property. George left a proviso in his will that 'no woman shall inherit', and there is no mention of his wife Catherine who died, aged 72, in 1846. One wonders what further story lies behind that brief stipulation? Apart from Buoys Cottage, George also owned the house called Laurel Bank in Sand Road, and John Burrel Millard moved down from Huddersfield and lived there with his family until his death. The orchard of Buoys Cottage was sold in 1899, for £100, to the Ecclesiastical Commissioners, and it became part of the Vicarage garden.

All houses of any age have an interesting history, and often the clues are buried in otherwise functional-looking title deeds: sales, leases, mortgages, attached papers, even modern typescript abstracts of earlier original documents which have been (unfortunately) discarded. Thanks to the generosity of Mr Paul Horley in allowing his deeds to be studied in detail, this is an instance where such deeds have not only clarified the history of a Wedmore house, but also yielded facts that can be linked to other parish documents, giving us an unexpected insight into the lives and times of some of its inhabitants.

Chapter 7
Ancient Landscapes

The other villages in the parish have a past just as ancient and interesting as Wedmore. Mudgley, for example, is today is a string of farmsteads along the southern slope of the Isle of Wedmore looking out over the Somerset Levels, but it has a very long and intriguing history.

The search for King Alfred's Palace at Mudgley

In 1878, to celebrate the 1000th anniversary of the Peace of Wedmore between King Alfred and the Danes, the Reverend S.H.A. Hervey, Vicar of Wedmore, obtained permission to dig the field at Mudgley called Court Garden.[1] When the new turnpike road had been cut through this field in about 1827, foundations of buildings were discovered. Folklore said that this was the site of King Alfred's palace; the field name Court Garden with its regal overtones caught the imagination. The idea of a royal connection had been enhanced in 1843 when a beautiful silver spoon had been found in this field. It was, however, identified as 15th century and is now in the Ashmolean Museum, Oxford.[2]

Hervey and his workmen opened up a large area and found substantial remains of several buildings. Before long he realised that the ancient buildings were nothing to do with King Alfred. The remains were later and were of a large country house belonging to the Dean of Wells, built in the 1100s. A chapel at Mudgley had been recorded in 1176 and this was probably part of the house.[3] A document of 1334[4] mentions the hall (house) and kitchen and in 1378 the complex consisted of houses, granges, bovaries (oxhouses) and stables with ancient chapel, garden and fishponds.[5] The 'Court' of Court Garden was not King Alfred's Court but the manorial court of Mudgley which had been held in the Dean's house, where rents were paid and disputes settled. Hervey's excavations concentrated on the main area of buildings, to the east side of the road which had cut through the site. The garden and fishponds on the west side of the road were not investigated.

Hervey's plan of the site in 1878-9 shows long stretches of fallen walls and buildings, and a cobbled road or yards. The remains of a large building found to the north of the main site was probably a barn. The main buildings seem to have been surrounded by enclosing walls. Hervey wrote up the excavations very thoroughly, but archaeology has moved on since the 1870s and modern methods such as geophysical surveying would show a good deal more and give a clearer picture of the site. Photographs were taken of the excavations in 1878[6] and drawings made from some of these were reproduced in the *Wedmore Chronicle*. Hervey was using the latest technology by taking photographs to record his findings and the original photographs show the walls very clearly. Dating the remains from photographs is rather difficult, but Hervey recorded the finds from the trenches. These included many pot sherds, tiles (some glazed), oyster and cockle shells, bones, arrow heads, keys, knife blades, coins and two pieces of slate.

The slates had music scratched on them. They were re-examined in 1979 when the music on the larger slate was identified as Kyrie *Pater cuncta*, probably from the mid 1400s. There

Ancient Landscapes

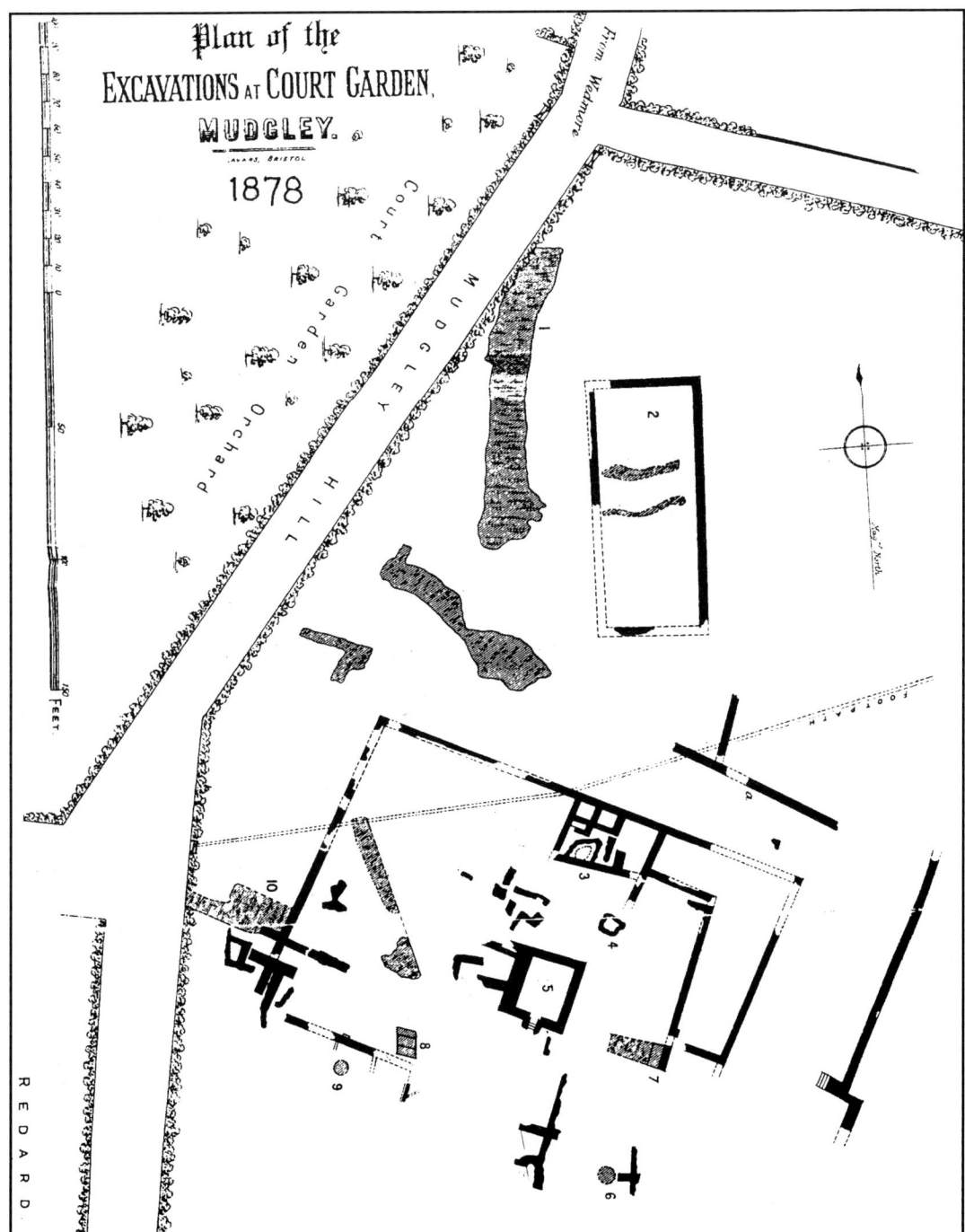

Plan of excavations at Court Garden, Mudgley, 1878, from Wedmore Chronicle *vol 1 (1887) facing page 17*

is a dog's head scratched on the reverse, and a name, probably Willelmus.[7] These slates are in Wells Museum.

The pottery found was of various periods. Some was clearly medieval but there was a lot of other pottery, including coarse black and brown ware. Some pieces were identified as cooking pots, being blackened inside. Hervey sent some of this pottery to 'Mr Franks, keeper of British and Medieval antiquities at the British Museum. He calls it Norman…pottery used in England in A.D. 1100' which fits the date of the Dean's house. However, when Hervey showed pieces of this pottery to 'Several authorities…some called it Romano-British'. The Roman expert Prebendary H.M. Scarth, a local member of The Bath Field Club, said that 'the pottery appeared to be of different dates from the very early to comparatively later times'.[8] Reading through the report there is a description of bones and black pottery being found underneath the foundations of at least one of the buildings 'some feet' down. This suggests that there was earlier occupation on the site, especially to the west of the main dig and near the present road.

So there we have the puzzle! Was the Dean's house on or near the site of a Roman building? This has happened on several of our oldest farmstead sites in the parish, and Roman pottery has since been found nearby at Fernhall Farm. The Revd Hurst of Somerset Archaeological Society is reported in the *Weston-super-Mare Gazette* 16th Nov 1878 as saying that he thought that the 'building had been raised on site of some older Romano-Celtic villa'. Did Hervey, rather inexperienced at archaeology at this time, rely too much on the word of the British Museum expert, ignoring the identification of local antiquarians? Was it that he so hoped to find Saxon evidence of King Alfred, that Roman finds were simply overlooked? While there may indeed have been a Saxon building on the site, it would probably have been of timber and it would have been very difficult in 1878 to have interpreted the changes in soil colour and marks of post holes which perhaps denoted earlier timber remains. Hervey would have expected a stone building for 'Alfred's Palace', but recognised that he had found instead the house of the medieval Deans of Wells. The most likely site for Alfred's *villa regia* or royal house was in Wedmore close by the church, where the Manor House stands today.

In the centre of the main area of buildings found by Hervey at Mudgley, at some depth, a small room 16x20 feet was revealed. Some of the walls were still standing and showed evidence that it had had a vaulted ceiling. Tufa stones found in the debris would have been used in vaulting the roofs, as they are very light. Hervey suggests this room might have been the chapel, first mentioned in 1176. Tufa outcrops occur at nearby Fernhall Farm.

While Hervey and his team of enthusiasts were digging, many visitors came to look over the site. In 1878-9 'Alfred mania' was at its height. The local press regularly recorded the work on the excavation.[9] Then, in the *Weston Gazette* of 16th August 1879, there appeared the astonishing headline

'THE SUPPOSED DRIVE OF KING ALFRED'

The reporter had been talking to the locals and to a 'popular and eminent man' about the area. This man seems to have known the landscape of Mudgley very well indeed, as the article describes in detail the hillside around and above Mudgley Hill Farm. This is the account from the newspaper, slightly abbreviated:

> '*The supposed drive of King Alfred which is about ¼ mile distant from the spot upon which the palace stood, the way to it and the description of it may be given in the*

Ancient Landscapes 91

Original photograph of part of the excavations of the Dean's House, Mudgley, 1878

following words. Adjoining King's Court Garden is a farm called Mudgley [Hill] Farm ... Passing through the farmyard we come to the foot of a gully ... through which a meandering gurgling brook passes southwards towards the supposed ponds of King Alfred. Whether this stream helped feed the fishponds is not known, but it is more than probable that there were fishponds in front of Mudgley [Hill] Farm house which were supplied with an excellent spring of water close by. Although the spring is now filled up it can easily be seen where it is...In ascending the steep incline from the gully, we soon come into the open fields and were it not for two hedges which were not there in King Alfred's time the wide open space would much resemble a park and here is the supposed drive of King Alfred. A very popular and eminent man in passing through the grounds the other day said "There was no doubt that King Alfred had walked there many times".'

The sublime confidence that King Alfred had actually trodden this hillside many times is a wonderful flight of imagination; but something in the landscape must have given the 'eminent man' this idea. What was 'King Alfred's Drive'? The report of 1879 continues with a detailed description:

'The drive runs very much like the letter Z, northwards, westwards and northwards, and comes into the Sand Road and there was once a beautiful avenue of trees on the

north and west route but there are only a few standing now. There are several trees on the westward route and all of them in a straight line but only on one side of the drive, and those trees appear to be very old...yet they might have been saplings from the parent stock standing in the time of King Alfred. We now come to the close of land called Kills Wall through which the drive runs. Here was a wall, and tradition tells us that the deer were driven and slaughtered for the Royal Palace. The drive passes through the gate of this field and onto the road leading from Wells to Mark ...'.

So ends the newspaper report. What can be made of it? What were the 'eminent man' and the reporter actually looking at and describing? And is there really a Saxon roadway running up and across the Mudgley hillside? They did see something, and it can still be made out on the ground today, albeit more faintly than a century ago. What they were looking at were archaeological features of the medieval arable open field system and the adjacent deerpark. Today one can still see what they saw. The gully and stream above Mudgley Hill Farm are still there, but below the farm, the traces of garden and fishponds and spring have been almost obliterated. There is, however, a zig-zag line with some ancient oak trees along part of it. The Wedmore parish map of 1791 shows that part of this Z-shape was an old field boundary.[10] By 1885 this boundary, destroyed when the fields were enlarged and reshaped, was just a low bank through the field, with some former hedgerow trees left standing along it.[11] The bank, now eroded almost completely away in places, can still just be made out, and a few of the trees still stand. Another part of the 'drive' is a bank which was in fact a former headland or furlong boundary, the bank on which the plough turned at the end of a block of medieval strips of ploughland. Some more ancient oak trees are standing on another bank, the last northward arm of the Z, which is much worn down but bigger than a mere field boundary. This is the bank formerly called Kills Wall, which certainly existed and gave its name to the adjacent field. The bank or mud wall, probably topped with a wooden paling fence, bounded this part of the Deans' medieval deerpark. It can just be made out, running from its junction with the Sand Road near Oldwood Lane, southwards across the hillside. The name Kills Wall occurs in documents of the 1700s,[12] and probably does refer to this part of the park 'wall' to which the deer were driven to be killed, as described in the newspaper. The deerpark, however, was medieval, and although deer were doubtless hunted over the Isle of Wedmore in King Alfred's day (indeed the name Wedmore is supposed to come from the Saxon words meaning 'hunting moor'), neither the park nor Kills Wall would have been in existence in Saxon times.

This splendidly imaginative story of King Alfred riding in state up his driveway from his Mudgley palace to Wedmore, must have died a quick death when Hervey confirmed that no trace of King Alfred's Palace had been found at Mudgley. It does, however, show how myths and legends can grow up; how they can provide clues to present-day archaeological remains; and how even a totally mistaken idea can still have its uses in unravelling a few more surviving details of our parish history. The archaeological dig showed evidence of the various periods of the Deans' house from 1100s to 1500s. There was probably earlier occupation on the site: Roman, perhaps Iron Age, and even earlier as suggested by the finding of several flints. Before the site was filled in many barrow loads of stone from the walls were removed for use locally. The site has since been 'listed' to safeguard it. The bases of these walls are presumably still there and modern archaeological methods of surveying and excavation might give us more answers about how long people have been living on this important site at Mudgley.

Alexander of Mudgley's farm, 1220

About 775 years ago two men exchanged some land in Mudgley. One of them was Peter, the Dean of Wells; the other was Alexander of Mudgley. The deed of exchange is dated about 1220, and survives in the archives of Wells Cathedral.[13] It is quite detailed, and it gives us our first written description of the landscape and farming of Mudgley at that time.

When the Dean of Wells built his country house at Mudgley in the 1100s, a deer park was created not far away on the west side of the road, to provide sport for the Dean and his guests, and meat for the table. We know from repairs described in 1378 that this deer park was enclosed, probably with a mud wall or bank and fence, to keep the deer in.[14] It included the area which is still known as Old Wood today; this is in Sand, which, together with Heath House, was part of the Manor of Mudgley.

Alexander held some land within the area enclosed by the Dean's park, and some more near the Dean's house. The exchange of land was made so that Alexander's holdings would all lie outside the park, and the Dean would gain more land close to his house. The original document is in Latin, and this is a slightly shortened translation:

'I Alexander of Mudgley have given and granted to Sir Peter, Dean [of Wells] and his successors, all the land, meadow, wood, alders and moor which lie within the circuit of the Park of Mudgley, and all the land which I had on the east side of the road from Wedmore towards Mudgley which extends itself in a straight line from the western corner of the croft which was formerly of Godfrey, eastward as far as the land of the said Dean, and from the same corner southward as far as the road which goes as far as the court of the same Dean; and half an acre which I had in Sand, which lies next to the land of David towards the east. In exchange for all the land which the said Dean Peter held in his demesne in the ploughland called Stanilond, and the meadow, alders and moor which lie next to the park of Mudgley towards the east, between my meadow and the said Park, and extending itself as far as the southern corner of the said Park; and a certain small piece of land of about ½ acre lying on the west side of the house which was of Malger; and two acres of land formerly of Robert Malherbe which lie together in the ploughland nearest to La Hethe; and half an acre in Hoverelulleg', which lies next to my land.'

The lack of punctuation in medieval documents (some modern punctuation has been added) makes the details at first seem confusing. The first part of the document concerns three blocks of land which Alexander held, and which he is giving to the Dean. One large area was within the Dean's park. The implication is that farmland was being cultivated there, before the deerpark was laid out over it, perhaps sometime not long before 1220. It must have been very inconvenient to hold land within a deer park, especially arable land with the deer nibbling all the crops! The circuit of the park stretched from the top of the hill where the arable 'land' or ploughland was, down the hillside through meadow and wood to alder groves and the moor at the bottom. The area of land which Alexander held and which he handed over to the Dean extended from top to bottom of the hillside, through all these different landscapes. In exchange the Dean gave him a similar belt of meadow, alders and moor lying to the east of the park, between it and some of Alexander's own meadow, and stretching as far as the south corner of the park. Missing from this part of the exchange was the arable land that Alexander gave up within the park. So, to compensate for this, the Dean gave Alexander some of his own (his 'demesne') ploughland in Stanilond. Stanilond or Stoneyland has not survived as a field name, but it was probably at the top of the Mudgley Hill, part of the great arable open field system. The name Stani or Stoney tells us what it was like for the medieval ploughman; Wedmore stone lay near to the surface. In the 1500s we know that there were stone quarries in the area to the west of Mudgley crossroads; and this may have been the medieval Stanilond.

The second piece of Alexander's land involved in the exchange was on the east side of the Wedmore-Mudgley road, running from the croft which previously belonged to Godfrey, east to the Dean's land and south to the road leading to the Dean's house. The Dean, by this part of the exchange, gained more land immediately around his house. The third piece was just ½ acre which Alexander held in Sand, which lay to the east of David's land; and may have been included in the exchange simply as a makeweight in equalising the arrangements. In exchange for these last two pieces of land, Alexander was given by the Dean three other pieces of land. One was ½ acre of arable land lying on the west side of Malger's house. Unfortunately there are no clues as to where Malger lived. The second piece was two adjacent acres of land which had previously belonged to Robert Malherbe, in an arable field 'nearest' to La Hethe, probably on the hill at Heath House. The last piece of land given in exchange was ½ acre in Hoverelulleg'. This land lay next to more of Alexander's own land, conveniently consolidating his holdings as a return for giving the Dean control over his new deerpark and space around his house. Hoverelulleg' is a strange field name; it is probably a corruption of Over or 'Upper' Lulleigh, 'Lull'-clearing.

Alexander, by these exchanges, transferred to the Dean one sizeable area within the park, land adjacent to the Dean's house, and a third small area in Sand. In return he received a block of land on the east side of the park adjoining meadow he already held, together with three smaller blocks of ploughland which cannot now be pinpointed exactly on the ground. The aim would be to make a fair exchange of land of equal agricultural value, while consolidating each person's holdings more conveniently. Alexander received no wood in exchange for that he gave to the Dean: perhaps extra alder groves compensated for this. We are not given acreages of wood and alder, so cannot make comparisons; but alder was a valuable timber tree in the medieval period. The Dean would appear to have an unencumbered deer park. The deer were left to graze in peace until the chase, and Alexander could grow his crops safely on his new land, adjacent to his existing holdings and outside the park bounds.

What is clear from the transaction is that Alexander is no mere peasant, passively subject to his manorial lord the Dean of Wells. He appears as a landholder of standing, in his own right, to whom the Dean has to grant away some of his personal 'demesne' in order to secure the other land he wants. The Dean of Wells' manor was surveyed in 1558. When this survey is plotted onto a map, it becomes clear that there is a gap in the middle of the area described - a block of land with a house on it which does not belong to the Dean of Wells, but is surrounded by the Dean's land. This block lies on the hillside at the eastern side of the boundary of Mudgley Park: that is, in the position of Alexander's main landholding with its new additions. Could this unit of land have been the nucleus of the separate estate of Alexander of Mudgley in about 1220? If so, Chestnut Farm, the isolated farmstead west of Mudgley Hill Farm and nearest to the former Mudgley Park boundary, could be the successor to the farmstead where Alexander lived.

The deed of exchange of 1220 shows Mudgley was then a thriving settlement. It gives a surprisingly detailed picture of the hillside landscape, with every scrap of land being ploughed, used as managed woodland, or as haymeadows. The landscape profile down the hillside, from ploughland at the top, through woods on the slopes to meadow land towards the foot and out to alder groves (a valuable source of timber) and the moor, is emphasised by repetition, and conjures up the landscape of 1220 on the hillside we can see today.

The document gives us the names of some Mudgley inhabitants at the time. It is too early for surnames to have developed properly; only Robert Malherbe has one, and his is a Norman-French name. He was a fairly important Somerset landholder who appears in other records of the time. He is described in another document of the 1220s as Robert Malherbe son of Henry de Mudesleg (or Mudgley) so he was obviously a local man. Alexander is just 'of Mudgley', while Godfrey, Malger and David do not appear to merit any additional names at all. Malger probably became the later local surname of Alger, a family flourishing in Wedmore in the 1500s.

This is a real document about real people and places, and gives a vivid picture of what Mudgley must have looked like over 700 years ago.

Theale landscape: The Battle of Kyppmerwalle

Theale lies on the edge of the north slope of the Isle of Wedmore looking over the moors and towards the Mendip hills. This is the story of a scene of conflict between Theale and Wedmore.

We are always hearing about disagreements between neighbours over their boundaries. Over 500 years ago, in 1494, neighbours in the parish of Wedmore actually fought each other over a boundary. The confrontations became so violent that the dispute was taken to one of the highest courts in the land, the King's Court of Star Chamber in London.[15] The neighbours in question were the estates of Wedmore and Northload. Wedmore belonged to the Dean of Wells, and Northload (now Theale and Panborough) belonged to the Abbot of Glastonbury. The argument was about the boundary between these two estates, which ran from Theale down to the River Axe.

This ancient boundary line separated Wells land from Glastonbury land. The dispute was caused by a large mud wall which the Wedmore tenants of the Dean had built along this boundary. It ran from just below the main road at West Well Lane in Theale, north to the Axe. Mud walls had been built for many years to protect low-lying land along moor edges from flooding. This particular mud wall was different in that, although its main purpose was to prevent Wedmore land from flooding, it was also the boundary between the two estates. It was called Kyppmerwalle.

Part of this Star Chamber case was published many years ago in Somerset Record Society volume 27,[16] but when the original documents in the Public Record Office in London were examined, some mistakes were discovered, as well as much more vivid local detail than was included in the published version. The mistakes had been made where writing was obscured, but under an ultra-violet lamp the words could be read more easily. The name of the mud wall was originally read as Kumnorwalle; but the lamp showed up the missing tails of certain letters, to give its real name as Kyppmerwalle.

Long before Kyppmerwalle had been built the tenants of Northload, Theale and Panborough had rights to turn their animals out to pasture on the common of Wedmore Moor. This ancient custom prevailed right up until the time of the enclosure of the moors in the late 1700s. The building of the mud wall made it rather difficult for the animals to scramble over, but they were still able to pasture in Wedmore Moor. After some years, however, Wedmore tenants prevented the animals from crossing over by building a fence of stakes along the top of the wall. Presumably it was intended to consolidate the wall against damage from the animals - but the effect was to outrage the Northload tenants. They were being deprived of their ancient rights of common. Also they claimed that when Wedmore built the wall they blocked off an ancient watercourse, causing flooding on the Northload side. At this time in the 1400s there was a river flowing north through the Panborough Gap, bringing water from Fenny Castle and beyond. In times of flood excess water was carried in a supplementary drainage ditch, which cut across Panborough Moor and Wedmore Moor until it reached Cocklake and joined the River Axe. Landcourse Rhyne, it is thought, is a surviving part of this ancient system. Kyppmerwalle cut across and blocked this ditch, and floods backed up on the Northload side all across Panborough and Yeo Moors, while Wedmore Moor stayed drier for longer. The Northload tenants, much annoyed, smashed down part of the wall to let the surplus water through, which in turn caused tempers to fly in Wedmore. The Dean decided to take Northload to court.[17]

Law court records can provide fascinating material for the local historian, but it is often buried in turgid legal language. In this Star Chamber dispute, however, the local participants come vividly to life. Wedmore's case was that on 2nd June 1493 several men from Glastonbury came 'equipped in warlike manner with bows, bills and other weapons .... encouraged by William Tyntenhull [Tincknell] of Panburgh, John Popham, John More, Robert Counsell, Robert Chalcroft, John Algare, William Algare, Thomas Theyre, John Collerigge of Theel and John of Martsey, they broke down, cruelly and with great force, a length of about 16 feet of the wall, letting water in onto the Dean's moor and land. At the same time they used their weapons to break up diverse barriers that stood upon the same wall in various places'. These barriers were designed to defend the wall itself from cattle and to protect Wedmore pasture. As a result the moor and land were flooded and greatly damaged.

When Wedmore tenants found that the wall was breached, they rushed to rebuild it, to stop the floodwater coming through. The Northload men and their supporters from Glastonbury, however, 'stood at the wall with bows drawn, and threatened to shoot', so that Wedmore was unable to make the repairs. Later, 'after the rioters had gone', Wedmore men succeeded in repairing the wall, 'to their great cost & charge.' When the Northload tenants realised that the wall was repaired, 'They once more broke it down in the same place and let the floodwaters in'. It was mended by Wedmore a second time. Six days later, at the instigation of William Tyntenhull of Northload, the Northload men 'came back a third time by night, armed as before, and broke down the wall in 6 other places.' Wedmore claimed in court that 'the land was so severely damaged by floods that it is likely to be useless for ever.' Faced with these accusations from the Dean, the Northload rioters all pleaded not guilty, except for Hugh Hardwich and Richard Dwale from Glastonbury. Hugh and Richard, spokesmen for the Abbot's case, explained to the court that although the tenants of Northload had 800 acres of their own moors, comprising Panborough and Yeo Moor, they also had 'common of pasture for all manner of beasts throughout the year in Wedmore Moor.' The wall and the fence of stakes deprived them of ancient rights of pasture there. Wedmore counter-claimed that the old drainage ditch often caused flooding in both moors but that Wedmore Moor always came off worse. On the instructions of the Dean, Wedmore therefore had built the new drainage ditch from Theale Well, at the top of West Well Lane, down to the river. The upcast from this ditch formed the mud wall called Kyppmerwalle. Hugh and Richard claimed that on 2nd June 'in daylight and peaceably [they] took down the barriers and stakes'; but where the barrier was fixed deeply in the ground across the old ditch, the mud itself broke down when the stakes were pulled out, blocking the new ditch and flooding Wedmore Moor.

Tempers became very frayed. The court record describes how Wedmore men were arrayed in warlike manner in jackets, helmets, mailcoats and with bows drawn, guns and other arms. The primitive guns of that time were dangerous to friend and foe alike! The bells of Wedmore church were rung, calling all to the cause. The Wedmore crowd marched to Kyppmerwalle and re-erected the stakes and banks as they were before. They also threatened publicly, in Wedmore church, that if any of the Abbot's tenants, whom they called churls - an insult in those days - should break down the wall again, 'they should be beaten and slain and fried in their own grease in their own houses.' These terrible threats never materialised, but some Wedmore tenants assaulted William Tyntenhull the constable and tithingman of Northload, and also Agnes More, who was pregnant. However, on the instructions of the steward of Glastonbury Abbey the wall was broken down yet again. It seems to have been at this point that the Dean decided to go to court to settle the troubles once and for all.

The individual witnesses' accounts of what happened in 1494 still survive in the Star Chamber Court records, in the Public Record Office at Kew. They describe, in their own words, the violent encounters between the Dean of Wells' Wedmore tenants, and the Abbot of Glastonbury's tenants in Northload and Theale, over the mud wall called Kyppmerwalle.

The first witness was William Lacham of Sand, who is described as a husbandman 'of thage of 63 or 65 or therabouts'. He was born in 'ye Zond' (the clerk needed three attempts to get anything like the name Sand, in a Somerset dialect!), in the house where he now dwells. He says that he knows the moor concerned, containing about 1500 acres, of which 600 acres have been enclosed into separate fields for the use of the Dean's tenants. The other 900 acres remained as open common for the Dean's tenants and also the tenants of the Abbot of Glastonbury. He says that when he was young, about 15, he heard 'divers of old folkes' such as his father who was 60 or more before he died, William Counsell who is still alive and aged about 80, and John Guylbert who was also about 80 before he died, all of whom dwelt in the parish, often say that the 600 acres out of the 1500 were 'several' to the

Dean's tenants and were 'enclosed with walles' by them, and no-one commoned there. Hugh and Richard claimed that on 2nd June 'in daylight and peaceably [they] took down the barriers and stakes'; but where the barrier was fixed deeply in the ground around the old drainage ditch, the bank itself broke down when the stakes were pulled out, blocking the new ditch and flooding Wedmore Moor. 'Several' was the term for land that had been drained and enclosed into separate meadows for which the tenants paid rent.

William Lacham says that 'on a Monday in June last' (i.e. 2nd June 1494) this wall enclosing the Dean's several was broken up by nine persons, of whom some were tenants of the Abbot of Glastonbury, and others came from Glastonbury Town. He named most of them, and saw them busy breaking up the walls 'and the Barryars the which were sett on high upon the said Walles to kepe out the bestes out of the severall. And they had with them 4 Bowes and a Swerd and other wapons.' He says that William Chalcroft and William Stone went to remonstrate with them; at which Richard Sydenham, one of the gang, drew his sword, and he and the others assaulted William and his companions, so that they were in danger of their lives unless they withdrew. Through this and other breaches, the moor was flooded. The Dean's tenants were afraid to repair the breaches because the rioters stood by them 'with Bulwerkes made with Fagotts before theym and with theyr bowes bent to have shot unto theym.' The breaches were eventually repaired, but broken down again at night. The breaches flooded the entire moor, both the severall and the common, and a great part of it was still drowned.

Thomas Prior, husbandman, aged 80 and also born in Wedmore, said that there had never been any trouble before. He quoted his aged father, many other old folkes including John Basset aged 80, and William Thurston of fast 100 years old, (that is, approaching 100 years old - people did sometimes live long in those days) who had said they were peaceably possessed of the 600 acres. William Chalcroft of 30 winters and more, said he asked the rioters why they did what had never been done before in his days nor his father's days, in breaking up the said wall; for which words, Richard Sydenham drew his sword and threatened this deponent's life. Five other witnesses from Wedmore all swore they saw the rioters and agreed with William Chalcroft's account. John Stone, husbandman (aged 50) said the rioters had 'bowes, Swerdes and long dych Crokes.'

The documents recording the outcome of the case have, frustratingly, not survived. So who won? The Dean and his Wedmore tenants won, despite the fact that they had deprived Glastonbury's Northload tenants of their rights to common their animals in Wedmore Moor. We know this because the troubles continued, and in 1535 the Dean of Wells once again took Northload tenants to the Star Chamber Court over trespassing in Wedmore Moor.[18]

Kyppmerwalle had been maintained and guarded by the Wedmore tenants of the Dean since 1494, but the underlying problems remained. The Dean claimed that great numbers of cattle had been bred on Wedmore Moor, and the mud wall had been built for their protection and to prevent flooding. Three Northload men - William Chalcroft, John Algar and Richard Mave - were accused with other riotous persons, about 20 in all, of knocking part of this wall down. This 1535 William Chalcroft is probably related to the 1494 William Chalcroft, but as a tenant of the Abbot of Glastonbury he appears on the 'other side' in this lawsuit. These rioters were said to have assembled on 23rd April 1535, and 'wyth fors and armys ... cutt downe two peces of the same walle', one 49 feet long and the other 28 feet. This caused the whole moor and 66 acres of several pasture to be flooded, 'to the great loss of the Dean, his tenants, farmers and commoners.'

The defendants William Chalcroft and John Algar denied everything (Richard Mave's answers do not survive) but admitted at last that the wall 'ys a great anoyaunce of all the Countrey adioyninge in the east side of the same walle, Forasmuche as Wedmore Moore is lower' than their grounds, and the wall caused floods to back up, drowning all their own moor and their several or enclosed fields. Over 200 acres were flooded, and the floods stretched right back into Godney Moor. The mud wall, they insisted, kept Wedmore Moor flooded for longer than if it was not there, because the water soaked through the wall and kept the land wet. They repeated the old complaints of 1494, that the ancient drainage ditch was blocked off by the building of the wall, and they had lost access to their common rights of pasture in Wedmore Moor. Whenever flooding seemed imminent, it had become the Northload tenants' practice to cut gaps in the wall to safeguard their lands and commons, cattle and hay. They denied cutting the wall out of spite.

Further questions were put to the defendants and their answers again tell us a little more of the goings-on. William Chalcroft said that he and John Algar pulled down the wall in one place, in the morning 'at 5 of the clocke', as he had seen it broken down diverse times within the last 20 years 'at every rage of water'. They had no weapons 'but eche of thym a spade in theyr handes'. He said that they 'pluckyd hyt downe of theyr owne myndes.' They would not have put up with the wall for so long, had it not been kept up by the Wedmore tenants 'wyth force of armys'

Again, the case-papers of the 1535 lawsuit have survived, but the court's decision has not. Who won this time, the Dean of Wells and his Wedmore tenants, or the Abbot of Glastonbury's tenants in Northload and Theale? Was the great mud wall knocked down and the flooding stopped? Did Northload tenants regain their common rights of pasture? It seems as if they did because no further cases appear.

Walking along the line of this ancient confrontation today, there is now no trace of any mud wall. The fields, drained in the 1700s, are seldom flooded; the rhynes carry water away to the River Axe. The watercourse that used to flow through the Panborough Gap was turned south to flow into the River Brue. All is now placid, where for well over 40 years in the time of Henry VIII, Wedmore and Northload neighbours faced each other angrily across their common boundary. Just one clue remains - the drove which now runs along part of the former boundary line is called Skitmore, a recent corruption of its name in the 1700s, which was Kitmore - a distortion, in turn, of that 1494 name Kyppmer(walle), especially if it is said with a Somerset accent.

Chapter 8
Ancient Landmarks

Many landscape features which give a clue to our past can be swept away by modern farming methods and the need for more housing. Landmarks can often survive for much longer: ancient crosses, because they are now protected; and wells, springs and streams, because water has to go somewhere! Our manorial pounds, however, although they were a feature of our medieval villages, have mostly disappeared

Ancient stone crosses

Wedmore is fortunate in having three medieval stone crosses still standing: the Market Cross, the Churchyard Cross, and Stoughton Cross. Each represents a different type and purpose, and each is a fine example of its kind.

The elegant 14th century **MARKET CROSS** now stands in a small enclosure in The Borough next to Cross Farm. It was erected in the 1300s as a market cross, because The Borough was then the market street of the village. The market was first granted in 1255, in the reign of Henry III, and was held weekly on Tuesdays.[1] An annual fair was also granted. This was to be held on the eve, the feast day and the morrow (the day after the feast day) of St Mary Magdalene, i.e. 21st to 23rd July. Later on, another fair was granted to Wedmore, to be held at the end of September.

Originally the Market Cross stood further north down The Borough, in the centre of the street at the point where it crossed over the Lerburne stream. The street, built to hold market stalls and pens, was originally much wider than it is today, when front gardens have encroached upon it. Where The Borough crosses the Lerburne, the parish map of 1809[2] and a clearer sketch-map on a deed of 1805,[3] show what looks

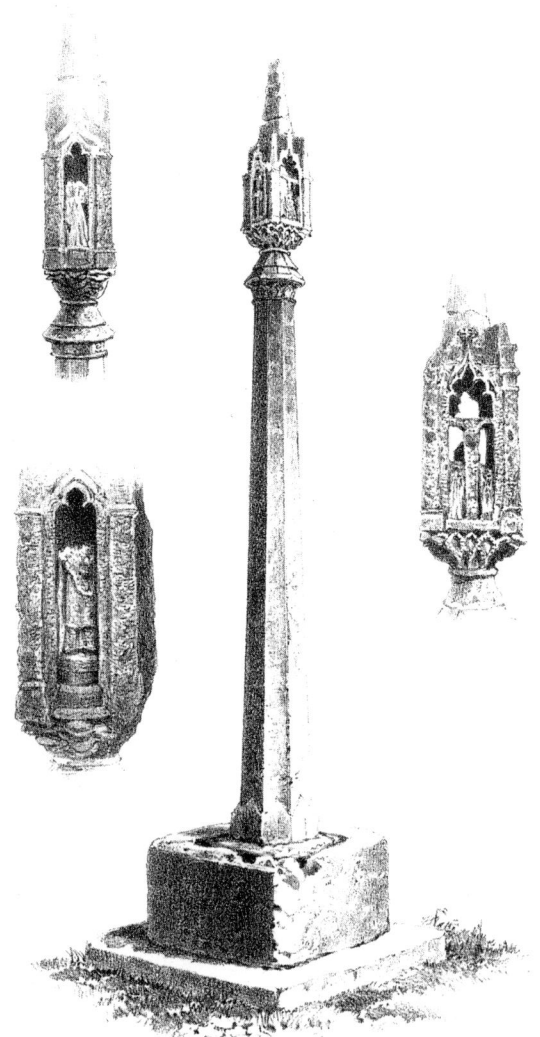

Wedmore Market Cross from C Pooley Old Crosses of Somerset (1877)

like a narrow bridge occupying the west side of the street, with a small enclosure in the middle and the fordable stream running across the east side of the roadway. Unfortunately the cross itself is not marked on either map, but it probably stood in this enclosure in the middle of The Borough, beside the stream. The earlier Wedmore Parish Map of 1791 is, alas, worn away at this point![4] The cross was moved to its present position in about 1820, perhaps when the old layout was obstructing the larger horse-drawn carriages then taking to the roads.

The cross we see today has suffered damage and erosion during its six hundred years standing in The Borough; but traces of its former beauty can still be recognised. The canopied lantern head is carried on a slender octagonal shaft, which stands on a small socketed base. The steps leading to the cross are 20th century. Originally the cross would have stood on a calvary or stepped base. These were often circular.

In 1877 Charles Pooley published his study of the ancient crosses of Somerset.[5] His detailed drawing reproduced here, shows the carvings on the cross head, and helps to identify the figures today, eroded as they are by a further century of weather and modern air pollution. On the west side are traces of Mary and John on either side of the figure of Christ on the cross. On the south side is the figure of a priest, perhaps a bishop, holding a pastoral staff in one hand. The carving on the north side is of a warrior, with right knee a little bent. The identity of this figure is open to conjecture; it might be King Henry III, who granted the market; or could it be intended for King Alfred? Alteratively, these figures on south and north sides may simply symbolise church and state. On the east side, but not drawn by Pooley, is a much-eroded Virgin and Child.

The head of the cross was originally much more elaborately decorated with pinnacles, which were already fragmented in the 1820s and have since largely disappeared. Above the canopied head rises a central pinnacle which once held an iron cross. The socketed base of the cross is square, and is unusual in that it has a channel running around the top, with a deeper scoop section and a plug-hole. It would seem to be designed to hold water, but we do not know how it was used.

The market or fair would have been declared open at the Market Cross, and took place around it, in the open street of The Borough. There were heavy penalties in the manorial court for secretive 'under the counter' dealings, out of sight or before the due time for trade (see Chapter 5). The cross, with its religious carvings, stood as a symbol for fair play and honest dealing in trade. It acted as a village landmark where market dues or tolls would have been paid, and proclamations made. The markets and fairs were managed by a Portreeve (market-reeve), who oversaw the good order of the market and collected the dues. The weight of bread had to be checked, and the ale tasted to make sure it was of good quality. The jobs of portreeve, assayers and ale-tasters were undertaken by villagers, usually for a year at a time.

Wedmore Churchyard Cross from C Pooley Old Crosses of Somerset *(1877)*

The 15th century **CHURCHYARD CROSS** now stands on the eastern edge of the churchyard. It originally stood outside the west door of the church,[6] and was removed to its present position in 1831, when £5 14s 0d was paid for 'taking down the cross'.[7] The tall cross shaft is square with recessed canopied niches. The ball on the top was replaced in about 1840; but whether the original top was a ball is not known. The shaft stands on an octagonal base, which is set on a calvary of circular steps.

One one side of the base are incised the names John Gray and James Brown C.W. 1700. John Gray and James Brown were the churchwardens ('C.W.') in 1700; but why they had their names carved on the cross is a mystery. The churchwardens' accounts for this time, which might have provided an explanation, have not survived. On the side opposite their names, an incised oblong shape can just be made out, but no lettering remains on it, and Pooley noticed nothing there when he drew and described the cross in 1877.

The purpose of this churchyard cross was to mark the graves of the hundreds of parishioners buried in the churchyard in medieval times. Individual gravestones were not usual before the 1600s, and this cross acted as a marker, and a sign of hallowed ground, for everybody. The churchyard cross was often the place where parish notices were read out. We know that the manorial court was occasionally held in Wedmore churchyard (see Chapter 5), and this gathering would meet around the churchyard cross.

STOUGHTON CROSS is a 15th century wayside cross, standing almost hidden in a small enclosure near the Wedmore/Allerton and Stoughton/Crickham crossroads. Pooley states, in 1877, that it originally stood at the actual intersection of the roads, so it like the others has been removed from its original position.[8]

It is the simplest of the three Wedmore crosses, with a fine tapering octagonal shaft. At some time this was split in two and has been repaired. The shaft sits on a square base with a calvary of square steps. There is now no top on the cross, and Pooley shows the top was missing in 1877. Luckily I have found a drawing made by John Buckler in 1844, which is in the Courtauld Institute in London: this shows that Stoughton Cross once had a fine decorative stone cross on top of the shaft.[9]

Stoughton Cross from C Pooley Old Crosses of Somerset *(1877)*

There is no record of exactly when or why a cross was erected here. The site must have been chosen for some reason. It is an ancient cross-roads, but there are many other ancient road crossings in the parish. Near the site of the present cross is a small wayside covered well, which provided water for travellers. There is no written record of this well, either, so we do not know which came first, the well or the cross. There is a tradition that such wayside crosses were used by passing friars who preached from the steps. According to Pooley, the Revd John Kempthorne, Vicar of Wedmore in the 1860s, 'revived the custom of preaching from the cross on certain days'.[10] A short service used to be held at the cross at Rogationtide until the 1990s.

Five hundred years ago these three crosses acted, in their different ways, as landmarks and meeting points for the villagers of Wedmore: at the market, at church, and on the road north out of Wedmore. Now their original purposes may have passed; but as landmarks we still have them today, firmly standing their ground and pointing to the sky.

The manorial pounds

The manorial pound or pinfold was once a common feature in most villages. There were at one time seven pounds in our parish. These small rectangular walled enclosures played a vital role in village farming life. The pound was used for 'impounding' stray animals which could cause a great amount of damage especially in the open arable fields. The strays were locked up by the haywarden or reeve, officials appointed annually from among the villagers by the manorial court. The owners of strays had to pay a sizeable fine to the manorial court before their animals were returned. Most animals were branded so that owners could be traced. However, sometimes a crafty owner would turn out his sick or elderly beast knowing that until it was claimed, it would be fed and sheltered in the pound. Fodder and fresh water were provided for the beasts. Local memory of pounds often survives in nearby property names such as Poundhay Orchard, Poundhay House – 'pound-hay' meaning in Old English the pound enclosure.

Wedmore manorial pound, 1953

Wedmore manorial pound is still in existence (2002). It stands on the south side of the road at the foot of Combe Batch, where the village ended and the open fields began. Until recently its walls were over 2 metres high. Formerly the entrance was narrower and closed with high gates to prevent animals from escaping. Fresh water from a nearby spring was diverted into the pound via a stone-lined drain.[11] Several Wedmorians still remember the pound in use at the early 20th century. In 1808 Philip Evans was paid £20 2s 0d for repairing the pound, and 'pitching it' - that is, repairing the cobbled surface which still lies under the present concrete.[12]

The pound belonging to Northload Manor at Theale has partly survived. This pound was rediscovered fairly recently. It is marked on the parish map of 1791,[13] and with a little detective work plus the co-operation of the owners, the floor of the pound was discovered still in place, and incorporated into the corner of a barn. This fine stone slab floor, with drain, is now preserved as part of the heritage of Northload.

Mudgley manorial pound was at Sand. It too is shown on the 1791 map, partly projecting out into the road opposite Lower Farm. All that remains is a faint indentation in the field edge. In 1558 it was ordered that 'all such strayers as are to be taken within the perambulacion [i.e. limits] of the manner [i.e. manor] ought to be brought to the Lordes Pound and there used accordinge as the lawe requireth to the best advantage of the Lord'.[14] The pound was destroyed soon after 1791.

The pound at Crickham stood in Crib House Lane in 1791. It was larger than the other parish pounds, but has now totally disappeared. This pound belonged to the manor of Churchland, a widely scattered holding of the Dean of Wells which was intermixed with the lands of several other manors. The administrative centre of Churchland seems to have been Crickham; hence the siting of the pound there.

There was also a pound at Clewer. At a manorial court held on 12th October 1550, it was decreed that all the tenants of the manor had 'to repair the Lord's pound there now decayed'. Thomas Moore was looking after an unclaimed stray, 'one horse, colour grey', until the pound was repaired.[15] We do not know where in Clewer it actually stood.

Blackford pound was in the heart of the village, near the ford and opposite the site of the house (now demolished) where the courts were held in the 17th century. Part of the pound still survives as the garden wall of the house built on the site in the last century. The pound was there in 1242-3 when Walter Cobbe accused John, sergeant of Blackford (the Bishop's manorial officer), of impounding five oxen which died. The jury found John guilty in that 'he chased and beat them so they died'. John the sergeant was put in custody, but paid ½ mark (6 shillings and 8 pence) as a fine.[16] This is the earliest reference to a local pound so far discovered. Blackford court records show that in 1637 it cost 10d 'for mending the pound Doore'.[17] In 1661 William Mitchell reeve of Blackford reported to the court that there were several strays in the pound including '2 naggs' worth 10s' and '6 oves [sheep] and a white horse.'[18] This pound was in constant need of repair.

Evidence of another pound, at Stoughton, survives only in references to its frequent repair. Stoughton was also part of Blackford manor, but distance, perhaps, made it sensible for the estate to have a pound there. The exact site of Stoughton pound is, however, now lost. Blackford court records show that in 1635 it cost 9d 'for mendinge Stoten pounde Doore' and a year later 'Nayles for Stoten pounde' cost 2d.[19] In 1640 the pound had 'to be made good'.[20]

Animals could stray many miles across the open moor. In 1620 the court at East Mark fined William Counsell of Wedmore 10s for two white sheep impounded in their pound. George Latcham of Wedmore was fined the same amount for his stray sheep.[21] This was a great deal of money to pay out in those days. The pounds were in use from early medieval times until the 20th century, although their usefulness declined with the advent of fields enclosed with hedges, fences or rhynes, where stock could be more easily kept from straying. The pounds are as much part of our ancient heritage as the market cross, but sadly most have not survived as well.

Holy wells and other springs

Every settlement needs a source of water. Wells and springs are an important feature of all periods in the history of Wedmore. Because they were so important, some had particular attributes - they were holy, curative or had other special properties. Well cults can be traced back to Roman and earlier times, and continued into the Christian period; vestiges continue to this day, with wishing wells and the practice, in some localities, of well-dressing.

DUNNICKS WELL is situated above Latcham at the side of an ancient green lane. The well bubbles out from the hillside. Originally it seems to have formed a small pool, but in the 19th century it was piped into a Draycott stone trough. This well was claimed to have healing properties, especially for eyes. The cure is only effective if the well is visited before sunrise, especially on Midsummer's Day. There are people still living today who have taken the waters.

The name 'Dunnicks' is a mystery. The Reverend S.H.A. Hervey, writing in the 1880s, suggested the name could have been derived from St Dominic or from Dominican friars who might perhaps have stopped and preached at the well in the Middle Ages.[22] There is, however, no positive evidence for these ideas; and there are, indeed, several more likely possibilities. The earliest spelling I have discovered so far is 'Donicks Well' in 1781, which is not early enough to give any clues.[23] It could be from the dunnock or hedge-sparrow, 'Sparrows Well', or from the name of a medieval tenant of that field. There is an Old English or Saxon phrase *dun ea* meaning a hill-stream, which although not very romantic seems a likely possibility.

As an alternative to Dunnicks at dawn there was **SUNSET WELL** in Guilo or Guildhall Lane.[24] A house has now been built over its site. Springing up beside Wedmore Brook, it was never known to run dry, and was cold even on the hottest day. This well was also renowned for its curative properties, and was supposed to benefit skin and eye ailments. In contrast to Dunnicks Well, Sunset Well water must have been most effective at sunset. Hervey never mentions this well, so it must have been disused long before the 1880s.

THEALE WELL or **WEST WELL** was at the junction of West Well Lane and the Wells Road in Theale, opposite the former Post Office. This was an ancient roadside well lying on the boundary between the manor of Wedmore, belonging to the Dean of Wells, and the manor of Northload, the property of Glastonbury Abbey. This boundary can be traced back to Saxon times; perhaps the well is equally ancient. The waters of this spring probably gave Theale its Saxon name (see Chapter 1). The well supplied travellers with a refreshing drink for many hundreds of years, and was still in use until the beginning of this century. West Well is its later name; it was originally Thele Wille in 1494[25]. In 1510, the Abbot of Glastonbury walked the boundary along here, and may have stopped for a rest and a drink from the well before climbing up the steep hill - unless Abbots preferred something stronger.[26]

There is another well at **STOUGHTON CROSS**, beside the 15th century cross. The stone sides of this shallow well are built up and curved to support a big Draycott 'pudding stone' slab as roof, making a traditional covered dipping well. It is the one remaining example of what the other wells probably looked like. Unfortunately there is no documentary record of this well at all, and no clue as to how old it is. It, too, would have been a roadside well for travellers, on one of our oldest routes over the top of the hill. As no folklore exists for it, it remains a nameless watering place.

CHARLWELL lies alongside Blackford Brook near Old Sexeys Farm, Blackford. It is a chalybeate spring, rich in iron, like the Chalice Well at the foot of Glastonbury Tor. Collinson, in 1791, writes that at Blackford there is 'a mineral spring which turns silver yellow'.[27] Charlwell may mean in Old English, the *ceorls* or peasants' well. However, in 1637 it is spelt Cholwell, meaning 'cold well'.[28] It was also claimed to have cured sore eyes.

MUDGLEY is built along the spring line, and every farm has at least one well or spring. Collinson mentions only one at Mudgley, 'a spring of a petrifying quality'.[29] Limey deposits from the very hard water form coral-like calcareous lumps, and coat any debris or objects left in the water, appearing to turn them to 'stone'. This spring could have been one of several, some of which have now disappeared; it is uncertain which one Collinson meant. One important spring supplied the Dean's house, built in the 1100s. The house was abandoned in the 1500s but the well, 20 feet deep, was discovered during excavations of the site in 1878.[30] Another spring until recently welled up in the field which contains the earthworks of the Dean's garden. It almost certainly fed the Dean's fishpond. It has now been filled in, so that we cannot know if it was 'petrifying'. A small petrifying stream still flows at Fernhall Farm. There is another spring rising at Sand Hall, in the manor of Mudgley, which certainly does have 'petrifying quality'. It bubbles down the hill alongside Sand Drove, where it forms curious calcareous 'stones'. This may well be Collinson's petrifying spring.

High above eastern Mudgley, away from any dwelling, was a well called Helie Well in 1538.[31] It was in Hely Thorn Furlong. Both names have since disappeared. 'Helie' or 'hely', spelt thus, may be derived from the Old English *halig*, meaning 'holy'. This raises an interesting possibility: have we a Holy Well sited in the Holy Thorn Field? There are no genuine medieval or earlier written references to the Glastonbury thorn. That legend was first written down in the early 1500s, when it was described in a life of St Joseph,

> *'Thre hawthornes also, that groweth at Werall*
> *Do burge and bere grene leaves at Christmas.'*[32]

The story of Joseph of Aramathea bringing the thorn from the Holy Land appears only after the dissolution of the monasteries in 1539. These dates would seem to make our Mudgley holy well and thorn of 1538 an intriguingly early reference. 'Helie' may mean something totally different, and all the romantic ideas of holy wells and thorns may be just that - romance!

Documents from the 1500s onwards provide us with several more wells. They are named, but not all can be identified on the ground without more information. **CHURCH WELL**,[33] probably the same as the well called **CASWELL** in 1609, is a very strong spring, which gushes out near Castle Farm, Heath House.[34] **RUGWELL** (1678) was at Rughill, Cocklake.[35] **ROWSHE WELL** (1558) was somewhere near Rushill Lane, Blackford.[36] **BUTTERWELL**

(1609)[37] was near West Stoughton, and **VYKERYS WELLS** (1558) or later **VICARS WELL** was in Maltfield.[38] The sites of **CRAYSWELL** (1756) or **GRAYSWELL**,[39] **WEIGHTS WELL**[40] and **COLDWELL**[41] are not yet known. There are other springs, which still flow strongly, but their names have been forgotten.

All settlements needed a water supply, and most houses had their own wells. A well on the top of Combe Batch supplied about fourteen houses, and several hamlets had their own village pump; the sites of many are now in danger of being forgotten. Sinking a well must have been a difficult and expensive operation. Collinson quotes a story from an earlier history: 'In sinking a well in some part of this parish [Wedmore] in the year 1670, there was found at the depth of thirteen feet the remains (as a certain antiquary will have it) of one of the Cangick giants, a people supposed to have formerly inhabited these parts. The top of his skull was said to be an inch thick, and one of his teeth three inches long above the roots, three inches and a quarter round, and after the root was broken off, weighed three ounces and a half.'[42] I have been unable to discover which well this was, or what the creature could have been. I have often heard people in Wedmore called thickheads; this must have been one of our antecedents!

Crossroad elms and boundary trees

Elm trees were once the dominant trees of our countryside. Shady lanes and the elm tree rookeries have been much missed since the devastation of Dutch Elm disease. Young elm trees keep reappearing in our hedges, only to die years before they reach maturity.

Two of our present-day placenames have 'elm' in them: Mudgley Elm and Crickham Elm. There were once three other elm placenames: Heathcross Elm, Stofftens Elm (Stoughton Elm) and Latcham Elms - all together an indication of the importance of elm trees as landmarks in the past landscape. Four of these elm names were on crossroads; obviously the large standing elm marked the road junction. *Elm* is the unaltered Old English or Saxon word for this tree.

MUDGLEY ELM is the crossroads where the Mudgley-Townsend Lane road crosses the main Sand-Bagley road. The name Mudgley Elm first appears in 1751;[43] its earlier name was **DELLY CROSS ELM**. Delly Cross Elm was one of the boundary landmarks in a description of the boundary of Mudgley manor in 1558.[44] The boundary coming from Sand goes 'to delly crosse elme which doth stand and growe in the higheway'. The elm was to be 'shrowded by Richard Edwardes',[45] one of the tenants of the manor. Shrowding or shrouding was the work of keeping the tree pruned so that it did not become a hazard on the road. In 1542 the lane leading down to Mudgley was called Delly Cross Way.[46] So far I have been unable to find out what 'Delly' means. It is possibly a personal name. The 1558 elm tree marking the spot has long since gone, but there are shrubby elms sprouting up in the roadside hedge at the crossroads today. Perhaps one day they might survive long enough and grow to maturity, to give the reason for its name back to Mudgley Elm.

The nearby crossroads on B3151 at the top of Mudgley Hill also had a name. In 1543 this was **COUNSELLS CROSSE**,[47] after the Counsell family who had lived in Mudgley at least since the 1300s. The 'cross' probably refers to the crossroads, both ancient tracks, rather than to a stone marker cross.

CRICKHAM ELM along Cribhouse Lane is another crossroad elm name. The lane running west is a track leading to the once open field, but the eastern branch, Crickham Lane, is now almost totally blocked. This lane used to be the main route from Crickham up on to the hill. The name Crickham Elm can be traced back to 1605.[48]

HEATHCROSS ELM is only mentioned in the 1500s. It was the name given to an area of arable field by the crossroads at Heath House, where the windmill once stood. It first occurs in 1544, as Hethecrosse Elme.[49] This was an important crossroads where the road from Wedmore to Heath House crossed the ancient Blackford to Wells road. Here again the elm must have stood out as a prominent landmark in the area of open field. The elm name perhaps failed to survive because when the windmill was built, some time before 1639, that became the more obvious landmark.[50]

STOUGHTON ELM was the earlier name of the Stoughton Cross crossroads. Although the cross is 15th century, Stoughton Cross does not appear as a place name until 1747.[51] Before that, the elm tree seems to have been the more important landmark. The latest reference to Stoughton Elm is in 1710.[52] In 1676 it is Stowtons Elm,[53] and in 1554 Stofftens Elme.[54] The elm tree probably stood in the centre of the crossroads, away from the cross site. Probably when the elm died, Stoughton Cross became the dominant feature and eventually the new name of the crossroads.

LATCHAM ELMS were something different. They were not at a crossroads, but stood on the roadside at Latcham, opposite Latcham Farm. Lachyham Elmes are first recorded in 1543,[55] and last appear in a document of 1682.[56] On the vacant verge where the elms had stood, the present wayside cottage with its garden was built in the 19th century.

When the great medieval open fields were enclosed, elm was used as one of the main hedging plants. The large standing crossroad elm became less prominent as a landmark in consequence.

Isolated standing trees were also often used as parish boundary markers. On the earlier parish Ordnance Survey maps 'Elm' appears on the boundary at Perrow between Wedmore parish and Brinscombe. This looks like a placename, but it refers to a boundary elm tree. This tree was still standing until the 1970s, and then survived for a long time as a stump, which has now disappeared. There were two ash trees marking the parish boundary between Panborough and Meare at Barrow Hill, until the great storm of January 1990; now only one survives.

Chapter 9
The Mills of Wedmore Parish

Everybody needs to eat, but reducing grain to something that can be cooked, whether as porridge or bread or gruel, is hard work. The story of efforts to ease this labour goes back a very long way. The most common way of grinding corn was by hand - a strenuous job. The water mill was the first complex machine invented by man, and revolutionised this task. Water mills first appeared about 100 BC in the eastern Mediterranean; windmills followed, in England, in medieval times. Every settlement had access to some sort of mill and we will look at the water mills and windmills of the parish of Wedmore, and the men who worked them.

Watermills

Domesday Book, in 1086, mentions 5,624 mills in England. These would probably all have been watermills, as windmills had not yet been invented. There were other types of mills, such as tidal mills, and treadmills, usually turned by animals but occasionally by men. The first watermills were small, nothing like the watermills we see working today. There were two main types: those with the very early horizontal wheels, or the more usual vertical wheels. The vertical wheel could be of 'undershot' or 'overshot' type. Undershot mill wheels needed very little water and only a slight drop to turn. They could run off a tiny stream. The overshot mill wheel needed more water with a longer fall to make it revolve, but it was more powerful. Even a small medieval watermill could do the same work as fifty people grinding by hand.

Despite the total number of watermills listed in Domesday Book, no mill appears in the entries for the villages of Wedmore, Blackford or Clewer in 1086. Yet in January 1559 Sir Thomas Gresham bought the Manor of Wedmore, which was said to comprise 8,200 acres of land, 200 houses, 10 dovecotes - and 10 mills.[1] Some may have been watermills, some may by that time have been windmills. This total, moreover, takes no account of any mills in the other manors within the parish: the Manors of Northload, Mudgley, Blackford, Churchland and Clewer. Clearly, between the blank of Domesday Book and the numerous mills of 1559, much had happened. There are certainly references to medieval mills in the parish, even though the actual number at any one time was never recorded. We will look first at the watermills, since they were invented first.

Northload Watermill

The first recorded watermill in Wedmore parish appears in 1310, when following a disagreement, a list was drawn up of the tithes to be paid by John of Northload, at Theale.[2] These included a tenth of the produce from his mill. This was a watermill and it was sited near his farmstead, Northload Farm, at the foot of the hill slope as it reached the moor. It was very probably an undershot wheel. The water was ducted through leats or wooden channels from a nearby ancient course of the River Axe, and penned up until wanted in a low-banked pond. It would then have been sent along the channel when needed. The mill would have been used only a few times a week, for just a small bag of corn at a time. The water was then led back out into the river.

The site of the watermill is now just a few humps and bumps, with traces of the water-channels as a clue to their purpose.[3] The Northload mill seems to have gone out of use by 1517, as it is not mentioned in a survey of Northload's estates made at that time.[4] A windmill had by then probably taken over the work of grinding corn.

Pillmead Watermill

There was at least one water mill in Wedmore Manor, situated on Wedmore Brook *alias* the Lerburne. The Revd S.H.A. Hervey, writing in *The Wedmore Chronicle* in the 1880s, mentions a folk memory of a watermill in the field called Benpool.[5] Benpool is the large field down the Lerburne Lane, opposite Worthington Close and behind the Borough Mall. Hervey looked at the field but apart from noticing a slight unevenness could see no trace of any mill; nor did he find any documents to prove its existence. There are, however, several documents among the parish records which show clearly that there had indeed been a watermill in Benpool. In 1765 John Thatcher, who owned Benpool, was paying a poor rate of 1s 10½d for 'the watermill' there.[6] He continued to pay rates for the mill until 1783. The journal of Dr John Westover of Porch House also contains a reference to a mill, called Pillmead Mill. In 1698 Dr John writes that he has four parchment deeds including Mary Thatcher's 'for Benpoole' and Thomas Hill's 'lease and counterpart for Pillmeads Mill'.[7] The old name for that part of Wedmore Moor close to the village is Pillmead Moor. The only trace of the name that remains today is Pillmead Lane, adjoining the cemetery and marking the northern edge of the Pillmead Moor area. Pillmead Mill was the name for the watermill in Benpool field. Mary Thatcher owned the field, and Thomas Hill was leasing the mill from her. The Thatcher family, it would therefore seem, were holding the mill at least sixty seven years before John Thatcher is recorded as paying his poor rates on it.

The mill itself had probably been there for a long time before 1698. In 1327 a list of lands in Wedmore shows that John Mylborne was holding 3 perches of meadow in 'Pulmede'.[8] John's early surname Mylbourne means 'the mill stream'; so perhaps he was actually the miller, and his 3 perches of meadow, a very small area, was the site of his mill.

Where did the water to run this mill come from? The parish map of 1791 shows that Wedmore Brook was divided into three watercourses as it flowed from Glanville Road down to The Borough.[9] Two of these streamlets were ducted towards Benpool, and acted as mill leats; the third and northernmost continued as the main Lerburne stream of today. The two southern leats would have fed a mill pond in Benpool. The name of Benpool itself is a bit of a mystery. The 'pool' part of the name is easy to understand but the meaning of 'Ben', sometimes 'Benja' (Benjapool) in documents of the 1700s, is unknown.

Although Hervey wrote that he could see no sign of the mill, there are actually still traces of the main water leat left today (2002). Part of a wall on the east side of the field adjoining an old orchard, could be remains of the mill. The rate books suggest that the mill ceased working about 1783.[10]

Glanville Road, Guildhall Lane and The Close watermills

Mills were usually held by families who made a trade of milling, who often held several mills at one time, and the job of miller often passed down through the family for several generations. There were probably more watermills situated higher up the Wedmore Brook.

There may have been one in Glanville Road, where the fall of the land suggests a natural site for a mill wheel. There was a tannery on this spot which also used water, but positive evidence for a watermill has yet to be found, except for this tantalising entry from the vestry minutes of September 16th 1840, 'To consult respecting enlarging the bridge at the Mill stream'.[11] This bridge is very probably the one in Glanville Road.

Upstream, behind Elmsett and in Guildhall Lane the abrupt and artificial bends in the stream suggest another possible mill site. Even further upstream at the edge of The Orchard estate, on land formerly part of The Close farmstead, the Wedmore Brook supported a small medieval watermill which was found during archaeological investigations in 1998, confirming my earlier suggestion that there had been a mill there.[12]

Mudgley: a possible watermill

There is no documentary evidence for any mill at Mudgley, but a very strong spring gushes out above Mudgley Hill Farm and runs down through a gully. Just above the farm, within the gully, are the remains of a series of dammed ponds, where a head of water might have been built up to run a small overshot watermill nearby.

Windmills

Windmills first appeared in England in the 1100s. It is not known who invented windmills, but the English soon exploited their immense commercial potential. The earliest recorded windmill in Somerset stood at Seavington St Michael in 1212.[13] These early mills were post-mills, where the whole mill turned around on its main post to face the wind. The tower-mill with which we are familiar, where just the cap and sails turn to the wind, was introduced in the 1300s.

Panborough Windmill

The first record of a windmill in Wedmore parish occurs in 1517, at Panborough within the manor of Northload, but windmills had probably been working in the parish long before that. The Panborough mill stood on the most eastern tip of the Isle of Wedmore, above Panborough village on the little hill now called Russells Hill. The 1517 survey of Glastonbury Abbey estates describes the holdings in Northload, and shows that several people held land near this mill. John Rylbury held half an acre 'next to Wynemill', and John Barghe [or Barrow] of Panborough held 'at Mylmote half an acre'. John Brownyng held 'At Wymyllmote one acre and one piece of ground called Mylmote'.[14]

John Brownyng was probably the miller, as he was paying rent for the actual mill batch or mote, the mound on which the windmill stood. The mill itself is not mentioned, so it is not known whether it was a post-mill or a tower-mill. This windmill probably took over the job of grinding the corn for the area from the earlier water mill down below at Northload Farm. There are no records surviving to say how long the windmill worked at Panborough, but it seems to have gone by the 1700s and no trace remains today.

East Windmill

Mill Lane in Wedmore takes its name from the windmill which once stood on the hilltop there overlooking the Latcham road. This mill was called East Mill as it stood in Wedmore's

East Field. The mill is first mentioned in 1554 when it is mentioned in a survey of the adjacent Mudgley Manor, but it was in fact one of the mills belonging to Wedmore Manor.[15] Unfortunately most of the documents relating to Wedmore Manor are lost, so no other early records survive to tell us about this mill. It is shown on Bowen's map of Somerset of c1760.[16] The enclosure map of Wedmore Moor in 1791 has a small drawing of the mill, when it was called Day's Mill after the then miller George Day.[17] The mill belonged to one of the joint owners of the Manor of Wedmore at that time, called Bracher.[18] It was a typical Somerset tower-mill. By 1815 it was held by George's son John Day, miller;[19] and in 1820 the miller was James Welch.[20]

Days Mill, Enclosure Map, 1791

In 1924 R.Stanton-Churchill published an article in *The Somerset Yearbook* no. XXIII, about his childhood reminiscences of Wedmore, where he came to spend holidays with his grandmother. She lived in Stanton House in the Sand Road, at the junction with Dandos Lane. He describes in the article 'a lane [Dandos Lane] which came all downhill from the gate of a bounding field where a windmill revolved its sails against the skyline.' This is the only known description of East Mill working. The millers at that time (c1870) were the Harvey family. In 1878 William Millard took over the mill. He put an inexperienced man in charge, and the mill 'ran away' - the sails went round so fast that they smashed.[21] The mill was never repaired, and the tower was demolished about 1886, although maps continued to show the site as a circle for some time thereafter. A bungalow was built on the site in the 1960s. Unfortunately no archaeological investigations took place before the bungalow was built, so an opportunity to find clues to its earlier origins was lost. As East Mill was close to Wedmore it was probably the main windmill for the village, and may have been in use for hundreds of years.

East Elms Windmill

Several years ago, while walking across the fields at Maltfield, along the Mudgley Road, I found a faint doughnut-shaped earthwork which was marked as a pond on the Ordnance Survey map.[22] However, this earthwork did not look like a pond although there was water in the centre of it. I thought it looked more like a very worn mill mound with traces of a ramp leading up into it. I had never come across any mention of a mill in this area. At that time I was working on a survey of the Manor of Mudgley, made in 1558. The day after my walk, I turned to the next page of the 1558 manuscript, and read the following description of one acre of land 'upon Lever Hill Lyinge betweene the too mylles'.[23]

I knew that the area I had been walking was once called Laver Hill, as three small fields there still had that name in 1820.[24] One of the 'too mylles' referred to in 1558 was East Mill, described above; and the other mill would seem to be the earthwork I had discovered out walking only the day before. That sort of coincidence was almost un-nerving. I eventually discovered references to an East Elms Windmill in deeds of 1682[25] and 1718.[26] Another deed of 1809 mentioned a field called Elms Millfield;[27] but by 1820 the same field was called Drag Furlong, and the mill had gone.[28]

East Elms Mill was on the hilltop only about 600 metres from East Mill. The part of the great Wedmore East Field, in which both mills stood, stretched right across the hilltop and was shared between both Wedmore and Mudgley tenants: this part of it was called Mudgley Field, and lay nearest to the Manor of Mudgley, although not in it. East Elms Mill was sited close by the road to Mudgley, and probably served the Mudgley tenants as their nearest mill. In 1689 Henry Fudge was miller.[29] It was a member of his family, Francis Fudge, who was a rebel during the Monmouth Rebellion (see Chapter 13).[30] The mill can be traced back even earlier. A few years after the 1558 reference, in 1599, George Rodney of Rodney Stoke sold his windmill and four acres in Wedmore parish, in the tenure of John Lydiat miller, to Nicholas Claxton of Rodney Stoke.[31] The Lydiat or Lythiat family lived at Mudgley. In 1609 there is a reference to 'Lovyattes Mill' in Mudgley Field - most probably another variant spelling or mis-spelling of the Lydiat family.[32]

A year earlier, in 1608, William Lytheat the miller had been living up to the Chaucerian reputation of his trade! Marjorie Chalcroft, a Wedmore girl, did penance in Wedmore church and swore before the whole parish that the father of her illegitimate child William, born in January 1608, was William Lytheat miller and not Edward Hopper who had previously been accused. William was summonsed by the overseers of the poor to pay 6d each week for the maintenance of the child, in the parish church at the end of morning prayers. Marjorie, when she was declared fit and able to travel, was 'to be whipped through the next market town'.[33] East Elms Mill ceased to work in the 1700s, probably because nearby East Mill could cope with all the corn that needed to be ground in this part of the parish.

Westover's Mill, alias Stone's Mill

It has been known for generations that a windmill once existed in Quab Lane. This mill was called Westover's Mill. The Wedmore tithe map of 1838 shows a small enclosure called Mill Batch, and the adjoining fields are called Westovers Mill Tyning. In 1678 Dr John Westover senior, 'chirurgeon', of Porch House, died. In his will he left 'to my son Henry my windmill during the stats that be upon the mill' (the 'stats' means the state or term of years unexpired on the lease). He also left three yards (a tiny area) of land by the mill to Henry during his life on condition that Henry paid 'widow steevens 3s and 6d, every Lady Day, 'but till after his mothers death he shall not have the profitts of the mill, neither the three yards neither shall he pay any rent concerning it'.[34] The widowed Mrs Westover senior thus had the benefit of the mill profits for the rest of her life; Henry in compensation did not have to pay rent during this time. Widow Stevens could have been a relative or old family retainer.

Signature of John Westover junior (1645-1706), physician

The mill was still in use in 1699, when it seems to have been run jointly by Henry and his brother Dr John Westover junior, physician, who lived in Porch House and who built the adjoining barn now called Westovers to house his mentally sick patients.[35] Dr John Westover is remembered for keeping a journal of his medical practice and his farming accounts.[36] In it he writes, in 1700:

> *'then lent Cozen William Westover my crane, fower pooley wheals one toung clavey and twooe toung clavey pinns, a payer of [s]crewes and plainke for ye screws. Lent him before 18 veallows to bare ye mill.'*[37]

It is not easy to understand the meaning of Dr John's cryptic note. A crane and pulley-wheels are clear enough; screws are probably big worm gears. A tongue clavey and clavey pins have so far defeated mill experts. Felloes, usually wheel-rims are here perhaps small, solid wheels to run in the track to carry ('bare' i.e. bear?) the revolving cap of the tower-mill. It seems that work is being done on a mill, but it is not possible to be certain that it was Westover's Mill in Quab Lane because the Westover family also held Ashton Mill at this time. The will of Dr John Westover senior makes this clear:

> *'Item I give unto my grandchild William Rowley ... Aisson [Ashton] Mill'* together with various lands in Allerton.[38]

Dr John the younger could have lent this equipment to his relation William Westover for work at Ashton Mill. The history of Ashton Mill has been written, but without any references to this period when it was held by the Westover family. Ashton Mill was still working in 1927, and still stands today, but it has probably been rebuilt or refurbished several times.[39]

By 1709, on the other hand, Westover's Mill at Quab Lane had ceased to work, because a deed of Llewellyn's Almshouse in Wells that year refers to 'that plot containing one yard of land whereof (*sic*, for 'whereon') a Windmill lately stood ... lately in the tenure of Doctor John Westover'.[40] Perhaps it was shut down about 1700, and it was as a result of this that Dr John Westover the younger was able to lend equipment to his cousin William.

The Westovers were thus the last in the line of tenants of the Quab Lane windmill, which had been there long before. A mill is first recorded on the site in a survey of the Manor of Mudgley in 1558. Then it is called either Weste Mill or Stone's Mill. The mill was in the Manor of Wedmore, in the old North Field which by 1558 was usually being called West Field - hence the name West Mill.[41] Tenants of Mudgley held strips of land in the field near the mill. This mill would be one of the ten mills mentioned in the sale of the Manor of Wedmore to Sir Thomas Gresham in 1559.[42] In 1576 Thomas Stone leased land in Wedmore North Field including the windmill. The appearance of the name Stone's Mill in 1554 shows that Thomas or a member of his family already had a lease of the windmill, before 1576.[43] The mill had been on Chantry land, but when the chantries were abolished in 1547, their lands were sold; the Stone family probably acquired it soon after. Thomas Stone was a wealthy gentleman, and when he died in 1606 he granted his lands in Wedmore to his 'natural brother' Edward Stone.[44] Edward was Thomas's illegitimate brother, but that did not bar him from becoming a footman to Queen Elizabeth I. Edward passed his lands, including the mill, to his son Edward, who sold it to Llewellyn's Almshouse in Wells. The Almshouse owned the mill until 1824 when the site was sold off as 'garden land' and the field name was by then Mill Batch, the name of Stone being forgotten.[45] It was the Llewellyn's Almshouse trustees who in 1621 drew up the 'Lease to John Westover of the windmill for 99 years, for the lives of Alice his wife and John and Richard his sons 12d per annum'.[46]

The batch or mound on which the mill stood can still just be seen in the corner of the field called Mill Batch adjoining Quab Lane.

Crannell Windmill or Burnt Mill

Stretching across the hilltop between Clewer, Crickham and the Stoughtons was the ancient open field system, one large block of which was called Crannell Field. Isolated at one end of this block, right on the boundary of Wedmore parish with Chapel Allerton, are two fields which in 1820 were called Burnt Mill.[47] This field name suggests that a windmill once stood there, and it burnt down - but when?

Over a hundred years earlier, on 9th July 1678, a deed mentions two half-acres of land in Burnt Mill Field, so the name went back a long time.[48] Another deed made the previous day, on 8th July, refers to ½ acre of arable land, in the same area, belonging to Crannell Mill.[49] The mystery was solved. The mill was called Crannell Mill, and had burnt down some time before 1678, but sufficiently recently for its proper name still to be remembered at that date. The mill was never rebuilt.

Crannell Mill stood on land which was part of the Manor of Churchland. This was a very scattered estate of the Dean of Wells, which included most of Cocklake and Crickham, and holdings in other nearby parishes. The mill site can still be found on the hilltop where several paths meet - no coincidence, for they are probably paths of ancient origin leading to the windmill. The area where the mill stood is hummocky, and there are two doughnut-shaped earthworks with a dent between. Perhaps these mark the site of one mill with its replacement alongside. Lying in the hedge nearby are two large Draycott stones. They may have had something to do with the mill, perhaps part of a platform for loading or unloading sacks nearby. Ashton Mill has a similar resting place. If Crannell Mill burnt down about 1678, its loss may not have been too disastrous for the local farmers as Ashton Mill was only just a few fields away over the parish boundary.

Clapp's Windmill: a lost mill

There are references in 1792 and 1804 to Thomas Tyley who, in addition to owning Pillmead watermill, was paying tax on 'Clapp's Windmill'.[50] The site of Clapps Windmill is a mystery, unless it was a shortlived alternative name for one of the known windmills.

Stoughton Windmill

Stoughton Mill once stood on the Blackford to Snipefield road, near where Quab Lane emerges to cross over it towards Stoughton. This mill is not one of the ancient mills of the parish. No windmill is shown there on the 1791 parish map, or on the 1805 map.[51] It first appears in 1811, in the first edition of the 1 inch: 1 mile Ordnance Survey map. The mill, then, was built between 1805 and 1811 on Blackford's East Field.

A deed of 1835 lists a 3 rood plot of land in Blackford East Field 'upon which in some time past a certain windmill for grinding corn and other buildings have been erected'.[52] The mill was then held by Jeremiah Wall. In 1840 it was held by Mr Wall and Mr Tucker. The last miller seems to have been John Burrows.[53] The mill had gone by 1886, as the 25 inch Ordnance Survey map shows only a small mound. This mound can still be clearly seen. It has the characteristic slight dent in the centre where the mill tower stood, and a ramp leading up to it on the southwest side.

Stoughton Mill had been built at the end of an era which had lasted for hundreds of years. The small local windmill was being superseded by steam-power, and the development of large flour mills using imported grain from America. Arable land in the parish had been replaced by pasture. Very little corn was grown locally, and flour could easily be bought in the village shops.

Heath House Windmill

Heath House Mill was the last working windmill in the parish of Wedmore. It stood near Heath House crossroads. It was sometimes called Westfield Mill because it stood in the open West Field of Wedmore. The mill belonged to the Manor of Wedmore but, as it stood near the boundary with the Manor of Blackford, it served as Blackford's mill for hundreds of years. There is no record of any medieval mill in Blackford Manor itself.

It is not known when the first mill was built at Heath House. The first time it is mentioned is in 1639, in the Blackford manorial court records, when tenants of Blackford are complaining about the mill.[54] The court was told that 'the mill is very predjudiciall unto the Tennantes by reason that they cannot pass by it with their ploughs without danger, And [it is] very dangerous for their Cattle, And alsoe for children to pass by it. Therefore it is Comaunded to Edward Tutton to reform it by our Lady Day next'. Edward Tutton must have been the miller. The mill sails, it seems, were too low for safety when they swept round. Mills were usually raised on a mound so that the tips of the sails were safely clear of the ground and passers-by. As there is no further court entry, it appears that Edward Tutton took heed of the warning, and either raised his mill or fenced it in. There was an accident, which was probably at Heath House Mill, when in 1807 the Wedmore burial register records the death of a daughter of William and Hannah Roper 'by accident, kild by ye windmill'.[55] William Roper and his family lived at Heath House.

From 1737 to 1780 the mill was run by the Emery family.[56] Richard Emery was the miller, and there was a beam in the mill with the date 1775 carved upon it. Then the Wilkins family took over, and indeed it was for a time called Wilkins' Mill. George Wilkins was the miller when he died in 1810. He is described in the Wedmore burial register as 'an honest man', which says a lot for George and not a lot for other millers! His son John Wilkins, aged 27, was struck dead by lightning in the mill, and was buried on 7th June 1833.[57] Jane Wilkins, widow of George and mother of John, continued the business as miller and baker for a time. George Wilkins, probably another son, was a 'labourer' there in the census of 1851. Edward Tucker was baker and miller at Heath House in the 1861 census, and John Spearing in 1871, before William Tucker took over as miller in 1876.

We know what William Tucker's mill looked like because photographs survive showing him standing on the mill steps. It was a typical Somerset tower-mill, with a thatched gable roof which, with the attached sails, could be turned into the wind. The four sails were wooden

Heath House Mill with William Tucker miller, on the steps, c1890

slats on which canvas could be unrolled and set as required. In 1898 the sails blew off the mill in a storm, and they were not replaced. William Tucker had a steam engine put into a nearby building to work the corn-grinding machinery. He died in 1902, and the mill business was then run by William Duckett, who installed an oil engine in 1909. The Tucker family, meanwhile, continued to live in the mill house. The tower of the old windmill stood until 1962 when it was knocked down and a bungalow was built on the site by William Tucker's granddaughter. The last pair of millstones are in the front garden. The old mill-house is still there. This building, dated 1856, replaced an earlier mill-house. William Tucker kept a diary, of which two years survive, giving brief entries about his day to day life as a miller, and we will look at this in the next chapter.

Conclusions

The previously known mills of the parish together with those I have discovered now total thirteen (possibly fourteen): six watermills and seven (possibly eight) windmills. Of these, two were within the Manor of Northload - Northload watermill and Panborough windmill. One was in Blackford Manor - Stoughton Mill, built c.1805. One, Crannell Mill, was in Churchland Manor, and there was possibly a watermill in Mudgley. No mill is known in Clewer. The remaining mills, were all within the boundaries of the Manor of Wedmore, although adjacent Mudgley and Blackford used those nearest to them - Pillmead and the Close Orchard watermills, and the windmills called East Mill, East Elms Mill, Heath House Mill, and Stone's or Westover's Mill. The location of the mysterious Clapps Windmill is uncertain, and it may have been an alternative name for one of the others. Thus of the ten mills which were supposed to belong to Wedmore Manor in 1559, only eight (possibly nine) have been accounted for. Perhaps the figure was just a rounded estimate, as my years of research among thousands of documents, and walking hundreds of acres, has not revealed written or physical trace of any other mills. The local historian, however, never ceases to hope that a trick of the light on the ground, or someone's early deeds, may yet locate and identify the remaining lost mills of Wedmore.

William Tucker, miller (c1859-1902)

A miller's diary

The life of a miller was not an easy one. The millers in medieval times did not usually own their mills, but paid rent to the lord of the manor. Mills were expensive to build and to maintain, and damage was easily caused by the vagaries of the weather. The miller often had a lifetime tenancy, and the job was usually kept in the family, with millers in surrounding mills often related to each other.

The miller made his money by charging the peasant or farmer for the job of grinding their corn or beans. The miller either took a percentage of the grain or flour, which he could re-sell, or a toll was paid. Throughout the country the percentage which the miller took varied greatly. In the southwest it was usually 1/32nd of grain, but in the north it would be as much as 1/13th. Hence the traditional unpopularity of millers, since the medieval period.

Millers worked hard, often dressing the millstones and repairing the windmill sails themselves. Windmills could only work when the wind conditions were right, so long periods of calm meant no work, and good wind conditions meant the miller might work all night. They usually kept horses to carry customers' corn or flour, and in the mid-1800s and early-1900s they often collected imported grain from railway stations to grind and re-sell. Milling was a very unhealthy occupation. Accidents were frequent, and the dusty atmosphere caused a nasty lung infection called 'miller's disease' which usually proved fatal.

Today we see the windmill as a romantic symbol of our past country life. I doubt, however, whether many people would actually wish to live the life of the miller if they knew the true facts. One Wedmore miller has left us details of his daily life in his diary - William Tucker, miller, born c1859, who took over Heath House Mill in 1876. Two of his diaries survive, for 1886 and 1887, when he was 27-28.[58] They give us an insight not only into his daily work as a miller, but also into his life in general. The diary entries are very brief, and one often has to search other local records such as newspapers to find out what he is referring to; nevertheless, quite a quantity of information is contained in his terse statements. His diary starts on 30th December, 1885.

DECEMBER, 1885
30 Wednesday
Charlie Bagg came to work at 12/- [12 shillings] per week.

Charlie was the miller's boy.

JANUARY, 1886
1 Friday
Shooting match at the Grouse and Pheasant.
The Grouse & Pheasant Inn was the pub in Heath House, now a private house.

21 Thursday
Went to Bristol. Stayed at Pantomime. Very cold.

William usually went to Bristol once a week, on Thursdays. He went by horse and cart to Cheddar Station, and then by train to Bristol. He enjoyed the pantomime so much that he went again the following week. At this time the Chute family owned the Prince's Theatre in Park Row, Bristol, and put on enormously popular pantomimes. This was probably the theatre which William visited.

23 Saturday
Cold Weather, Busy day.

24 Sunday
Heavy fall of snow.

27 Monday
Went to Highbridge after cake.

This was cattle-cake for re-sale, as most millers at this time were also corn and cake merchants, selling cattle food to farmers.

FEBRUARY
1 Monday
Windy Day. Stayed up Grinding untill 12.30

3 Wednesday
Fine Day. Good Wind for Grinding

4 Thursday
Went to Bristol. Bought Garden Seeds

9 Tuesday
Horse Bad. Very fine Day.

The next few days are just weather observations.

17 Wednesday
Cold Day. Mill Window smashed.

20 Saturday
Fine Day. Hard frost in morning. Emily & George came up.

Emily and George were his sister and brother-in-law.

> *22 Monday*
> *Went to Missionary Meeting at the Baptist Chapel, Wedmore.*
>
> *23 Tuesday*
> *Went to Cheddar and Bought a Horse of Mr Harvey for £25.10s.0d.*
>
> *25 Thursday*
> *Fine Day. George Wilkins Sale.*

The Wilkins family had formerly held the mill; this was presumably a relation.

MARCH

> *1 Monday*
> *Heavy fall of snow.*
>
> *2 Tuesday*
> *Cold Day. Dressing stones.*

The stones were the millstones, which needed regular 'dressing' to ensure they were smooth and the grooves were clean-cut.

> *3 Wednesday*
> *Cold Day. Snow.*
>
> *4 Thursday*
> *Went to Bristol, Very cold day.*
>
> *6 Saturday*
> *Cold Day. Very Busy. Went to Wedmore to see the vet.*

The horse William had bought was not fit.

> *8 Monday*
> *Went to Wells for a certificate and returned mare to H. Harvey. Very cold.*
>
> *9 Tuesday*
> *Bought a Horse of F. Page for £32.*
>
> *13 Saturday*
> *Fine day. Paid for Horse. Hauling hay.*
>
> *15 Monday*
> *Cold day, began planting seeds in garden.*

APRIL

> *5 Monday*
> *Went to Highbridge Market and sold Horse for £10.*
>
> *10 Saturday*
> *Stormy Day. Very busy.*
>
> *14 Wednesday*
> *Fine day, finished gardening, went to Wedmore in the evening.*
>
> *19 Monday*
> *Fine day, went to Temperance Meeting in evening. E. Cooper came dressing stones.*

Mr Cooper came from Bridgwater.

24 Saturday
Very hot day. Heavy hail stones and thunder.

MAY

1 Saturday
Had Mr Tucker's mare on Trial. Went to Cheddar. Cold

3 Monday
Went to Highbridge Market. Returned Mr Tucker's mare.

5 Wednesday
Hot Day, finished Stable carpenting.

8 Saturday
Fine Day. Hauled Bricks for stable.

The bricks probably came from Wedmore's brickworks.

13 Thursday
Wet Day. Mark Wall finished stable.

19 Wednesday
Went to Blackford and bought Reed for the mill at Mr Holes. Bought C. Champeny wheat.

21 Friday
Busy day. H. fetched Reed for the mill.

31 Monday
Wedmore Rioters tried at Taunton. Stormy Day.

The rioters were men arrested for disturbances during the recent elections (see Chapter 14).

JUNE

2 Wednesday
Stormy Day. Agricultural show began at Bristol.

4 Friday
Hot Day. Went to see C. Cook's mare. Lot Roe started to America.

Lot Roe was one of many agricultural workers who left Wedmore to seek a new and better farming life in America. Members of the Roe family still live in the parish.

7 Monday
Bought mare of W. Puddy for £20.

11 Friday
Fine Day. Sheep shearing match at Axbridge.

14 Monday
Stormy Day. Went to Burtle in the Evening.

15 Tuesday
Windy Day. Busy.

16 Wednesday
Fine Day. Went to the fete at Wedmore. Began Thatching the Mill.
He would have used the reed bought on 19th May for thatching.

17 Thursday
Put Down Floor in the Stable. Went to Crickham in the Evening.

18 Friday
Sent to Shepton after Grains.

19 Saturday
Busy Day. Finished Thatching Mill.

20 Sunday
Fine Day.

29 Tuesday
Hot Day. Sent to Highbridge after cake.
i.e. cow cake

JULY
3 Saturday
Hot Day. Mr Sperring committed Suicide.
Mr Sperring, probably a member of one of the milling families, was found drowned in a pond in a hayfield near his home. The *Wells Journal* of July 8th noted that he had suffered sunstroke a few days earlier.

12 Monday
Stormy Day. Grand show at Weston-s-Mare. Saw the Baloon.
An advertisement in the *Weston Gazette* of 10th July records that this show was 'GEORGE SANGER'S GRAND CORONATION FETE AND JUBILEE In honour of Her Majesty's Long and Prosperous Reign.' The day started with a procession all through Weston to the recreation ground. The procession included the 'HANDSOMEST CAR IN THE WORLD.' and 'BRITANNIA WITH A LIVING LION.' During the day there were Roman sports, including chariot racing. Three circus rings were working at the same time. At some point, according to the advertisement, 'A MONSTER BALLOON WILL ASCEND.' Later on a 'MONSTER TORCHLIGHT PROCESSION' was led by 10,000 torchbearers on horse and foot followed by 'Lady Godiva ... presented by the beautiful Miss Hastings,' with knights in costume and trades of the ancient city of Coventry. The day concluded with a 'GREAT FIREWORK COMPETITION.' Admission to the whole seven hours of continuous amusement was one shilling. No wonder even the terse William found it 'grand'.

14 Wednesday
Windy Day. C. Bagg drove a load to Cheddar. To the circus in the evening.

19 Monday
Fine Day. Went to Wedmore Fair.

27 Tuesday
Stormy. E. Cooper came Dressing stones.

Entries from William Tucker's diary, 1886

The millstones needed dressing regularly.

AUGUST
3 Tuesday
Went to Yarrow [Mark] and Wedmore Choir Festival in the evening.

6 Friday
Fine Day. Went to Wedmore and paid Coal Bill.

12 Thursday
Weare Cricket Match. Wet Evening.

13 Friday
Very Wet Day. Charlie Drove a Load to Burnham. Heard of Aunt Jane's illness.

16 Monday
Stormy. Morgan Jumpt Rhine.
Was Morgan one of the horses getting loose by jumping a local drainage ditch?

18 Wednesday
Went to Highbridge. Mother & Charles went to Burnham Flower Show.
Charles was his brother, and had a hunch-back.

20 Friday
Blackford fete and dancing. Hot Day.

25 Wednesday
Banwell Horse Show. Horse fell down and broke shaft.

30 Monday
Hot Day. Put Sail Cloth on.
He was replacing old canvas on the mill sails.

SEPTEMBER
7 Tuesday
Went to Brent Harvest Home. Fine Day.

8 Wednesday
Emily came from Dorchester here. Stormy.

9 Thursday
Stormy. Stayed up grinding until 12 o'clock.

11 Saturday
Fine Day. Bought 6 pigs of George Wall, 26s. 6d. each.

13 Monday
Emily went home.

21 Tuesday
Went to London to the Exebition, started at 3.40 a.m.

Great Western Railway inserted an advertisement in the *Weston-super-Mare Gazette* for Saturday 18th September, to announce this day trip to London by 'a special excursion train' leaving Cheddar at 3.50 a.m. The 3rd class fare was 5s.

22 Wednesday
Came back from London at 6.30 p.m.

27 Monday
Went to Wedmore Fair.

Wedmore had two fairs a year at this time.

28 Tuesday
Went to Baptist Harvest Thanksgiving at Wedmore. Went to Axbridge Court Office.

OCTOBER

After many days of stormy weather in the first weeks of October:

17 Sunday
Fine day. Horse bad.

30 Saturday
Fine Day. Busy. J. Banwell's horse died.

William Tucker does not seem to have had much luck with horses!

NOVEMBER

1 Monday
Went to Highbridge Market and to Wedmore to Tate's Minstrils in the Evening.

4 Thursday
Went to Bristol, sold 4 pigs to Mr Porter. Went to Wedmore in the evening. Old Horse killed.

8 Monday
Stormy. Sent to Bridgwater after cake. Sow went to pig.

15 Monday
Fine Day. F. Fear sent to Axbridge lock-up.

22 Monday
Fine Day. F. Fear tried at Axbridge, case dismissed. Went to Mark and bought Root Pulp and 18 sacks Barley at T. Fishers.

The *Wells Journal* of 25th November reported that Frederick Fear was a boy lodging with Michael Duckett of Heath House. He was accused of stealing £6 10s from the bedroom of Michael's son William, and £1 from Michael's daughter. The theft was supposed to have taken place while most of the family were at church. Fred was only out of the sight of a witness for ten minutes, but was accused of the theft and arrested by Sergeant Gilbanks.

After he had been a week in the lock-up at Axbridge, the case was heard and dismissed after such flimsy evidence. The magistrate said 'it is a great shame that they should have brought the boy before us.'

> *25 Thursday*
> *Went to Bristol. Bought chair, lamp and fruit trees.*
>
> *26 Friday*
> *Fine day. Finished Potato digging.*
>
> DECEMBER
> *28 Wednesday*
> *Very windy day, had 5 pigs from Bridgwater.*
>
> *10 Friday*
> *Went to Wedmore to a Sale in the Evening.*
>
> *20 Monday*
> *Frosty, went to Wedmore after Malt Mill*

What was a Malt Mill?

> *25 Saturday*
> *Very Fine Day. Mother and Charles went to Lympsham.*

Sister Emily married a farmer and lived in Lympsham.

> *26 Sunday*
> *Wet Day. Snow in the Evening.*
>
> *29 Wednesday*
> *Fine Day. Busy grinding.*

The next year is full of similar entries. The diary finishes at the entry for Tuesday 29th November 1887, which reads 'Got married.' No further diaries survive - perhaps they were never written. William married Eliza Duckett, and died of miller's disease on April 18th 1902 at the age of 44.

This selection from the daily events of one year in the life of a Wedmore miller shows that although he worked hard, he still had time to enjoy himself in Wedmore and elsewhere. It also shows just how much entertainment was available to, and enjoyed by, the people of a Somerset village before television. As the last local wind-miller of a line stretching back over many centuries, William Tucker has left us a particularly vivid picture of his varied life, and its mixture of hard work and pleasureable pastimes. There are more pictures of William Tucker and his mill in *Wedmore Past* (1993).

Chapter 10
Local Industries and Transport

The Wedmore Gas Company Ltd.

Wedmore Gasworks was built in 1870 on a plot of land at the end of the garden belonging to Stone's Bakery in The Borough. This site was probably chosen because it had good access to the main roads, being on Wedmore Moor Lane just beyond The Lerburne, yet tucked away out of sight of most of the village.

Gasworks had been springing up in towns for some time, and companies were spreading to larger villages. It is not known who made the decision to build the gasworks in Wedmore, but the advent of gas certainly changed the way of life in the village. The Wedmore Gasworks today form an attractive group of brick buildings. A plan of 1918 shows that apart from the gasholder itself, which has now disappeared, there was the retort house and buildings for production of gas, linked by a range of low workshops to a neat manager's house and office.[1] All are built to match, with architectural details in coloured brick, decorative ridge tiles on their roofs, and elaborate chimneys. A datestone of 1870 is fixed over the door to the retort house.

The first manager was James (Jimmy) Batten. He retired around 1918, having worked about fifty years running the works almost single-handed. He was married and had several children, and his wife Mary used to work as well, shovelling the coal for the boiler. She was reputed to have become deformed from this hard work. Jimmy Batten was a very clever engineer, but he could neither read nor write. His wife read to him, and he learnt from diagrams. He could also repair early motorcars before the advent of garages in Wedmore. Dr Bracey cared for his family when they were sick, and Jimmy Batten in return took care of the Doctor's car! When the meters had to be emptied and the money counted, a collector went round to help him.

James and Mary Batten at the Gasworks, c1910

Local Industries and Transport 127

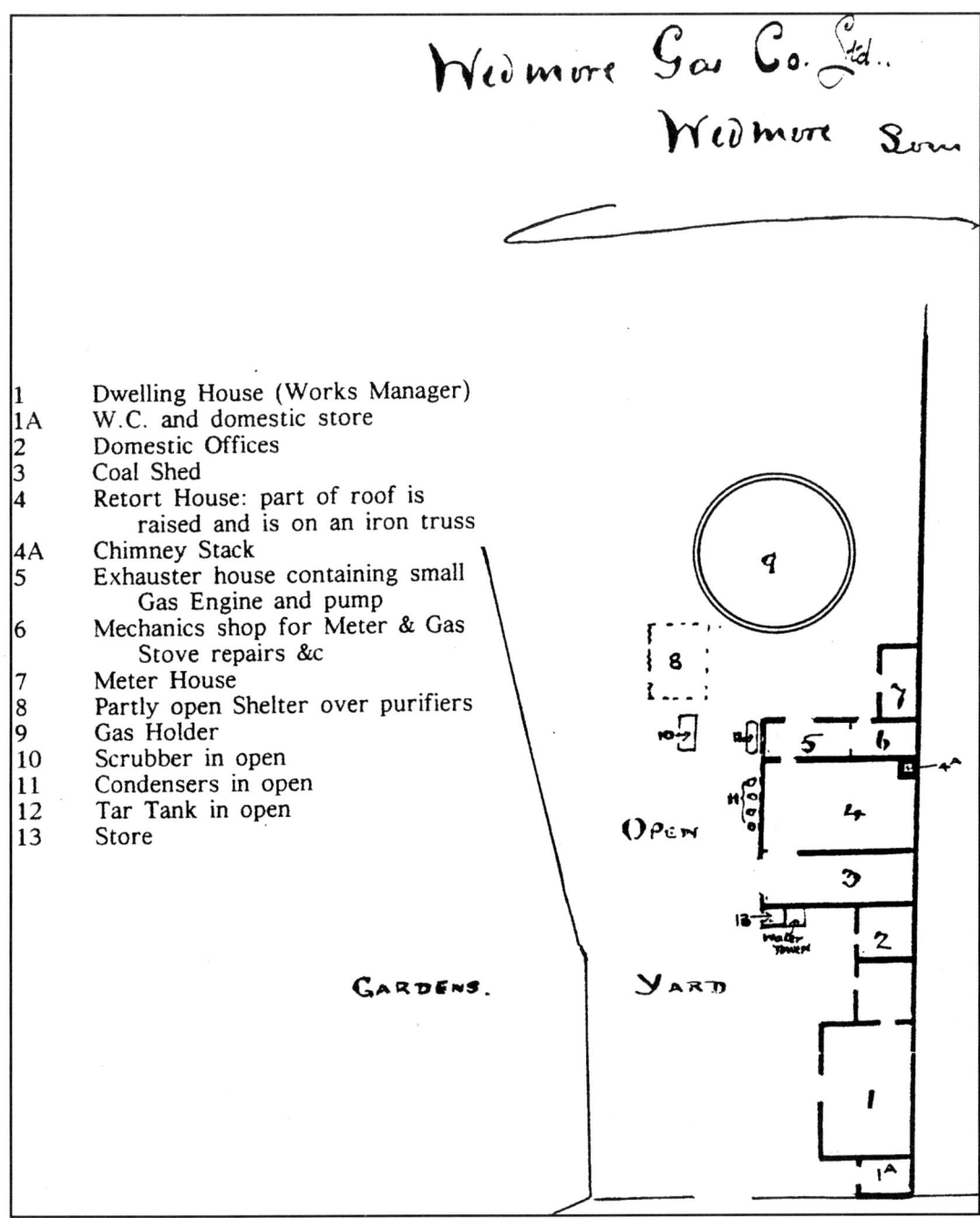

Plan of Wedmore Gasworks, 1918

When Jimmy retired, the works were run by William Webb. A photograph taken in 1921 shows his two sons William Cecil and Charles Ernest standing outside the retort house.[2] The elder of the brothers, William Cecil Webb, has told me that the family arrived at Wedmore Gas Works in 1918. His father's main problem was 'keeping the Gas Holder full for the demand for Sunday's lunches: if too much gas was made it would escape - if too little then the holder would empty'. He also remembers that when the purifier was emptied and cleaned, the local children who had whooping cough were brought to the Gas Works 'and stood around, inhaling the vapour given off'. The retorts were continually heated and topped up with coal every six hours. The work was very hot and heavy. Mr Webb left in about 1923, when J Freckingham took over.

One of the first uses of gas was for street lighting. This proved a great boon to Wedmore on dark winter nights. Jimmy Batten and his successors would go around with their lamp-lighter's sticks, lighting the street lamps. The village was lit by electric light in about 1911 but changed back to gas again in 1936, when the gasworks tendered a lower price than the Electric Company.[3] These gaslights still lit the village until December 1952, when the decision was finally made to change over to electricity. This was because of the cost of the gas, and of the new gas fittings and extensions that were by then required. Wedmore's street lighting had been run by a Street Lighting Inspector's Committee. This was started c1870, and in 1952 was chaired by Cecil Puddy (my father). There were only three of these village committees in the whole country. Due to the need to raise money for new street lighting after the South West Gas Board's contract ran out, it was decided that the parish council should take over the committee's duties, and subsequently electric lights were installed in place of gas.[4]

Before the coming of gas, turf or peat was the main cooking fuel in Wedmore. The decline in the use of turf must have been a disaster for the peat-diggers in the moors. Many people took up the Gas Board's offer of rented gas cookers, and found the gas cleaner and more efficient than their solid fuel ranges. The parish church was lit by gas in the early 1870s. The lights were held on standards fixed in some of the pews. Other meeting places in the village found gas lighting most convenient, including the Methodist church, where pendant gas chandeliers were installed.

The gas was produced from coal. This was brought by rail from Radstock to Cheddar, and then by horse and wagon to Wedmore. In 1908 the Wedmore Electric Light and Power Company started producing electricity. This provided competition for the Gas Company, and they found they had to reduce their prices! A report in the *Wells Journal* of March 25th,

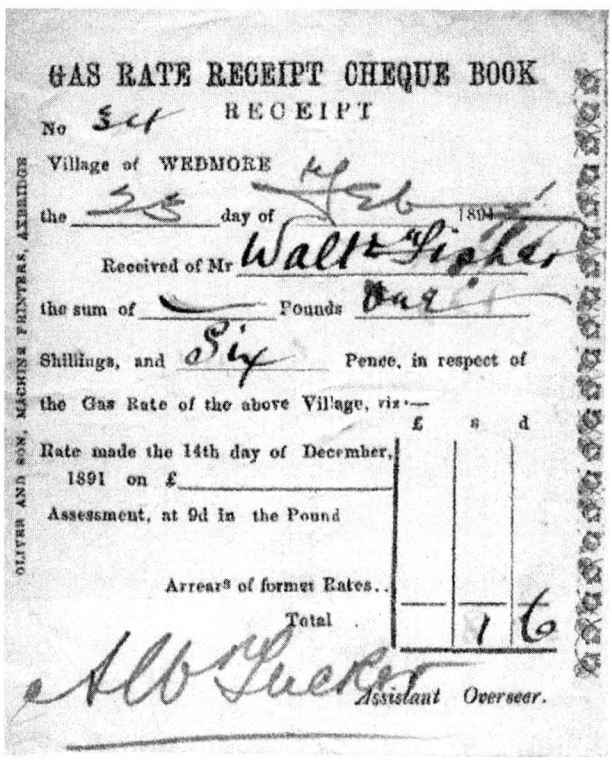

Gas receipt from Wedmore's Gasworks, 1894

1909 states 'The Gas Company are waking up, and intend offering cheaper gas, the lending of cooking stoves and general overhauling of existing meters and plant, so that thanks to the new [Electric] Company Wedmore will benefit to the extent of cheaper light and up-to-date apparatus which will be the envy of much larger communities.' The two companies ran in competition with each other until they were both taken over during the nationalisation of the gas and electricity industries in the late 1940s.

The imminent demise of Wedmore's gasworks came to the attention of no less than *The Times* newspaper in 1947, when the following appeared on 30th January:

> 'THE LORD HIGH GAS-MAN:....Here and there ... is a man upon whom the whole life of the community really does depend, and one such seems to be MR WHEATLEY of Wedmore in Somerset. He is, we are told, the manager, engineer, stoker, meter collector and general clerical assistant of The Wedmore Gasworks; he also does all the maintenance work and looks after the cookers in the houses and the street lamps. Everyone has heard of a one-man band but a one-man gasworks is unique. MR WHEATLEY and the gasworks are synonymous expressions, and - here is the tremendous fact - if ever he let the furnace or the oven go out there would be seven days of cooling down and seven more days of warming up again, and during all that time Wedmore would be gasless. The responsibility of the vestal virgins was as nothing to his .... Now, after twelve years of working from six in the morning to seven at night for seven days a week, MR WHEATLEY is to lead a comparatively otiose life. The gas undertaking of a larger neighbour, Weston-super-Mare, is to swallow up Wedmore's tiny works, and, when once the main is laid from Weston, MR WHEATLEY will devote himself merely to maintenance and meter-collecting. He is said to be looking forward to an easier time. No one has ever earned one better, for never perhaps have so many owed so much to one man. And yet life may seem a little empty at first, so that he looks back with tender regret to the days when he was Lord High Everything Else at Wedmore ... MR WHEATLEY, his day's collecting done, will drop now and then into a neighbour's house and give a friendly glance at the cooker, to see that all is well'.

The Wedmore Gas Works Company was purchased for £3017 and when the gas main from Weston to Cheddar, and from Cheddar to Wedmore, was finally finished in 1947, Wedmore Gas Works closed down.[5] At the time of writing, the manager's house and offices still stand, along with the retort house and some of the other outbuildings now converted into a workshop. It is hoped that these buildings will remain as a reminder of one of the village industries that changed the life of Victorian Wedmore.

Wedmore Electric Light and Power Company

In 1908 Mr William George Burrough, a local solicitor, started an electric company in Wedmore. The business began in a shed behind the house called South Bank in Grants Lane. Mr Burrough lived opposite, in Hill House. Within a few months the demand for electricity grew so great that the premises were too small. The machinery was moved to 'The Electricity House', a purpose-built building in part of Mr Burrough's property above Grants Lane. The electricity was originally provided by a large steam engine powered by an

William George Burrough (1876-1940), with a brother on the left

anthracite boiler. Storage batteries were kept in an adjoining room. The first engineer was John Hankinson.

Mr Burrough's son Charles remembers as a child the huge rolls of wire for the lines, stored in the yard. One day he rolled one of them down the hill - I don't know what the result was! Such was the interest in Wedmore's electricity works that many newspapers reported on its success. This was because it was a novelty to have electricity so early. Wells did not receive electricity until 1924, sixteen years after Wedmore.

Wells Journal and Somerset Advertiser, March 25th 1909, reported:

'WEDMORE ENTERPRISE

The Electric Light Company having installed their light in numerous public and private residences and promised the current at eight pence a unit, now announce that they can supply at 6d. This compares favourably with the cost in the large towns in England. They are also prepared to put in plant, where wanted for power for driving machinery such as apple mills, corn and cake crushers and chaff cutters, as well as cooking stoves, at a much reduced cost per unit.'

The *Weston-super-Mare Gazette*, August 15th 1911, announced:

'*Wedmore is in the throes of an epidemic ... not so many months ago a couple of very enterprising gentlemen were struck with the idea of lighting the village streets with electricity and put down a small plant for that purpose. Probably they never anticipated that the 'lighting fluid' would be put to such extensive use as it is today. The inhabitants of the village saw the splendid effect of lighting the streets by this method. Then they woke up, the people of this sleepy, old fashioned, out of the way place simply woke up. They wanted the innovation in their homes, and they got it! They were not content with mere illumination: they craved more, and all the forces of electricity are now being brought into play. The little company has had to extend its plant, for the people are having electric fans fitted into kitchens, parlour and bedroom. The bakers are kneading their dough by electricity, [farmers are] grinding their corn, churning their butter and making their cider by means of the new force. Indeed, the demand for electric power is growing apace and soon we may expect to find established the unique example of a village tramway and all the multitudinous operations that we have come to believe are possible through the power of the dynamo.*'

The electricity business was really taking off. By August 1911 most of the shares of the company had been taken up, and the works was now a public company instead of a private enterprise.[6] On September 16th 1911 the company wrote to Axbridge Rural District Council:

'We desire to extend our area a little towards Cocklake and apply to you to kindly grant us permission to erect poles at the side of the road in positions meeting with the approval of your surveyors. We would go off the road into the field below, where the footpath runs'[7]. Electricity had already reached Blackford as Sexey's School installed lighting in 1910.[8]

An article in the *Weston Mercury* of October 21st 1911 entitled 'Progressive Wedmore' reports that:

> *'It would be instructive and interesting to anyone to see the small electric motors at work driving the apple mills and other agricultural machinery at minimum cost. We do not think anywhere else in the country would be found such a novel and progressive practice.'*

The First World War put a strain on the company by taking away its workmen to fight at the front. In February 1918 this report from the *Wells Journal* shows the problem:

> 'WORKING 16 HOURS A DAY
>
> *Mr W.G. Burrough solicitor of Wedmore applied as managing director of the Wedmore Electric Light and Power Company for the exemption of Ernest Bond, the company engineer. Bond, 33, was in grade two. He was married and lived in Grants street [sic] Wedmore. He was the only man employed to look after the gas plant, dynamos, batteries and to do all the necessary repairs and renewals. He also repaired breakdowns on motors throughout the district. The electric current was not only used for lighting purposes but extensively for power by farmers and others. He was absolutely essential. The company had tried to get a substitute but had failed. Bond was now working 16 hours a day. Conditional exemption granted.'*

A photograph of 1916 shows there were then three or four men employed, along with John Hankinson the manager and Edward Batten the engineer.[9] After the war ended in 1918, the Wedmore works employed more men and extended its operations. In 1920, Alfred E Goodridge came to Wedmore to take over the running of the company which he ran until about 1931. His son, Mr Charles Goodridge, put me in touch with his sister Mrs Joan Cresswell, who has written the following vivid personal account of the Electric Company building at that time:

'My father, Mr Alfred E. Goodridge, who was always known as AEG, came to Wedmore in 1920 to take over the management of the Wedmore Electric Light Company. He had been recently employed in making electricity for two large private estates, one in Devon and one near Frome, in Somerset. This new post was therefore much more important in that it was to supply light not only for Wedmore, but for Theale and Blackford as well.

The entrance to the Electric Light station looked out over Wedmore and the Church could easily be seen across the valley. One noticed the warmth underfoot, and felt the vibration, and heard the thump, thump, thump of the engine exhausts. Entering meant passing between two large circular furnaces, one for each of the engines. These were probably of cast iron and were lined with fire bricks. They heated coke to produce gas which was led away at the top and washed before being conveyed by pipe to the engines themselves. The engineers used to wash their hands in the warm basal water of the washers and I remember clearly the packet of Hudson's soap always available there.

Then came large wooden double doors with a smaller door set inside them. Beyond was the engine room itself, which was rectangular, and mainly taken up by two gas engines. They were bolted to the concrete floor, and wiped clean with oily rags. Each had a large flywheel driven by a piston which slid to and fro. Oil pots like small round lanterns decorated each engine chassis. The large 4 ton flywheel carried a substantial woven belt, the floor being recessed to carry the belt to a round, solid, humming generator at the far end of the engine room. I imagine that the gas engine, belt and generator accounted for about 20 feet of the length of that room. It was, of course, the generator which produced the electricity, which I remember to be direct current (DC) and not the alternating variety (AC) which is used nowadays. The smaller of the two engines was used during the day; the larger one took the responsibility of making power for the evening. The one was watched and oiled from about 8.30 am to 4 pm, and the other from 4 or 5 pm to 10.30 pm at night.

The engineer in charge had quite a large black switchboard at the end of the engine room, on the right hand side. There were switches which dipped into open reservoirs of mercury, and others which resembled large light switches. Dials, with needles which flickered, told how much power was being made and also what load was being carried. Bearing in mind that most homes in this area used electricity only for lighting, the main load came on at lighting-up time. I have seen AEG standing anxiously at the entrance to the station, looking at the church on Sunday nights. When the sermon began, the nave lights were mostly turned out, and this helped to reduce the load. On nights when the full moon was very bright, the street lights (only Wedmore had this advantage) were turned out too, to save the load. Normally they operated from autumn to spring, from lighting-up time until 10.15 pm. They were inspected on Wednesdays and Saturdays, by walking the route to see if, and how many, bulbs needed replacing.

Of course, there needed to be power available for all the 24 hours, and so at the far end of the engine room on the left side there was a room which I remember to be about 10 or 12 feet square, which housed row after row of accumulators. Each consisted of a thick greenish glass open-topped 'box' which was filled with sulphuric acid, into which the 'plates' dipped. They were linked with terminals and wires and must have worked in sections. They stored the electricity overnight, and during the interval while one engine was silenced and the other took over its task. I clearly remember the atmosphere in the battery room - the sulphuric acid made the nose tingle and there was a feeling of 'power lying in wait' there. 'Do not touch', although not written, was the feeling one had.

The engineer had a little office in which I remember an old slanting-topped desk, a slate and pencil for messages, cotton waste to rub it clean, shelves of electric bulbs for sale, an old heavy kitchen chair and a stool or two. There was a round coke stove for winter nights, shielded by sheets of grey asbestos. A jug of cocoa would keep warm at its base. It might even have made toast! The station also charged accumulators for wireless sets which were becoming common. I only remember one electric fire which came in for repair. It consisted of a large sausage-shaped bulb on a stand, with metal reflectors sending its heat forward. It belonged to the Manor House near the Church. The day's work consisted of engine-watching, oiling and filling the coke furnaces (I think each was called 'the plant') with buckets of coke carried to the top by the engineer up a metal ladder.

The outlying villages also called upon the Electric Company. When gales blew a tree down onto the overhead lines, repairs had to be made, and casual labour was brought in when poles had to be replaced. A flat-topped, two-wheeled truck was pushed to the accident area. The creosoted poles were lowered into hand-dug holes and packed in with rammed stones. The copper wire lines were fastened to china cups and strained to the correct tension. Poles had stays to keep them upright when a change of direction in the line occurred. The voltage requirement for Wedmore was 230 - so one bought 230 volt bulbs. Because of voltage drop (which I believe was characteristic of DC current) the villages of Theale and Blackford bought 210 volt bulbs. Just outside the extent of the company's overhead lines, places had no electricity. I well remember the former village school on the Cheddar Road had no electricity, and on the rare occasion when it was used for an examination in winter, it had to to be lit by oil lanterns. People realised the benefits of electric lighting and the engineers were often sent for, to price the extension of the wiring to another part of the home.

Every aspect of this service was dealt with by the local team. AEG at one time had an engineer called Jim Beveridge, but he decided to return to his native Scotland. Then there was Bramwell Freckingham (Bram),[10] who also watched engines and pushed trucks, and Lionel Rogers, a delightful young man from Blackford who was unfortunately a diabetic and who only lived to 21 years. They kept the service going with the aid of an engine fitter, a Mr Hathaway, who came from a Bristol engineering firm at intervals and, with AEG, took the engines, one at a time, to pieces to overhaul, reassemble and re-tune them in perfect working order. I suppose the hours of work those days were overlong, except for the evening shift. This was taken alternately, for a whole week at a time, by AEG and by Bram.

In later years AEG had a second-hand Douglas motorbike and sidecar to travel around the company's area. He replaced the sidecar with a black coffin-like box in which he could carry tools all over the area for wiring installations. I remember the motorbike had a drive belt which kept shedding its connectors.'

Mrs Cresswell goes on to describe how in 1928 the Wedmore works were taken over by the North Somerset Electric Light Company. The main centre of production was eventually Portishead Power Station. Wedmore became a sub-station. A building added to the south end of the old works housed very complicated switch gear.

'This was the end of the gas engines and generators - no more loads of coke or carboys of acid. The engine room looked desolate with everything stripped out. AEG kept his Morris 8 there, having constructed a ramp up which to run the car, and he made the belt race of one of the engines into a car-inspection pit.'

This description by Mrs Joan Cresswell is an outstanding example of the value of writing down memories of the village, so they are safe for the future. She has given us hitherto unknown details of the workings of this Wedmore industry. The village would not have had its own electricity so early, without the entrepreneurial spirit and foresight shown in 1908 by WG Burrough, first chairman of the company. He died on 30th December 1939, having lived to see his dream of Wedmore running on electricity come true.

The final part of the story of the Electric Station is based upon the Company Minute and

Shareholders Books from 1912 to 1928, which tells the story from a different angle, that of the boardroom.[11] The private company set up in 1908 by William George Burrough, solicitor, and John Hankinson, engineer was sold to the new public company, Wedmore Electric Light and Power Company Limited, for £3,300. The first meeting of the directors was held in a room in Mr Burrough's offices on the Cheddar Road. William Burrough was appointed Managing Director. The other directors were Mrs Edith Mary Smith of The Manor House; Dr William Edelsten Bracey of The Uplands, the village doctor; William Owen, draper, whose shop is now Lloyds Chemist; and two farmers from Sand Road, William Duckett of The Myrtles and Albert Tucker of The Laurels.

The new company issued £1 shares, and 3,500 were taken up by thirty-five shareholders. These were all local people except for two or three who were friends and relatives of Mr Burrough. William Burrough himself held 1165 shares, and his wife 100. Mrs Edith Smith of the Manor House held 790, and the other directors 100 each. Mrs Clara White of Sand House held 300 and Samuel Price, the Headmaster of Wedmore School, had 100. Most of the other shareholders held blocks of 50, 25, 15 or 10 shares. They came from a cross-section of parishioners. There was an insurance agent, a boot-maker, a butcher from Blackford, a baker from Plud Street, together with several ladies and some local farmers. Ernest Bond, engineer, brought 20 shares. He lived in Church Villas at the top of Church Street and later became the company engineer.

The directors decided to rent a room at Mr Burrough's offices, in which to hold their meetings, for £1 2s 6d per annum. The minute book gives a little insight into the day-to-day running of the business. In September 1912 Sand Hall was being wired for electricity, and neighbours Edward Hawkins and Mrs Toogood had asked to be wired as well. In October it was decided to buy a testing set jointly with Winscombe Electric Power Company. On 2nd January 1913 the company's auditors, Samuel Price and Frederick Curtin, resigned. They were replaced by Harold Davis of Glastonbury. Frederick Curtin later became company secretary. The decision was also made to 'let out on hire' the firm's vacuum cleaner, at 2 shillings and 6 pence a day. It would seem that this scheme was very successful as in February another one was bought, and the charge for renting one of the vacuum cleaners was raised to 3 shillings a day. Roger Hembury was appointed as a clerical assistant at 2s 6d a month, presumably as a part-time job.

In March it was agreed to extend 'The Electric House' at a cost of £128. WR Withers was to do the work. He had built 'The Electric House' in 1908 and lived opposite it in Grant's Lane. It was 'Agreed to take on P.C.Hansford's son as apprentice electrician.' The little company was proving a useful source of local employment. To increase the capital of the company a further 1000 £1 shares were issued.

May 1913 saw the decision to buy 'engine and plant' from Messrs Crossley Brothers Limited for £266, and a complete dynamo from Newtons Limited for £49 15s. It was also agreed to apply to Somerset County Council for licence to erect poles in Theale Road. In July the cable and poles had been delivered, and the engine and dynamo 'were promised'. William Burrough was to arrange for the old engine house to be whitewashed and the woodwork in the new engine house (the extension) 'to be pickled'; this cost £3. The sign 'Electric Station' in black letters was to be fixed over the door of the building.

New cells for the batteries were purchased in October on the advice of Mr Parfitt, who had originally designed the battery. As Mr Wilkinson the secretary had resigned, Mrs Smith proposed that Frederick Curtin should be appointed, at a salary of £15 a year. He remained as secretary until 1928. The meeting of 7th February 1914 reported that the cost of the extension had exceeded the amount raised by the new share issue; but the company continued busy during the early years of the First World War. On 12th October a letter was received from Mr Henson, demanding the removal of a pole in Glanville Road. Mr Henson (actually Dr Henson) lived in Elmsett Hall, and perhaps the pole obstructed his view! Mr Burrough reported a fault in the casting of the new engine; this had been replaced without cost by Crossley Brothers.

On 19th November the company received a letter of thanks for fitting a light free of charge to 'The Belgium Refugee Home.' These Belgian refugees are also mentioned in Wedmore School Logbook; they came to stay in Wedmore for about a year and lived in the house now called Whitegates in Glanville Road. It was agreed to purchase a booster to increase voltage from 230 volts to 300 volts for Blackford and Theale. The current supplied was still DC (direct current), with a consequent loss of power at the end of the line. Mr Ernest Bond the engineer requested a rise in his salary in February 1915. It was agreed that he should receive an additional £10 a year, on condition that he also did 'petty work'. By July 1916 the First World War was having an effect on the company, due to the 'great increase in the price of coal oil etc.', and the price for electric current had to be increased by one penny per unit; the charge paid by Sexey's School was increased by 5 guineas.

A typical dividend of 4% was paid in both January 1916 and January 1917. The directors discussed purchasing War Bonds and Government Bonds, and took on Percy Bethel as apprentice at 2s a week. £300 worth of bonds were bought, and in March another apprentice, Francis Vowles, was to be given his indenture at the end of his term. Both Bethel and Vowles were, presumably, local boys.

Ernest Bond was given 6 months' exemption from military service by Axbridge Tribunal in July 1917. The company had to apply for a further exemption for him in 1918. In March 1918 prices rose again. The cost of lighting went up 1d per unit. Power was priced in bands: under 100 units a quarter cost 6d a unit; between 100 and 300 units a quarter cost 5d a unit; and 300 or more units a quarter cost 4d a unit. Many houses at this time had only electric light, not power. February 1919 saw another increase in Ernest Bond's salary, by 7s a week, bringing it to 55s a week. It was agreed to consider raising the price of electricity by 1d a unit. It was suggested that information should first be obtained from other electric companies at Burnham, Winscombe, Bridgwater and Weston to compare prices. In the event the company decided to increase the price by 2d a unit. It is in the spring of 1919 that we find, along with this price increase, the first clues that all is not well with the little company. A new engine and gas plant is needed, and they have to borrow money to purchase it. In May, the old engine was sold for £250. The new engine and suction gas plant was due to be delivered at the end of August, but this was delayed until September. At the September meeting the directors wrote to the Lighting Inspectors that 'We are prepared to light the streets on the same terms as last year viz ½d per lamp per hour, but owing to the difficulty in getting delivery of our new engine ... due to strikes, we ask that the date for the actual lighting of the streets may be deferred.' In January the new dynamo had burnt out and Newtons General Electric Company had sent one on loan.

In January 1920 Ernest Bond resigned. The suggested replacement was Percy Bethel, and he was engaged in March at £2 a week. The price of current for light was to be increased from 10½d to 1s 0½d. William Burrough purchased a generator for £60 in September 1920. It was to be hired out to Wedmore Cinema, at £12 a year. The cinema was at this time in the Church Schoolroom (now the Village Hall), but later on films were shown in the Assembly Rooms (now the Masonic Hall). Percy Bethel and FW Bowyer resigned in December. William Burrough had already interviewed Mr AE Goodridge from Chitterne in Wiltshire, and he was appointed engineer at £3 a week. Mr Smith was appointed as his assistant at 50s a week. By June 1921 the company again faced financial problems. Bills were unpaid. It was resolved to increase their borrowings from £1000 to £1400, and, in September, to ask for a temporary overdraft. The money problem seemed to be solved for a while, as in 1923 the company produced a 5% dividend.

Mr George Vowles, carpenter, had his house and carpentry workshop at Blackford connected up in October. Good news for customers came in 1925, with two reductions in electricity prices. In February, the cost of lighting was reduced by 1d, and of power by 2d; and in June domestic supplies were to be reduced to 6½d a unit. It was also resolved in June to improve the supply to Theale Church, at a cost of £350. In October Mr Goodridge broke his leg while putting up a pole at Theale.

The end of the company was approaching. Electricity was on the way to becoming a national commodity. The Electricity Commissioners wrote to the Wedmore Company regarding their compliance with the Electric Lighting Act of 1888 (section 4). Mr Burrough as Managing Director reported that equipment had been 'overhauled and increased in capacity.' At the same time the directors realised that the advance of the North Somerset Electric Company (NSEC) across this part of Somerset, using AC (alternating current) would mean expensive changes if Wedmore was to stay in business.

By April 1927 Christy Brothers, who made the equipment for NSEC, were proposing to extend their mains supply from Axbridge to Cross, Weare and Chapel Allerton, and made an offer to supply Wedmore as well. A takeover of the Wedmore company was in the offing. On 1st May, in accordance with a resolution made at the AGM, 'the chairman was asked to obtain particulars in writing of obtaining a supply from the North Somerset Electric Company.'

The end came on 19th May 1928, when NSEC offered and the Wedmore directors accepted a buy-out at 15s a share, for all the shares in the Wedmore company. It would have cost £3000 to adapt the Wedmore DC transmission to AC, as all the plant would have had to be written off and replaced. The price of buying in a bulk supply to Wedmore was too expensive. The company was wound up and the last meeting took place on 16th June 1928. From then onwards Wedmore, like other communities in the area, obtained its electricity through big outside suppliers. The 1908 'Electric House,' is now no more. It was burnt down in 1999 when it was struck by lightning and a house is built on the site. Mr Burrough's enterprise in setting up his company in 1908 gave the village a head start of two decades in the advantages of the modern miracle of electricity. Who can imagine, nowadays, living without electricity?

Wedmore Brick and Tile Works

Sometime during the 1830s or 1840s a brick and tile works was established in Wedmore by John Tonkin. It was sited down Wedmore Moor Drove off the Lerburne, where Brickyard Farm is today. Clay was dug from the ground at the southern edge of the brickyard site. Later on clay pits were dug in Wedmore Moor. The clay at the brickyard was yellow, while that dug from the moor was blueish-grey. These pits flooded and provided a place for the local lads to swim, but were filled in after a boy drowned there. There are very few surviving records to show the original extent of the works, but a wide range of products were made: roof tiles, bricks, floor bricks, water pipes and ornamental garden urns.

The buildings which stand on the north corner of Church Street and the Borough, now Lloyds Chemist and Minstrels Gallery, were built as their shop and house by the Tonkin family, using their own bricks and tiles. The roof tiles were of a special design, like fish scales, which was produced solely for these buildings. The brickyard became a secondary enterprise to the Tonkin family's drapery business and general emporium (see Chapter 6). There are probably Tonkin tiles still on some other Wedmore roofs. John Tonkin (junior) was still the owner of the brickyard in 1863 when he is described as 'brick, tile and drain-pipe manufacturer'.[12] John was busy running his shop in Church Street, and had a foreman, Charles Savage, in charge of the brickworks. According to the 1861 census Charles Savage was 35 and had five children, one of whom was actually called Charles Wesley. His father was a local Methodist preacher and nicknamed 'Wesley Savage'. This census does not indicate where the Savage family were living, but there may have been a cottage on the brickyard site at this time. Staying as a boarder with the family in 1861 was William Pople, aged 24, tile maker. There were also two other workers, brick makers called Samuel Collins and Thomas Perry, who lived elsewhere in the village.

In 1875 Charles Savage is described in Kelly's Directory as brick, tile and drain manufacturer, but the works were still owned by John Tonkin. An article in the *Weston-super-Mare Gazette* of March 20th 1880 reported an accident in the brickyard:

> 'A boy aged 13-14 by the name of Cook who has been employed by Mr Savage's brick and tile yard for some months past had the misfortune to put his hand too near the machinery while it was in motion, the consequence was that his fingers were lacerated, some of them afterwards amputated and his thumb set. Under the care of Dr Tyley we are pleased to learn that he is going on very well.'

Not every report was quite so gruesome. In 1886 the *Wells Journal* gave a long account of a cuckoo which laid an egg in the nest of a water wagtail,

> 'in a row of tiles about five feet from the ground near the engine-house door in Mr Jo. Tonkins' brick and tile yard, where they were minutely watched by the foreman and the manager of the yard who saw a cuckoo fly from the nest where she had deposited an egg.'

The men watched the baby cuckoo hatch and grow until it was mature enough to fly away.

Soon after this the brickworks were sold to Mr Henry Harvey, who employed Mr George Harris as manager. The business, however, declined so Mr Harvey bought in machines to replace some of the hand work. Business still failed to improve, and in July 1900 Henry Harvey went bankrupt, owing £700.[13] He said that for the last seven or eight years he had lost between £2000 and £3000, and 'ascribed his insolvency to working with bad machinery'.

Henry Harvey produced many thousands of bricks, which are instantly recognisable with their characteristic maker's stamps. Note the reverse D in WEDMORE!

Henry Harvey lived in Lerburne House in The Borough, but after being made bankrupt he sold this house to Frederick Morgan in 1901 for £770.[14] Frederick Morgan was Henry's son-in-law, and he carried on the brickworks. Things did not, however, run smoothly for Fred. In July 1902 the *Weston-super-Mare Gazette* reported a case at the Assize Court. Frederick Morgan had

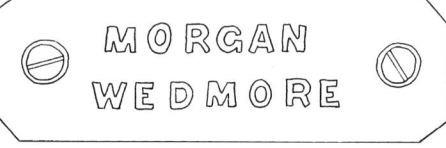

Stamps on Wedmore bricks produced by Henry Harvey (c1887-1901) and Frederick Morgan (1901-6)

> 'bought a tile making machine from Whitehead and Co. Ltd., Boston, Lincs, which he had returned to them claiming it did not make as many tiles per hour as the manufacturers claimed. His tile makers George Webb and Walter Adams could make much better and more Roman tiles by hand'.

The brickworks closed in 1906. Some Morgan bricks can be found today, but they are much rarer than Harvey bricks. All that remains of the brickworks is the brick drying shed and ancillary furnace room.[15] The drying shed dates from about 1850. It was a long building with hinged wooden shutterflaps all along the sides for ventilation. Bricks and tiles would be stacked in the shed before firing. Warm air was ducted from the furnace room into the shed to speed up the drying process.

Thus after about seventy years, brick making in Wedmore came to a close. It was one of many such little brickworks which sprang up wherever the clay was suitable. Although not in production today, the survival of this distinctive drying shed is a bonus for the history of small industries in Wedmore. The Wedmore bricks and tiles which were produced there can be identified in the walls and roofs of many village houses. They testify to this final 19th century phase of locally produced building materials, which have since been lost to the modern mass-production that makes houses look the same all over Britain.

A Wedmore Tannery

Walking past the pretty cottages in Glanville Road, it is difficult to imagine that 200 years ago this was the site of one of Wedmore's smelliest industries. Behind the pair of houses now called Nyland View and Mendip Cottage was a tannery. The tannery was sited here beside Wedmore Brook because water is an essential ingredient in the messy and odoriferous process of cleaning, soaking and curing the raw animal skins to produce the finished tanned leather.

References to a tannery or tanhouse appear in various parish documents but trying to pinpoint its site was rather complicated. The starting point was in 1792 when John Gardiner held a tanhouse for which he paid 3s 8¼d land tax.[16] Grace Taviner also paid 11¾d for part of a tanhouse in the same 1792 land tax list.

In 1814 Richard Banwell held 'Gardiners tan house', and he was still paying 3s 8¼d land tax for it.[17] The Highway rate of 1815 shows that Richard Banwell held property number 1748.[18] Plot no.1748 on the Wedmore parish map of 1791 is the site of the cottages in Glanville Road.[19]

Grace Taviner, who was holding part of a tanhouse in 1792, is holding part of plot 1748 in 1820, so she was involved in the same site.[20] The rest of the plot, in 1820, was held by Joseph Stickland. Joseph was a carpenter and the family lived there for about 150 years (see Chapter 13). Their house plot was called, significantly, Gardiner's Orchard.

John Gardiner and Grace Taviner were thus sharing the tannery in 1792. The parish poor book shows that Grace Taviner, in the late 1700s, was making 'soap and lye' for Wedmore Poor House - and presumably for anyone else in Wedmore who wanted to buy it.[21] The Poor House stood just outside the west gate of the Church, opposite the end of Glanville Road. The soap was made from rendered-down animal fat, and lye was an alkaline solution used for washing and scrubbing in those times. Both the fat and the alkaloids were leftovers from the smelly business of the tannery; this probably explains Grace Taviner's connection with the site. John Gardiner must have obtained a good supply of animal hides for his tanning business from the local butchers. Wedmore's annual fair was renowned as a cattle-fair.

The 1791 parish map shows that Wedmore Brook had a secondary stream, a channel or 'leat', branching off at the site of the tannery above Glanville Road. It ran through the property, providing the quantities of flowing water necessary for the cleaning and tanning processes, and then ran under the road, eventually rejoining the main brook lower down. This leat is still there today, but it is culverted underground until it emerges below Glanville Road.

This tannery can be traced even further back in time. It is described as a tanhouse when John Gardiner held it in 1792: but still earlier, in 1778,[22] John Gardiner is recorded as holding a property called Thatchers, after a previous owner. Back in 1766 John Thatcher was paying 7s 5½d land tax - for a tanhouse.[23] The water supply, vats and tanks of a tannery were such major fixtures that a tanhouse tended to stay on the same site through successive owners: and though we have no documentary evidence beyond the name to prove that John Thatcher's tanhouse in 1766 was the same as the later Gardiner/Stickland tanhouse, there is one other clue to connect him with it.

According to the date stone on the front, the tanhouse was rebuilt in 1882 as the present pair of cottages, by Edward Stickland, grandson of Joseph Stickland who held the property in 1820. A photograph of about 1880 shows that the earlier house was an old thatched cottage with a wing alongside the brook.[24] This wing is now a separate residence called The Old Cottage. On the chimney stack of The Old Cottage is another date stone. When Edward Stickland rebuilt the tanhouse, he removed this date stone from an old chimney and placed it where it is today. The late Miss Kate Stickland, his grand-daughter, did not know who or what the date stone commemorated. The lettering on the stone is a monogram in the style of the late 1600s: with the letters **S & M.T.**, and part of a date **16...** . Does the T stand for Thatcher? A search through the Wedmore parish registers shows no marriage of any S... and M... with a surname starting with T in the late 1600s - but then, the bride might not have come from Wedmore and the marriage might well have taken place in her home parish. The Wedmore baptism registers, however, show that John Thatcher, who held the tanhouse in 1766, was the son of Samuel Thatcher and Mary his wife - **S & M. T.** They had four children, all baptised at Wedmore church between 1692 and 1697; which suggests that they were probably married in about 1690-91. John Thatcher was the eldest son and would have inherited his father's property: the cottage and tanhouse with the datestone commemorating his parents' marriage. Samuel Thatcher's occupation is not listed anywhere, but he too may well have been a tanner in the house by the stream.

The earliest reference of all that I have found to a tannery in Wedmore, is in 1640. Richard Thomas of Wedmore made his will on 16th December 1640, and died just three days later. His executors made a list of his belongings, to go with the will.[25] This inventory shows that he was a prosperous villager leaving £57 3s 4d, a considerable sum of money for those days. Among the usual household goods were listed 'rushes 20s' and 'leather fates [vats] and other things belonging to the trade of a tanner, £101'. Richard Thomas had two sons, John and Richard, but there is no mention of either of them continuing their father's trade in the village; by 1643 the family had gone from the parish. We cannot prove that Richard Thomas's tannery was on the same site as the Thatchers' and John Gardiner's, but it seems highly likely.

John Gardiner died in 1793,[26] but Grace Taviner was still making soap there after that date. Probably someone else took over and carried on the tanning side of the business. The tannery had finally ceased to work by about 1820 when Joseph Stickland the carpenter took over the property. After more than 180 years Wedmore brook could run a little sweeter down through the village, and the smell from the tanning process faded into a memory of the past.[27]

The Highbridge, Wedmore & Cheddar Light Railway

In 1899, about thirty years after 'railway mania' was at its height, two professional men decided to apply for an Order authorising a Light Railway from Highbridge to Wedmore and Cheddar.[28] This was to link up with the existing stations at both ends. At the Highbridge end the railway would connect with both the Great Western Railway line from Bristol to Exeter, and the Somerset & Dorset Railway from Burnham-on-Sea to Glastonbury. At the Cheddar end it would link with the G.W.R. line from Wells to Bristol. The steam engines were to have a maximum speed of 25 miles an hour, and five years were allowed for construction.

The two men behind the scheme were both local solicitors: Mr WG Burrough of Hill House, Wedmore and Mr JC Smith of the Manor House. Mr Smith did most of the paper work.

The proposed route started at Highbridge Station, and swung northeast then eastwards towards Mark and Blackford. The line was to run north of the two villages, parallel to but a quarter of a mile north of the main road. Approaching Wedmore, the route was supposed to turn northeast again across the top of Lascot Hill, and descend the steep hillside to cross

Local Industries and Transport 141

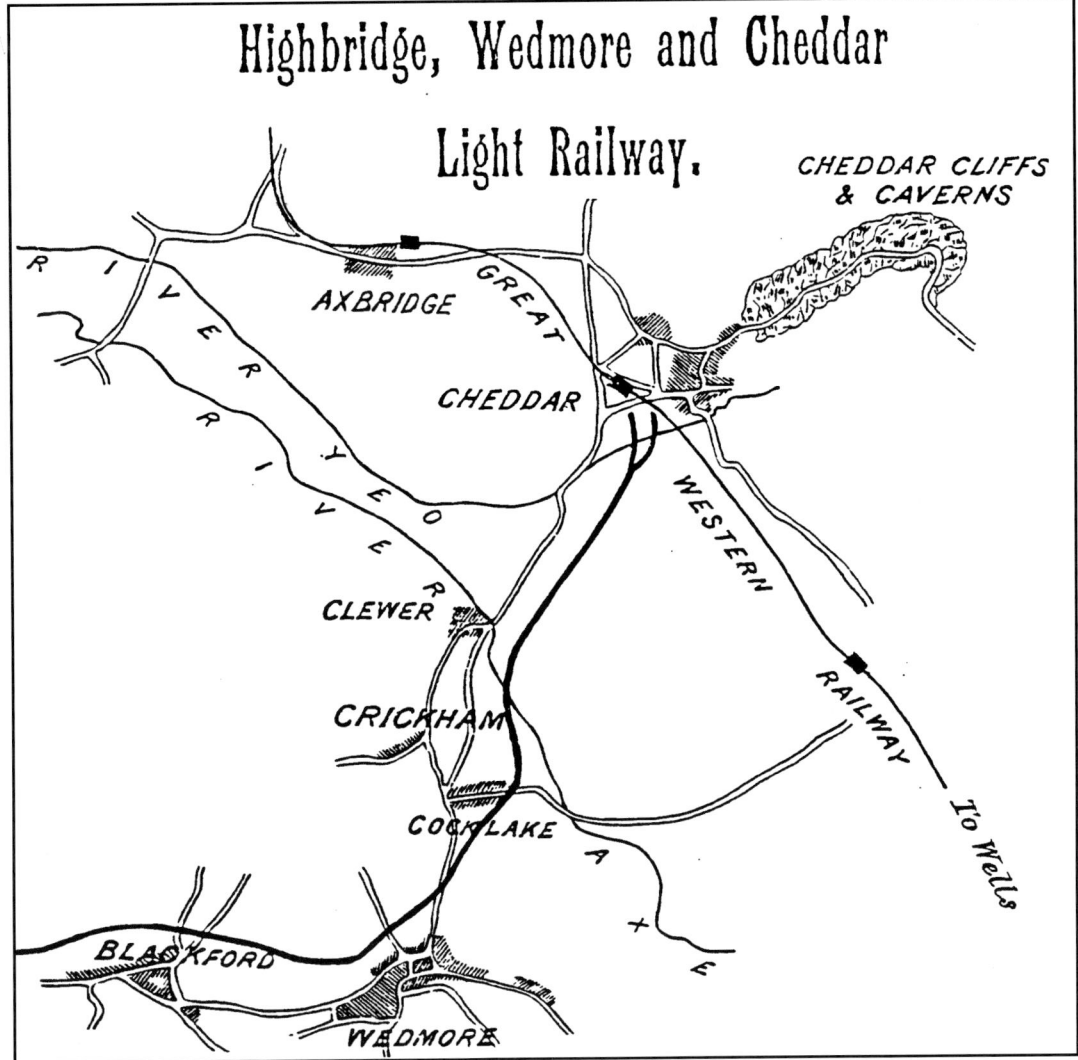

Map of the proposed Highbridge, Wedmore and Cheddar Light Railway, 1899

the road near the present cemetery. Passing just east of Cocklake and turning north, it ran parallel to the Clewer-Cheddar road, and a quarter of a mile east of it, to Cheddar Station.

The application was lodged in May 1899, and all the local parish councils and other interested bodies were informed for 'assent or dissent'.[29] They were only given one month in which to make their submissions, but discussions with local interested parties had, however, already taken place. The proposal seems to have been greeted with much enthusiasm. Farmers and growers would benefit greatly from the new line, which would provide an important link with the town markets and the wharves at Highbridge. The line would carry milk, cheese, fruit and vegetables more quickly and smoothly than the usual horse and cart.

In February, the Visitors of the Hospital of Hugh Sexey, who still owned most of Blackford, recorded in their minute book that they 'approved the construction of a Light Railway from

Highbridge to Wedmore and considered that it would be beneficial to their property and tenants.'[30] They would not however 'commit themselves further without seeing the plans'. In March Mr JC Smith met the Visitors and said that £500 was needed locally towards preliminary expenses of obtaining the Order. He was confident that the Order would be obtained, and said that 'Persons subscribing would be entitled to shares in the Company for the amount of their contribution. After looking at the map and on ascertaining as nearly as Mr Smith could point out the proposed route of the line, the Visitors unanimously arrived at the conclusion that it would not only be of advantage to the district generally but of decided benefit to their tenants.' They resolved to subscribe £50 towards the cost of obtaining the order, on the understanding that they would receive an equivalent amount in shares.

Concern about the proposed line came from the Somerset Drainage Commissioners, who were very worried about the many bridges which would be required over the rhines and the Rivers Axe and Yeo.[31] The bridges proposed were not considered sufficient. The Drainage Commissioners suggested that the bridges should be at least 4 feet, and some up to 12 feet, wide. They were also concerned that the construction of embankments might cause flooding. The engineer appointed for the line was Mr Russell, who defended his narrow bridges, stating that wider bridges were unnecessary, and that drainage would not be affected, as some rhines would be diverted.

The *London Gazette* July 1900 reported that an Order made by the Light Railway Company authorising the construction of a light railway in Somerset between Highbridge, Wedmore and Cheddar had been granted. However, at this point the whole idea foundered because insufficient funds had been raised, and the Great Western Railway did not offer any financial help. It is not just our age which has difficulty in raising money.

The project had not really been thought out carefully enough. The number of bridges and new rhines needed would have been vastly expensive. The idea of a great incline slanting down the steep side of the hill from Lascot to Cocklake is audacious but hardly practical, and the cost for such a small scheme would have been prohibitive. If this little railway had been built, it would have had a considerable impact on the area. Buildings and industry might have been attracted along its route. Of the light railways that were built, few survived very long, but even these have left permanent scars today. The area around Wedmore in particular would have looked very different.

Wedmore's first bus service

A 1905 photograph shows one of the first omnibuses in Wedmore.[32] The letters G.W.R. can be seen very faintly on the side of the bus. This clue led me to a long report printed in the *Weston Mercury & Somersetshire Herald* on Saturday April 8th 1905.

On Thursday 6th April 1905 'the inaugural trip of the motor omnibus service which the Great Western Railway are on Monday next initiating between Burnham and Cheddar' took place. The service was to link Burnham-on-Sea and Cheddar, after the scheme for building a light railway between the two had fallen through.

The route started at Cheddar Station, and went through Wedmore and Mark to Highbridge. There were to be four trips in each direction on weekdays. Three motor omnibuses built by

Messrs Clarkson Ltd of Chelmsford were used. They worked by steam power generated by paraffin, using one gallon per mile. The buses were '18 horse power at the road wheels, with 2½ inch Turner tyres on the front and 3½ inch on the back.' Luggage went on the roof, and there was room for 19 passengers. Each omnibus weighed 2 tons 5 hundredweight.

Special invitations were sent out for the inaugural trip by all three omnibuses, and the photographer for the day was CH Collard of Cheddar. Those present included superintendents, engineers and officials from the G.W.R. and prominent residents of the area. From Wedmore came WG Borough, solicitor, T Hawkins of the George Inn, JB Millard the Board School clerk, EH Smith, Headmaster of Sexey's School, and F Crease who ran a carrier service to Cheddar Station, together with residents of Mark and Burnham.

The three omnibuses were waiting to collect the passengers at Cheddar Station. The journey

> 'started at 12.40 to hearty cheers. The weather was of an ideal character and once fairly launched on the Wedmore road, the scenic panorama opened up well suggested the great vogue which the service will enjoy among pleasure makers apart from its more practical uses. The trip certainly gives one a full conception of the rugged grandeur of the Mendip scenery and the peaceful restivity of the lowland district .... En-route common flocks of sheep and other quadrupedal obstacles were encountered, but the Great Western Railway, unlike the ordinary motorists, discourage such frivolous delights as murdering mutton .... As Wedmore was reached and passing Glendale Farm [see below 'The Cheddar Cheese School'] the lady students therein acquiring the art of butter making .... threw dignity to the winds, rushing out in a mass of attractive femininity in equally attractive butcher blue overalls, for a closer view of the illustrious voyagers, alas, time and tide and the G.W.R. motor omnibus can wait for no man, and with a hurried hand wave to the blushing butter makers, the chapter of romance closed and the guests awoke to dull realisation of the fact that they were mostly middle aged and considerably married.
>
> At Wedmore school the youngsters lined the wall of the playground and delivered themselves of salvoes of cheers and later the main street was found to be crowded with spectators .... Someone wanted to see somebody in the George Hotel, and in order that he should not miss his way, most of the others went with him and emerged wiping their lips, a pleasing little 'extra turn' which (ordinary patrons of the omnibus please note) is not included in the ordinary service.'

Schoolchildren at Sexey's, Blackford, and Mark schools cheered them on their way. Spectators gathered, and bunting was hung out at various points.

> 'The journey was completed by the arrival at Burnham shortly after 2 pm and all sat down to luncheon in the Royal Clarence Hotel .... Toasts were proposed to the prosperity of Burnham and Highbridge, Cheddar and Wedmore'. Mr Kislingbury, the GWR superintendent from Bristol, said that 'Some few years ago application had been made .... to construct a light railway from Cheddar to Highbridge, a scheme which had the sympathy and support of the G.W.R inasmuch as they had felt it was a district entirely shut off from rail communication and they had then considered the scheme would be a success. As those present were aware, however, effect had never

*Inaugural trip of the G.W.R. steam omnibus, April 6th 1905.
A refreshment stop at the George Inn, Wedmore*

been given to the Order and for a variety of reasons, principally because money was scarce (laughter). Since that Order had been obtained, road-motors had come very prominently to the front .... The district was thoroughly well adapted for a motor road service and .... they were on the eve of introducing such a service.'

Mr WG Burrough, replying on behalf of residents in the district, 'thanked G.W.R. for having introduced the service. He and his partner had been interested in the earlier scheme for a Light Railway from Cheddar to Highbridge', but that was never carried out for lack of funds. 'Now however the G.W.R. was helping to open up the district' with this new bus service.

After many more speeches, the company climbed aboard the omnibuses again and returned to Cheddar.

The Wedmore Cheddar Cheese School

The newspaper report on the first omnibus to run from Cheddar to Highbridge (see above) gave a lyrical description of the encounter on 6th April 1905, with the 'blushing butter makers' of Glendale Farm on the Wedmore/Cheddar road. Glendale Farm at Cocklake was then owned by Mr W Porter; and the school, for making Cheddar cheese (not butter), had in fact only been opened three days earlier, on 3rd April.

A report in the *Weston Mercury & Somersetshire Herald* of March 18th 1905 gives a few details of the school. The farm premises were described as 'suitable and commodious'. There was provision at the farm itself for the comfortable lodging of students. Miss Emma Cannon of Evercreech, who had been thoroughly trained in cheese making by her parents, was appointed teacher. Her mother had won prizes valued at over £2000, an enormous sum of money in those days, for her fine cheeses. The school was set up on behalf of the Agricultural Instruction Committee of the Somerset County Council, by the Bath & West of England Agricultural Society. Students were to be 'thoroughly instructed in the use of the Acidimeter and in the keeping of complete records of each day's work.' These 'cheese schools' had been running since 1890, and were held in a different farm each year. The school ran for the cheese making season, from April to the end of October and the fees were 'moderate': £5 for the complete four-week course plus board and lodging. Some people came for a week or just for a few days, to practise the new and improved techniques.[33]

The Glendale school seems to have been a great success. The *Weston Mercury* of August 5th reported

> 'the first draft (nearly 31 hundredweight) of this year's cheese made during the month of April ... at Glendale Farm has been sold at 56 shillings per hundredweight. 3,701 gallons of milk made 3,655 pounds of green cheese, which when sold in the middle of July, weighed 3,453 pounds. The school has been well attended, 30 having already entered.'

The *Weston Mercury* report of September 2nd shows that the second draft was even better. 40 hundredweight was made during May which was sold at 62 shillings per hundredweight. 5,235 gallons of milk made 4,942 lbs of green cheese which when weighed showed a shrinkage of about 5½%. Thirty-three students had already entered, with applications still being received.

The school followed the methods laid down by Miss Edith J Cannon (later Mrs Sage), a relation of Miss Emma Cannon, who had published a small booklet in 1900 with FJ Lloyd FCS, FIC, entitled *The Manufacture of Cheddar Cheese*. This booklet was incorporated into the students' notebook in which they kept their daily record.[34]

At the end of 1905, the Somerset Agricultural Instruction Committee had decided to discontinue the cheese schools, run for it by the Bath & West & Southern Counties Society since 1888. The school at Glendale, however, re-opened on 3rd April 1906 as 'The Western Counties Cheese School', still with Miss Cannon in charge. The notebook of one student, Florence Hooper of Stowell Farm, near Sherborne, still survives.[35] It shows she attended from 4th August to 1st September 1906. The notebook is a printed diary with 39 points to be observed during the cheese making process. It includes such things as how many cows were milked, temperatures attained at various points during the process, amounts of rennet and salt used, the weight of the curd, etc. Space was also given for notes on the weather, taints in the milk and anything unusual. The teacher then added her comments. It was a very thorough and scientific approach to cheese making, using the Cannon family's proven method. The school seems to have been held intermittently for several subsequent years, at least up until 1910.

Cheese has been made for many hundreds of years and the type called Cheddar has become one of the most popular, probably because it travelled so well. It is now made all over the world. Its origins are lost in time. In 1586 Camden wrote that 'just under the Mendippe-hills, lies Cheddar, famous for the excellent and prodigious great Cheeses made there, some of which require more than a man's strength to set them on the table.'[36]

Daniel Defoe visited Cheddar in 1722 and saw the farmers working as an early co-operative to make cheese.

> 'The milk of all the town cows is brought together every day into a common room, where the persons appointed or trusted for the management measure every man's quantity, and set it down in a book; when the quantities are adjusted, the milk is put together, and every meal's milk makes one cheese, and no more; so that the cheese is bigger, or less, as the cows yield more, or less, milk. By this method the goodness of the cheese is preserved, and, without all dispute, it is the best cheese that England affords, if not that the whole world affords.'[37]

In 1722 Cheddar cheese sold for 6d to 8d a pound, while Cheshire sold for about 2d. The milk producers did not receive any money until the cheese had been sold. Cheddar cheese continued to be made in the farmhouses of the Cheddar Valley and beyond throughout the 19th century. The advent of the Cheese Schools must have given a great boost to the industry. What would the student cheese makers think today of our supermarkets stacked with so many varieties of cheese, and with Cheddar cheese from Canada and even New Zealand?

Chapter 11
Schools

Early Schools in Wedmore

A new era began in Wedmore in 1990 with the advent of a new school along the Blackford Road and the closing of the old familiar school building along the Cheddar Road. Those of us fortunate enough to have attended the old school, as did perhaps our parents and grandparents, felt a little sad at its closure.

We do not know when Wedmore had its very first school, but it was over 300 years ago. In 1692 on the 30th July, Thomas Stone of Wedmore was granted a licence 'to teach an English school in the parish of Wedmore'.[1] Thomas Stone (1635-1693) was a member of a well-to-do local family; he possibly lived in Lascot Hill. In 1680, aged 45, Thomas is described in a deed as Thomas Stone, scrivener: that is, a professional writer.[2] This was the age of 'fancy' writing, and Thomas was an expert in the art. His licence for an 'English School' meant a school which taught in English subjects such as writing, reading and accounting. It was for local boys to have practical training, perhaps boys who were not destined for University and who did not therefore require Latin or Greek which would have been taught at Grammar Schools.

The School was probably held in a house which stood near the west gate of the church. This house was church property, but the Stone family had some interest in it. For many years a rent of 2d a year was paid to the Stones out of the Church rate, for the use or part use of this house.[3] Thomas Stone died aged 58 in 1693, but the school seems to have continued, for in 1707 the Vestry paid 1s. 6d. 'for mending Schoolle house windows.'[4] On March 6th 1732 the same minutes record that 'We whose names etc. doth agree to give a School Master £4 a yeare to teach such Poor Peopels children as the Parish shall think proper and to be payed every quarter out of the Parish stock.' Signed, Wm. Sheppard, James Counsell Churchwardens and 12 others.[5]

On November 20th 1733 they decided to make life more comfortable for the pupils: 'We ... do consent and agree that there shall be a fier place made in the School house for the use of the Schollars'.[6] It may not, however, have been built, as another similar resolution was noted in 1761.

In 1711 Samuel Vigor of Falkland left 50 shillings a year in his will for the schooling and teaching of two poor children of the parish of Wedmore, and two poor children of Hemington (the parish east of Radstock in which Falkland is situated) for ever.[7] The money was to be raised from his lands in Wedmore. However, this money was not forthcoming. Legal action was taken in 1773 as later owners were not fulfilling the intention of the will.[8] It is not until 1775 that we find an entry in the church accounts, 'Paid the schoolmaster his salary for Lady Day £1 5s'.[9] This may have been the half of Samuel Vigor's bequest due to Wedmore. In 1781, 4 shillings is paid out for 'a fourm in the School'.[10]

Who were the pupils? Unfortunately only two scraps of paper survive.[11] One is a schoolmaster's bill. This gives the names of pupils on 15th September 1787: 'Barrot, Burnett,

Bodman (sick), Bisgrove, Creese, Drew, Hembury, Lader, Morgan (absent last week), Martin and Vowles' A quarter's salary was £1 6s 6d. The other paper, dated 1789, lists children's names 'att the school: Benjamen Court, John Banwell, John Carsley, Jeffery Burnett, Solomon Bunn, George Andrews, William Heggs, John Court, Edward Cole, William Vowles, John Parker, John Barnett, Henry Harvey, Isaac Martin, Richard Drew, Edward Tyley and John Bunn.' Some of these, it would seem, had attended for at least two years, since 1787.

In 1781 Joseph Chapman was appointed master for £5 a year.[12] He was succeeded by John Rickard in 1787.[13] Sometime after John Rickard came William Nicholls. On 28th March 1796 William Rickard son of John was appointed to take care of the parish school.[14] His salary on April 25th 1798 was £1 6s. 3d. a quarter for 'teaching 10 poor Boys to Read.'[15]

So had the past hundred years of schooling produced literate villagers? If we look at signatures on deeds and various documents we find that most local men could sign their names with confidence, and sometimes with style; so most of them could at least write.

Hannah More at Wedmore

A momentous year in Wedmore's history was 1798, with the coming of Hannah More and the establishment of a Sunday School for the poor. Many writers have described the varied facets and talents of this famous Somerset lady, from writer to philanthropist.[16] I shall concentrate on the bare bones of her involvement with Wedmore. My main source is *Mendip Annals*, the published diary of her sister Martha.[17]

In 1798 Hannah's acquaintance Mr Fry, a young Oxford cleric, visited Wedmore with some friends. Hannah's sister Martha wrote that he 'met with some striking exhibitions of ignorance ... They were very warm in their accounts of the populousness as well as the wickedness of the place - and urged us to take it in hand!'

Since 1784 Hannah and Martha had been running Sunday Schools for the poor in Cheddar and nearby Mendip villages. They considered Wedmore 'an impossibility' because of its distance from their home in Wrington and the cost, but 'overcome by the shocking and increasingly shocking accounts of their sins and ignorance', they broached the subject 'though with fear and trembling'.

Hannah More (1745-1833)

Mr Fry had visited many people including John Barrow of the Manor House, whose wife had declared a school to be 'a very wrong measure, the poor were where they ought to be and where they were placed by providence. They were intended by Him to be servants and slaves, it was pre-ordained they should be ignorant and it was a shame to alter the decrees of God.' John Barrow said that 'when they gamed or rioted in the churchyard on Sundays, he sometimes went and cursed and swore among them a little and as he was Overseer, they then dispersed, what did people wish for more?'

Hannah and Martha then visited Wedmore, and found the village 'immensely large with a prodigiously great church ... and in a state of great depravity'. Hannah wrote that the great opposition which they met in endeavouring to 'establish an institution for the religious instruction of these people would excite your astonishment'. However, many people 'were clamourous for the school'.

So on a summer morning Hannah, Martha and Mr Boake, rector of Brockley, arrived to take a service with the blessing of the curate William Eyre, 'our fast friend'. During the service much emphasis was put on the fact that the full cost of the school would be borne by Hannah. At the end 'the enemies of the cause shuffled off as quick as possible'. The remainder drew up in the middle of the church, declaring to Hannah their 'thankfulness for the intended scheme'. One old woman exclaimed 'now my grandchildren will be taught the way to God'.

A fortnight later during Sunday Service the clerk read out a paper requesting all those intended to oppose the school to meet Mr Barrow on Friday. Mr Drewitt, the preacher, immediately countered with 'parents and children to meet next Sunday at 9 o'clock as the school will be opened'. The result of Barrow's meeting was that although he used threats to induce men to sign against the school, all refused, even those who owed him large sums of money. One man 'on whose estate he had a considerable mortgage', Barrow, 'with all the impudence of considerable wealth, in vulgar language ordered him to sign'. His reply was - 'Mr Barrow, though I am much in your power, yet I am still a man,' and another declared 'I will never put my name against this school'. Barrow then 'vented his rage, in the most abusive language, upon the poor powerless curate, foaming with passion, and declaring that the day the school was opened would be the beginning of rebellion in England as had taken place in Ireland and France. On finding he did not succeed, he left the church and was pursued and hunted to his own house'.

The Sunday following saw the school opening in an orchard. Martha described them 'standing up to our ankles in weeds and grass. We taught in the afternoon dividing our time betwixt this orchard and a poor dark kitchen, or in a shed in the orchard'. No suitable house had been found, and John Barrow made sure the church was not used. After many months Hannah got a 'comfortable house ready' and built a large schoolroom.

Mr Harvon 'a very promising master' was appointed teacher and everything went well, '300 to 400 were under instruction'. In March 1799 Hannah and Martha 'began to be a little uneasy about Wedmore'. By the summer opposition from Barrow and friends had grown so much that 'a violent explosion took place'. Members of the Vestry drew up and signed a series of Resolutions, still in the Minute Book above all their signatures. This formed the basis of a petition to the new Dean of Wells, the Very Revd George W Lukin, citing among other things that 'the school erected by the Miss Mores is offensive to us'. They claimed it had no licence and was 'a meeting place for people not respectful to the regular ministry of the church'. The school also had the 'Doubtful if not Dangerous tendency of innovation'. They resolved to 'meet again upon the plan of a school' for poor youth at their own expense.[18]

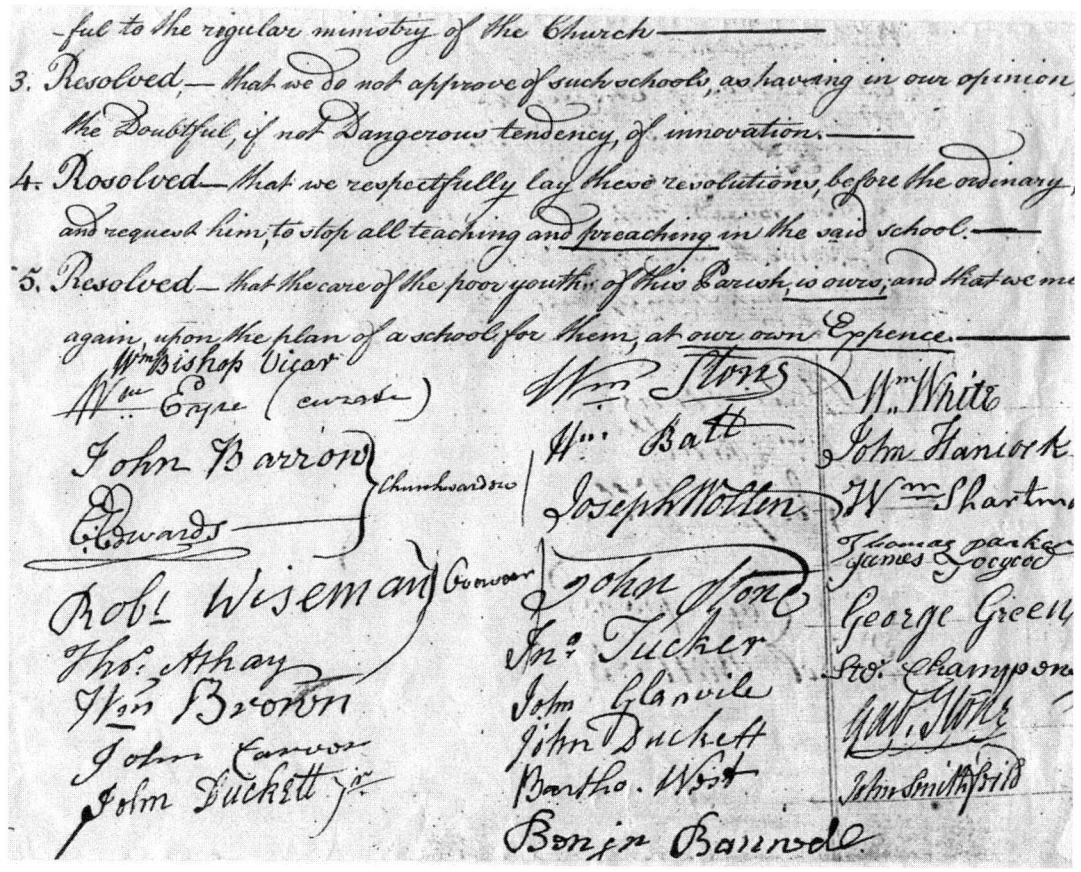

Part of the resolutions made at a Vestry Meeting 1799, opposing Hannah More's school in Wedmore, signed by John Barrow and church members. Wedmore Vestry Minutes

The Resolutions were signed by the Vicar, who lived in Bath and rarely visited Wedmore, and William Eyre the curate who it is clear had not been able to remain Hannah's 'fast friend' under such pressures. There are a further twenty five signatories headed by John Barrow himself, followed by William White the surveyor from Sand House, Joseph Wollen the lawyer from Wedmore Hall, and farmers including Benjamin Banwell, John Duckett and John Green many of whom were John Barrow's tenants.

Hannah wrote many letters to save her school and reputation, including one to the Bishop of Bath & Wells. She was found to have no case to answer, a licence was not needed any longer. The cause of the problem was Harvon the master, who was removed. He had been a local Methodist preacher in Bristol. Methodists were much hated and feared in Wedmore at this time; Hannah wrote, 'the parish would prefer a Mahomadon to a Methodist'.[19] Mrs Carol from Axbridge was appointed teacher and in 1800 Martha wrote 'Wedmore not as full as we could wish yet some appearance of improvement but the Parish depraved and shocking as ever'.[20] The Dean of Wells gave the school his support, and Hannah in 1801 wrote to her great friend William Wilberforce, who first encouraged Hannah to start her schools, that 'things look very smiling in Wedmore ... our persecutors have become our admirers'.[21]

The Sunday School started by Hannah More was in Pilcorn Street, but the actual building has not yet been identified. It has been suggested that it was Fernside; but this house is much older and does not fit with the description in Martha More's journal of 1798 that 'they were building a large schoolroom and getting a most comfortable house ready',[22] or with the fact that Hannah writes to a friend that 'I am building a house [at Wedmore]'.[23] Fernside, moreover, is known to have been the home of William Rickard, the schoolmaster appointed to teach the poor boys in 1798, and it is very unlikely that Hannah's teacher and William shared the same house![24] More probably, local memory of a teacher living at Fernside has been mixed up with Hannah's school somewhere nearby.

Hannah's Sunday School continued after 1801, when Martha's journal finishes. Sellick Sweet, who lived in Quab Lane, told the Revd S.H.A. Hervey in the 1880s that her eldest sister Sherah (born 1781) took over from Mrs Carrol as teacher.[25] Sellick herself (born 1800) went to the school, and remembered the Misses More very well. Sherah Sweet's family were one of the literate village families, and had been supplying parish clerks since the 1600s. I discovered that Sherah was one of my great-great-great-grandmothers, and William Rickard one of my great-great-great-grandfathers.

The writings of Hannah and Martha More give their side of the story of Wedmore's 'depravity'. Was it really so bad? There had been no resident vicar for twenty years, as he preferred to live in Bath. The parish was run by one poor curate who often could not cope. In my research I have discovered many couples unmarried, and many babies not baptised, a great disgrace in those days. There was no religious instruction, and communion was held just four times a year. Hannah taught the way to God, hoping this would cure all the economic ills of the poor. She taught reading, but rarely writing. The parish may have been depraved, but it was certainly not totally illiterate. The school for the poor boys had been run by the church for over a hundred years. Many dame schools catered for the slightly better-off, girls as well as boys, and the 'well-to-do' could afford private tutors.

In 1818, the Select Committee on Education of the Poor described three schools in Wedmore. There was 'a school in which 10 children are taught supported by £5 per annum allowed from parochial rates'. This is the village school for poor boys. Another school was 'annexed to the Bath and Wells diocesan school, usually attended by from 50 to 60 children'. The third was 'a weekly school containing from 30-40'. The report observed that 'A considerable number of the poorer classes have not sufficient means of educating their children'. One of these two latter schools was the survivor of Hannah's school. This school was held in 1818 in the upstairs room of what was called 'The old poorhouse' - the same building which had housed the first school of 1692.

The Revd William White (born 1793, and the first incumbent of the new Theale Church opened in 1828 - see chapter 13) was educated in one of the many dame schools, one run by Priscilla Latcham.[26] Another dame school, Mrs Sprake's, was held in a house in The Borough. Cross Farm now stands on the site. A sampler by Mary Harvey aged 14 shows that it was made in 'Mrs Sprakes School Wedmore. 1817'. Mrs Sprake was mother-in-law of William Rickard the schoolmaster. As with the Sweet family, literacy and concern for education ran in families. A dame school was also held in Bench House, Combe Batch, two more in Glanville Road, and another started in Cocklake in 1883. One in Eglantine House, Sand Road, cost 5d a week. Most of these dame schools were very short lived.

Some children had private tutors or a governess. A Miss Toomer taught John and Betsy Latcham of nearby Stone Allerton in 1828.[27] The bill survives to tell us that 20 weeks' education cost 7 shillings; 2 writing books and a catechism cost 1s, pens and ink 6d. In 1851 the Vicar of Wedmore, the Revd John Kempthorne, was also supplementing his income by boarding four little boys for private tuition.[28]

By the 1820s the main school was the Church or Free School. This was held in a building which once stood on the site of the village hall. It had been the old Methodist Chapel. A pupil remembered attending in 1827 when the pulpit and seats were still there; the master then was a Mr Newton.[29] The census of 1841 lists George Redman, Robert Turner, Martha Spencer and Elizabeth Stickland as schoolteachers in Wedmore. Elizabeth Stickland kept a school with 14 live-in pupils, ten girls and four boys. By 1851 the census lists 14 schoolteachers in Wedmore village alone.

With the passing of the Education Act of 1870 and the introduction of compulsory schooling in 1876, new Board Schools had to be provided in the parish. With the size of the parish, three schools were needed: Wedmore, Blackford and Bagley Close.

Early schools in Blackford and Theale

Schools were established in Blackford and Theale before the Board Schools were built. At the turn of the 18th century Mrs Mary Savidge lived in The Cedars at Blackford. She was the wealthy widow of William Savidge. Mary's family, the Counsells, were an old Wedmore family who owned much property in the parish. After William Savidge died and her daughter Anne was married to William White the surveyor of Sand House, Mary became a consid-

Blackford Old School, built 1832

erable local benefactor. One of her projects was to provide a school for Blackford.[30] Most of Blackford belonged to the Sexey's estate so free land was scarce. However, in 1817 a site was chosen on 'wasteland' alongside the brook, just below the Sexey's Arms. The little building still stands today, with slate roof and 'Regency windows', opposite Blackford church which was built in 1823. The cost of building the school was £193 18s 3d. Mary paid for the building. John Barrow her neighbour and friend was in charge of the project and was paid £5 5s for supervising it. The school was originally a Sunday School, but seemed later on to have become a day-school. On 14th April 1818, Mary Savidge paid a bill for 18 weeks' schooling for Jane Cridland at 3d a week, totalling 4s 6d. Jane was the daughter of her coachman. Apart from providing the school for Blackford, Mary also gave an annual subscription of £3 3s towards the free school at Wedmore. The plaques commemorating the little school built by Mary Savidge now hang in Blackford Village Hall.

No records survive to tell us who were the schoolteachers in Blackford in those early days. In the census of 1841 Joseph Pearce aged 35 is listed as the only schoolmaster in Blackford. In the 1851 census there were 40 children called 'scholars' with just two 'Sunday scholars'. The schoolmistress then was Ann Harvey, aged 37.

Theale also had its own school. Opposite Theale Church is the building now used as Theale Church Hall. This little brick building has an inscription and date on the gable end: 'Theale National School 1864'. A National School was a voluntary school connected with the National Society for Promoting the Education of the Poor in the Principles of the Established Church. We do not know who set up this school, but it was probably one of the worthy Vicars of Theale. Unfortunately, few documents survive to tell us much about the history of schooling in Theale. There was a school in 1841, when the census lists Mary Hooper as schoolmistress. By the 1851 census there are 47 scholars listed in Theale and Panborough. Sarah Summers, 40, is schoolmistress; John Haynes, 28, and his wife Sarah, 22, are school teachers. Ann Rickards, aged 18, from Mudgley, is listed as a schoolmistress; and at Mudgley and Bagley there are 29 children who are scholars, and 11 who are Sunday scholars. The new school built in 1864 may well have superseded an earlier school building on the same site, because in 1861 the census shows that Sarah Summers is living in 'Theale Parish School.' Robert and Ann Taylor, schoolteachers, are living at Bagley but no doubt teaching at Theale school.

Theale National School, built 1864

On Thursday 23rd June 1887 a vestry meeting was held in Theale Church and it was decided to build a new school in a more central part of the parish.[31] The existing Theale National School building had many times been condemned by H.M.Inspectors on account of want of room, difficulty in separating classes, and defective sanitation. The vestry minutes note that 'the smell with a south wind being reported so offensive that no windows on the south side could be opened.' Mr Champeney strongly advocated building a new school, and he proposed that the Wedmore School Board should carry out their suggestion and build a new school at Bagley on top of the hill between Bagley and Theale.[32]

Altogether three Board Schools were built in the parish and their history can be traced in some detail up to the end of the 1914-18 war.

Wedmore Board School

The site of the Wedmore Board School on the Cheddar Road was purchased for £106 in 1876.[33] The plans were drawn by Mr Spencer of Taunton, and the cheapest tender from Mr James Wensley was accepted. The cost of this stone, purpose-built school was £1,925, very cheap even for those days, and this included the adjoining headmaster's house. Wedmore Board School opened its doors to pupils on 6th January 1879. Much of our information about the Board Schools comes from the headmaster's logbooks.[34] School logbooks usually deal with changes in timetables, visits of managers, inadequacies of school staff and with the mundane everyday running of the school. We learn little of the schoolwork except for comments such as 'What is learned in Geography is quickly forgotten' (Wedmore 1902). Fortunately for Wedmore and Blackford, however, their headmasters included in the logbooks occasional snippets of information which give us details about local school life that we would not otherwise know.

Wedmore Board School, c1900

The first headmaster of Wedmore's school was Tomline Dungate. He had quite a task ahead of him. The school building was unfinished, and several windows were not fitted. As partitions separating the boys and girls classrooms were also missing, he decided to 'work the school as a mixed school'.

The first job was to put the children into classes. He writes in the school logbook, 'found them backward beyond all my powers of description, the majority (including girls of 12 or 13) never having held a pen or pencil in their hands before - did not know anything of figures, could not count and some hardly know the alphabet ... of 46 boys admitted only 6 have any knowledge of arithmetic'. The village schools, which through the 1840s-1870s had provided successfully for those who wanted education, would seem to have lost their effectiveness with the arrival of the new system. Those who did not wish to attend school now had to do so - with the results noted by the despairing headmaster. Parents were quite keen to send their sons to school, but girls and infants were often kept at home or else sent to 'some non-effective dame schools of which there are several in the neighbourhood'. Schooling was not free: each pupil paid 2d a week; if the parents could not afford 2d, the fees were paid by the School Board.

On 20th January 1880 the headmaster received complaints from the police that boys were throwing stones at the telegraph wires. Several boys were caned for this. Horses and passers-by were also bombarded - there was at this time no wall between the school and the road. On 19th April 1880 Albert E Puddy was punished for stone-throwing. The name caught my eye as I studied the logbook - for Albert was my grandfather!

By July Tomline Dungate had had enough. After a gap in the logbook, there is an entry in a different hand, saying he had 'absconded'. He seems to have disappeared overnight, and Samuel Price was appointed as headmaster.

Attendance at the school was often poor, especially if the weather was bad, because of course all the children walked to school, some coming several miles. On 9th March 1891 it began snowing. By 11th March the roads were impassable, and 'snow level with tops of hedges, men engaged today with opening the road from Wedmore to Cocklake.' The snow continued and the school was closed for nine weeks, which included the Easter holidays as well.

Wedmore Board School class, 1893

entered in the log, 'Keeping the school in such weather as we are now having is very trying, especially to the children; even whilst I write the ink freezes on pen.' On Saturday 9th February, 'The temperature yesterday morning at my desk from 9 to 12 was never higher than 28 degrees [c. -2° Centigrade]. We had no pen work whatever for our ink was frozen. In writing this entry before this I dipped my pen 4 times into the ink bottle held at the stove.' This entry is written in red ink and the effort of trying to write it can be clearly seen. Not surprisingly, only about forty of the usual 240 pupils were present!

Six boys were admitted from a Dr Barnado's Home in September 1889, and five more in October. The following February two ladies came from the home and 'made thorough examinations of each as to his physical state, his personal cleanliness etc. Edgar Frost and Fred White ordered home because of ringworm'. Presumably these boys were sent to the country for the good of their health, and were boarded out. Several also went to Blackford and Theale Board Schools. There is a sad little entry on 9th June 1890, 'Admitted Alfred Richardson from Dr Barnado's - the age of most of these children is not known'.

Wedmore School had its accustomed holidays for village events: the Oddfellows Fete, the Choral Festival, 'Wildbeast Shows' and once a 'Teetotal Demonstration'. On 8th August 1893, 150 children went on the Band of Hope outing to the Mendips. The most important village event was Wedmore Fair. Two fairs were held at this time, in July and September. The September one was a big cattle fair, and on one occasion the children were told 'not to be cruel to the cattle when helping the drovers'.

The children suffered the then common childhood illnesses. The school was closed for epidemics of measles, chickenpox, whooping cough, diphtheria and scarletina. In April 1897, Katie Stickland's father called and said that 'his two little girls were very delicate, and were generally unwell when they were not at school. The elder, Kate, talked of schoolwork in her sleep. He would like her to be treated leniently at school and not pressed onward. I promised she should work easily. I excuse her from our monthly exams'. Regular monthly exams were obviously an accepted feature of education in the 1890s. Delicate little Kate Stickland, whose home was Mendip View in Glanville Road, in fact lived to be 97; she died in 1984. All her siblings lived to a good age, and her youngest sister Mabel died in 1997 aged 98.

The school well was often contaminated, and fresh water was brought from Cocklake. A new well was sunk in 1893, as the headmaster writes, 'September 20th, well sinking apparatus borrowed by Sperring of Latcham'. This did not solve the problem entirely. The contamination seems to have come from the nearby lavatories. On 3rd March 1884 Bessie Clarke had her fingers caught in the lavatory door, and cut the tips off below the nails. She was immediately sent to Dr Tyley who lived nearby. On 25th March the four lavatory doors were taken down 'as they are a danger to the children and are not wanted'.

On March 1st 1900 a telegram was read to the school at 10.25 a.m. It said 'Ladysmith relieved'. The school was closed for the afternoon in celebration of the event. On May 24th a whole day's holiday was given on account of the Relief of Mafeking and Queen Victoria's 81st birthday. The Boer War had a considerable impact on the village, although South Africa was so far away. Wedmore was kept in touch with events by the family of the local chemist Mr Stanley Tomson. Mr Tomson's uncle was a reporter in South Africa, and sent telegrams hot from the war front to his family in St Ives, Buckinghamshire, and they immediately telegraphed the news on to Wedmore.

On 8th July 1901, 'Edith Price was given a wedding present, she has been here for 17½ years as pupil and assistant teacher'. Mr Price was writing about his own daughter. Edith married James Merriman, the assistant master who later became headmaster, first of Blackford and then back at Wedmore. Their wedding photograph survives, showing the wedding group and guests gathered in front of the school house.

The weather must have been very hot in September 1901, as on the 17th September Walter Larder, Edward Cook and Arthur Cope played truant and walked to the river Axe in the dinner hour and had a dip. 'Mr Cope caught his truant in the water and flogged him, Larder was caught later on by his father and flogged. Cook was flogged and sent to bed on reaching home'. It was quite a long walk from the school to the river Axe. After their punishment I doubt if the lads repeated their swim. It was usually the head who meted out punishments in the form of caning. On May 28th 1903, Edward Cook was again in trouble, this time with William Cotland. They were caught 'throwing stones at a cripple', and they received 'two strokes on each hand'.

The nasty illnesses of those days such as diphtheria took their toll of the pupils. 'The knell rang last evening [September 30th 1901] for Edith Puddy, who died at Bristol Hospital; she was in her seventh year.' Little Edith was my aunt. She died of diphtheria after her tracheotomy tube was removed by an inexperienced nurse.

Some events were given special holidays, such as the Coronations of 1902 and 1911; but any event was an excuse to miss school. Mr Price writes on the 10th April 1902 about the 'reopening of the Wesleyan Chapel [Wedmore] after restoration, this afternoon, has kept more than the usual number away this morning. Some habitually stay away.' The girls had a wonderful excuse for not attending in the morning, because of 'their hair being in curlers'.

December 18th 1902 was an emotional day for Mr Price. 'This afternoon the teachers and many of our children met at 2 p.m. unknown to me in the infants room. A messenger called Mrs Price and Myself from our house to come into the school to meet them. We found the room full … They formally said farewell to us and asked us to accept an armchair, a cushion and a pair of bellows' to mark 'a well-earned retirement from school life'. A few days later on December 27th at 7 p.m. a meeting was held in the Church Schoolroom (now the Village Hall) to say farewell to Mr and Mrs Price. Over a hundred people were present, and the Vicar, the Revd R May, made a farewell speech. They received gifts of a Russel Desk, a revolving chair, a brass inkstand with silver penholder, and an illuminated address bearing the names of the seventy-seven subscribers. On the same day Mr Price wrote in the logbook, 'Here I lay down my stewardship after 19 years work. Samuel Price. Headmaster'.

12th January 1903: 'I commenced duties as headmaster of this school today'. This comment in the logbook does not say who was writing it, but Thomas Henry Mitchell, former headmaster of Blackford School, had been appointed to the position. He was disturbed to find that 'there is insufficient of books, pens, blackboards and stationery for use in the school'.

For several years the water supply at the school was a problem. The new well which had been sunk in 1893 often ran dry, and so did the rainwater tank. Water had to be hauled in milk churns from Wedmore. Summers may have been warm and dry, but winters were very cold. In January 1907 the headmaster writes, 'It was impossible to do ordinary work in school: the boys have taken to sliding on a pond for 1½ hours each morning while the girls have been allowed to sit round the fires and teachers read to them.'

December 2nd 1907 was the day that 'Miss Merritt commenced her duties as assistant in charge of the infant class this morning.' The name 'Miss Merritt' still strikes terror into many of her former pupils. I can remember spending hours sewing long seams on a nightdress, only to have her rip it apart saying 'blown together, do it again!'. She spent 42 years of her teaching career in Wedmore School, and the last four at Blackford.

In 1909 cookery classes were started for the older girls. To begin with they were held in the infants' classroom. Blackford school girls came for cookery lessons one afternoon a week. Later, probably to save the disruption to infant classes, the cookery classes were moved to the Church Sunday Schoolroom, now the Village Hall.

To try and combat the irregular attendance of the pupils, the Board School managers of Wedmore introduced the idea of giving a half day's holiday a month if attendance reached 90%. This was achieved by Wedmore School on June 3rd 1909. A half day's extra holiday was much enjoyed by the pupils.

In the autumn of 1911 Mr Mitchell felt unwell. He wrote, 'The illness has now developed into nervous debility. I am ordered to go away immediately for a change of life and scene'. Mr Hoyle the assistant master was left in charge. Mr Mitchell returned after a fortnight, but was 'far from well'. The following June the doctor again ordered 'me to go to Harrogate at once for a course of the waters. I am hoping to be back in the course of a week or two.' It seems as if teachers have always suffered stress. Mr Mitchell returned, and as no more mention is made of his illness he seems to have recovered.

Pupils were often involved in accidents. Mercen Lukins was worthy of a special note as in November he returned to school after he 'had met with an accident with a traction engine'. From 1913 the health of pupils was taken more seriously, with medical inspections including eye tests. Spectacles were issued to several children. The dreaded school dentist arrived on the scene in 1914.

The First World War is hardly mentioned in the logbook, except to say that many children were staying away to help on the farms and with the harvest, 'as so many farm hands have volunteered' for active service. One curious entry in the school logbook for August 9th 1915 reads, 'The Belgians are leaving Wedmore and taking their children with them'. The Belgians were two families of refugees and were living in a house in Glanville Road, now called Whitegates. When they arrived all the village children came to stare at them and the village policeman P.C. Hansford came and made them go home.

Sadly, on May 23rd 1918 the headmaster Mr Mitchell died suddenly, and the school was closed for a week. Miss Merritt took charge of the school until the new headmaster was appointed on June 21st. This was Mr James Merriman, the former assistant master. The school carried on under his headmastership, and the logbook continued to mark the special events in the village. In July 1919 there were many belated 'Peace Celebrations being held in neighbouring villages, some children away'. Little change seems to have taken place with the change of headship. We leave the Wedmore School logbook with the comment of October 27th 1919 'Admitted child 6½, very backward, hitherto only attended a so-called private school'.

Theale and Bagley Close Board School

Wedmore and Blackford Board Schools (see below) had been purpose built, and both had opened in January 1879. The third of the Wedmore Board Schools had already opened on 1st July 1878. This was Theale Board School, for pupils up to the age of 14 years. In contrast to the other two new schools, it opened in the premises of the former National School opposite Theale Church.

Bagley Close Board School, c1900

The school logbook shows that George James Hitches commenced duties as Headmaster in 1878, with his wife as sewing mistress.[35] In the first week 36 children were admitted, and 20 more the following week. As at the other schools, the headmaster found the children very backward: 'quite one half of them do not know their letters. Some of these are over seven years old. Only one boy has ever done Compound Rules in Arithmetic. Only two more can do anything beyond simple addition'.

As soon as the children were enrolled they began staying away, working in 'the haymaking fields'. Throughout the years headmasters despair at the absenteeism. 'The children stay away from school on the most frivolous pretences. They come when they like and stop away when they think proper, no-one troubles whether they are at school or not'. However, the attendance officer was soon kept busy, and many parents were eventually fined for the non-attendance of their children. One cause of absence was the potato crop. The potato fields were in the Heath below Bagley. The children had to plant potatoes, hoe and then pick them. It must have been a very valuable crop to their parents, and probably worth a fine from the court for non-attendance at school.

On 7th August 1878 many children were away 'on account of the Anniversary of the Peace of Wedmore'. Unfortunately Theale children were not given a holiday for this special occasion. Theale School did not have so many holidays for events as the other two schools, perhaps because there were not so many things going on in Theale. They did have holidays for Sunday School trips, Panborough Club Day, Theale Harvest Festival, and for Wedmore Choral Festival because the teachers were singing in it.

On 7th April 1893 'Attendance was very small owing to a visit of a Menagerie to the neighbourhood'. Sensibly, the head gave a half-day's holiday and took the children to see this 'Wild Beast Show'. In October 1893 a circus passed by on its way to Wedmore; this again caused 'a great falling off in the attendance'. Again the remedy was simple: half a day's holiday, 'there being an afternoon performance'.

The first two headmasters at Theale did not keep such detailed records as those of Wedmore and Blackford. Often the entry 'usual routine' covers several weeks of school life. Only if the weather was very severe were any comments written, and the school seems to have stayed open when the other schools were closed. On 8th December 1882, 'weather very strong preventing children from attending school. Five came on Wednesday and Thursday'. On 11th November 1884, 'Pelting rain the whole day' and on 15th November, 'Only 84 present this morning. Several families in The Heath and at Blakeway having their homes flooded have been driven to the hills for shelter. The flood is the highest within the memory of the oldest inhabitant'. The moors were still flooded a week later.

Theale School had very many changes of staff, not always by choice. On 15th March 1880 the headmaster's wife Mrs Hitches, who was the sewing mistress, died. Just over a year later, on 15th June 1881, Mr Hitches died quite suddenly. Temporary staff took over; most suprisingly, Tomline Dungate - the former head of Wedmore School who had 'absconded' in July 1880, stood in as headmaster for a few days! In August 1881 Mr and Mrs Ryman were appointed as headmaster and sewing mistress respectively. They stayed until 1891 when Mr Ryman was asked by the school board to resign. No reason was given in the logbook. Standards in the school seem to have slipped, and there were problems with the staff and parents. On 1st December 1882 'George Wall father of two schoolchildren burnt their exercise and home lesson Books, refusing to allow them to learn any more lessons at home'. It was common practice in the school to give children homework, but clearly Mr Wall had had enough! In 1885 Miss Bancroft, an assistant mistress, asked for an afternoon off but refused to give a reason. When the headmaster said he would not let her go, she replied that she 'would tell the Board of the times I had been absent, staying out of school taking photographs etc.' It does not record if the blackmail worked.

On 29th April 1890 the logbook records 'Admitted 4 Dr Barnado's orphans, 3 of them over seven have never been to school before.' Three more boy orphans came later, and they all lived with farmers at Panborough and Theale. They stayed about three years and then returned to the 'Home in London'. Presumably the Dr Barnardo's boys attending Wedmore and Blackford schools also came from London. I hope they enjoyed the experience.

After the dismissal of Mr Ryman, John Vowles was appointed headmaster in August 1891. He found the school rather backward, especially in the infant department. For four years he struggled with an overcrowded school, smelly lavatories and constant absenteeism. On 3rd January 1895 his patience was rewarded with the opening of the new Board School built on the hilltop at Bagley - Bagley Close School. On that special day there was a free tea for the pupils at 3.30 p.m., followed by a public tea at 4.30 and a concert at 7.00 p.m. On 7th January the children 'assembled for work for the first time in the New School'.

Sadly just a month later Mr Vowles' youngest child died. There were other sad occasions to follow. On 9th October 1896 Amy Hellier the pupil teacher died from diphtheria, and on 21st September Stephen Hellier died from measles; we do not know if they were related. This outbreak of measles was very severe. It continued after the Christmas holidays and the school was closed on 19th February 1897 for three weeks while the epidemic raged. It was then followed by an outbreak of mumps. In 1898 Mr Vowles himself became very ill with pleurisy and pneumonia and was off work for five months. He returned in good health, to continue as head.

The year 1900 started off badly, with attendance down due to the surrounding moors being flooded, followed by heavy snow falls. There was again 'wretched attendance' on March 6th due to 'a Wild Beast Show in the neighbourhood'. Only 73 children were present out of the roll of 178. Previously half-day holidays had been given for this annual event, but during this year the extra holidays were saved for more important happenings. On May 26th a half-day was given for Queen Victoria's 81st birthday, and to celebrate the Relief of Mafeking. Wedmore School was given a whole day's holiday for these celebrations. Bagley children made up for it by playing truant and taking time off to visit a circus a few days later! By September Mr Vowles was despairing again over attendance, 'only 69% of children are at school'. There were so many more interesting things than school to go to. There was Theale Harvest Festival, then the Baptist Chapel School Treat; Godney Harvest, Wedmore Fair and Bridgwater Fair followed.

1901 dawned with heavy snow falling, and an epidemic of whooping cough. The school closed for a fortnight. Mr Vowles visited the homes and found 65 children suffering from whooping cough. Despite these setbacks, the school inspector found 'discipline good and the instruction thoroughly satisfactory', and the children 'kindly managed'. In June Mr Vowles took a couple of days off to consult a physician in London about the state of his health. He was suffering from 'phlebitis and thrombosis'.

On June 1st 1902, 'Peace was declared.' This was the proclamation bringing the Boer War to an end. June 26th and 27th were two days' holiday to celebrate the Coronation of King Edward VII. All the children were presented with Coronation medals generously given by Mr JC Smith of the Manor House, Wedmore. No school was held on August 27th, which was the day of Theale's Coronation festivities. The delay in the celebrations was because the Coronation itself had been postponed, the King having been taken suddenly and seriously ill with appendicitis.

A surprise visit was made by a school inspector in September. He suggested that the children should be interested in and 'acquainted with their surroundings, e.g. Glastonbury'. The timetable was amended accordingly. In 1905 Henry Amesbury was rewarded with an attendance certificate for his 'excellent attendance during the last five years'. He was the only pupil at any of the three Wedmore Board Schools reported to have received this honour.

Mr WG Burrough, the chairman of the managers of all three Board Schools, was married on February 7th 1907, and all the schools were given an extra day's holiday. This, the wedding of the year, took place in Wedmore Church. Mr Burrough married Lilian Pople, daughter of William Pople the village photographer and sister to Mrs Vowles.

During these years there were many changes of staff at Bagley. Mr Mitchelmore was appointed as assistant teacher in March 1907. However, he was soon called away to Devon as his father was very ill. On returning, he was taken so ill himself that he had to hand in his notice. While the school was thus short-staffed, Mr Vowles had to go to Bridgwater Hospital for an operation on 'a fistula'. He was away for a month, and Mr George Wright was employed as deputy head meanwhile to run the school. The deputy writes in the logbook on September 7th, 'Weather very oppressive. No physical drill taken owing to the heat'. He was also appalled at the state of the school toilets. These were earth toilets, and they were not being cleaned properly. I remember these toilets when I was at school there - they were not much better after the Second World War!

One member of staff, Mrs Cook, did stay for some time. She was given leave in May 1908, 'on account of the near approachment of her accouchment.' It was not usual to employ married women in those days, although the headmaster's wife often 'filled in' when necessary. Marriage was often the end of one's career. Mrs Cook, however, returned to the school on July 1st, but it is not recorded whether she had a baby boy or girl.

As in the other schools the boys had, for several years, been having gardening lessons. The gardens were regularly inspected. In September 1908 cookery classes were started for the older girls.

The winter of 1908-1909 was very cold. The classrooms were often only just above freezing, and it was too cold for the children to write, so oral lessons were given. No school was held on June 22nd 1909 as the Prince and Princess of Wales visited Wells. Unfortunately we do not know if any of the children went to Wells that day.

Mr SN Cock the school attendance officer came regularly once a fortnight to check on the absentees. On September 19th attendance was down again because of the Sunday School Treat at Tealham Chapel. This little tin chapel still survives, used now as a barn at Chapel Farm, Blakeway. Not all children wanted to miss school, and some were keen to learn new skills. In 1911 two girls were chosen to attend 'Milking lessons at Wedmore'. These milking classes were held by the County Council.

At the outbreak of the First World War in 1914, staffing again became difficult. Mr Barnett the assistant master left, 'having enlisted for foreign service'. During the year Ivy Freckingham began duties as a monitress. She will be very well remembered by generations of children at Wedmore School, where she taught for most of her career.

Although education had been compulsory for many years, children were still being admitted who had 'never been to school before', such as the three who came to Bagley in 1914 aged 9, 7 and 5 years. It was decided early in 1916 that 'during the period of war the school would commence work in the afternoon at 1.30 p.m. and cease work at 3.30 p.m.'. This was to make the most of the daylight. On January 28th the school was closed by order of the Medical Officer of Health, 'on account of measles'. This epidemic was very severe. The school was closed until March 6th, and even then less than half the pupils were well enough to attend.

A year later, on March 9th 1917, a blizzard prevented all but 20 pupils getting to school. On April 2nd heavy snow fell again, and only 36 were present. By May 1918 the headmaster himself was involved in the war effort. He attended military duty at Minehead, and Miss Merritt from Wedmore School came to assist during his absence. On September 9th children and teachers were engaged in picking blackberries. During September and October 18 half-days were spent picking. This, again, was on behalf of the war effort. Mr Vowles writes, however, that 'the unsettling effect of time off is becoming more and more apparent'. The school picked 3,303½ lbs of blackberries. The fruit was probably taken to the jam factory in The Borough, Wedmore, which was working day and night to produce jam for the troops. The school was closed again from November 8th until December 7th due to influenza. Little schoolwork was done during the latter part of 1918.

On June 2nd 1919 Mr Barnett resumed his duties 'on demobilisation from the army'. He was one of the fortunate young men to come through the war unscathed. He left on November 11th to go to Bristol University Training College.

In 1895 a separate house was built for the headmaster next to the school. This was bought by the last headmaster, Mr Horace Parfitt, and he and his wife continued to live there after the school closed in the 1970s.

Blackford Board School

Blackford Board School stands on a triangle of land between Hugh Sexey Middle School and The Sexey's Arms. This piece of land had been chopped off when the Wells and Highbridge turnpike road was pushed through in the 1840s.[36] In 1876 the tender for building Blackford School was given to Mr Wensley, the builder of Wedmore School.[37] The cost was £1,100, which included the Headmaster's house. Blackford School was opened in January 1879 and, sadly, closed in July 1976 with 79 primary children on the roll. Originally, like the other Board Schools, it was a mixed school for children up to the age of fourteen. The school logbook provides most of our information.[38] The school building, now converted into a house, still stands today, on its a piece of land just east of Sexey's School.

The headmaster Edward Arnold wrote in the school logbook on the first day, 7th January 1879, 'Attendance poor, because not generally known in the neighbourhood'. By the end of the next week, 26 pupils were enrolled. However, teaching was not going to be an easy task, as he wrote: 'most of the children unable to make out or point out a letter or a figure'. The weather was bitterly cold.

On 24th January, the headmaster noted that the children were very backward, particularly in writing and arithmetic'. By the end of the month 57 children were registered. In March an epidemic of diphtheria struck, and five children died including Amy Puddy, the young daughter of the landlord of The Sexey's Arms. Many parents kept their children home because of the infection. In August attendance was very good, and the children had a special treat - a tea party. Sadly, however, diphtheria struck again and Benjamin Francis died. The sanitary inspector came to check the drains, lavatories and water supply.

One of the problems in running the school was the constant absence of the children, not because they were playing truant but because their parents kept them away. The children were needed to help with the haymaking, picking potatoes, the harvest, and picking blackberries. On 24th October 1887 the headmaster wrote 'as cider making has become general in the neighbourhood, some of the children are away apple picking'. Boys were often punished for scrumping apples from adjoining orchards, and the children were warned of the evils of eating 'un-ripe apples'.

Children from the Heath rarely attended school. They were kept home to cut turf, and often the bad weather prevented them from coming to Blackford. During the 1880s-1890s, the winters were particularly severe. Snow fell almost every year. In January 1881 the school logbook records 'roads impassable on Wednesday to Friday on account of snowdrifts.' On 11th March, Blackford was 'entirely cut off from all the surrounding villages, the roads are all blocked, some drifts 10-12 feet'. When the snow thawed the moors flooded. The Heath children were often trapped for weeks in their houses. December 3rd, 1881: 'Children from the Heath cannot attend without rowing on account of the water'. The moors also flooded after heavy summer rain. The local weather recorded in the logbook is often fascinating. On 26th April 1894, 'There was a phenomenal hailstorm this morning, some of the stones measure 3 inches in circumference'.

Full and half-day holidays were constantly being given for such events as 'The Foresters' Fete', the Band of Hope trip, and 'Ginnetts Circus'. Blackford School was not usually given a holiday for Wedmore Fair, but the children went nonetheless! On 13th September 1892 many children went to see 'a novel wedding' at the church, 'the bride being 70 and the groom 83'. The Blackford marriage register records the marriage on that day of Charles Champeney, 83, widower and farmer, and Laura Redman, spinster, who was in fact only 68. Being so near to Blackford Church, the children would be drawn away from school by any wedding taking place there. The playtimes and dinner-hour were adjusted so that the children did not miss the ceremony.

Thomas H Mitchell became headmaster on 1st October 1885. After the first week he wrote in the logbook, 'We are without the following materials for school work, viz.: Chalk, Pencils, Copy Books, Pens, Ink, Foolscap, Arithmetic Books and Test Cards'. One wonders how they had managed without all these things, but of course most work was done on slates.

Quite often children would turn up to register for the first time well past the age of entry. These children caused a problem, as they were beyond the infant class age. However, when Edward Watts first came to school at the age of 12, 'having never been to school', the head entered him on the infant register. On 12th May 1890 '5 children called White' were admitted. They had previously attended a private school and the head found them 'extremely backward, the eldest, 14, hardly knowing the multiplication tables'. However, almost two years later he wrote: 'April 1st 1892. The White 5 bright intelligent children have gone to reside in America'. He was sorry to lose them; several other families emigrated at this time.

In November 1891 the School Board decided that to encourage regular attendance, rewards were to be given for the 'greatest regularity'. To raise money for these rewards a concert was given by the school children to their parents. The grand sum of £4 5s 0d was collected. On

13th May 1892 the Vice-chairman of the School Board, The Revd S.H.A. Hervey, Vicar of Wedmore, presented the prizes. The bribe had worked, for attendance greatly improved.

The children were always suffering from some illness: measles, mumps, scarletina and 'the itch' (scabies) were prevalent. In 1896 another diphtheria epidemic claimed the life of little Kate Hudson (no relation). Whilst the epidemics spread, the school was closed. Even the staff were prone to the usual ills. On 23rd September 1898 Mr Mitchell wrote that he was 'suffering from strain, insomnia and depression'. He was advised by the doctor 'to take a week or so at the seaside'. He found this of little use, and returned to work on 5th October, when he 'resumed duties, though still unwell'.

On 30th August 1897, when Blackford School reopened after the summer holiday, the head was concerned that 'a new Technical School' had opened at Stoughton and was drawing away some of his older pupils. This 'Technical School' was the start of Hugh Sexey Middle School at Blackford.

The year 1900 opened with Thomas H Mitchell still in charge of the school. The weather was very wet and the Heath was flooded again preventing the children who live there from attending school. Some did manage it whatever the weather, as they had the use of the flat-bottomed boats used by the peat diggers. Following the floods, heavy snow fell on February 14th, making it 'impossible to open the school today owing to the roads being blocked.' The snow melted within two days, causing more floods!

On March 1st, Mr Mitchell wrote 'In honour of the Relief of Ladysmith it is intended to give the children a holiday tomorrow'. This event was celebrated in all the board schools On March 7th the school inspector arrived. After he had given a fairly good report of the school, the headmaster decided on March 16th 'as it is the usual custom to give the school a holiday after the visit of the inspector, there will be no school this afternoon.' Mr Mitchell seems to have been a very good and patient teacher. He spent extra time on handwriting in the lower classes, 'helping the children acquire a running hand' - i.e. joined-up writing.

Events held in Blackford and neighbouring villages often kept children away from school. A special holiday was given on May 24th both for the Queen's birthday, and to celebrate the Relief of Mafeking. The 'Oddfellows fête' on June 13th drew many pupils away although the sports were rained off. When the sports were re-held a few days later, the children were away again. July was very hot and when the inspector called again he was pleased to note that 'In spite of about tropical heat ... vigorous good teaching is in progress and most satisfactory discipline prevails'. In September the School Board decided to nominate Saturday as 'Waif Saturday', when a collection would be made on behalf of Dr Barnado's Homes. The children 'received the idea with enthusiasm, and £2 0s 9d was raised'.

Few children were punished with the cane, but it was sometimes thought necessary. In October, Victor Norris received three strokes 'for insolence', and the following year Clifford Norris received 'several cuts' for insubordination and swearing. After repeated warnings about stealing apples, William Wall was punished 'by a cut on each hand from the cane'. In November many of the boys were 'away playing and did not hear the bell'; after repeating this offence several times, they were all given 'one cut on the hand'. They did not turn up late again.

In 1901 the school was closed for several weeks because of an epidemic of whooping cough. The school had children from 27 families ill with it in one week in January. One of the local doctors 'has forty cases in our school district'. An epidemic of mumps followed. It was not surprising, therefore, to find Mr Mitchell writing 'The children have forgotten a great deal ... we shall not be able to attempt any new work'.

In September 1902 Mr Mitchell was offered the headship of Wedmore Board School, which he accepted. He writes on December 15th, 'This is the last week I shall be in charge of this school'. On January 12 1903, James Merriman became headmaster. He had been assistant master of Wedmore. To prevent the constant absenteeism among the boys, Mr Merriman, a keen sportsman, hit upon a brilliant idea. He wrote in the school logbook, 'As a reward for good attendance in upper classes, the boys were taken to Mr Duckett's field for a football match very much enjoyed'. If the boys made '10 attendances' they were taken to play football each week after school, at 3.30 p.m. He notes that 'the attendance of the elder boys ... has been 100%'. They often played matches with Sexey's School, almost next door. Once the spring arrived, Mr Merriman introduced cricket practice after school; this was 'much enjoyed by the boys'.

On one of the inspector's regular visits, it was noted that 'Seats should be provided for the teachers, it is not fitting that a delicate female monitress should be without the means of resting herself for a moment'. The monitress was a young girl, just finished school herself, who helped the teachers and supervised some activities. She might or might not go on to train as a proper teacher. There were then 153 children on the school roll, ranging from 4 to 14 years old. High daily attendance (145 or more out of 153) was rewarded by school finishing an hour early.

Some children were taken away from school to go into service. Helen Dodd had been put into service in September 1903; but she was found to be under age, at 13 years old, so she was forced to return to school. In December 1903 a special Christmas Treat was arranged, 'A lantern entertainment was given to the children' and 'oranges were distributed.' This treat was continued for several Christmases. Wet weather continued to cause problems. In March 1904 the logbook entry states, '3 of the Heath children have now returned after a continuous absence of 6 months.' After years of overcrowding, a new schoolroom was finally built, and was in use by March 1907. The lavatories and playground were improved.

It was decided that secondary education should include gardening for boys, and cookery and dressmaking for girls. The garden started at Blackford by Mr Merriman in 1907 was a great success and at least an hour a week was spent gardening. The crops grown were entered in the Annual Wedmore Flower Show, and, of course, a day's holiday was given for this event. The school came away with several prizes, including first prizes in the open classes for marrows and onions. They won prizes in the show regularly thereafter.

Over the years the school logbook reports mainly on attendance figures, gardening progress and changes in the daily routine. The staff were always given time off to sing in the annual music festival in Wells Cathedral, and the school was closed for Blackford's Annual Cricket Festival - Mr Merriman being a very keen cricketer. March 7th 1911 saw electricity being put into the school, but there is no other comment to tell us whether the electric light was useful or not!

During the years of the First World War, 1914-1918, little comment was made on the national struggle. On June 7th 1916, there was no Bank Holiday 'because of the war'. There was a circular from the Board of Education in September 1917, as a result of which 'children commenced a collection of horse chestnuts'. It does not say what the conkers were to be used for, in the war effort, but probably as cattle feed.

On June 14th 1918, Mr Merriman learned that he had been appointed Headmaster of Wedmore School, in succession to Mr Mitchell, who had died suddenly. On July 19th, Mr Merriman writes in the logbook, 'This is the last day of the mastership of the Head Teacher, who concludes a period of 15½ years with a considerable amount of regret, as the time spent here has been very happy'.

The new headmaster, Mr Ernest H. Phillips, commenced his duties on August 26th 1918. During the blackberry season the school spent many days picking blackberries for the war effort. The children picked 1179 lbs. in three weeks. There is no mention of the end of the war, except that the children had been given an extra week's holiday during the summer, 'for Peace'; and on November 11th 1919 the headmaster writes, 'Armistice Day celebrated by the 2 minutes silence at 11 a.m'.

Hugh Sexey and Sexey's School, Blackford

Hugh Sexey Middle School, Blackford, is named after Hugh Sexey who lived over 370 years ago. The story of Hugh's link with the school is quite a long and dramatic tale.[39]

Hugh Sexey was born in Bruton about 1537 before baptismal records were kept. Very little is known of his early life; the traditional story that he started life as a shepherd boy or stable lad is probably just that, a story. He may have been one of the sons of Robert Sexey (1500-1587), a rich merchant and one time mayor of Bristol. Hugh attended school, King's School, Bruton. He later studied law and became an attorney in London. For thirty four years he was clerk to one of the seven Auditors of the Exchequer of Queen Elizabeth I. On 29th June 1599 he was appointed as an Auditor himself, and continued in this post under the Queen and her successor King James I, until he died in 1619.

During his lifetime Hugh amassed great wealth, mostly through lending money to the spendthrift sons of gentry, whom he charged 10% interest. He bought land and property in Bruton, and estates including six manors in Somerset. One of these, purchased in 1610, was the Manor of Blackford.

Hugh Sexey married Dorothy Uttley in 1583. It seems to have been a happy marriage, but sadly they had no children. They both decided to use their wealth to help others. Dorothy died in 1597; the charitable trust she founded still exists today. Hugh bought houses in Bruton to provide accommodation for poor men and women; pensions were provided for others, to give them a better life.[40]

Hugh's nearest blood relation was Anne, his cousin's daughter. Anne married Thomas Banckes, and they both lived with Hugh. Thomas became Hugh's clerk, managing the older man's affairs; and their son was Hugh's godson. It was understood that when Hugh died, Thomas and Anne would inherit something from his estate.

On 19th December 1611 Hugh Sexey, then well over 60, and very rich, suddenly married again. His second wife was Ursula Campernoun, of Montgomery in Wales, who was a step-daughter of Thomas Horner of Mells.[41] Just before they married Hugh gave her a share in the revenue from his Manor of Wanstrow. Before long Hugh realised that he had made a disastrous marriage and that Ursula was a gold digger just after his money. Hugh decided to disinherit Ursula except for her interest in Wanstrow. In 1617, he began to set up a charity and appoint trustees of his landed estates, so that after his death these estates 'should be employed to such charitable and good uses as the said trustees should appoint, and to settle the same accordingly'. His final wishes would be set out in his will.

Hugh's town house was in St Giles without Cripplegate, London, and it was here that Hugh died on 19th August 1619. The story of Hugh's last hours is vividly described in court cases brought by Anne and Thomas Banckes against Ursula in a dispute over Hugh's last will.[42]

As Hugh lay on his deathbed in the presence of his servants, the vicar and Thomas Banckes, Ursula suddenly arrived from the country. According to Thomas she immediately tried to make Hugh revoke his will, but he refused. She then asked Hugh's friend Sir Francis Goston, who was also present, to set something down in writing. They both 'stood at a window remote from the bed' and Francis began to write. However, when he realised that Hugh was very weak, he refused to proceed, saying that Hugh was not fit to make a will, and left. Ursula, undaunted, did not call upon any servant or clerk present to help her, but sent for 'some other instrument' to complete the will. About half an hour before Hugh's death she had the supposed will read to him, and, although Hugh was not by now able to understand what was going on, had him lifted up. She put a pen into his hand, guiding him to write 'two imperfect letters' H.S. under his supposed will. Ursula then put wax on the will, made an impression with the seal, and procured witnesses including Thomas. Thomas later admitted he was so 'overcome with sorrow' that he did not realise what he was signing. Hugh died within minutes of the will being signed.[43]

For several years after Hugh's death, Thomas Banckes tried to prove that this will was void, and that his family had been deprived of their rightful inheritance. Thomas swore that Ursula, having destroyed Hugh's earlier will, made this new one whilst Hugh was dying and when he did not understand what was going on. What did this controversial will say? Dated 19th August 1619, after the usual preliminaries about 'beinge weake in bodie but of sound memorie' (which last, according to Thomas, was far from true), the will is brief: 'I give to Thomas Banckes and Anne his wife my kinswoman one hundred and fortie pounds. I give to the rest of my kindred to be equally divided amongst them Five hundred pounds. I give to my cozen Georg Attley Five hundred pounds. I give to Martyn Prechard and Thomas Laud my clerk twentie pounds a peece. I give to the rest of my servants now dwellinge with me forty pounds to be equally divided amongst them. All the rest of my goods and chattles whatever I give to my deere wife Ursula Sexey, who I make my Executrix of this my last will and testament And doe also further give and appoint unto her my Mannor of Blackford, for and duringe her natural life.'

It is a very basic domestic will, not at all what one would have expected from a man of Hugh's earlier charitable actions and intentions. Thomas and Anne Banckes were left £140, which although quite a lot of money in those days was not what they had expected. Ursula came out of it as the wealthy widow, in charge as sole executrix, with property to the annual value of £1,000 and Lady of the prosperous Manor of Blackford for life. The Manor then consisted of more than fifty farmsteads, and about two thousand acres of land. Ursula was now extremely wealthy, and soon after Hugh's death she married Sir Gerard Sammes, knight.

Thomas lost his case and Ursula kept her money and lived for another fifteen years. Until she died little could be done about Hugh's charitable trust because there were no instructions in the will. Eventually the trustees, after talking to Hugh's friends, decided that it would have been his wish to continue the charitable works in Bruton. In 1632, therefore, they erected an Almshouse called The Hospital of Hugh Sexey. In 1638, almost twenty years after Hugh's death, the charity was finally 'incorporated' or formally established. One aim was to be the education and training of eighteen poor boys, of whom at least one was to come from Blackford. They were 'to be maintained, clothed and educated in reading, writing and arithmetic'.[44] At the age of 14 they were apprenticed for seven years, usually to the trade of a carpenter or blacksmith. John Harbett from Blackford was apprenticed in March 1663 to William Smart of Bruton, shoemaker, for seven years.[45] Schools were set up and financed in Bruton. In 1897 it was decided by the Trustees, or 'The Visitors of the Hospital of Hugh Sexey' as they were now called, to build a senior or secondary school in Blackford. It was the Blackford estate which had always provided the bulk of the money to keep the charity running, and this gesture acknowledged its importance while maintaining the link between the Sexey funds and education. The Visitors gave the site and buildings, and an endowment of £100.[46]

While the buildings were being erected, the school started in August 1897 in a barn belonging to The Cedars at Stoughton, which is now converted into the house called Highbury Barn. There were twelve pupils, seven boys and five girls. The headmaster, the Revd EH Smith and his wife lived at The Cedars, and Mrs Smith took charge of the domestic arrangements as a few of the children were boarders. Among the first pupils were Herman Cock, C.Comer, Ethel Champney Margaret and Mary Duckett, Francis Latcham, Grace Owen and Elsie Vowles.[47] Clifford Champeny was the first boy boarder.

Sexey's School, Blackford, 1899

Sexey's School was officially opened on 25th September 1899 by Sir Henry Roscoe FRS, one of the eminent scientists of the day.[48] There were about fifty seven pupils, with fourteen boarders who lived in the hostel which was the original house left on the site when the school was built. Distant pupils were taken to school by the Sexey's brake, a horse-drawn waggon. A photograph survives of Mr Wall of Blackford driving the Sexey's brake in about 1912.[49]

The original idea of the school was to train pupils not just academically, but also in domestic sciences and agriculture. An old farmhouse opposite the school in Wells Way was later acquired, to be the 'farm school'. Here pupils learnt skills in farming techniques, bee-keeping, cooking and suchlike.

The Farm School, 1913

The school eventually became Sexey's Grammar School, and then with the change to the comprehensive three-tier school system, Hugh Sexey Middle School. If Hugh Sexey could return today he would be amazed and no doubt very proud to see his name on the school board. The Sexey's estate still holds much of Blackford, and the income still goes towards the charity. Unfortunately there is no surviving document which records that Hugh Sexey ever actually visited Blackford himself. To him, it was probably just a good investment. As a young pupil at Sexey's Grammar School, I was regaled with tales of Hugh Sexey's ghost haunting what was then the boys' dormitory. Several pupils swore they had seen this Elizabethan gentleman. I am sure we can let Hugh's ghost rest happily in peace, knowing that without his great benefaction Blackford and its neighbourhood would have been a much poorer place, and many thousands of children would not have been educated in such pleasant surroundings.

Chapter 12
Chapels

Wedmore Methodist Chapel

Wedmore Methodist Chapel celebrated its 175th anniversary in 1992. There had been a Methodist congregation in the parish for well over 200 years.

In 1795 a chapel was built and granted a licence 'for the worship of God by a congregation of dissenters of the Methodist Denomination'.[1] Before the chapel was built, services were held in various private houses. The chapel was built on the site of the present village hall. The land was given by Abraham Dyer, a staunch member of the village Methodist congregation, and lay behind his shop and house, later rebuilt, and now Lloyds Chemist and the Minstrels Gallery (see Chapter 6).

There seems to have been much opposition to Methodism in Wedmore in its early years. When Hannah More came to start her school for poor children in 1798 there were objections to the schoolchildren singing Watt's *Hymns for Children*, as it was suggested that they were 'Methody'.[2] Hannah had to remove her first schoolteacher, Mr Harvon, as it was discovered that he had once been a Methodist local preacher in Bristol; there was such violent local opposition to him that the school was threatened with closure. 'Farmer Stone the Methody man' sent his children to Hannah's school; but, for the rest, Hannah wrote in a letter that 'the parish would prefer a Mahomadon to a Methodist'.[3]

Eventually this opposition died down. In 1799 there were thirty Methodists in Wedmore and by 1801 this had increased to three hundred.[4] With such a large congregation it was decided to build a new chapel on the Sand Road, which was opened in 1817. The old chapel was sold to the Church of England and it became the Free School. Pupils in the 1820s and 1830s remembered the pulpit and seats still being there.[5] The old chapel was knocked down in the 1870s to make way for the Church Schoolroom, now the Village Hall. Burials had been made in the graveyard of the old chapel, and some of these were removed to the new site. No records survive of the building costs of the new chapel in Sand Road, but we do know the names of some of those involved.[6] They included Abraham Dyer, Jeremiah Wall, George Millard, Joseph Stickland and John Tonkin. John Tonkin was a fervent Methodist from St Ives, Cornwall, who bought Abraham Dyer's business and eventually built what is now Lloyds Chemist and Minstrels Gallery on the site.

The chapel was built of brick and faced with local stone. Its hipped roof was tiled and the semi-circular windows filled with clear glass. The simple Georgian meeting-house exterior belies the exuberant interior, with its plaster ceiling of nine panels of rosettes and circles of flowers. The hexagonal pulpit and font at the east end face the gallery, which has wrought iron inserts and stands on two slender pillars. The charming chamber organ with its decorated pipes is contemporary with the building, and originally stood in the centre of the gallery.

In 1895 it was decided to build a Sunday School room adjoining the chapel. It was to cost about £175.[7] To help raise funds a bazaar was held. The *Wells Journal* of 13th June 1895 reported that

Wedmore Methodist Chapel, built 1817

'On Wednesday and Thursday a bazaar was held in the Church Schoolroom lent for the occasion by the Vicar [Revd S.H.A. Hervey] .... the bazaar was opened by Mrs Tonkin of Bath, and concerts were given each day. The bazaar was arranged in a novel and attractive manner as a series of prehistoric huts, and was very largely patronised.'

More money was raised by subscriptions. One novel method of attracting such subscriptions survives: I have a large red and white patchwork tablecloth embroidered with the words WEDMORE WESLEYAN BAZAAR JUNE 4th 1895 around the central block of squares. On each of the 165 patchwork squares is an embroidered signature. In places where a few stitches have worn away, it is possible to make out the faint pencil signature underneath. Unfortunately I have not been able to find any written record of this tablecloth; but I assume each signature was embroidered in recognition of a subscription to the building fund. Many of the signatures are of prominent local people, but by no means all of them are Methodists. They include the Revd S.H.A. Hervey, the Vicar; William G Burrough, solicitor of Hill House, Sand Road; William Owen and his family, all active Methodists, who had taken over Tonkin's shop at the bottom of Church Street; Samuel Price, headmaster of Wedmore Board School, and his wife and daughter; William Pople, the village photographer and newsagent, who was also the chapel organist and choirmaster; and many people from other villages.

According to Meeting Minutes, the profit from the bazaar was £116 14s 8d.[8] The accounts show that out of four craft stalls, each run by three Methodist ladies, the one organised by

Mrs W Owen, Mrs JB Millard and Mrs W Pople brought in £36 19s 6d, more than double any of the others. Mrs Owen's drapery and sewing department at the shop would have had facilities for working the names on the patchwork cloth. The patchwork squares themselves, moreover, are stiffened with cut-up pieces of old advertisements for William Owen's shop. From these clues, I surmise that it was Mrs Owen's stall that organised and displayed the embroidered cloth to such good financial effect, although I cannot find out how much each signatory had to contribute.

The Sunday School room attached to the east side of the chapel was designed by Edward Wall, architect, of South Bank in Grants Lane, and built by John Larder with Edward and George Stickland as carpenters. The building was opened on Friday April 10th 1896 at 3 p.m. by the Revd Walford Green. At 3.15 p.m. the Revd WD Walter, President of the Methodist Conference and elected head of the Methodist Church in England and Wales, preached. A public tea was held at 5 p.m., followed by a public meeting. About £108 was still outstanding, which included money for furnishings. It was hoped that this would be raised during the services on that day.[9]

In 1901 the chapel was restored.[10] A front porch was added, and the roof was partially slated to match the schoolroom. Floor boards were taken up, and a block floor put down. Pitched pine pews replaced the old benches. The organ was removed from the gallery to the north-east corner.

Mr JB Millard of Laurel Bank, Sand Road had lost one of his sons as a result of the Boer War. Private JC Millard, former bank clerk in Bampton, Devon, had gone out to South Africa with the 26th Company of Imperial Yeomanry but died of pleurisy in Johannesburg on 6th October 1901.[11] The Millard family gave £13 to have a coloured glass window in memory of their son, and the church members decided to fill the remaining windows with glass to match.[12] JC Millard's signature is on the 1895 cloth.

When the chapel came to celebrate its centenary in 1917, 'nothing was needed' for the Wedmore building. It was therefore decided to raise £100 to build a mission church where need was greatest.[13] At the centenary service on 6th June the £100 had been raised. The money was sent to India and a church was built in Kastur, a poor village near Mysore. The church building was also used as a school. Photographs of the substantial building and the villagers are still kept at the chapel. Later a small hospital was built, and a bore-hole and pump provided the drought-ridden village with pure clean water. Kastur church is still thriving, and they have built a leprosy centre there.[14] The enterprise and generosity of the Wedmore Methodists in 1917 expanded from their own village needs, to have a lasting effect on another community the other side of the world.

The Mission Chapels of Wedmore

At the end of the 19th century there were eleven churches and chapels in Wedmore parish. The parish church of St Mary's, Christ Church at Theale and Holy Trinity at Blackford served the Church of England members. The other eight nonconformist chapels belonged to various subsections of the Baptist and Wesleyan Methodist persuasion. Three of these chapels began as mission chapels. The story of their origins was published in the winter issue of the *Methodist Recorder* of 1905, a copy of which was discovered in an attic.

The article, entitled 'The Story of Tealham Heath. The Baker, the Blacksmith and the Peat Cutters', was written by Thomas H Rauns. It begins with these words,

> 'Can you conceive of a place in England where a clergyman or minister of religion has not been for six or eight years? If you try, you will probably suppose it to be in the heart of some of our great city slums ... or some wave beaten island ... it is but a dozen miles away from Weston-super-Mare in rural England. Tealham Heath is a part of the low-lying boggy plain of Somerset. Really it is in the parish of Wedmore, but it is five miles from the nearest church or place of worship'.

Thomas Rauns had visited the area and describes it:

> 'the roads stretched out for miles ... dykes on either side ... a few cottages dotted here and there and in some fields might be seen a few cattle, or, maybe a pig or two. The distinctive feature of the neighbourhood was the peat fields, where both men and women were at work. When the top earth has been removed', he continues, the peat 'is cut into slabs about nine inches square and four inches thick, these are placed in long rows on the bank of the trench which has been cut, and dried by wind and sun. Then they are stacked in big heaps which have the appearance of huge bee-hives, whence they are carted away as required'.

This formed the main livelihood for 'these dwellers on the Heath'.

Richard Drake baker, 1889

'Some five miles from Tealham Heath is the straggling village of Mark. The village baker is a man named Drake, a staunch and true son of the Wesleyan Church, a pious man and a devoted local preacher. As much may be said of James Cavil, the village blacksmith. These two men are the heroes of a most romantic, arduous and successful piece of Home Mission Work. Some sixteen years ago [i.e. 1889] Drake was driving his cart along ... when he noticed a group of rough turf diggers. At the sight of them his spirit was moved within him and jumping down from his cart, he stood on a stone and exhorted them to come to Jesus. His hearers were greatly wrought upon, and one of the roughest came to him and said in broadest Somerset, 'You do make Hoi roar' meaning that he had been moved to tears'. As Drake jumped into his cart to drive away, 'a chorus of voices requested him to come and speak to them again'.

Richard Drake and his friend James Cavil began their mission. They started holding meetings in a cottage on the Heath. After a while Richard Drake decided to find a more permanent place. 'He conceived the idea of getting a railway carriage in which to hold services'. He sent £5 to Swindon, and got what he wanted. The carriage duly arrived and was 'planted as

Chapels

a rock in a weary land' by the side of Blakeway, probably where its successor still stands today. The Blakeway causeway was the only raised ground which was reasonably safe from flooding. With an established meeting place or 'chapel', Drake decided to approach his Wesleyan Minister in Burnham-on-Sea. He walked into Burnham and asked the Revd James Goudie to help him in his work.

Soon the chapel was filled every Sunday with *'sixty people coming from far and near and the magnetic sound of the gospel ... some of the most notorious and depraved characters on the Heath were reached and claimed for the Master'.*

James Cavil, blacksmith, 1889

A Sunday School was started, followed by a Band of Hope. The railway carriage became a recognised chapel and was put into the Weston-super-Mare circuit. The Revd James Goudie was at this time third minister in the Weston-super-Mare circuit, but resided in Burnham. A circuit is a group of Wesleyan or Methodist churches under the care of a superintendent minister, assisted by other ministers and lay preachers.

The autumn of 1891 was very wet, rain fell day after day, and the moors flooded. Soon some of the little cottages were submerged and in others the residents moved upstairs 'using the windows as doors ... The only means of locomotion being by boat'. The poor peat diggers were suffering dreadfully and James

The Reverend James Goudie, 1889

Floods in Tealham Moor, 2000

Goudie wrote about their plight in the local paper. Soon money and gifts of clothing and food poured in. Richard Drake and the Revd James Goudie delivered the goods to the stranded people. They worked 'often to twelve at night ... in a flimsy punt'. They paddled from house to house handing in food and clothing. Most of the people were living in the single upstairs room. The work was dangerous in the flooded conditions, and Drake and Goudie had 'many a narrow escape ... in the darkness on the water'.

Turf worker's cottage, c1900

The Revd James Goudie published a report each week, in the Weston-super-Mare Gazette, of the help received and gifts distributed. When this came to the attention of the Vicar of Wedmore, the Revd S.H.A. Harvey, he was incensed. He wrote 'in great anger to know who this J Goudie was, who was interfering with things in his parish which did not belong to him'. The Revd James Goudie defended himself and the work, and 'the controversy ended disastrously for the Vicar, who was clearly shown to be acting only in a 'dog in the manger' spirit'(see Church v Chapel below).

When the flood subsided, Richard Drake and his friends thought about providing 'a more substantial structure than the railway carriage which had suffered considerably'. The Wesleyan Circuit erected at Blakeway a chapel of corrugated iron which they bought by mail order. In 1905 this chapel had a congregation of between 60 and 100 people, and a Sunday School of 40 children. Richard Drake and James Cavil had shown 'pity and ready sympathy' for another place - Heath House. There, part way up the hill, they erected another railway carriage. Every Sunday and on one day in the week they went to preach until this 'chapel' too was put onto the Wesleyan Circuit. In 1896 a brick chapel replaced th carriage. The foundation stone was laid by Richard Drake, and John Day on behalf of Mr Sidney Hill of Langford House. Mr Hill of Langford, near Churchill, was a Wesleyan and a great benefactor to the church. The chapel opened just two months later, on October 25th.

A third railway carriage was also bought for Bagley, but soon afterwards, in 1904, it was handed over to 'Baptist friends' as it was too far out of the circuit for the Wesleyans to manage. Worthington Cousins, a deacon from Wedmore Baptist Church, took charge of it and walked to Bagley each Sunday to take the Sunday School.[15]

Blakeway Methodist Chapel, which replaced the railway carriage. The chapel is now a barn.

What has happened to those chapels now? The corrugated iron chapel of 'Tealham Heath' is still there (2002), beside Blakeway. It closed many years ago and is now a barn. The brick chapel at Heath House was only closed in the 1990s and has been converted into a house. Bagley railway carriage continued in use as a Baptist Chapel until 1911, when it was removed to Worthington Cousins' farmyard in The Lerburne, Wedmore, and used as a store. A new 'tin tabernacle' or corrugated iron chapel replaced it. This arrived at Cheddar station and was carried to Bagley on a horse-drawn wagon. In 1966 the tin chapel was knocked down and the members themselves built a new chapel on the site, which is now being enlarged (2002).[16] Bagley Baptist Church is thriving today, a legacy of those missionaries from Mark in 1889.

Church v Chapel, 1891

The establishment of the Mission Chapels and the involvement of a non-conformist minister in the parish led to a confrontation between him and the Vicar of Wedmore. The occasion was caused by flooding of Tealham Heath in 1891. Local records rarely describe the social conditions in which the poor were living, but this confrontation gives vivid descriptions of their plight. The story begins in the autumn of 1891, which was the wettest for many years. Soon the low-lying land of Somerset was flooded. Roads, railways, houses and crops were under water. The local scene was described in the Weston-super-Mare Gazette of October 29th: 'standing on the Mudgley-hill near Wedmore, ... nearly the whole country thus viewed being under water'. The Revd James Goudie, the Wesleyan minister of Tealham and Heath

House chapels, saw the plight of his churchgoers and their neighbours, and decided to do something about it. However, the reaction he got from the Vicar of Wedmore, the Revd S.H.A. Hervey, was far from friendly; and for over two months controversy raged between more than fifty contributors to the letters page of the *Weston-super-Mare Gazette* and other papers.[17]

In October Revd James Goudie wrote a letter describing the terrible conditions of the moor peat diggers. Many had abandoned their houses or were living crowded together upstairs. The floods were the worst for about 30 years, and the people were in great distress. He wrote that people were always responding and sending money to foreign famines and floods, and was it not now more important to help 'the suffering poor who are at our very doors'. He mentioned that 'the Parish of Wedmore ought to show its practical interest', but that 'the present distress is more than any single agency will be able adequately to deal with'. Donations were to be sent to him through the *Gazette* office.

The Revd S.H.A. Hervey took strong exception to what he regarded as outside interference. His reaction was, perhaps, all the sharper through some feeling of embarassment that the situation should have been exposed publicly by someone from outside the parish, although he was not going to admit this. A man of outspoken views, and a staunch Liberal in a strongly Tory parish, he was used to controversy. In a letter published the following week, he objected strongly to subscriptions being asked for the relief of the people by

'a Mr Goudie of Burnham. *The duty of helping these people lies first upon their landlords and fellow parishioners. I have no doubt that these will be ready to help to do all they can, and if it needs to be done, then an appeal to the outside public may be made. Without a word of consultation, ... he* [Mr Goudie] *fires off a letter ... as if there is was nothing left of Wedmore above the water'.*

Hervey wrote that Mr Goudie

'*does not give a single fact or figure to show how much is needed, whether £10 or £1000. He does not even give any idea as to the number of people involved, whether 10 or 1,000. All this is a bit of meddling patronage which was not needed. ... we won't try to puff one denomination at the expense of another ... if we find it necessary to make an appeal ... we will make that appeal at the proper time'.*

It does seem rather odd that Hervey himself does not know how many people in his parish were flooded, and yet complains about outsiders 'meddling'!

The Revd S.H.A. Hervey, who was no fool, might have foreseen the incensed reactions which his letter understandably provoked. One correspondent, Mr Elthelred W Moon, wrote that he had lived in the area and, knowing the people, expressed his surprise and regret at Mr Hervey's letter. He saw no

'puffing one denomination at the expense of another'. Mr Hervey should have been 'thankful for such assistance. ... *What has been done by the landlords and fellow parishioners? ... apparently nothing ... According to Mr Hervey's theory these poor homeless and penniless individuals should wait until the floods subside and then see if they have anything left. But what are they to do in the meantime? Starve, I suppose'.*

Mr Moon urged people to take no notice of Mr Hervey's letter and said it was 'a pitiful exhibition of despicable jealousy, and certainly not becoming to the vicar of any parish'.

Mr Charles Watts, who lived on the Heath, wrote that he had 14 children, 8 still alive; he describes previous floods, and said that they had never had any help from landlords or farmers – 'we might just as well look for help to the North Pole'. One winter flood they were starving, and his pregnant wife 'hunted up some old newspapers and took them to the grocers … to buy us some bread'. This year he had lost 10 wagon loads of turf and all his potatoes 'are rotting'.

The Revd James Goudie wrote in response to Hervey's letter,
> 'It would appear that I have provoked him to anger by appealing to the public for aid on behalf of the poor of Tilham Heath without his knowledge or consent … The letter betrays an utter ignorance of the facts of the case .. he [Hervey] sets to bring our appeal, which was made in the kindest spirit, … into the heated atmosphere of sectarian bigotry and narrowness … I have according to your correspondent committed a grave offence by interfering on behalf of the poor residents in his parish. I am the curate in a Methodist parish, which is larger than the vicar's. It includes Tilham Heath, consequently I have duties to attend there .. I have had to wade through mud knee-deep and pass from door to door in a boat … I did wrong according to your correspondent in not consulting him … only yesterday I tried to administer a little comfort to a poor woman whom I found sitting in a hovel, destitute of furniture, pale and haggard with a child of tender years by her side – a mere skeleton clothed in rags. She told me that for three weeks they had existed almost solely on potatoes, and those had been begged from a neighbour and the good vicar stands by telling the public "to take no notice of our appeal as the time for helping has not yet come".'

The Revd James Goudie objected to the inference that he was 'puffing his denomination'. He said that he just pleaded the case of over 30 families 'irrespective of creeds or churches'. Then follows a list of subscribers to the fund which had now reached £23 13s 0d. Much more was to follow. Many shops gave food including sides of bacon, and tinned meat and peas, while many people sent parcels of clothing.

There were a couple of letters supporting the Revd S.H.A. Hervey, although both wrote under pseudonyms, and neither seems very sure of the district they are writing about. One states that there were only 6 cottages under water, when at least 30-40 families were flooded out. Hervey's letter had provoked a response from a national paper called *Truth*, which was edited by an MP, Mr Labouchere. In this paper, Hervey was condemned for his 'depreciation of the appeal of a Dissenting minister for help for the sufferers by the flood'. The editor commented that 'Mr Hervey was so ill-advised to write this letter'.

On November 25th Hervey wrote again to the *Gazette*. The letter begins with an attempt at an apology to Goudie, but soon changes into accusations that he is still meddling, not because he was a Wesleyan, but because he was an outsider interfering within Hervey's parish. Hervey said that if the Wedmore Wesleyans 'had started the matter he would have been ready to join them in it'. He wrote another letter accusing 'busybodies at Weston who write arrogantly upon a matter that they know nothing at all about' – although several of the letters were actually from his own parish church members. Hervey's two letters caused

Goudie to write yet another very long letter, patiently explaining that he was within his rights to take action as

> 'Tealham Moor was within his Wesleyan circuit, and that he [Hervey] does not seem able to grasp the fact that Methodist circuits extend sometimes over an area of ten miles, and I am morally bound to advance the moral welfare of the people in this circuit'.

During early December Wedmore had been shamed into calling a public meeting about the flood victims. The Revd S.H.A. Hervey presided, and a committee was set up which consisted of the Vicar of Theale and members of the Baptist and Methodist Churches of Wedmore. Hervey had already been sent £160 to help in the relief, so clearly something had been done at last. People as far away as Cardiff had contributed. This meeting was reported in the *Bridgwater Mercury*, but not in the *Weston-super-Mare Gazette*, which on December 8th received another letter from Hervey:

> Sir -
> In your last issue you state that the Vicar will be pleased to receive any donations etc. I write to say that the officious person who told you that was not asked nor authorised to say anything of the kind.
>
> Yours truly
> Sydenham H. A. Hervey

By Christmas the controversy seemed to be over. The floods had subsided, and hopefully the poor of Tealham had received money, food and clothing and could start to rebuild their lives again – until the next flood. People in the main part of Wedmore probably never again ignored the plight of the folk on the moor during flood times, although one correspondent's attitude was that 'they will insist on living there'.

The Revd James Goudie's descriptions of the suffering of the people bring vividly to life the darker side of local society in the late 19th century, on our doorstep. It is not often that documents give such an insight into the conditions in which some of our forebears lived, not so long ago. One is particularly touched by the account of an old woman of over 70 who was

> 'a victim of leprosy, who had only one set of clothes and when these were wet she had to take them off and try to dry them by a fire while she sat shivering in the cold with an old blanket wrapped round her'

while nearby another family was described as living in abject poverty:

> 'the mother of a large family [was] sitting in a hovel of the meanest description, the water was still washing up to the door; the poor woman is advanced in consumption. The damp walls were reeking with filthy fumes, and there she sat, pale and worn, only able to speak to us in a whisper. On the other side of the smouldering turf on the hearth sat her three little boys on a bench, their bodies clothed in rags. A daughter was preparing dinner by cutting the sound pieces from potatoes. This was the only fare at the command of the sick woman and her family'.

This is why James Goudie pleaded for help as he said, 'Instead of going abroad with our charity, shall we not keep it at home?'

CHAPTER 13
People

Jeremy Horler and Ann Hodges – a Civil War love story?

In the chancel of Wedmore Church are two memorials, mute reminders of an intriguing story of three people. On the wall at the north side of the chancel steps is a memorial of inscribed slate, with a decorative stone surround, ornamented with hourglasses, skulls and coffins as reminders of mortality. It is an exuberant piece of 17th century design, once coloured; traces of paint still remain. Below the coat-of-arms of the Hodges family, and three naive winged angels' heads, is the following inscription:

> Near to this Place
> Rest ye Bodies of George
> Hodges Esq, & Ann his
> wife, since the wife of
> Jeremy Horler Clerk in
> hope of a joyful Resurrection
> Christus Nobis vita
> Mori Lucrum

On the floor of the chancel just below this memorial is another more sophisticated incised lias memorial slab to George Hodges and Ann. They are buried beneath this stone, which although much worn gives more details about them.

> To the memory of George Hodges Esq. who deceased the [illegible] day of February and in the 43 yeare of his age an. domini 1654. To the memory of Ann ye wife of Jeremy Horler, clerk, formerly the wife of George Hodges Esq. abovesaid who deceased the 26th July 1684. In the same grave lyeth Mary [their eldest daughter and co-heiress who was first married to Henry Wogan of Weston in Pembrokeshire Esq. and afterwards to Edmund Clerk of Falstone in Wilts. Esq. whose widow she dyed] May 24 1709 aged 68.

The words in square brackets are now too worn to read, and have been supplied from a copy made by the Revd S.H.A. Hervey in the last century.

Who were George and Ann Hodges - and who was Jeremy Horler, the third name on the memorials?

The Hodges memorial, St Mary's, Wedmore

George Hodges, born 1611, was the Lord of the Manor of Wedmore. His family had been living in the manor house since the mid-1500s. He married Ann Mansell of Monmouthshire about 1640. George was then about 30, but Ann may have been only 16 years old. They had two daughters, Mary born 1641 and Jane born 1643.

George died aged 43 in February 1655 (still 1654 by old-style dating), and was buried on 7th March. As Lord of the Manor, he was responsible for repairs to the chancel of the parish church, and this is why he was buried there. Within three months, on 17th May 1655, his widow Ann married Jeremy Horler. Jeremy Horler was the Vicar of Wedmore, who had only been appointed shortly before. Church organisation in England during the Commonwealth (1649-1660) was in a muddle. The victory of Oliver Cromwell and the Parliamentarians in the Civil War meant that great changes had taken place. Instead of having christenings and weddings in the parish church, lay registrars recorded births, deaths and marriage contracts. Couples intending to get married had to have their names published on three consecutive 'Lord's Days' (the Puritans did not approve of the name 'Sunday'), either in the church or in the local market place. The marriage ceremony was then performed not by the vicar but by a Justice of the Peace.

When Jeremy Horler married Ann Hodges, however, the name of the person who performed the ceremony is left blank. The Wedmore parish registrar, John Petheram, recorded the three announcements, 'April 22, 29, May 6, Betwene Mr Jerimy Horler & Mrs Anne Hodges, both of this parish: and were married May 7 before [blank]', adding a further touch of mystery to the occasion. This abrupt marriage of the newly-widowed Lady of the Manor and the new young vicar must have set the tongues wagging in Wedmore. One can imagine the gossip: 'hardly cold in his grave', 'he's after her money' , and so on. Jeremy and Ann were about the same age, Jeremy being thirty and Ann perhaps a little older. Ann's two daughters Mary and Jane were fourteen and twelve respectively.

The circumstances and timing of this marriage, and the Horlers' later life until Ann reappears in Wedmore, buried beside her first husband, have hitherto remained something of a mystery. The Revd S.A.H. Hervey speculated that Horler might have been a Puritan with Baptist leanings, but there is no evidence for this.[1] I have now discovered that, shortly after the Restoration of King Charles II in 1660, Jeremy Horler completed his qualifications (probably interrupted by the Civil War) by gaining an MA at Oxford - the Royalist stronghold - on 6th December 1660.[2] Far from being a Baptist and puritan, this timing might well suggest he was a supporter of the established church and the restored monarchy. He was, almost immediately, appointed Rector of Yate in south Gloucestershire. The family moved from Wedmore to Yate in 1660. Mary, the eldest daughter, had meanwhile married Henry Wogan in 1658. When Henry died in 1661 Mary, then twenty years old, went back to live with Jeremy, Ann and Jane at Yate until her second marriage to Edmund Clarke in 1665.

Jane Hodges 'of Yate', the younger daughter, married John Strachey of Sutton Court near Chew Magna in 1662, when she was nineteen. John Strachey was a landed gentleman of some learning, and Jane herself seems to have been a bright, intelligent girl who could well have been taught by her stepfather Jeremy Horler. He certainly helped Jane to run the Hodges and Strachey estates, including the Manor of Wedmore, when she was suddenly widowed in 1674 at the age of thirty. Jeremy Horler's name occurs on several of her family deeds and documents. He seems to have been a caring stepfather to his stepdaughters who both made Yate their home.[3]

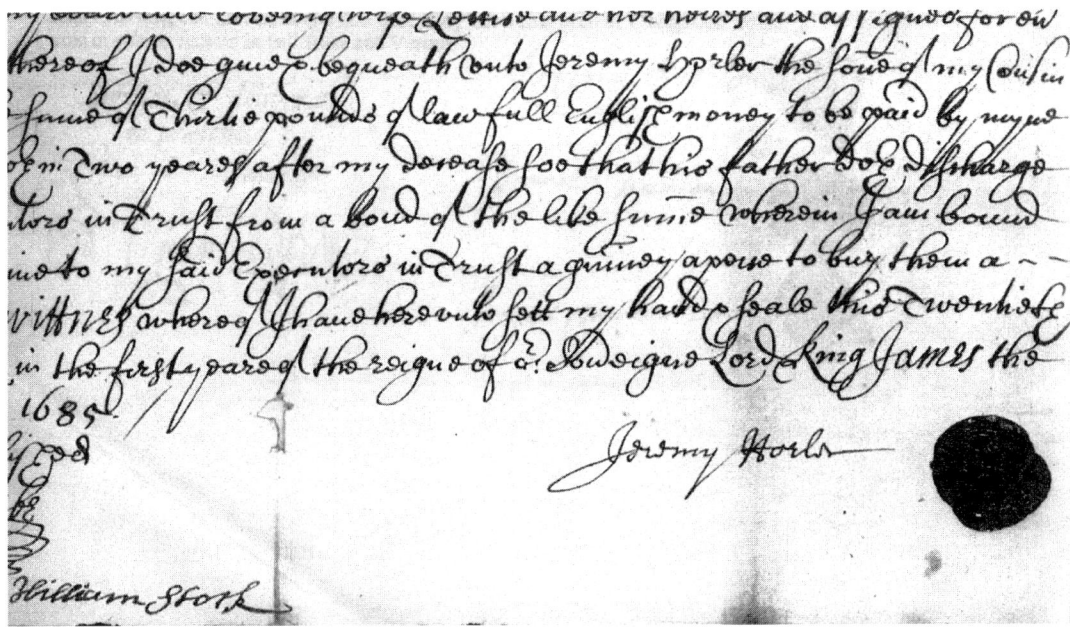

Signature of Jeremy Horler, 1685

Ann Horler died in July 1684. Her body was brought back to Wedmore and interred in the Hodges family tomb in the chancel of the church. Daughter Jane inherited the whole of the Wedmore estate after the death of her sister Mary in 1709. Jeremy Horler stayed in Yate and within three months of Ann's death married a young widow called Letitia Trewman from nearby Westerleigh in Gloucestershire.[4] Just over a year later Jeremy too died. There is a brass plaque in Yate church to 'Jeremiae Horler A.M. hujus Ecclesiae'. It records that he had been rector for twenty six years, and died at the age of sixty in 1685.

There is a postscript to this story. Jeremy made his will on 20th November 1685 when he knew he did not have long to live. He left his estate to 'my deare and loveing wife Lettice' and to 'my child with whome my wife is now great'.[5] Sadly, Jeremy died on 3rd December 1685, before his child, a son, was born. This boy was called Jeremy after his father. He matriculated from Oxford in 1702 aged 15, gained his BA in 1706 and his MA in 1709.[6] Jeremy Horler junior subsequently became Rector of Little Sodbury, not far from Yate, in 1717.

The two memorials to George, Ann and Jeremy in Wedmore church hide a complicated story of relationships in the aftermath of the Civil War. Was it a story of passionate love between the manor house and the church? Only Ann and Jeremy could tell us - the memorials remain silent.

Wedmore and the Monmouth Rebellion, 1685

The Monmouth Rebellion of 1685 was such a momentous event in Somerset that stories of the exploits of the rebels were still being told two hundred years later.

On 11th June 1685 the Duke of Monmouth landed at Lyme Bay, Dorset with a party of just 80 men. James, Duke of Monmouth was Charles II's illegitimate but favourite son. Charles II died on 6th February, 1685, to be succeeded by his brother James II who was a Roman Catholic. The Protestant James, Duke of Monmouth retreated to exile in Holland, but was encouraged to lay claim to the English throne.

Men flocked from all corners of the west country to join Monmouth, and soon an army of four regiments was formed. The number of men who took part in the final battle against James II's professional troops at Sedgemoor on 6th July 1685 will never be known, but estimates vary betwen 3,200 and 7,000.[7] This huge support for the cause was probably why the government reacted with such savagery against the rebels they caught. It also explains why so many men were reported to be 'at large' or 'not taken', having disappeared into a countryside prepared to shelter them. Wedmore, like many other Somerset villages, developed its own folklore around the Monmouth Rebellion and the terrible Judge Jeffreys; what, if any, truth is there behind these stories?

We have two sources for our Monmouth stories: Charles Pooley's book on Somerset Crosses, published 1870, and the Revd S.H.A.Hervey's *The Wedmore Chronicle*, 1881-1898. Pooley had been told a story about Wedmore Churchyard Cross, that 'the cross was erected to the memory of the victims who fell under Judge Jeffreys' displeasure'. This was because of the engraving on the cross 'John Gray and James Brown C.W. 1700'. The cross, as Pooley points out, is at least 250 years older than this inscription. John Gray and James Brown were the churchwardens ('C.W.') in 1700, and the inscription has nothing to do with the Monmouth Rebellion.

Pooley then writes
> '*The Village Cross* [market cross] *stands in the small garden in front of the house which tradition has marked as that in which Jeffreys lodged. It was on this Cross, when it stood in the village by the shambles, that he is said to have hanged a doctor because he helped dress the wounds of a dying Puritan.*'

Cross Farm (1880) now stands on the site of the house in which Judge Jeffreys was supposed to have lodged. We know exactly where and when Judge Jeffreys held his Assize courts, and there is no record of any visit to Wedmore. Looking at the cross today it seems impossible to hang anyone from it. It might originally have had a surround like that at Cheddar, from which one might contrive to hang someone, but there is no evidence for this. We do know, however, that after hanging in the Assize towns, the traitors were disembowelled and quartered. The gruesome remains, tarred to preserve them, were sent around the rebel villages of the area for public display, as a lesson to the local inhabitants. It would have been perfectly possible to suspend a part of these grisly remains of a rebel from the Wedmore cross. This brutal lesson was so burnt into local memory that it is easy to understand how such an exhibit might, in time, be remembered as a local rebel physically executed there. Only a little more imagination was needed to see Judge Jeffreys, who certainly gloated over his victims at the Assize courts, as the bogey-man leaning out of a nearby window to watch the proceedings in Wedmore.

There are in fact no records of rebels from Wedmore being hung, but there was a village doctor caught as a rebel. His name was Robert Thatcher and he is described as 'Chirurgeon [surgeon] of Wedmore'.[8] He was tried at Wells, and the court records show that he was 'remaining in custody' at the end of that Assize. This entry is deleted, and Robert's name added in another hand to the list of those to be executed for high treason. A document in the Public Record Office shows that Robert Thatcher was executed for treating Colonel John Bovett.[9] Robert Thatcher's land was therefore forfeit and put up for sale. He held a tenement and 3½ acres of arable land on a long lease. We do not know where he was finally executed. Some prisoners' families bought pardons; the price was £60, but unscrupulous lawyers exacted anything from £200 to £400 from frantic relatives. Robert's family may have been trying for a pardon, during which time he was kept in custody after the trial.

The Wedmore parish registers show that among the Thatcher family there were three Robert Thatchers, all alive in Wedmore at that time, but none identified as a doctor or chirurgeon. They had married in 1653, 1660 and 1666. There is no further record of any of them, except that Alice Thatcher, who had married one of the Robert Thatchers in 1660, was buried in 1686, the year after Monmouth's Rebellion, as a 'widow'. Might her husband Robert have been the rebel doctor executed in 1685, and might his quartered remains have been strung up on the cross? As we do not know anything about the other Roberts or their wives, the question remains unanswered.

There was another well-known doctor in Wedmore in 1685. This was Dr John Westover of Porch House. He kept a journal recording his daily life as doctor and farmer.[10] The journal begins in 'January 1685', but this date, by the modern calendar, is in fact January 1686, six months after the rebellion. A few pages are missing from the beginning of the journal; but much as one would like to think that they were deliberately torn out to save the Doctor's or some rebel's skin because they contained some reference to the rebellion, this can only be speculation.

The Revd S.H.A. Hervey, in *The Wedmore Chronicle*, writes of a story he was told about rebels at Porch House. 'Two rebels are said to have been concealed by the ladies of the house, but to have been found out and executed, and their heads fastened up on the porch.'[11] In 1685 Dr John Westover's mother and sister Ann were living with him at Porch House. There is no official record of any rebels being caught in Wedmore, or being executed. This story may have grown up around the Doctor's house, confusing Dr Robert Thatcher with Dr Westover.

Hervey was also told that the field called Hangacre near Combe Batch was so named because Judge Jeffreys had rebels hung there for taking part in the rebellion.[12] The name Hangacre is, however, more likely to be from the Old English or Saxon *hangra* meaning a wooded slope. Another story he recorded was that two men were hung as rebels on the same bough of an elm tree at Combe Batch, adjoining Hangacre. The royalist troops became notorious for unofficial lynchings of rebels they hunted down. The Combe Batch story was told to Hervey in the 1880s by 'old Sally Leigh', the washerwoman, who had it from her husband. He had been much older than her, and he in turn had heard it from his father or more probably his grandfather Leigh. Curiously, this could well take the Leigh family and the story right back to the late 1600s – back, in fact, to the time of the Rebellion; and there were two Leighs or Lyes from Wedmore involved in the rebellion, although as far as we know they escaped hanging. There may well be an element of truth behind this story. The survival of so many local stories, this one which could have been handed down from about the time of the event, and likewise another story of a man hiding in a gout (a drain or ditch) near Theale Great House, preserve small vivid local details, and do suggest that royalist soldiers might well have gone on a rampage through Wedmore after the rebellion in 1685.

The Monmouth Roll or Constables' Presentments taken in 1685 show that there were 21 rebels from Wedmore.[13] Most of these are described as 'absent [from their homes] and in the late rebellion'. Nearly all were never traced by the officials. They stayed hidden, or perhaps had been killed and buried unknown on the battlefield at Sedgemoor. I have searched the parish registers to try and find any local information about these men.

The Wedmore Rebels

Robert Barrell	'absent'	No Barrell in register; could be error for Barrett: A Robert Barrett died in 1711
Francis Bussell	'absent'	No trace of a Francis Bussell [see below]
Edward Buxton	'absent'	No trace of any Edward among the Buxton family
William Carter	'absent'	A William Carter married in 1687, died 1709
John Charell	'absent'	No Wedmore family of this name
John Counsell	'absent'	Several John Counsells at that time
Robert Cox	'absent'	No Robert among Cox family
Nicholas Fear	'absent'	A Nicholas Fear died in 1709
Charles Fisher	'absent'	No Charles Fisher of the right age
Francis Fudge	'excepted from General Pardon' [see below]	
Richard Honan	'absent'	No Honan family, probably error for Homan. A Richard Homan died 1725
William Jenkins	'absent'	A William Jenkins died 1708
William Lader	'absent'	A William Lader or Larder died 1690
Richard Latchem	'absent'	A Richard Latcham of Stoughton died 1692 [see below]
George Lye	'absent'	A George Lye of The Borough died 1695
William Lye	'absent'	A William Lye or Leigh died 1733
John Smith	'absent'	A John Smith died 1692
Thomas Smith	'absent'	A Thomas Smith died 1733
William Taylor	'absent'	A William Taylor of Stoughton died 1710
Robert Thatcher, chirurgeon.		Tried at Wells, to be executed [see above]
William Walch	'absent'	A William Welsh died 1707

Without further records it is impossible to say whether the parish register entries are really those of the rebels or other men with the same name. There is one other problem in trying to trace these rebels. Nonconformity was strong in Wedmore, so that some of these men might never appear in the parish church registers. Nonconformists flocked to Monmouth's Protestant cause, although the exact number is open to debate. In 1675 several Wedmore men had been fined for assembling illegally to listen to George Stert, a nonconformist, preach in John Bussell's house at Stoughton.[14] A Francis Bussell was among the rebels, and so was Richard Latcham who was one of the men fined in 1675 for the gathering at Stoughton.

One rebel, Francis Fudge, was 'excepted from General Pardon'. The Fudges were local millers, but there is no Francis among their family register entries. Francis was not pardoned, we do not know why. He seems still to be at large after the General Pardon. Whether he was ever found is not recorded. Of the 21 Wedmore rebels, perhaps 12 may have returned home. These rebels were not labourers and peasants as so often depicted, nor were they professional soldiery. They were yeoman farmers, artisans and tradesmen, the middle strata of village society. Perhaps this is why the Monmouth Rebellion has given rise to so much folklore and has stayed so vivid in local memory.

John Tucker of Blackford, 1700–1779

Through the ages many people have left bequests to Wedmore church. Some of these have survived the passage of time. One such bequest was left by John Tucker of Blackford, and we see it every time we go into the church. It is the oldest of the three brass chandeliers hanging in the nave.

John Tucker lived in the farmhouse called Sexey's Farm (now Old Sexey's Farm), which was part of the Sexey Estate, as was most of Blackford. He was born in 1700, the son of Henry and Grace Tucker, and his brother William was born in 1711. He also had a sister, called Grace after her mother.[15] John took over the tenancy of the farm about 1730,[16] and quite late in life married, in 1761, Mistress Elizabeth Saunders of Bridgwater, spinster. John is referred to in the register as 'Mr' John Tucker, showing his status as one of the local gentry. John and Elizabeth had a son John in 1765, and probably a daughter Hannah in 1770, but neither are mentioned in John's will, so they probably died young.[17] In 1772 he was a church warden in Wedmore Church along with William Brown of Wedmore. During their term of office they had two new bells hung in the tower. One still bears the inscription

Chandelier in St Mary's, Wedmore, donated by John Tucker, 1779

**MY TREBLE VOICE
MAKES HEAR TS REJOICE**

In January 1779 Mr John Tucker, probably in failing health, made his will.[18] It is very long, and it lists all the lands which John held, and all his bequests to family and friends. His executor was his kinsman John Tucker, to whom he left several acres of land, out of which £20 was to be paid 'in four parts' every year to his wife Elizabeth. Henry Tucker, another relation, was to get land from which he had to pay John's brother William £8 yearly during his lifetime. Another relation, Robert Tucker, was to receive land, and he had to pay John's sister Grace Mayne £6 a year for her life. He left money to the following relations: Elizabeth Mayne £30, Ann Medlam £30, Hester Latcham £40, Henry Tucker 20 guineas, Robert Tucker 20 guineas, sister Grace Mayne 20 guineas, and William Stanfield 5 guineas, kinswoman Mary Tucker £30, and Hannah Binning £30. It is the will of a local man of some substance.

After these quite considerable sums of money comes a request that 'William Melliar shall be provided for and sustained in sufficient meat, Drink, washing, Lodging and apparel during the term of his natural life'. William Melliar, 27 at the time of the will, was born in 1752, and was the illegitimate son of John Redwood and Ann Melliar. It is noticeable that the bequest is not a sum of money. We do not know why John Tucker made this bequest to the young man, or what was the connection between the two. William Melliar did not in fact live much longer; he died in 1783, aged 31 years. This leads us to wonder whether he was an invalid or handicapped; possibly (as he does not seem to have been any relation) he lived or worked on the farm, and John Tucker felt a philanthropic responsibility for his welfare. John Tucker's apprentice on the farm was Samuel Andrews, aged 15. He was left 10 guineas and a new suit of clothes, on condition that he 'faithfully and honestly serve his apprenticeship until the full age of 20 years'.

The will then reads, 'Also I order and direct that the sum of half a guinea shall be laid out and distributed in Bread unto the Poor of Blackford aforesaid on the 5th January yearly for ever'. The money for this was to come from the profits of three acres of land at Droveway. This bread charity for the poor of Blackford seems to have finished by 1820. January 5th was old Christmas Day.

Elizabeth, John's wife, was to keep all the household goods she was 'possessed of before her marriage, and a chest of drawers'. Sarah Chandler was given 'my best cow'; Sarah, in 1781, married John's kinsman and namesake John Tucker. Mary Barnes was to have 'the white cow'. Mary, aged 29, lived in Blackford, as did Hester Latcham who was left 'the cow she used to call her own'. Hester, aged 25, was the daughter of William and Hannah Latcham who lived in Grove Cottage. Had some, or all, these girls worked as dairymaids for the farmer?

Then John makes his generous gift to Wedmore Church: 'I give and bequeath to Wedmore the sum of twenty guineas to be laid out and expended in and towards purchasing a sconce or candlestick for that purpose within half a year after my decease'. He then leaves a further 10 guineas for a gravestone. The end of the will lists his clothing: 'to my wife my best shirt and all the rest of my linnen apparel unto my brother William Tucker ... All my woollen apparel to William Melliar ... The rest of my estate to my kinsman John Tucker ... [signed] John Tucker'. The will was dated 28th January, and was proved in September.

The bequest to Wedmore Church for the purchase of a 'sconce or candlestick' was soon fulfilled. The easternmost of the three elegant chandeliers hanging in the nave, the one nearest the chancel, bears the inscription

THE GENEROUS GIFT OF MR JOHN TUCKER OF BLACKFORD IN THIS PARISH 1779

This chandelier must have provided much-needed light for the congregation. It was almost certainly made in Bristol, which was noted for its brass industry at this time.

Later it was joined by two more chandeliers. In 1854 Ann Redman of Wedmore left a similar bequest. Her money was sufficient to provide two chandeliers, one a virtual match for John Tucker's, and the other somewhat smaller. We know that Ann Redman's chandeliers were made in Bristol by Thomas Hale and Company. When gas lighting was installed in the church in the 1870s, the chandeliers were thrown out into the barn of the Manor House. Fortunately the Revd S.H.A. Hervey rescued them in 1881, and they were re-hung where they are today.[19] John Tucker still lives on through his generous bequest to the church, and the hearts of Wedmore churchgoers still rejoice when all the candles on his chandelier and its two partners are lit, for the annual Christmas carol service and on other special occasions.

The story of Mary Hardwick, 1752–1813

From several documents in Wedmore parish records, I have been able to piece together a story which despite its sad ending gives an unusual insight into the life of a Wedmore lady facing difficult circumstances, two hundred years ago.[20]

On 7th January 1787 Mary Hardwick of Wedmore appeared before a Justice of the Peace. Evidence was given to show that Mary had been abandoned by her husband, and so she was now applying to the parish for relief. Mary had married Edward Hardwick in March 1769 in St Leonard's Church, Shoreditch, London. Edward was an excise officer, and four years after their marriage he was sent to Wedmore. Fourteen years later Edward disappeared, leaving Mary with seven children to care for. Before long Mary was penniless, and owing money: she was £5 behind with payment of her rent. The Overseers of the Poor of the parish, who gave relief to the poor from the rates, gave Mary some money to tide her over. Edward did not return, and a few months later Mary was again having money problems.

Mary, meanwhile, discovered that her husband Edward had returned to London. She decided to go to London to find him, planning to stay with relatives and find work in the silk manufacturing industry at Spitalfields. Her debts, however, still had to be paid off. The solution was to sell up the entire contents of her home, and Mary sold her household goods to William Cullen of Wedmore for £10. He may have been an agent of the Overseers of the Poor, because they afterwards sold it all at auction, presumably to recoup the £10 which William Cullen had paid over on the spot.

The Hardwicks had been renting a house in Wedmore from a Mr James Tucker. The Tuckers had several substantial houses in the village, and the one in which Mary lived might have been the one that formerly stood on the corner of Pilcorn Street and Glanville Road, opposite the west gate of the churchyard.

Before the sale, however, on 4th June 1787, an inventory was made of Mary's belongings, showing the prices they might reach at auction. The inventory is very interesting because it is unusual to find a document which gives us such a vivid idea of what the well-furnished house of a middle-class family of those times contained, down to the last pot and pan. The public auction was held on the 29th June, and a note was taken of the buyer and the prices paid. I have drawn up the list of Mary Hardwick's household belongings from the inventory and the auction note together. The prices in £ s d may seem ridiculously cheap, until one realises that a labourer then only earned about 1s 6d a day.[21]

Mary Hardwick's household goods

Goods	Suggested price	Price paid
In the kitchen		
Round tea table	3s. 0d.	1s. 9d.
Two stools	1s. 0d.	9d.
Five chairs	5s. 0d.	9d.

Another tea table and stool	2s. 0d.	1s. 3d.
8 pewter plates	10s. 6d.	5s. 1d.
Coffee Pot	9d. }	
Coffee Mill	1s. 6d. }	2s. 3d.
3 Candle sticks	1s. 6d.	1s. 0d.
3 spits	4s. 0d.	2s. 9d.
Cleaver	1s. 0d.	9d.
Earthenware	6d.	1s. 0d.
Frying pan	1s. 6d.	1s. 2d.
Fire shovel, tongs and poker	1s. 0d.	1s. 9d.
Iron pots	1s. 6d.	2s. 6d.

In the Parlour

Writing desk	10d.	11d.
Elm tea table	3s. 6d.	5s. 9d.
Square table	2s. 0d.	1s. 10d.
5 chairs	6s. 0d.	7s. 3d.
Japan waiter	5s. 0d.	not sold
Clothes baskets	4d.	8d.
11 pictures	2s. 6d.	2s. 1d.
Looking glass	10d.	7d.
Cupboards	3s. 0d.	9d.
Clock	7s. 6d.	6s. 0d.

In the cellar

Browning kettle	10s. 6d.	10s. 0d.
Tin oven	9d.	1s. 3d.
One hogshead and wooden horse	5s. 0d.	4s. 3d.
One horse clog	9d. }	
Wood hook	6d. }	1s. 2d
Iron pot	2s. 6d.	not sold
3 wood bottles	3s. 0d.	1s. 4d.
Mug and lanthorne [lantern]	9d.	7d.
Bird cage	6d.	3d.
Pail	1s. 2d.	2s. 0d.

Inner Chamber

One bed and bedsteads	£2. 15s. 0d.	£1. 11s. 0d.
One chest	3s. 6d.	2s. 8d.
Trunk	1s. 0d.	10d.
Looking glass	10d.	8d.
Barrel	1s. 6d.	1s. 2d.

Outer Chamber

2 beds and bedsteads	£1. 10s. 0d.	£1. 1s. 2d.
4 barrels	10s. 6d.	12s. 9d.
Side saddle	2s. 6d.	10d.
Picture	not valued	7d.
Total	£9. 16s. 6d.	£7. 2s. 1d.

The hogshead (a large barrel) and other barrels with the wooden horse or trestle to support one of them, were probably something to do with Edward Hardwick's work as an Excise officer. A horse clog was a heavy lump of wood used to 'anchor' a tethered or hobbled horse. The wood hook was a small, heavy type of sickle for cutting brushwood. The 'wood bottles' might have been small wooden containers like small barrels. The iron pot and browning kettle, both big items to judge by their valuations, suggest the house had an inglenook equipped for cooking over the open fire: but Mary also had a 'tin oven', a modern device for doing her baking. The 'japan waiter' would have been a salver or tray decorated in Japanese lacquer work: this is an early date to find such a fashionable item in a village house.

There is a noticeable difference, in many cases, between the value put on an item and the price actually paid. The auction attracted much local interest, with some of the wealthier inhabitants such as Joseph Wollen, Joseph Redman and William Drew buying some of the attractive pieces of furniture and sophisticated items such as Mary's coffee pot and mill. It must have broken Mary's heart to have seen all her possessions sold. Out of the £7 2s 1d raised at the auction, 17s 7½d went on auction fees, while £5 5s 0d was owing and paid as a year's rent to James Tucker. That left just a meagre 19s 5½d which the parish officers used to pay any other remaining debts.

The Overseers of the Poor agreed to send Mary and her children to London, where she had relatives and hoped to find work. Overseers were officers of the parish, elected from local residents for a year at a time, and the job was probably not generally relished. The overseers collected the poor rate, and used it to help the very poorest of the parish in all sorts of practical ways. No doubt the overseers were quite glad to get rid of Mary and her numerous children, and they paid the family's fare to London.

The journey to Bristol cost 12s 0d, and the fare, probably by coach, from Bristol to London cost £10 11s 0d. This came to £11 3s 0d altogether, more than all the money raised by the sale of Mary's household goods. It would have taken a farm labourer many, many months, to earn this amount, even if he could afford to save it. Today, he would only have to work for a few days to raise the present-day cost of the cheapest tickets for an adult and seven children to go by bus to Bristol and on by train to London. The overseers complained bitterly, after Mary had gone, that the parish was by now £10 4s 1½d out of pocket.

This, however, was not by any means the end of Mary's story. Things did not work out as she had hoped. In September a letter arrived in Wedmore from Edward Hardwick. Edward had been trying to get back into excise work, but was finding it impossible because of his debts. His letter to the Wedmore Overseers of the Poor is in a flamboyant, educated hand although the grammar suggests that it was written in a hurry and under considerable stress:

'London Sept. 9th 1787

Sir,

My Wife and Familly waits on you, Hoping these few Lines will Find you and all Enquiring freind in good Health at Wedmore. As for me and all my Familly have Been very Ill, Ever since at London, and no vew of Getting Better. At Present I have an Opportunity of Getting in to The Excise again, By a Petition as I have nothing *against me to Hinder the same, But them few Debts at Wedmore, Which Sir must Beg the Favour of you to Inform my Creditors that when Mr Jerman the supervisor Enquireis for the same to tell him that the [y] Have heard from me, and settled on the Matters Concerning the same, Which if the [y] Agree to shall be Restor'd again, wich as soon as the same, shall Let them know, and Pay the same to every One that Indeted to; Also shall Have an Opportunity of Removing my Familly from the Parish as soon as assesd in another wich favour Sir I hope you will not faile Immedtly to do.*

I am sir your most Obt. Servt.
Edward Hardwicke

N.B. Sir Please to Direct to me. To be Left at No.8 The Duke's Head in Red Lyon's Street Near Spittlefeilds Church.'

This request for his debts to be cleared was ignored by the Wedmore Overseers. They probably knew that there was no chance of Edward paying them back.

Two months later, in November 1787, Mary Hardwick in her turn sent a letter to Wedmore. It is addressed 'For Mr Joseph Comer at Sand in the Parish of Wedmore Near Wells, Somerset.' The letter cost 3½d to send. Joseph Comer lived in Sand Hall and was one of the wealthiest and most influential people in the parish. Mary writes, also in a good though less practised hand,

'*Worthey Sir*

this Waits on you humbly beging of your asistance with the Rest of the Gentelmen my few Goods is once more taken for a quarters Rent at 7 pounds a year my Situation at Presant is very deplorable I have had none but my own hands to Suport myself and four children and ther unworthy father is in the hosptal with bad Legs my Landlord has Given me a fornight to Redeam them I therfore hope you will pity my misfortunes as I must be forced to bringe back the famaley Please to Grante me an answer as soon as posabele from

Sir your homble Sarvant
Mary Hardwick
London November 14 1787

Please to Dierect to me at the Blue Coat boy No.5 Northenfolget.'

Signature of Mary Hardwick, 1787

Mary is again in debt because Edward is in hospital, and she has to return to Wedmore. The parish was responsible for its own poor and could not 'pass them on' to other parishes. Her plea was answered with a curt note from George Tutton the parish Overseer of the Poor, a copy of which is jotted at the bottom of Mary's letter:

'Madam,

We are sorry to hear of your Distress but cannot think of sending any money to London if you cannot support yourself & family the Law directs that you must be carried home in which case the parish will place out the Children Apprentices and you will be alone to maintain yourself.

I am for &c.
G.T.'

In December Mary and six children returned to Wedmore and were placed in the poor house, which stood outside the west end of the churchyard at the top of Church Street. They were all suffering from 'the itch', the skin complaint scabies. The parish overseers immediately ordered a surgeon to attend to them, and they were soon cured. The Poor Book records that the family was now costing the parish about 15s a month.

Mary's two eldest daughters were put into service, and two others were apprenticed. Her eldest son, aged about nine, was to be apprenticed to William Stone of Wedmore, but when Mary learned that Stone intended to pass the boy apprentice on to a tradesman, she, clutching at the last remnants of her genteel upbringing, refused to permit it and immediately left the poor house. She tried to support herself and the two little boys for several months. When the winter of 1788 set in, however, life for Mary again became difficult. She applied for poor relief, but the Overseers refused to help her unless she agreed to live in the poor house and give up her children as apprentices. Mary then applied direct to the magistrate for help; but after hearing from the two Wedmore Overseers, George Tutton and Joseph Wollen, the magistrate too refused any assistance.

Mary, however, was not going to give up. She issued yet another warrant to the magistrate. This time George Tutton the Overseer spoke up for her. Was his conscience touched by this well-brought up, articulate lady reduced to such a situation? We do not know. At last Mary was granted relief of 1s 6d a week - but then Joseph Wollen the Overseer's agent refused to pay it over to her. There followed a succession of court cases at Axbridge between Mary and the Overseers' agent Joseph Wollen, with Mary trying to get the relief payments, granted to her in court, which Wollen was witholding. She at length agreed that her older son should be apprenticed, but said that her younger son 'was infirm'. The magistrate declared that she had fulfilled all the other conditions, and added that as soon as her youngest son was declared fit by a surgeon, he too should be apprenticed. The magistrate further ordered that Mary's indictment against the Overseers should be lifted, and that they should pay her relief to her. Eventually the whole sorry business was sorted out. Mary got her relief, although Joseph Wollen still disapproved. Joseph Wollen was a rich man who later built The Hall, in Sand Road, Wedmore. Why was he so against Mary Hardwick? Was he taking a stand against the unfamiliar challenge of an educated lady of spirit, to his parochial authority?

Whether Mary ever heard any more of her husband Edward is not known: he certainly never returned to her in Wedmore. In 1795 Mary, now aged 45, gave birth to a son baptised 'George Toogood': but, Edward having vanished, Mary could not have got a divorce and remarried, even if she could have afforded it. The child was obviously the offspring of a George Toogood. George Toogood died in 1801, and described as 'a poor man' in the parish registers. Mary and George were probably living together in the poorhouse.

On December 24th 1797 the poor book records that Mary Hardwick was given a quarter of coal (that is, ¼ cwt or about 12 kilos, about enough for fires over Christmas). The next year she received a blanket, and in 1801 a shift (the most basic form of gown, for a pauper) and a woollen shawl. From then on, usually about twice a year, Mary received from the poor fund a single item, such as a shift, shoes or a blanket. Presumably she was by now permanently in the poor house.

Mary died aged 61 in August 1813, and was buried in a pauper's grave on August 27th. Two of her daughters, Ann and Hannah, had died years before, but at least one of her other children, Sarah, survived her, married and stayed in Wedmore.

So Mary's sad life ended in dire poverty. Once she had sunk to this level, there was no way that she could ever get back into her former middle-class comfort and affluence. Her last 26 years had been a struggle for survival. Probably she was one among many of life's losers in the Wedmore poor house; but she stands out, among the records of fleeting, anonymous individuals, as an articulate fighter whose hard life survives vividly, in the parish records, to move us today.

Joseph Stickland, 1773–1824: an apprentice and his descendants

In 1788 Joseph Stickland was apprenticed to John Buxton, carpenter, of Wedmore.[22] The Stickland family lived in Wedmore until recently, and it was through this Joseph that their story here began. Joseph was not a local boy; how did he gain his apprenticeship in Wedmore, and where did he come from? Joseph's apprenticeship indenture survives in the archives of the Hospital of Hugh Sexey. By searching the Hospital records, parish registers and other archives, the story of Joseph and his family can be pieced together.

Joseph Stickland was one of the poor boys who was lucky enough to have been elected to attend the school run by the Hospital or Almshouse of Hugh Sexey in Bruton. He started at the school in 1785, and spent the usual three years there learning reading, writing and arithmetic.[23] Boys were elected from poor families who had several children and were 'unprovided for'. Only boys who lived in one of the parishes which were part of the Sexey's estates could be elected. The system of election was quite complicated. Most of the income to run the Hospital came from the rents of Hospital estates at Bruton, Lyncombe and Widcombe (near Bath), Wanstrow and Blackford. Each year five new boys were elected to the school, as five older boys finished their three years' schooling and became eligible for apprenticeship. Four boys were chosen from Bruton each year, and one boy in rotation from one of the other places.

Each boy when elected was provided with a suit of blue clothes, two shirts, two cravats, one pair of stockings, and one pair of shoes, as well as any clothes left behind by the boy who had now become an apprentice. In the second and third years each boy was allowed yearly two shirts, two pairs of stockings and two pairs of shoes. Once in two years an allowance was made to each boy of a blue gown and cap; these were given at Christmas.

Every year, therefore, there were fifteen boys altogether at the school. They were taught by a master who, in the 1800s, was paid seven shillings a week for each pupil. Out of this money the master had to provide board, washing and mending. The boys were lodged in three bedrooms.

Each year a special service was held in Bruton, followed by dinner. All the local dignitaries and trustees of the Hospital attended. At this service new boys were elected and old boys bound as apprentices. Craftsmen within a radius of about fifteen miles of Bruton were notified by advertisement that five boys were available for apprenticeship. The advertisement described the boys and gave notice of the premium and terms. Each boy was given a testimonial of his character from the local minister and churchwardens, and proof given to show that he was a member of the established church. On gaining his apprenticeship, the boy received two suits of clothes, one a working suit and the other a Sunday suit; also two shirts, two cravats, two pairs of stockings, a pair of shoes, a hat, a Bible and a Common Prayer Book.[24]

This would have been how Joseph Stickland spent his three years at the school. He was the son of Joseph and Judith Stickler of Bruton, born in 1773, and one of several children. Nothing is known of his father except that he was literate, being able to sign his name, Joseph Sticklin, with a flourish in the marriage register.[25] Changes in the spelling of a surname was quite common. On 25th May 1788, at the age of fifteen years, Joseph Stickland, as he was now called, was bound apprentice for seven years to John Buxton, carpenter and wheelwright of Wedmore.[26]

Apprenticeship was a very serious undertaking. During those seven years the apprentice promised to serve his master faithfully and diligently, and to obey him, keeping his trade secrets. He was not allowed to marry or to have any relationship with women. He was not allowed to visit any taverns, inns or alehouses unless it was about his master's business. He was not permitted to play cards, dice or any other unlawful games. He was not to waste his master's goods nor lend anything without permission. He also promised 'to behave and demean himself towards his said Master and all his [master's family,] ... as a true and faithful apprentice'.

The master in turn made promises to teach and instruct the apprentice in his trade. He also had to provide for him, in sickness and in health; and provide good, wholesome and sufficient meat, drink, washing, lodging, apparel and mending. At the end of seven years the master had to provide the apprentice with two suits: a working-day suit suitable for his trade, and a suit for 'holy days'.

The Sexey's Trustees initially paid John Buxton £12 for Joseph's apprenticeship, and a further £10 after four years. After Joseph had completed his seven years, he decided to stay in Wedmore and follow his trade as a carpenter. In June 1800 Joseph married Hannah Clap, who was probably a member of a local milling family who owned a house in Glanville Road adjoining Elmsett Hall. The house is now the three cottages called The Old Cottage, Nyland View, and Mendip Cottage. Sadly, their baby son Matthew died in 1801 aged about nine months, and Hannah died the following year. In 1804 Joseph remarried. His second wife was Mary Tucker, and they had three children. Their son John (a carpenter) married Joan Hudson of Cheddar. Of their eight children, Edward (carpenter) married Mary Wilmot in 1858. Edward and Mary had two sons, George Chilcott (carpenter) and Albert Edward.

George married Amelia Williams. They had five children, including Kate who was still living in the family home in the 1980s.[27] Their only son Edward (Ted) Stickland was the last in this long line of carpenters. After his retirement, Ted and his wife Dorothy emigrated to Australia in 1960 to live near their daughter and only child Ruth Moore. He died in Australia in 1982.

The apprenticeship of the Bruton Hospital schoolboy Joseph in 1788 thus led to Wedmore having a family of five generations of carpenters spanning 150 years. No doubt many buildings in the parish contain Stickland craftsmanship. One which can be definitely identified with the family is Wedmore Methodist Church. The new Methodist Church Schoolroom was built by John Larder with Edward and George Stickland, father and son, constructing the roof in 1895, and its exposed timbers are evidence of the quality of their workmanship.[28] The Sticklands usually worked with Solomon Wall, builder, and most of the houses built by Solomon Wall contain roofs and carpentry work by the Sticklands, such as Glendale (built 1880), and Cross Farm (also 1880); and in 1902 he worked on what was the former Victorian Vicarage now Whitfield House. The link between the Stickland family and Sexey's schools came round full circle when in 1898-1899 Edward Stickland helped equip the temporary Sexey's school at West Stoughton, providing desks and fittings and a workbench. He and George made furniture including desks at £1 each, and provided timber for woodwork classes.[29] In October 1899, George Stickland moved school furniture from Stoughton to the newly built Sexey's School at Blackford, and provided twenty new desks at £21. 12s.

The Sticklands' work book, October 5th 1899

10d including carriage, and a new workbench at £1. 3s. 0d. including screws and carriage. Just eight years later the Managers' Minute Book of Sexey's School records that on 16th September 1907 E.Stickland (Ted) was awarded a scholarship.[30] His daughter Ruth, who also attended Sexey's school at Blackford, is the most recent link in the long chain stretching back to the election of the poor Bruton boy to school in 1785. There are probably many other Wedmore houses containing woodwork that forms a silent memorial to the successive generations of Stickland carpenters, and a legacy of that Wedmore apprenticeship.

The Reverend William White, 1793–1867

George Stickland and family outside their house in Grants Lane, 1897

In 1860 the Reverend William White of Wedmore, who became the first incumbent of Theale church, published his autobiography, *The Life of the Reverend William White*. His book gives us the story of the life and thoughts and doings of this local 19th century clergyman; but perhaps of even more interest, he includes unique snippets of parish history which might otherwise have been lost for ever.

On 3rd February 1793 a baby boy was born to John and Abigail Tucker of Wedmore. Abigail was the sister of William White, the renowned surveyor and mapmaker who lived in Sand House. Three days after the baby's birth Abigail died, probably of puerperal fever, leaving the baby very weak and sickly. Just after Abigail's death, her sister-in-law Ann White had a vivid dream in which she saw Abigail holding the helpless infant out to her. Ann, believing that Abigail wished her to look after the baby, took the tiny sickly boy to Sand House; there, through her loving care, the baby survived.

Baby William was named after his uncle, and was brought up by William and Ann White, who had no children of their own, as their son. William was not baptised until he was five and a half years old, in October 1798, when he was given the name William White Tucker.[31] The reason for his late baptism is not known. At the age of eighteen, however, William discovered that he was not the son of John Tucker. He was very distressed to discover that 'I was born in sin, and that in sin did my mother conceive me ... I was nothing more or less than a fallen child of Adam'. He does not reveal whether he knew the name of his real father.

At the age of four, William was sent to a local dame school, run by a 'truly beautiful specimen of a dame' - Priscilla Latcham. Priscilla's school was kept 'in a little cottage in a lane surrounded by trees'. After a few months he was sent to another school in Wedmore. At six he went to Bleadon, to a school run by the Reverend John Price. Here he was educated with the sons of neighbouring gentlemen and Bristol merchants. During the six years William spent at the school, he found study hard, particularly Latin which he 'could not love'.

When he was 12, William was sent to Bristol, to a school at The Fort, near Tyndall's Park - now part of the University campus. He still, however, found study arduous, and at 15 he returned home to Sand. His uncle William would have liked him to have entered his own profession, that of a land surveyor; but William had no desire to do this. Two years later he became articled to a Bristol lawyer. For five years he studied law, but was often so low in spirits that he thought of taking his life. During this time he began to attend church. He was particularly drawn to the preaching of the Methodists, but he decided not to 'forsake the established church'. One day, William walked out of his lawyer's office, and kept on walking. He walked all the way to Wales. On his return, he gave up his law studies and returned home to Wedmore, to consider his vocation for the priesthood.

During the early 1800s times were very hard. The weather was very bad, resulting in poor harvests. Prices of basic necessities were exorbitantly high. England was at war with France, and in the parish the gentry were at odds with one another. There was no resident vicar, and there were 'frequent squabblings' even 'in the house of God itself'. There was no vestry room in which to hold meetings about church or parish affairs, so all business was conducted in the church itself. The arguments seem to have been largely political, and William's uncle William White, one of the leading lights of the village, was often 'agitated by parochial commotions'. Arguments raged on for years, but ceased for one day in 1815. Ann White wrote of this occasion in a letter to her nephew, 'when all, save one or two, consented to unite in friendship, harmony and peace'. This special day was the day when peace was celebrated, after the great English victory over the French at the battle of Waterloo.

Ann writes:
> 'last Friday you can scarcely imagine how gay we were. A subscription dinner on a very large scale, for the poor, was given in Mr Barrow's field on Lascott's Hill. Two sheep were roasted on the spot; a band of music and a troop of horse attended ... in the midst of our gaiety down came the rain in torrents on the dinner table. Surrounded by at least 800 persons it was indeed most woefully unfortunate ... All party animosity seemed on that day totally laid aside. Mr Barrow [The Manor House], Mr Wollen [The Hall], Mr Cattle [the curate], Mr Batt and Mr Giles and Mr White [Sand House] presided at different tables. For once at Wedmore general amity was the

conductor. Mr E— alone refused to join in.

You would have laughed to have seen Mr Green dressed in Mr Barrow's scarlet coat, and Major S—'s military hat, mounted on a very young white steed, parading around, and, at every corner halting to read a peace proclamation. Mr E[dwards] did not return from his excursion until last Sunday. He is vastly pleased with all he saw and heard. He does not consider shaking hands with the Emperor of Russia and Blucher among inferior gratifications'.

It was Wellington's ally General Blucher, with his Prussian troops, who turned the balance of the battle of Waterloo. Mr Edwards was a neighbour of the Whites, and lived at Sand Hall, but what he was doing in the victory celebrations, whether in London or in France, is not clear.

The harmony in the parish did not, however, last long. Discord returned again. William White senior 'exerted himself to his own injury' trying to help with Church and parish affairs. His health declined, and he died 30th May 1816. Nephew William stayed at home with his aunt for a year, and then he left, not to return for six years. During that time he travelled extensively, making friends, visiting churches and studying theology.

On 2nd September 1821 William took holy orders, and on 22nd December 1823 he was ordained priest. He took charge of the parish of Dewsbury, in Yorkshire, from 1821 to 1823. He had met with many setbacks in his efforts to be ordained. One stumbling block was the Very Reverend George Henry Law, then Bishop of Chester and later to become Bishop of Bath and Wells, who said that on principle he never ordained 'anyone who had been brought up to any trade or profession'. William had studied law. He had not studied theology at university, nor at the renowned college of St.Bees. The Bishop of Gloucester was more kind and helpful to the hopeful William White, and he was actually ordained at Durham Cathedral in 1821 by the Archbishop of York himself.

In 1823 he returned to Wedmore and became engaged to Jane Tyley, a local girl. He worked and preached in Wedmore church and in the newly-erected (1823) Blackford Chapel. He accepted a year's curacy in Devon, before his marriage. William and Jane were married at Wedmore on 3rd February 1825. William was now looking for a position nearer home, when the decision was made to build another new chapel at Theale, and he was offered the position of priest there.

A subscription list for the new chapel at Theale was opened, and money poured in 'from every quarter'. Soon enough was raised to commence the building, and a plot of ground was given by Thomas Knyfton Esq., and Mr Batt of Theale. The foundation stone was laid in January 1826 by the Vicar of Wedmore, the Reverend Joseph Richards. The day was 'cold and bleak ... and few were present to witness the ceremony'. When the chapel was opened in 1828, the services were conducted by the Bishop of Bath and Wells (Bishop Law, formerly of Chester), and the Bishop of Lichfield and Coventry (the former Bishop of Gloucester who had befriended William earlier). The Bishop of Bath and Wells dedicated the church and burial ground, and the Bishop of Lichfield and Coventry preached the sermon. The chapel of Christ Church, Theale was duly consecrated, and after the services the guests 'were entertained by many a generous farmer, who opened wide their doors ... whilst at the

Parsonage House, a building just completed for the residence of the minister, the two Bishops and as many as the snug little mansion would contain, received a hearty welcome'.

When William White was appointed to Theale, he felt it was ironic that the bishop who had refused to ordain him because he had studied law, was now consecrating his chapel and was 'to be a

Theale Church, c1900

welcome guest at my table'. William took up his living on 13th January 1828 and so became the first incumbent of Theale Chapel. This had been built as a chapel-of-ease in 1826-28, to save Theale people the long walk to the parish church. William White was an evangelistic preacher, greatly influenced by the Methodists, and he was determined to bring the gospel to the folk of Theale.

His biography includes memories of his time as curate of Theale Chapel. William and his wife Jane moved from their home at Sand House into the Parsonage House at Theale. He soon discovered that the contractor who had built the chapel had gone bankrupt, and 'the labouring men lost all their money'. This weighed heavily on William's mind. He did not have sufficient means to pay them himself, so he decided to publish some of his sermons. Within weeks he had obtained enough subscribers to be able to pay the workmen their money.

The first Sunday that Theale Chapel was open, there was a very small congregation. William White was at a loss: 'either the inhabitants were not sufficiently aware that the chapel was to be opened on that day, or else they were so unconcerned about religion that they did not think it was worth their while to attend the service'. Soon the chapel was better attended, but not so much by 'the people for whose benefit the Chapel was built, as by persons coming from a distance'. He soon, however, had 'a Sunday School, consisting of about 80 children; nor were we at a loss for Teachers as several kind persons, both young and old, came and volunteered their services'.

The first sermon which William preached in his new church showed his concern for his flock. He objected strongly to their indulgence in the 'dangerous evils' of drinking and fighting. For many years the local 'revels' held in the spring in Wedmore and surrounding villages had become days of excessive drinking, gambling and back sword or single-stick fighting. A revel was originally a religious festival, but the religious significance of the day had long been forgotten. William White had seen the over-indulgence, and its effects. He was appalled by 'these scenes of iniquity', and was determined to stop the revels. He said that backsword-playing was 'falsely called the glory of Wedmore, but rightly called the shame and disgrace of Wedmore'.

Back sword or single-stick fighting was a violent sport. The two opponents fought, each with a long stick held in one hand, and proceeded to batter each other on the head. The first to draw blood above the neck was declared the winner. The Reverend S.H.A. Hervey, writing in the Wedmore Chronicle in the 1890s, says that he was told that players used to drink gunpowder to stem the blood flow. As any bleeding above the neck counted, players would frantically lick away any blood on their mouths, quickly - but spectators would shout 'Blood, blood, blood'.[32]

There had been many exponents of the sport in Wedmore, and fortunes had been made at it. Two brothers of the Wall family won a great deal of money by their single-stick fighting. William Stone Wall (Wedmore had its longstanding Stone and Wall families; the conjunction of names was because of intermarriage, not as a joke) rebuilt the house in Pilcorn Street now called Grantchester with his winnings. The Wall brothers did not drink, so perhaps this is why they were so successful.

William White, in his sermon, warned husbands 'not to squander in drunkness and folly, the money you have so hardly earned, but feed your wives and children'. The wives were called upon to be 'keepers at home and endeavour to prevail on your Husbands to follow your example ... To Husbands and Wives! If you love your children, keep them from the revel'.

On Tuesday 19th April 1830, some time before Theale revel, a meeting was held at Panborough where 'several respectable inhabitants' decided that instead of a revel they would form a 'Friendly Society for the relief of sick members etc.'. These village Friendly Societies always held a special day, with a parade and church service, and this was to replace the revel. The innkeeper at Panborough said that the revel would still be held that year (on 18th June), because it was too late to cancel it; but he promised that there would be no fighting.

The locals, however, were not deterred. Even if the revel had no official contests, fights were still being held. One evening William White was told that a fight was to be held 'between Mr W- of Mark and Mr P- of Mudgley ... They were to meet about 9 or 10 in the morning'. Next morning William set off to Mudgley on his horse, and met the fighter, who refused to give up the contest as 'there is money paid down'. Undeterred, William rode off to the Panborough Inn. Eventually the two contestants arrived, and sat in opposite sides of the chimney corner. William tried to persuade them to give up the fight, but suddenly 'three or four men rushed towards the fireplace, and tore the man away from me, and conducted him into a field allotted for the fight'. 'Well', said William, 'they have seized one man, I will make sure they shall not have the other, so we kept him in the chimney corner, until the time fixed for the fight was long past'. The crowds who had come to watch found that no fight was taking place, and the prize money was returned. Some of the people came into the inn and William distributed religious tracts among them. He admitted that it had been 'one of the most painful trials I have ever experienced'.

The fighting at Theale may have been stopped, but it continued in Wedmore. The Wedmore Revel was held on the Wednesday after Whitsunday. William's influence, however, began to take effect. He managed to stop more fights, especially one at Wedmore where one morning he saw 'a multitude of people' walking 'in great haste'. When he asked where they were going, they said 'There is a fight today'. William walked with the crowd until he met one of the fighters. His 'poor wife was sitting in a ditch by the roadside, lamenting her husband'. William tried to persuade the man not to fight, but he said that the prize-money was already laid down. 'Never mind,' said William, 'if you will return, and not go to the fight, I will take care that you shall not lose your money'.

After a while some people came to help William, and undertook to conduct the man safely home. William then went to the field where 'several hundreds if not thousands of people were assembled together, what for? To hear the Gospel? No: but to see two of their fellow creatures disgrace themselves by fighting!' He then addressed the crowd on 'the folly of such proceedings'. After he left, he discovered that the remaining fighter was taken outside the parish, where a new opponent was found for him - 'who soundly beat him'.

The Reverend William White's opposition to single-stick fighting eventually stopped the sport in the parish. His health, which had never been good, began to deteriorate. After three years at Theale, he was allowed to employ a curate of his own to help; but two years later, he had to resign his living, and retired back to Sand House. His beloved aunt had died in 1831, and William had inherited the estate.

During William's years at Theale he and Jane had one son, but he longed for a daughter. He learned that two of his great friends who had been missionaries in India had died, and that their daughter, who was his god-daughter, was orphaned. William, himself the adopted son of his uncle William White the surveyor, decided to adopt her, 'not believing that God would ever gratify my wish for a daughter'. The girl, Elizabeth Dawson, was put in a good school and became 'a useful member of society'. A few years later, William and Jane had a daughter and then another son.

The Reverend William White continued to preach on occasion, during his retirement. His influence in Theale and in the parish of Wedmore as a whole was greatly felt. He changed some of the social habits of the time. The revels and single-stick fighting ceased, and with them the enormous sums spent in gambling. People perhaps became a little more sober. His autobiography, however, is not just about a clergyman's local zeal for improvement; nor just the account of the otherwise quiet existence of a leisured rural clergyman of the day. It is clear from the earlier chapters that after his difficult start in life, and against the background of the comfortable affluence of his generous uncle and aunt, he found his own way in the world, and worked out his true vocation with a determined independence of mind. In addition, his book shows he was quite an adventurer. After that initial walk from Bristol to Wales, made in some agony of mind, he walked and rode many hundreds of miles across England, Wales and Scotland, and even went to Paris, making thirteen tours in all. His autobiography includes his descriptions of the places he explored, and the people he met, and shows clearly that he could enjoy life in all its variety. He died on 3rd June 1867, aged 74 years. His memorial is on the east wall of the south chapel in Wedmore Church. It records, simply, that he led 'an exemplary Christian Life'.

Richard Lyde Scott, 1816–1899: the Bard of Wedmore

Entering Wedmore Church through the little door from the porch, you will see facing you on the wall of the southwest chapel a handsome memorial to Richard Lyde Stott, 'a composer of patriotic and religious poems'. This epitaph arouses curiosity among those who read it, as perhaps they search through their memories. Who was he? Did they learn his poetry at school?

The whole epitaph reads thus:

NEAR THE SPOT
WHERE HE WORSHIPPED FOR 52 YEARS
THIS TABLET
IS ERECTED BY HIS 2 DAUGHTERS
IN LOVING MEMORY OF
RICHARD LYDE STOTT
A KIND FATHER,
A FIRM FRIEND, A TRUE CHRISTIAN,
AND A COMPOSER
OF PATRIOTIC AND RELIGIOUS POEMS.

HE DIED OCTOBER 13th A.D.1899,
AGED 83 YEARS:
HIS BODY RESTS AT CHRIST CHURCH, THEALE.
'UNTIL THE DAY DAWN.'

Being one of those inquisitive readers of epitaphs, I have tried to find out a little more about him. The quest led next to Theale. There, standing in Theale churchyard, is his elaborate tomb. It consists of a marble cross standing on four steps. The cross is decorated with a carved spray of passion flowers, and a dove with an olive branch. The grave is surrounded by decorative iron posts, with chains, set on a stone plinth. In lead letters set on the steps of the cross is:

In loving and affectionate remembrance
of
RICHARD LYDE STOTT of Wedmore
who was called to his eternal rest
October 13th AD 1899
aged 83 years
Requiescat in Pace
Make him to be numbered with the saints in glory everlasting.

and below this is a verse, perhaps from one of his poems:

Where Thou art now adored - wilt be
by all the heavenly host above
How dear to be transformed to see
And be with him we long have loved.
Thy presence to enjoy alway
In endless everlasting day.

So who was Richard Lyde Stott? He was a farmer who in his later years lived in The Borough, and then in Redhill Villas on the Cheddar Road. He was married and had two daughters. One remained single, the other, Althea, married a Mr Norman from Marchey Farm near Theale. They had two sons. The *Wells Journal* 26th October 1899 recorded the death of Mr Lyde Stott, who passed away at Redhill, Wedmore aged 83; friends 'esteemed him as an authority on Church architecture and for his literary tastes'.

Quite by chance while looking for other information in the *Wells Journals* of the 1880s I came across a couple of poems by 'L.S.' A further search revealed other, later poems duly signed Lyde Stott. The poems are fairly lengthy, so I am only including shortened versions of the first two. His poem on *The Cuckoo*, which begins:

Richard Lyde Stott, the Bard of Wedmore, (1816-1899)

> *Oh! Albion dear, thou favoured Isle,*
> *The cuckoo comes to thee...*

ends

> *But why so transient is its stay,*
> *And it so short time here?*
> *Why in such haste to fly away,*
> *Are foreign lands more dear?*
> *Cuckoo! cuckoo! cuckoo! We'll listen while we may,*
> *And wish, with all our hearts, it would make a longer stay.*
>
> *Oh! listen to the cuckoo's song,*
> *Oh! listen aye, I say;*
> *Oh! listen to its well known song*
> *In April, June and May.*

Richard Lyde Stott seems fond of writing about birds. Another poem is dedicated to the Lark:

> *O! get me from the busy throng,*
> *The noisy, dusty, smoky mart,*
> *To hear my favourite bird in song;*
> *The sweet and dear aerial Lark.*

There follow another ten verses in similar style[33].

On 2nd December 1886 the following poem was printed in the *Wells Journal*. It is reproduced here in its entirety:

THE VILLAGE BELLS

How dear to hear the village bells,
Their welcome sounds how mild;
How sweet to hear the village bells,
They please a lisping child.

Their peal delights a minstrel's ear,
Bards give their rhymes a spell,
When friendly zephyrs bring them near
And mellow every bell.

The bridegroom dressed in gay attire
And his sweet bride so fair,
will listen to the well-strung lyre
And every pleasing air.

Elate to hear the village bells,
Hung in the distant tower:
Charming the woods, the hills and dells,
And every ros-y bower.

When the blest of Christmas vigil comes,
We keep when Christ was born;
Oh! how they waken Zion's sons,
To hail the suspicious* morn!

'Tis joy the village bells resound,
(Save when a knell be rung)
They swell the echoes with their sound,
From every silvery tongue.

Oft many a one, now fled the night,
That sleeps in Death's embrace,
Has heard their music with delight,
With smiles upon his face.

Oft yet a one that's yet unborn,
In ages yet to be:
Will catch their notes on zephyrs borne,
And hail their sounds with glee.

Then if such music be below
Beneath the starry spheres,
Where troubles in abundance flow,
With cares, and doubts, and fears,

> *Let's muse! ah, muse on happier climes,*
> *Where love each bosom fills;*
> *Where music rivals earthly chimes*
> *On Beulah's happy hills.*

*sic, presumably for 'auspicious'

Richard Lyde Stott was also supposed to have sent a poem to Queen Victoria on her Jubilee. His grandson Stuart Norman was fond of quoting one of his grandfather's poems. This deathless verse was recited to me by a friend of Stuart, the late Mr Geoffrey Pavey.

> *The lights, the lights, the Draycott lights,*
> *Shine out across the lonely moor,*
> *You look a little to the left,*
> *You see the lights of Clewer.*

Presumably this was written when Richard was living at Redhill Villas, where on a clear night he would see the oil lamps shining from Draycott windows.

However awful this last piece of doggerel, and however dated we now find the high-flown sentiments of his other poems, this should not detract from the efforts of Richard Lyde Stott, the self-taught farmer-poet. He clearly was a man who loved the Wedmore countryside, and who loved words; and by putting the two together he no doubt enchanted many local people in his time.

CHAPTER 14
The Wrong Side of the Law

The Wedmore Riot, 1885

The imminence of a General Election nowadays hardly fires up the population, and very often apathy reigns. We may think an election dominates the present-day media; but in Wedmore in 1885, before television, before radio, before widespread newspapers, electioneering could be an altogether more rowdy affair. Friday December 4th 1885 was the date on which Wedmore voted in a General Election - polls taking place, at that time, on different days in different places. Wedmore was in the Wells Division and the local Conservative Member of Parliament, Colonel Richard H Paget, was seeking re-election. The seat was contested by Mr Pandeli Ralli, an established Liberal politician who had been MP for Wallingford for ten years. On that Friday in Wedmore, political fervour spilled over into mob violence, and the 'Wedmore Riot' achieved local notoriety. Several men were charged and later appeared in court. After the rioters appeared at Axbridge Petty Sessions, the reports of the riot filled the local newspapers for weeks, and revived again six months later with their trial at the Somerset Assizes. The story has been woven together, with some difficulty, from the copious, complex and overlapping reports and witness statements made during the court cases that followed that eventful day.[1]

There were 704 electors (men only, of course) in Wedmore eligible to vote, and 550 recorded their vote. The majority of voters in the parish were true-blue Tories, and it was a brave or foolish man who declared himself to be a Liberal supporter. The polling station was probably the Church Schoolroom, now the Village Hall. The morning of December 4th began according to an eye-witness 'quietly with the Liberals who were not afraid to show their colours voting early and going away quietly. About 9 o'clock the Tories began to pour in, coming in wagons bearing flags and banners. These voters were mostly farmers bringing in their men. There were also farmers standing at the door of the polling station to receive the labourers, persuading them who to vote for and in some cases using intimidation. About 10 o'clock the carriages of the resident gentry were called into use to pick up villagers'.

During the morning a boy rode through the streets on a pony; both the boy and the pony were painted bright blue. Long before midday liquor had been given away very freely, and its effects were soon apparent; but beyond a little horse play nothing serious happened until about 4 o'clock.

The trouble started when James Binning, George Tutton and Mark Wall, with about twenty men, came down from the New Inn in Combe Batch. They were making a considerable noise, and when they came opposite the house of Mr Robert Redman, tailor (now called Barnards) on the corner at the top of The Borough, they stopped. The Redmans were Tories and were flying a blue flag. James Binning went up to the front door and said, 'If you don't open the door, I will break the door down'. He believed Mr Redman was in, but only his wife and son Walter were in the house. Binning then tried to pull down the flag which was hanging out of the bedroom window. He jumped up and down, and managed to grab it and the flagpole. Walter Redman watched them cut a piece of iron off the pole and fling it on the lawn. Binning and the other carried the flag off in triumph to the New Inn, shouting 'Come up here you blue, we are waiting for you'.

Barnards in The Borough, Wedmore, with Victor son of Sidney Redman, c1936

About half an hour later, Walter Redman with a group of Tories went up to the New Inn. There he saw Tutton, Wall, Binning and George Parker, whose mother Annie Parker kept the New Inn, assembled outside with about 30-40 others. They were all armed with big sticks or bludgeons. Walter Redman asked them to return the flag and 'to let us go back quietly'. Parker, however, replied 'Come on you blue, come on in,' and they began to fight. Redman saw Parker strike Thomas Stott of Panborough with a large stick 'called a gamble'; this was a pig-killing stick, massive and with a pointed blade on the end. Parker then struck Redman on the right hand with it, and Walter Williams on the back.

Binning and his Liberal friends then went into the New Inn and out into the garden at the back. Soon a volley of stones flew over the roof and fell into the crowd standing at the front. In no time, everyone was throwing stones and the windows of the inn were being smashed. The road had recently been re-made, with beaten stones (this is before the age of tarmac) so plenty of ammunition was to hand. Inside the inn someone was trying to tear down the gas pendant. Walter Williams of Cocklake described how he saw everyone fighting with sticks, and he was sure Binning had a whip stock with brass on it. George Tutton pointed his gun at the crowd; he 'snapped two caps, but the gun did not go off'. William Millard the corn dealer who lived near the New Inn shouted 'Stop this flinging my lads, and I'll go and get the flag quietly'. Mr Millard went into the inn and eventually obtained possession of the flag, and then he went home. The flag was passed around the Tories, and after a while they marched back down into the village with it. P.C. Edwin Davis, stationed at Clewer, was called to the New Inn at about 4 o'clock, when he said that the mob 'were in a very noisy and excited state about a flag. The flag was brought out, and some of the crowd dispersed'.

The New Inn, Combe Batch, Wedmore

Some, who had been hurt by sticks and stones, went home. The hard core of Tories, however, gathered more supporters together and marched back up The Borough at about 6 pm. They reached the New Inn, having smashed the windows of Liberal supporters on their way. This time when they reached the inn, they overran the garden, cutting down some young apple trees, and 'forced their way into the cellar, peremptorily demanding beer'. They smashed the rest of the windows, and even some window frames. Some miscreants even tried to set fire to the inn.

George Parker of the New Inn 'appealed to them to stop, but he was met with a shower of stones and curses, and threats. His forehead was cut open, and the bone laid bare, and he received another similar wound over the left eye, both wounds being of a ghastly nature' and leaving him with permanent scars. The mob then threatened to raze his house to the ground 'if only they had pick axes'. Someone threatened to drag George Parker out and take him down to the George Hotel. They were beaten off, and the crowd of Tories moved away for the second time, probably back to their base at the George Hotel. However, they soon returned a third time, having no doubt boosted their courage with yet more free drink, and brought reinforcements, increasing the crowd to between 200 and 300 people. This time the people inside the New Inn were in fear of their lives.

Suddenly the crowd outside realised they were being shot at. 'Someone from within fired upon the mob'. The gun was loaded with shot, with the result that several people were injured, two of them badly. Witnesses saw Alexander Alves (Parker's brother-in-law) fire his gun from a bedroom window and William Hembry fell, 'blood flowing from his left thigh and left arm, and he was in a fainting condition'. Dr Tyley was sent for and Hembry was carried off, blood oozing from his trousers, to Mr Redman's house where the doctor attended to him.

Dr Tyley, called as a witness, said that William Hembry was in a state of collapse and there were 70 shots in his body. He was badly injured and bleeding, and was ill for about a fortnight. One of the other people injured was Robert Brice of Clewer. He claimed that he was just 'passing the New Inn when he was shot in the body'. Twenty-nine shots penetrated his skin. He then went into the inn and asked who had shot him. Mark Wall replied, 'If you pull that colour out of your coat you shall not be hurt'. No doubt he was wearing a blue Tory 'favour' in his lapel. He saw Mark Wall and Alexander Alves load their guns in the kitchen and then they left the room. Shortly afterwards he heard the report of firearms. Robert Brice then sat down in the inn, and drank two or three quarts of free cider! When asked by the court how he knew he had received 29 shots, he replied 'Because I and my wife picked them out and saved them; some we picked out with a stocking needle'. Outside, the fighting continued.

Inside the inn, furniture and crockery was being smashed up and all the windows were shattered. While all this was going on, one man was determined to carry on drinking. As he lifted up his mug, a stone flew through the broken window, smashing the mug and leaving just the handle in his hand. Edmund Hole was seen by one witness to knock down Mary Rogers; he then picked up a shovel and smashed the shutters of the inn. He later knocked down Robert Rogers. Other witnesses denied this happened. It was also reported that an old man called Somers was thrown to the ground and had two teeth knocked out.

On Friday January 15th 1886 the Wedmore rioters appeared in the magistrate's court at Axbridge. The defendants who were accused of rioting on the night of the General Election on December 4th 1885 were George Parker (New Inn), Mark Wall, George Tutton, James Binning and Alexander Alves. They were charged, on the information of Superintendent Gillibanks, 'together with divers other people, to the number of 10 or more' with 'having unlawfully and riotously assembled to disturb the public peace, and to make a riot and disturbance to the terror and alarm of Her Majesty's subjects there'. Mr Hobbs of Wells prosecuted on behalf of the police, and Mr Poole was counsel for the defendants. Colonel Hesse was chairman of the bench, but objections were raised as he had witnessed the event; he thereafter took no part in the proceedings.

There were six policemen on duty in Wedmore on that day, four of them engaged at the polling station. The two policemen on duty in the village - Sergeant Green and Police Constable Davis - could not cope with the crowd of two or three hundred rioters. Some of the police in the polling station were called upon to help. PC Gilson of Wedmore and PC Edward Short from Mark came to assist and 'Sergeant Green, after the first outbreak in the afternoon, telegraphed to Axbridge for assistance, and as quickly as possible Superintendent Gillibanks arrived at the village with a dozen constables, who with those already there made up a force of nearly twenty'.

Meanwhile, some of the prominent residents of the village came to see if they could calm things down. Colonel Hesse, the local magistrate, and Dr Ford addressed the crowd, but 'the Riot Act was not read, as sufficient constables were not at hand to put its provisions into force'. Their efforts did however have some effect, and Colonel Hesse, Sergeant Green and the other available policemen 'after great exertion, ... managed to clear the streets, though they were pelted with stones and several of them hit with sticks'. As soon as they arrived, Superintendent Gillibanks 'marched his men to the scene of the riot, and drove the mob from the neighbourhood of the inn'. The mob quickly moved off, some going to the Swan and others to the George, both of which were where the 'blue' Tory gangs drank.

The report in the *Wells Journal* of December 10th disproves the long-held village tradition that the Riot Act was actually read in the streets of Wedmore on this occasion; but the arrival of Superintendent Gillibanks and his band of 20 policemen, marching purposefully through the village, must have un-nerved even the most befuddled rioter.

By now the windows of several houses in Combe Batch and The Borough had been smashed. These seem mostly to have been the houses of known Liberals. Mr Millard's house near the New Inn was wrecked. The houses of John Wall, builder (Bench House), Miss Tucker, Mr Roper, A Lea, Moses Sawley, tailor (now Sally's), Ralph Woodward, grocer (Allington House), and Henry Harvey (Lerburne House) were also damaged. The crowd then moved along the Cheddar Road. The house of the Baptist minister the Reverend Edwin Edginton, had its windows smashed, as did that of W Pople (now the solicitor's office). Further along, the crowd attacked the homes of William Harvey senior and William Harvey junior at Redhill, again smashing windows.

One of the most prominent Liberals in the village was the Vicar, the Reverend S.H.A. Hervey. He had been out for the day. When he returned home later that night he discovered most of the vicarage (now the Old Vicarage) windows had been smashed. Hervey referred to the matter of the riot in his sermon on the next Sunday morning, and a number of the congregation at once left the church. He again spoke about it in the evening service, and said he would rather preach to empty pews than hold his peace on such matters. Afterwards it was reported in the local newspaper that the Bishop of Bath and Wells and Lady Hervey, his parents, had been concerned for their son's safety. A member of the Cathedral cruelly remarked 'Surely Mr Hervey might easily escape unhurt by disguising himself in the garb of a clergyman, for none of the mob would then recognise him'. In past accounts of the Wedmore Riot, there has been some confusion between the Vicar, Revd S.H.A. Hervey, and the two William Harveys of Redhill.

Mr William Harvey senior lived at Redhill Farm, and was a staunch Liberal who was picked out by the Tory mob for persecution. The faults were not all on one side, because it would seem that all day long father and son had been aggravating the crowd. Benjamin Tyley happened to be walking by Harvey's house 'cheering Colonel Paget in company with others, when out came the old man [William Harvey senior] using abusive language, hit Tyley in the face and knocked him down ... In consequence over 200 came to throw stones' during the evening rampage, but worse was to come. The details were described in a separate case, when Sidney Redman (another true-blue, and brother of Walter Redman) was summoned for assaulting William Harvey senior that same night. About seven o'clock William Harvey's windows had been stoned, and his wife fled to safety after hearing Sidney Redman shouting outside, 'Come out you —, we will murder you tonight'. Redman thought that William was at home, but he was actually at his son's house in Redhill Villas, next door. The crowd moved away to the son's house, and William Harvey junior fired two shots to frighten them away. Stones were thrown by the crowd, and they even smashed the windows of the adjoining house of the semi-detached Redhill Villas, where one of the village policemen lived!

The crowd dispersed, returning to Redhill at 11 o'clock that night, after the pubs had finally closed. William and his son heard them coming. Benjamin Tyley came up to William senior, shouting and yelling and 'calling the Liberals generally all kinds of ill-names'. When Mr Tyley threatened to knock his head off and shook his fists in his face, William knocked him down in self-defence. Then two other men, Frank Tucker and Mr Tincknell, started shouting at William Harvey senior, who by now was trying to cross his son's garden and get to his own house. Suddenly shouts of 'Where's Will Harvey, let's murder the —' were heard, and Sidney Redman rushed up 'like a madman' striking William Harvey 'on the head with a stick, which caused him a deep wound'. William, not wanting to be hit again, struggled with Redman and they both fell to the ground. During the struggle Frank Tucker was stabbed in the arm with a pick. William's son and the police came to his rescue, beat off the assailants, and got him safely home at last. According to the newspaper report, the 'attitude of the crowd was so threatening ... that Mr Harvey, who is by the way between 60 and 70 years of age, would have been killed, had the mob got hold of him, there can be no doubt'.

The magistrates dismissed the case against Sidney Redman and also a complaint from Benjamin Tyley that William Harvey had assaulted him. The bench thought that there had been a great deal of provocation on both sides. The case against the rioters, however, was treated very seriously. The magistrates decided that James Binning, Mark Wall and George Tutton should be committed to the next Assizes on bail of £20. George Parker from the New Inn, however, was dismissed. Alexander Alves, who fired the gun from the New Inn, was also dismissed. The Bench decided that the charge of rioting could not be maintained against them. On June 4th 1886, at the Assize court in Taunton, Binning, Wall and Tutton together with John Tyley Wall, John, Edmund and James Hole, William Sweet and Benjamin Ham all pleaded guilty to the charge of rioting. The Chief Constable 'considered it his duty … to prosecute the ringleaders, Conservatives and Liberals alike'.

After hearing the case, the judge gave a very long speech on law and order in elections, and the excitement of the occasion. Each defendant was bound over to keep the peace on penalty of £25 per person. 'If the neighbourhood remained quiet, they would hear no more about it, but if any more trouble occurred in the neighbourhood they would be brought up and punished - not for future troubles for which they might be responsible, but for the offence to which they now pleaded guilty'. The defendants were all then discharged.

There must have been many sore heads in Wedmore at the end of that notable day, both from the sticks and stones wielded by the crowds, and from the copious drink which had been all too 'freely given' to supporters of both sides during the day, which one suspects was a root cause of all the trouble. The next day was a Saturday, 5th December and was wet and windy; the atrocious weather ensured Wedmore remained very quiet. The twenty extra police remained on duty, but with nothing to do.

The result of the election on December 4th 1885 was 'received in the village soon after one o'clock on Saturday' [5th December] and was a victory for the Conservatives by a majority of 866. Colonel Paget received 4201 votes, while his Liberal opponent Pandeli Ralli received 3335. This election had been vigorously fought. Wedmore was not the only place to have suffered 'rioting', as many other villages and towns experienced 'disorderly behaviour'; but

Wedmore was probably one of the worst affected. At the declaration of the poll in Wells, between 50 and 70 police were drafted in, and 40 special constables sworn in, but 'perfect order prevailed'. At Wedmore, the news 'caused great rejoicing. The bells of the parish church were rung, and a flag hoisted on the tower'.

General Elections in Wedmore now may lack most of the colourful enthusiasm of the 19th century - nowadays the RSPCA would hardly approve of painting a pony bright blue - but is probably rather quieter and safer for us as residents.

A village burglary in 1909

Reading about the increase of crime in the parish prompted me to look back through old newspapers at some of our former 'criminal cases'. Often these cases give us a little insight into village life at that time and the type of punishment meted out. The newspapers of the 1800s and early 1900s print lurid and minutely detailed descriptions, which make our present-day newspapers, for all our complaints about them, look comparatively restrained.

We will look at the story of Henry Coles, who was involved in a particularly nasty incident.[2] Henry Coles was a Wedmore blacksmith, aged 62, who lived in Pilcorn Street on the corner of Lascot Hill. He was charged at Axbridge Petty Sessions in January 1909 with unlawfully and maliciously wounding P.C.Robert Woolcott, stationed at Wedmore, with intent to do him grievous bodily harm.

On the night of January 15th 1909 P.C. Woolcott was patrolling around West End at 4 a.m. - something we don't have nowadays. He saw Coles coming from the direction of Plud Street. Coles was carrying some iron carriage steps and was stopped by the constable who asked him what he had. When P.C. Woolcott asked Coles to hand over the goods and to come with him, Coles replied 'I shan't', so the constable tried to hold him by the collar. Coles retaliated by grabbing the constable's collar and then the constable felt a stunning blow on the left side of his head. Although the blow rendered him partially unconscious, he struggled and both fell to the ground. P.C. Woolcott's helmet fell off, and Coles then proceeded to beat him 'about the head with the iron bar', which was produced in court.

Coles then got up, picking up various items including the steps, and went away. The constable followed and overtook him, and pulling out his truncheon ordered Coles to put down the things he was carrying. Coles said 'I'll give thee some more of it' and brandished the iron bar over the constable's head. The constable then struck the prisoner across the head with his truncheon, knocking him down. Coles got up and another struggle ensued, Coles repeatedly hitting the constable, whose truncheon was underneath him. Eventually Coles allowed P.C. Woolcott to get up, and promised to allow him to go home unmolested. However, Coles followed the constable and outside the police station threatened to kill him.

At the police station, the constable asked Coles to put down the goods, and tried to arrest him. They both fell to the ground again, Coles grabbing the constable by the throat. P.C.Woolcott shouted for assistance and his wife, Frederick Crease and other neighbours came to his aid. They were, however, unable to handcuff Henry Coles as the handcuffs were too small! He was finally arrested by Sergeant Hubbard and another constable.

The Police Station at that time, where the Woolcotts lived, was probably Sunnyside in

Pilcorn Street, close by Henry Coles' house. Mrs Woolcott told the court that while they were fighting she got her husband's truncheon and threatened to hit Coles with it if he did not leave go. Frederick Crease also corroborated her story.

Dr Maurice Hickie of Wedmore gave evidence of the injuries received by the constable. He stated that the constable 'was so covered with mud and blood that it took him some three quarters of an hour before he could see what the real injuries were.' There follows the full description of these horrendous injuries, which included extensive wounds on the head and face, two black eyes, wounds on the cheek, ears and lip. His left wrist was sprained and useless, and there was bruising on his trunk, left thigh and knee. This is a shortened version of the full gory details given in the newspaper.

William Parker, blacksmith, c1908

Coles was committed for trial at the Taunton Assizes and the Bench commended the 'plucky manner in which the constable had acted and the pluck of his wife.' Coles was also charged with breaking and entering the house of William John Parker and stealing 'a pair of iron steps, a die stock, dies etc.' William Parker lived in Walnut House, Plud Street and was also a blacksmith. The dies and the stock or handle onto which they were fixed for use, would have been used by the blacksmith for stamping or branding impressions on leather, barrels or suchlike.

On February 25th Henry Coles stood trial in Taunton for theft and grievous bodily harm to P.C. Woolcott. He was defended by a Mr C Garland. Evidence was given by P.C. Woolcott, Mrs Woolcott, Mrs Frost, Mrs Alice Crease, Samuel Cock and Elizabeth Ann Hooper; these last three were the neighbours woken up by the disturbance, who helped restrain Henry Coles.

Mr Garland, defending, said it was a most extraordinary case, and a remarkably sad one. He tried to prove that there was inherited instability in the family, by describing how Henry Coles' uncle was for twenty five years in the Wells lunatic asylum, where he was sent because he wrote a threatening letter to her late Majesty Queen Victoria. For forty seven years Henry Coles himself had been a respectable and well-to-do ironmonger and blacksmith; but within the last two or three years he had become a changed man. He had suffered a bad epileptic fit in the street some time previously, and he had become moody and lachrymose. Mr Garland sought to show that on the night in question Henry Coles was incapable of controlling himself. Mrs Frost, a niece of Coles, said he had had several epileptic fits 'and in January three slight fits and his body was very rigid.' Mr Vachell the prosecuting counsel said that Henry Coles was a widower and five years ago wanted to marry a Mrs Tucker. Mrs Tucker had however married P.C. Woolcott instead!

Dr Frederick St John Bullen of Clifton, a doctor with twenty years' experience in these cases, gave evidence on the mental state of Coles. He said Coles was very dull and apathetic, generally weak-minded, and had very marked defects in memory. The judge decided, however, that there was no evidence of insanity. The jury retired to consider the verdict, and returned after a few minutes, finding the prisoner guilty of theft. He had already pleaded guilty to the wounding of P.C. Woolcott. The police constable had been 'laid aside for five weeks' after the assault. The judge sentenced Coles to 18 months hard labour in each case, the terms to run concurrently, and remarked that but for his age Coles would have been sent to penal servitude, with its regime of solitary confinement followed by hard labour.

The judge expressed a hope that Mrs Woolcott would receive a reward, and that the Chief Constable might remember P.C. Woolcott's actions 'when there were promotions to be made'. Frederick Crease received a reward for coming to the rescue of P.C. Woolcott, and also a letter of thanks from the Chief Constable. A few months later Henry Coles' house in Pilcorn Street was sold for 'the good sum of £505'. This price did not include the stock in trade of his blacksmith's business. During his trial two letters were read out giving Henry a good character. These were from the Revd AR May, Vicar of Wedmore, and Mr Samuel Price, former headmaster of Wedmore School.

Although no-one approved of the crimes that Henry Coles had committed, there was some sympathy towards him as he clearly suffered epileptic fits at times. Several days after his committal, all the prisoners from the Somerset Assizes passed through Cheddar, and a brief notice in the local paper reported that 'Henry Coles looked much better and was in good spirits. An opportunity to speak a few encouraging words to him was taken advantage of by a well known resident.' Local interest in the case is perhaps reflected in the printing of a special extra sheet as a supplement to *The Cheddar Times* of Saturday February 27th 1909, with an outsize headline in bold type proclaiming **'HENRY COLES gets 18 MONTHS!'**

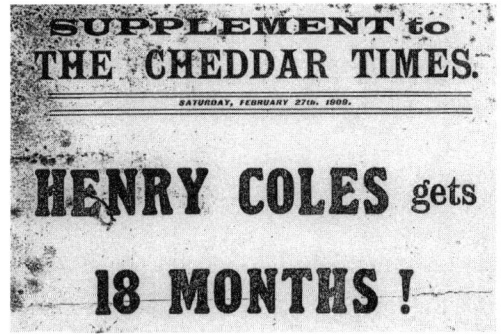

The Cheddar Times *February 27th 1909*

The Tin-Pot Band

One hundred years ago certain attitudes in the parish and indeed in the country were very different from those of the present day. If anyone was seen to be living together without 'the benefit of parson', the local community registered its disapproval in a particularly public and humiliating way.

In January 1900 a reporter from the *Weston Mercury* was passing through Blackford when he heard 'the most awful, discordant and dismal noises' that he had ever encountered from a band.[3] He came to the conclusion that the 'musical talent of some of the young villagers had certainly been neglected'! On enquiry, he discovered that the band consisted of instruments made from 'anything from a stove pipe to a broken zinc bucket'. The purpose of the band was 'to serenade a couple who had departed from the strict laws of virtue'.

The lady had once been a 'Salvation lass' and it appears that she had won the heart of a travelling merchant. This man was very well known, both in the area and in other parts of the country. Unfortunately, he was already married and had a family. However, he had told his beloved that his wife was dead. He must have been very surprised when his wife turned up, very much alive, to spoil the 'honeymoon' of the happy couple.

For three nights the Blackford band gave their musical entertainment outside the couple's house, and according to the reporter 'conducted themselves in a very orderly manner and no damage was done' - or at least, none that he saw, for it later appears there was some misbehaviour. On the third night the couple were burned in effigy, to the derisive shouts of a large company of villagers.

The lady in question, Selina Summers or Somers, was not to be intimidated and because of the harassment she had suffered she called the police. At Axbridge Petty Sessions on February 17th 1900, twelve young men from Blackford were up before the bench.[4] They were Thomas Edney, Robert and Benjamin Wall, Henry Isgar, Albert Kingsbury, Walter and Charles Tucker, Frank, Richard and Henry Long, Herbert Dinham and Augustus Latcham. They were summonsed for disorderly behaviour in Blackford on January 13th. The Wedmore solicitor William George Burrough appeared on their behalf and all the defendants pleaded not guilty.

The local policeman, Constable Standen, had been on duty in Blackford on one of the nights. He appeared as a witness. Describing the scene, he saw 'a number of men coming from Arthur Wall's premises, they had a spring conveyance [a light, horsedrawn waggon] with them, containing two effigies. Some were beating tins, blowing horns, ringing bells, playing fifes, flutes, and making a great noise'. P.C. Standen asked them to desist, but they took no notice. He asked them a second time, and they promised to do so but actually continued and went back to the starting point. They were creating 'a regular uproar and caused several complaints'.

Selina Summers then gave her evidence. She was a single woman from Blackford who said that on the night in question she was in Wedmore. When she returned home she saw that bricks and stones were being thrown into her house. At this she informed the police, being 'considerably annoyed by the defendants'. She believed the row was 'in consequence of Mr Franks living with her'.

Mr WG Burrough said that there was no case against his clients of annoying Miss Summers on that day. The real annoyance took place the previous day when the lads had got up a band and annoyed Miss Summers. The magistrate after listening to all the evidence decided to fine each defendant one shilling, and the costs to be divided between them.

There had been a similar case a few years earlier in the adjoining parish of Allerton in 1896.[5] Martha House, a young woman from Chapel Allerton, went to work as a barmaid in the Anchor Inn at Combwich near Bridgwater. Within a few months she and the landlord, John Lillycrap, had eloped. He left behind his wife and six children. Mrs Lillycrap found that her jewellery was missing, and the police eventually discovered the couple in Abertillary. Most of the jewellery was recovered, but a valuable ring was missing. Martha House was later apprehended in Allerton, with the ring which she claimed to have had for over two years.

Martha House returned to Chapel Allerton again a month later. Whether she had been found guilty or not, was not reported. The villagers were 'determined to hail her arrival with the respect they considered due to such an important event'. A large crowd assembled outside her house on the Tuesday evening and 'exerted themselves in fine style on their various instruments ... tin pots and pans, kettles etc., calculated to inspire harmonious melody. The heroine made her appearance during the serenade and was received with great enthusiasm, but probably on account of the warm reception or for another reason, hastily withdrew. There has also been talk about the burning of effigies representative of the elopement case'. This report also appeared in the *Weston Mercury*, and the headline of the 'Combwich Elopement' was flashed in big letters on several occasions.

I have been told that there was a 'serenading' of a couple in Wedmore in about 1906, a very late occurrence of this ancient local tradition. Perhaps this was the last time it happened locally. I have been unable, so far, to find out whether this practice had been going on in the Isle of Wedmore for hundreds of years, or whether it was a fairly recent development. The ritual was known as making 'Rough Music'.[6] John Giles in his diary in 1854 mentions rough music in 'rustic Oxfordshire'.[7] A related local custom called Skimmington (or Skimmerton) Riding, or Riding Skimmetty, was designed to ridicule suspected adulterors or henpecked husbands. It was described by Thomas Hardy in *The Mayor of Casterbridge*, published in 1886, where it was called the Skimmitty Ride. The couple, or effigies of them (sometimes called 'mommets') were tied back-to-back on a horse, and led through the streets to the rowdy and shaming 'music' of the tin-pot band. At Montacute House, a screen depicts 'Riding the Skimmington'; here, one scene shows a hen-pecked husband, whose wife has left him to tend the baby, consoling himself with a pint of beer. His wife finds him and hits him over the head with a shoe. A neighbour tells what has happened. The husband is then shown 'riding the Skimmington' - sitting on a pole, and being carried round the village for the villagers to mock him.

These two episodes are the only time this ritual is recorded in the Wedmore area, and then only because the events made the magistrate's court and the newspapers. Did it happen more often, but as a tradition of an unwritten, unrecorded rural sub-culture? And for how long had this folk-practice been handed down? The custom is certainly recorded in the early 1600s, and could be very much older. The meaning of the word 'Skimmington' is obscure, but thought to be similar to 'simpleton' as a term of derision. There was a well called Skimmington Well at Rock Hill, near Curry Mallet; people danced there on Midsummer Day and its water was supposed to cure rheumatism - but apart from the name, there does not seem to be any link with the noisy local disapproval of 'the Skimmington Ride'. Was Selina Summers being particularly brave to take the lads of Blackford to court, and did her stand mark a change of attitude, and the end of the tin-pot band playing in Blackford? Was the rumoured 1906 episode perhaps its final manifestation in Wedmore?

Chapter 15
Wedmore in Wartime, 1939–1945

In 1995 the parish celebrated the 50th anniversary of VE Day, the end of World War II in Europe, with an exhibition of memorabilia from those dark days of the war. Against the world-wide scale of events between 1939 and 1945, and compared with the official histories of that time, events in Wedmore may seem small scale and memories of fifty years ago fade all too easily. What happened during those war years is, however, an intrinsic part of our village history, now half a century away. What did happen; were we bombed; how did Hitler's threat affect our lives, and what did we all do about it? To help answer these questions I have talked to a number of villagers who were involved at that time. I have to thank, especially, Alan Banwell, Bert Ticknell, George Harding, and the late Tom North, Leslie Cook, Geoffrey Pavey, and Ida Hobbs for their memories. There is value in writing down these local recollections because they will not necessarily appear in any official record.

Wedmore had many voluntary groups during the war, in which everybody played their part. It is through their memories of what they did in these groups that a picture of Wedmore at war can be built up. These groups included the Home Guard, the Air Raid Precaution Wardens and the First Aid Unit, the Auxiliary Fire Service, the wartime Special Police Constables, the 'Secret Home Guard' Auxiliary Unit, the Women's Voluntary Service, and youth groups.

A large number of the younger men and women disappeared from Wedmore, having been called up to serve their country. Others, however, were in reserved occupations such as farming, or related industries. My father ran an agricultural merchant's business supplying farmers with cattle food. Those who were not called up joined a group. At first they could choose which group to support; but later on people were put where they were most needed. Every man between the ages of 17 and 65 who was 'fit enough to walk about' had to volunteer. After a full day's work farming or in other reserved occupations, they would spend at least one and often two or three nights a week on duty. If an emergency happened there was a general call-out, and everybody available came to do their bit. In case of invasion, the church bells were to be rung.

The central meeting place was the old Police Station. This stood opposite the west gate of St Mary's Church where the car park is now. The house was knocked down in about the 1960s, to widen the road on that dangerous corner. This Police Station became the headquarters and billet for most of the voluntary groups, although one group - the Auxiliary Fire Service - was based at The Swan. If a bomb had hit the Police Station it would have knocked out Wedmore's wartime nerve-centre.

After the evacuation of Dunkirk and the fall of France in 1940, there was a general fear of invasion, and the LDVs (Local Defence Volunteers) came into their own. They later became the Home Guard. The Wedmore Home Guard was in the capable hands of Ernest Banwell, farmer, of Westholme Farm at West End. Bill Boley of Combe Batch was second in command and Sid Cook was the sergeant. The Home Guard was based at Westholme Farm, and ammunition was kept in a hut at the top of the orchard; there was also a post at the Police

Station. The office was in another hut at the top of the garden at Westholme Farm - it is still there today (2002). The volunteers had no weapons to begin with, and their own shotguns were checked to see if they were suitable until rifles arrived for them. Later on, sten guns were issued. Major Ernest Banwell was decorated with the MBE for his work with the Wedmore Home Guard some months before the war ended. Organising the men was sometimes a problem. Two men from Mudgley were not up to the mark, and would have let the group down on parade. There was a need for stretcher-bearers, so Major Banwell suggested these two - which would solve the problem, as they would be excused from parade. However, the plan backfired when one of the men came to 'Farmer' Banwell and said 'We could shoot the b.....s but we wouldn't pick them up after they were dead!' The Home Guard was eventually issued with khaki uniforms, their forage caps bearing the Somerset Light Infantry badge. Their first rifles were American, and they were allowed just five rounds of ammunition each. They were trained by NCOs of the Suffolk Regiment who had recently been evacuated from Dunkirk. Training took place in the Church Schoolroom (now the Village Hall). Practices were also held at Yoxter Rifle Range on the top of Mendip; and spigot mortar practice took place at Cross Quarry. Later they were organised into patrols. One of the Home Guard observation posts was near Bagley, which gave an excellent view both north and south of the Isle of Wedmore. Tom North joined the Home Guard, and on Sunday mornings he trained in signals in an old chapel at Stone Allerton, before he left to join the RAF.

In 1940 a report came that German troops were landing in the Moors south of Heath House - the feared invasion had come! The church bells were rung, and the Home Guard rushed out with guns, pitchforks and clubs, only to find it was a false alarm. There are two stories about this 'invasion'. One is that the haycocks out in the moor had been swept up into the sky by a whirlwind. Searchlights picked up the shapes, and it was thought they were descending parachutes. The other version is that the 'Germans' spotted were in fact farmers coming home from milking the cows out in the moor late at night. The Swan Inn, apparently, did a roaring trade that night - 'the best night's business for years', quenching the thirst of everyone who had been 'rushing about after Germans'.

One night in March 1944, four parachute bombs were dropped near Wedmore. One landed at Quab Lane, another near what is now the Golf Course, the third at Snipefield and the fourth, which did not explode, at the top of Lascot Hill. I have been told of another unexploded bomb which landed in the orchard of a farm at Crickham, which may or may not have been part of the same episode. The craters left by the bombs were quite large. A small cottage in Quab Lane was damaged and the doors blown off a house in Snipefield Lane, but the only damage in Wedmore itself was some smashed glass. Mr Geoffrey Pavey, who was in the wartime force of Special Police Constables, under the command of P.C. Hill of Wedmore, remembered taking over from the Home Guard to guard the unexploded bomb at Lascot Hill. It was the size of a pillar box and lay at an angle half-embedded in the ground. The road at Lascot Hill was closed, with a notice 'UXB' (unexploded bomb) barring the way. The army bomb disposal squad came to deal with it, and blew it up in a controlled explosion. It was reported, on a different occasion, that another bomb fell below Castle Farm at Heath House. It did not explode, and soon sank into the peat. Presumably it is still there. Also remembered are incendiary bombs falling across the hilltop towards Maltfield.

There was a unit of regular soldiers on duty in Wedmore, who had charge of searchlights, which dotted the countryside to track enemy aircraft at night. One searchlight was set on Lascot Hill, and another where the Bowls Club carpark is today; there may have been others. Most of the soldiers who manned the searchlights were billeted in their headquarters, which consisted of lines of huts either side of Kelsons Lane. There was also a cooking block, and toilets: the drains are still there. The RAF also had a Radar Observation point up Quab Lane, on the Wedmore side of the lane. It was in the centre of a field near the large barn. The concrete base still shows through the grass during dry summer weather.

There was also the special Auxiliary Unit, which was separate from the Home Guard. These secret units were formed across the country to go 'underground' and carry on local resistance should the worst happen and Britain be invaded. It is still difficult to find out locally about this unit. They were sworn to secrecy and were not allowed to keep records. It seems worthwhile setting down here what I have learned. In Wedmore, this unit of nine men was based at Sand, and included Captain Francis Banwell of Sand, and Sergeant Arthur Duckett who lived in Billings Hill. Their secret underground headquarters were in Francis Banwell's orchard near Old Wood. Explosives and incendiaries were stored in one of the derelict cottages in Old Wood. If the invasion came, the job of the Auxiliary unit was to go missing. There was enough food and water to last a fortnight. Everyone was sworn to secrecy, and not even their families knew what they were involved in. They were trained to use the latest explosives, and would have destroyed all lines of communication. In our area, this would have meant blowing up bridges over the rivers Brue and Axe, and destroying our roads to hinder the enemy. One of their secret lookouts was a hut down the Lerburne, watching the Axe. Despite all this secrecy, one photograph survives!

Wedmore Patrol 203 Battalion, Home Guard Auxiliary Unit, 1944

By contrast there was an 'official' Invasion Committee made up of a representative from each group. Charles Pavey (Geoffrey's father) was the wartime police member. The Invasion Committee did keep records, and the Invasion Committee War Book still survives.[1] In December 1942 it records that there were 649 houses in the parish. The committee went round each house, checking and counting spades, shovels, forks, ladders, wheelbarrows, buckets, carts, lorries - anything and everything that could be brought into use if needed. It may seem amusing to us today to think of someone going round counting every bucket, but this list could have made the difference between death and survival.

There were many groups besides the Home Guard and the wartime Special Constables; and memories of their activities add vivid details to the history of wartime Wedmore.

The Wedmore Auxiliary Fire Service was set up in 1938 under the charge of Chief Fire Officer WJ Egan, of Axbridge Rural District Council. Wedmore men went to Cheddar for instruction, and met for regular practice sessions. The ten firemen included George Harding and Bert Tincknell. To begin with, they had no uniforms, helmets or proper equipment. My father Cecil Puddy, another auxiliary fireman, bought an old Armstrong Siddeley for £5, to act as 'the engine' and tow the pump. The car was rarely used and, when needed, was difficult to start. Later a Bedford lorry was provided, in which all the firemen could sit; the pump was still towed behind. The firemen were based at the Swan Inn, because there was room to house the 'engine' in a barn there. Mr Patterson, the landlord, who was one of the firemen on it, also had a telephone! Two men were on duty each night. They slept in the harness room and according to Bert Tincknell had to watch out that the rats did not eat their supper.

The officer in charge of the Auxiliary Fire Service in Wedmore was Ernest Stock. He was manager of the milk factory which stood where the Borough Mall is today. Ernest Stock could not drive, and sometimes he would pedal off on his bicycle to see whether a fire justified calling out the firemen. Once he raced to a chimney fire at Heath House on his bicycle, getting there and putting out the fire before the 'engine' towing its pump arrived. The fires they dealt with were usually in chimneys or hay-ricks. The firemen were also called out to gorse and heath fires on the Mendips. These fires had to be put out as a matter of urgency, to prevent the flames lighting up the night sky and attracting enemy aircraft.

The firemen never had to put out a fire caused by the enemy in Wedmore, but they were called out to assist at Weston-super-Mare and Bristol. Weston was bombed on several occasions, and Wedmore firemen helped to clear bombed buildings, including an hotel on the seafront. For volunteers coming from their country occupations this was a particularly harrowing experience. In addition a fire-watching scheme was set up in the parish, with every road or area having two men on duty each night. They were given 3 shillings for their supper. This scheme, essential in urban areas, proved hardly necessary in Wedmore, and was soon discontinued.

The Air Raid Precaution wardens (ARPs) played an important part in Wedmore during the war, checking on blackout, measuring people for gas masks and training in first aid. Leslie Cook and Tom Puddy joined the First Aid Unit in 1940. Later that year it branched out and became the St John Ambulance Brigade. They were linked with Cheddar, and trained in Wedmore Manor House stables. Their training included how to deal with gas attacks.

The first aid team did not have an ambulance. They had the use of a van, which belonged to a lady from Allerton who did duty with the ARP wardens. When the bomb went off on Lascot Hill bits of the shrapnel were salvaged and used to give added reality to practice nights. The first aid unit was also called to Weston after a big air raid. Leslie Cook helped to clear rubble and bodies from the Bournville area in January 1941, where a whole road of houses was destroyed. Thirty-four people were killed in this, the first raid on Weston. The unit also helped in Bristol.

Keith Puddy off to Wedmore School with his gas mask in 1942

The first air raid warning of the war in Wedmore came at midnight on 24th June 1940. The all clear was given three hours later at 3.10 a.m. My brother Keith remembers the man who used to cycle around the village ringing the ARP bell to warn of the approach of enemy aircraft. Local school children had to be alerted to the dangers of war on their doorsteps. On 31st July 1944 the Wedmore School logbook records that a talk was given to the children by Sergeant Curtis of the Somerset Constabulary, on 'the dangers of touching unknown objects which might be explosive.'[2] He warned against what were called 'butterfly bombs.' I was sitting in my place in the infant class that day, and this phrase stuck in my mind - so that not only did I never kick a tin can for many years afterwards, but I was also terrified of butterflies!

Several people remember a dog-fight over the village between a Spitfire and a Messerschmitt, as the one chased the other southwards across Somerset. On another occasion, a British glider, which had become detached from the aeroplane towing it, came down in the moor. Advantage was taken of this to further the war effort, by making people buy National Savings Certificates as tickets of admission to the field to see the glider close to.

On 27th March 1944 a German bomber, a Junkers Ju88A-4, crashed in Tadham Moor. The plane was reportedly shot down by anti-aircraft fire from Weston-super-Mare. As it flew, in trouble, over the village the crew ditched some items to try and keep it flying. It was said that canisters, bomb doors and other things were dropped, but no bombs. Some of the bits landed in the grounds of The Hall, Sand Road, and one piece was said to have been the gun turret. Before the plane ditched, the four members of the crew baled out. The parachute of the wireless operator Heinrich Schink failed to open, and he was found dead in the moor the next day. He was buried in Ashcombe Road Cemetery, Weston-super-Mare, with full military honours. The remaining three crew members were captured making their various ways to the coast. One was captured in the moor near Heath House by Stanley Tucker. He was taken to Wedmore Police station by P.C. Freddy Hill and interrogated. He was the pilot Lieutenant Wolfgang Fritz, and he wanted to return to his aeroplane to pick up his papers. The aeroplane had crashed into the peat near Blakeway and had gone down about 30 feet. The crash site was guarded by the special constables; the late Leonard Wall stood guard all the first night. In 1986 Mervyn Sweet of Blakeway, who owns the field (now called The Aeroplane Field by locals), decided to try and dig up the Junkers.[3] Pieces of the fuselage, cockpit, rudder and wings were found but the engines had gone in too deep to be recovered, and are still buried there. It was reported at the time that some petrol had leaked from the fuel pipes, and it was ignited with a match forty-two years after the aeroplane crashed.

It is hard now to realise just how little food people were officially allowed to buy each week or each month. No-one actually starved, but the diet was boring - although, being in the country, there were ways of getting extra food. Blackberries, mushrooms, nuts, rabbits and crows were free. The hedgerows were usually stripped bare of fruit very quickly. Farmers were allowed to kill two pigs and two calves a year, themselves; and everybody made sure that the animals were fattened up as much as possible - no nonsense in those days about not eating fat. Sometimes a farm animal met with an unfortunate accident, and had to be slaughtered! Once a year also, farmers were allowed to make up one day's milk into cheese for their own use; and many people churned their milk into butter to supplement their ration. Many people, also, kept a pig somewhere, and chickens scratched around almost every door. 'Dig for Victory' was the famous motto. My father Cecil Puddy grew peas on the field behind his house, Stonecroft on the Mudgley Road; and local 'pea-ladies' came to pick them. A percentage of pasture had to be ploughed and cropped, although often the land was unsuitable for cropping. Some land army girls came to work on the farms. Ernest Banwell first had two girls for training, for just a fortnight; then two, both from Weston, came to live in. Their names were Vera and Peggy. Peggy married John Scourse from Cheddar and became one of the pillars of the community at Cheddar.

In 1939 Hove College was evacuated to Elmsett Hall; when the boys were on holiday, their fat ration was often still available, and several people did quite well by it! Mr Geoffrey Pavey and his father kept a grocery and hardware shop in The Borough, and Geoffrey remembers the difficulties of trying to keep a correct account of the points on everybody's ration coupons. These points were sent to the food office in Axbridge for checking. When clothing was first rationed, margarine coupons were used until official clothing coupons were issued.

Ironmongery and household items were in short supply for most of the war, and the wholesalers sent whatever they had. One day a load of kettles arrived in Wedmore and were sold before they even got into the shop. The little cottage at the foot of Grants Lane, now part of Bridgwood, was then normally used as the hardware store for Mr Pavey's shop. During the war, however, it was used instead to store emergency food rations in case of invasion. The Ministry of Food paid rent to store tins of food there, but these tins were never needed and may eventually have gone to France.

William Owen, who kept the large shop now Lloyds Chemist, was the Home Guard quartermaster sergeant. In a shed at the back of his premises he kept the Home Guard store. Alan Banwell remembers going with his father Ernest when clothing was issued, and seeing the boots and leggings that were stored there.

The women of Wedmore worked very hard for the war effort. Many had to do the work of their menfolk who had been called up. They also took in evacuees, knitted for the soldiers, collected for National Savings and for appeals, and many joined the Women's Voluntary Service, the WVS.

Ida Hobbs was a keen member of the WVS who met at The Old Vicarage. They undertook many and varied activities. Ida remembered in particular the fire-fighting team. They met at Wedmore School playground (on the Cheddar Road) for fire practice. The demonstrator set fire to buckets of wood shavings or straw which had been impregnated with petrol. The teams of three then worked to put out the fire, one member carrying water, one pumping the water with a stirrup pump from the bucket, and one directing the jet of water onto the fire. After much practice, an exercise was held in the Swan yard. There they demonstrated their expertise at putting out a fire in a hut, and were congratulated by the fire service for their skill and effort. Twenty-five members of the WVS joined the Fire Guard team. Their expertise was, luckily, never needed, but they were ready and well trained, and to keep their hand in, they took part in competitions with other groups. Doctor Kemm from Cheddar came to teach members first aid and they became experts in the art of bandaging. They also learnt hay-box cooking, to save fuel and for use in emergencies. The food was boiled up on a primus stove and then put into the hay-box to continue cooking. Ida Hobbs went to Winscombe once with Emmie Hole and cooked a hay-box dinner there to feed the parish council, demonstrating how successful the method could be.

Many hundreds of pounds of jam and preserves were made for the war effort, using local fruit in season. Samples of each boiling were taken for testing, to keep a high standard, and careful records kept. Between March 1941 and January 1944, 15 hundredweight of jam, 160 jars of bottled fruit, and 300 pounds of chutney were made, and 1000 pounds of fruit were canned.[4] Women and children spent hours during the autumn gathering rose-hips from the hedgerows. These were collected to make rose-hip syrup, a valuable source of vitamin C which was supplied to young children.

In the early days of war evacuees arrived, mostly from Bristol and London. Some moved into condemned houses, but most were taken into local homes. Ida Hobbs, who also housed some serving soldiers stationed at the searchlight on Lascot Hill, had several lots of evacuees, including two young children, mothers with their children, and two Indian boys who went to Hove College at Elmsett Hall, as some of the boys were boarded out. When a group of evacuees arrived, the police often just 'delivered' them to the door. Ida found it hard coping with the evacuee children, for she was also working their smallholding, as her husband had been called up. She had her own two small children to look after as well, and also spent many hours a week on various activities in the WVS.

Part of the men's club in Church Street, now the Masons' building and Westminster Bank, became a rest centre and meeting place for evacuees. There the mothers could gather and compare their lives in Wedmore with their old lives in town. There were piles of blankets and good second-hand clothing to be sorted and handed out. A nursery school held in the Methodist Schoolroom on the Sand Road was run by Mary Edney. Originally it was for evacuee children, but some local children also went. Evacuee teachers arrived to help in the schools, where the classes had sometimes increased considerably. Many of the evacuees returned to the parish after the war, to spend holidays at their 'foster homes', remaining firm friends and recalling their happy days in Wedmore.

In 1942 a new group was formed within the WVS. This was 'The Housewives Section' and drew many more women into the organisation. This group of about 30 helped the ARP wardens. Each member was responsible for looking after the welfare of one road. The housewives did their training and were then allowed to put blue cards in their windows to show they were qualified. They assisted the Invasion Committee in getting the 1941 census up to date. It was important to know exactly how many people lived in the parish. On January 14th, 1943 the parish held an Invasion Exercise.[5] This included all the various groups, ARP wardens, First Aid Unit, Home Guard, special constables, Auxiliary Fire Service, rest centre staff and the WVS. This day was declared a great success, with all the groups working together.

Everybody collected salvage. Railings outside some houses, but oddly not all of them, went for the war effort. Waste paper was collected, mostly by children. My brother Keith had a little hand-cart in which he pushed the waste paper from our office down to the collecting point at the George. Children were paid a small amount for what they brought in, and given a distinctive small badge in the form of a cog inside a wheel, with the motto 'Junior Salvage Steward - A Cog in the Wheel'. The WVS collected bones at the Old Vicarage, presumably for bone meal and glue. People turned out their attics for jumble to raise money for efforts such as Wings Week in May 1943.

In March 1943 a 'pie van scheme' came into operation. This served food to workers, such as farm labourers, who had no access to canteens. Wedmore's delivery round entailed a 55 mile round trip every Wednesday. Other places delivered on other days. Up to October 1945 it was calculated that 71,766 pies, 32,318 sausage rolls and 18,698 jam tarts had been sold.[6] The van was driven by Mrs Tom Hole of The Close, West End. Many of the WVS members must have been sick of the sight of pies, rolls and tarts by the time the enterprise finished. Mrs Hole also took surplus garden produce to the Saturday market in Wells.

Axbridge Rural District Council had adopted HMS Goathland. Wedmore women decided to send parcels to the crew. Some people gave up half their sweet rations, others saved shaving and toilet soap. Such a quantity of books and games were collected that when the parcels were wrapped they were so heavy that the railway refused to handle them and they had to be repacked.

During 1943 vast areas of the county were taken over by British and American troops, in what was later known to be the build-up to the D-Day invasion of June 1944. Who can remember the cheery Americans going through Wedmore, tossing out chewing gum? When, however, the Americans left their base at Burnham-on-sea for the south coast, hundreds of trucks trundled through the village all one day, all full of American soldiers - and it is remembered that some were crying as they went to embark for France.

One of the roads near Charterhouse on Mendip was filled for miles with army vehicles, all in combat order. Military vehicles such as these needed to be disguised with camouflage nets. Wedmore took a hand in the production of these nets, 'garnishing' them with strips of multicoloured camouflage material made from scrim, cheap, loosewoven cloth. The WVS got a netting team together, including some men and the older Girl Guides. The team met in the barns of Wedmore Manor House which were lit and heated. The nets were spread out and the lengths of scrim were woven into them to make the camouflage pattern. The scrim had to be cut into lengths. Mrs Morgan, the Vicar's wife, was often seen trundling home her wheelbarrow full of coloured scrim to cut up during the evening. When the nets were finished they were baled and sent off. The nets were 'garnished' from 18th October 1943 to 29th March 1944. By the end of the first month, 13 nets had been finished, but by 1944 the team was so expert that in March 1944 167 nets were garnished. It is recorded that 98¾ miles of scrim were used, 3,084 hours were spent working, and the total number of finished nets was 568. Wedmore was the top team in Somerset, and Somerset the top county for 'garnishing': so Wedmore was the best in the country for this particular wartime undertaking.[7]

Wedmore W.V.S. Netting Team, 1944

Everybody was involved in some way towards helping the war effort. There were other activities which there is not space to describe in detail here. In particular, boys trained as army cadets. They camped at Yoxter Rifle Range on Mendip, and went on training courses. The Reverend Daven Morris was the officer in charge.

It was not all hard work during those years. Dances were often held in the Church Schoolroom (now the Village Hall), and the Americans used to come. Bill Lukins took the front and top off the piano, and played as loudly as he could. The Americans taught everybody to jitterbug, throwing the girls over their shoulders. Those dances were thoroughly enjoyed by all.

VE (Victory in Europe) Day was celebrated in May, 1945 on a beautiful day. The villages were hurriedly decorated with flags - even Christmas decorations appeared. Coloured lights were strung up in Wedmore, including a spot-lit picture of Winston Churchill making his V-for-Victory sign. Fireworks were let off in one garden, and the Home Guard let off some 'loud bangs' in Church Street, which shattered some windows. The telephone box was stripped of its blackout, and the George and the Swan were lit up. It is recorded that people entered the pubs that night who had never previously been over the threshold before! There was a service of thanksgiving in the church, remembering the fact that Wedmore parish had lost twelve of its finest young men, never to be forgotten. The day ended with dancing in the streets. Music was provided by a gramophone lent by a teacher from Hove College at Elmsett, and Herb Urch rigged up an amplifier. Refreshments were supplied by Mrs Tom Hole and her pie van. Those who could, took along a packet of biscuits. The church bells rang out at midnight, to celebrate the official start of peace at 00.01 hours on 9th May 1945. As it was put in a letter from Wedmore, written at that time,

'EVERYBODY WAS HAPPY.' [8]

Chapter 16
A Field Name Alphabet: A–Z

When I started looking at the history of Wedmore parish many years ago, one of my primary objects was to study the names of fields. Fields are all around us: mostly now pasture, but some ploughed. Some are high on the hill, others are low and damp on the moors. They come in a vast variety of sizes and shapes: some tidy rectangles, others like pieces of a jigsaw. They are enclosed with hedges, fences, or watery rhynes. And every field has a name.

As we drive past them at speed, we can too easily overlook this astonishingly simple fact. People named their fields so that they knew what was theirs, and what was somebody else's; and to identify who was going to work where. When your fields were the raw material for your survival, their identification was important. This naming of fields is a vast resource for the local historian, for these names preserve local memories that can go back centuries. What people chose to call their fields can tell us about the landscape, soil conditions, crops and stock, ownership, and folklore; even, occasionally, their wry sense of humour, their exasperation, or their own sense of history.

What is more, while many fields are old, their names are often older still. Even when a field was radically redesigned, the old name might be passed on to the new field - garbled, perhaps, but a surviving fragment of a much older past.

At the outset, studying field names seemed a relatively simple task. The Revd S.H.A. Hervey had already looked at many local field names in his *Wedmore Chronicles*.[1] Scholarship, however, has progressed far since the 1880s, and ideas are constantly changing. A new assessment of our field names seemed overdue. I started by looking at the parish and tithe maps of 1791-1839, with their accompanying schedules, to match the names listed in the schedules with the numbers on the map.[2] The field name could then be marked on a tracing of the map, and thus pinpointed on the ground today. In a parallel study, Judith van der Meulen collected some field names used by farmers today, and showed how a good many of them have survived since 1839 in more or less recognisable form.

The map and survey names of 1791-1839, however, were far from the whole story. It was apparent that some names, either because of their innate meanings, or because they seemed to have become garbled, were much older. What was needed was the earliest version of any field name. The task suddenly became far more complicated. As, in the course of a more complete study of Wedmore landscape history, I began to search through as many deeds and other early documents as possible, I made many additions to the basic list from the maps and schedules.

I have come across the earlier and more genuinely original versions of some of the 19th century names. I found others which had disappeared by the time of the maps, and which cannot now be precisely located on the ground. Fields appeared in the Somerset landscape in Roman and Saxon times, and were well developed over Wedmore by the early middle ages; and with these fields came field names. Though it is not normally possible to date the origins of names precisely (they may already be very old by the time they were first written

Wedmore field names in a Highway Rate book, 1818

down), some that I found in early documents have an ancient, rough dialect sound to them; they are certainly at least medieval in origin. Often we cannot now tell what these names mean. Other field names are descriptive words we still use today, but the words themselves are Old English in origin, in use from Saxon or early medieval times. Are the names, too, that old? I have found field names in documents dating from the 900s to the 1900s. Wedmore is a very big parish, and there are nearly 4000 named fields, although many are variants of the same name. Allowing for this, and for fields that gave their names to adjacent roads, or took their names from nearby features like mills and wells, I have identified about 800 distinct field names, and will look at some of the more interesting examples.

Field names, like place names, are a study to which there are not always certain, cut-and-dried answers. It will be seen how often a name, despite all research efforts, remains an unsolved mystery. What, for example, are we to make of

Alwoshulleisballe

This wonderful field name is found in Clewer in 1365.[3] There is no trace of the name in later documents, and there are no clues as to exactly where it was or what it means. *Ball* means, in Middle English (ME), a boundary mound. *Hull* is Old English (OE) for hill, usually a hill with a broken outline - perhaps referring to the cliff edge at Clewer. *Alwo* could be a personal name. So does Alwoshulleisballe mean the field with the boundary mound at the hill belonging to Alwo?

Abovedoores

A name for the field next to, and uphill from the house. Abovedoores is found in Blackford in 1612.[4]

Aeroplane Ground

This field, at Blakeway, is our newest field name, and one of the great rarities, a field name that can be precisely dated. It dates from 1944, when a German bomber, a Junkers Ju88A-4, crashed there. Part of the aeroplane still lies in the peaty ground (see Chapter 15).

Allermoor

This name is given to a whole large group of fields below Sand. Aller is from OE *alor*, the alder tree. Alders flourished in wet ground, and were a valued medieval timber tree. The name is in fact much older than the fields: it was first recorded in 1533, when it was the name of the open common moor.[5] This was divided up into fields and drained under one of the Wedmore Enclosure Acts, in 1785. The old name was transferred to the new 1785 fields, perpetuating a memory of the landscape they replaced.

Amerell

There are two fields called Amerell (1517)[6] or Ameral in the parish. One is in Theale, and one in Blackford. It may be just coincidence, but Northload Manor owned two nameless fields, one in Theale and one in Blackford, in 1189; and it may be that these two fields with the same distinctive name are the ones in question.[7] In 1414 a Blackford field of 6 acres was still held by William of Northlode; this was very probably Amerell, although not named.[8] However by 1636 the Blackford field was called Greate Amerell.[9] What Amerell means, however, is a complete mystery.

Ballardes Lyee

This romantic-sounding field name occurs once, in Mudgley, in 1529.[10] The field is above the village on a steep slope. Lyee or leigh comes from OE *leah*, a wood-clearing or pasture in a wood clearing. Ballard is a Somerset dialect word for a castrated ram lamb - so we have a record of the field conveniently close to the original hamlet where the medieval peasants of Mudgley carried out their farming practices.

Barley

A large area of Wedmore's East Field between Mudgley and Sand was called Barley or Berleye. In 1538 there was Over (Upper) and Nether (Lower or Further) Barleye.[11] Was this the large area of ploughland where the barley crop was grown? The barley would have been used to make ale, the staple drink in medieval times. The name could, however, be *bar-leah*, the boars' woodland clearing; or *baer-leah*, the barley woodland clearing; both ancient names that conjure up Saxon times when the hilltop was still wooded and relatively wild, with just a few clearings for the first tentative fields.

Benpool

The large field below The Borough Mall towards the moor is called Benpool. In the 1700s documents show that the name was sometimes spelt Benjapool.[12] The pool can be explained easily. From the 1300s to the late 1700s there was a watermill at the edge of the field on Wedmore Moor Drove. The mill pool was formed behind in Benpool. Traces of the mill and the mill-leat can still be made out, although the pool has totally disappeared under farmyard dumping. What the Ben- or Benja- part of the name means, remains a mystery.

Blackland

Several examples of the field name Blackland occur in different parts of the parish - but they are all found only in older documents. The name does not survive today and this makes locating it difficult. This is particularly exasperating as the name Blackland is one that excites archaeologists and local historians; it often indicates an ancient settlement, usually Roman, where the later medieval ploughman noticed the black, nitrogenous soil contrasting with the more usual colour of his plough furrows. Only by linking documents through the ages can field names which have disappeared be pinpointed today - and this game of historical dominoes does not always work out. So far, several of our Wedmore Blacklands have been roughly located: there is one somewhere at Theale, another in the Crickham area. What is needed is the discovery of Roman pottery to confirm the sites. Just one definite Roman site, on the edge of Wedmore, has been matched with a field formerly called Blackland, but that must remain secret for now.

Blackpitt

Two separate fields in Blackford Manor are called Blackpitt. The name is first mentioned in 1621.[13] Both fields are on the top of the hill well away from the black soil of the peat moors. So what was the black pit? In early medieval times these fields would have been in or on the edge of ancient woodland. They may have been where charcoal burners worked and the traces of burnt earth and charcoal remained in the soil, to give the name.

Breach

Breach, from Old English (OE) *brec*, means land which is newly broken up for cultivation. The field name Breach is first recorded in Wedmore in 1342,[14] and occurs in several places in the parish, always next to a stretch of ancient woodland, suggesting that these were new fields pared from the edges of the woods. A large block of land in Mudgley was called Breach in 1559,[15] and seems to have been fields cleared from the wood in the 12-1300s. Such new fields provided more ploughland to produce more food at a time when the population was growing fast. The manorial tenants had to pay an extra rent for this new land, which was called 'overland'.

Another area of fields called Breach adjoined the former Westham Wood in Blackford. The woodland here had already disappeared by 1559, so the Breach fields must be earlier than that date.

Brewers Hay

Brewers Hay orchard at West End has given its name to a house now standing there: but the field name is the older of the two, and is probably medieval. It is the fenced enclosure (OE *[ge]haeg*) belonging to a brewer or where there was a brewery (OE *breow-aern*).

Calvecroft

Calvecroft is an early medieval field name. It occurs in Blackford in 1189, and shows that here was a small enclosure (OE *croft*) where the calves were kept.[16] The name disappears by the 1500s, so it is not possible to say exactly where in Blackford it was.

Chitterley

Below the village of Sand is a block of fields called Chitterley. These fields take their name from John of Chudderlegh, who held them in 1332 - so that in this field name we have a record of a local farmer of the 1300s.[17] John was taking over this land, in 1332, from David de Holbrook. David and William de Holebrook are living in the parish in 1299,[18] and at this early date their name, 'of the hollow brook', may have been derived from the strong little spring which bubbles out of the hillside into these fields, and which would have carved a gully for itself down the steep slope. The spring is a petrifying spring, where leaves, twigs and small stones get covered and preserved by limescale deposits.

Clyfforlange

This is one of the earliest field names I have found in Clewer. It is mentioned in a document of 1334.[19] The 'forlange' is a furlong, which was a subdivision of the medieval open field, a group of ploughed strips all lined up the same way; it was originally said to be as much land as could be ploughed by a team of oxen without taking a break to rest. The OE *Clyf* is our word cliff, a very steep slope not just (as usually nowadays) on a coast, but then also on a hillside or river bank. The name of Clewer itself has been interpreted as meaning the dwellers at the cliff: the steep bluff that juts out so prominently towards Cheddar, around which the village has developed. The 'cliff' itself is too steep to have been ploughed, but the furlong is probably the level land above, ploughed right up to the edge of the drop.

Coudenesham

Coudenesham is one of our oldest known field names. It was a landmark on the boundary of the Northload estate, described in the Panborough Saxon charter of 956.[20] Coudenesham or Cowdenesham means the enclosed pasture (OE *hamm*) belonging to cow valley (OE *cow dene*). It gives a descriptive picture of the fields below Daggs Lane at Bagley in the 900s. This is also a good example of how field names can change with time. In the mid 1300s Cowdenesham had become corrupted to Cumessam.[21] By 1510 it was Calsham - neither words giving any clue to the real origin and meaning of the name, so clear in the earliest version. Today the 'ham' pastures all have tenants' personal names: Fishers Ham and Davidges Ham; the Saxon cows have been forgotten.

Culvercroft, Culvershays and Culver Close

The common factor in these three field names is Culver, from the OE *culfre*, meaning dove. Doves or pigeons were a good source of food in medieval times, both eggs and birds being eaten. The fledgling pigeon squabs were regarded as a luxury, and the lord of the manor could build his dovecote where the birds could feed at the expense of his tenants' crops. Wedmore Manor, in 1559, had ten dovecotes scattered over its extensive territory.[22]

Culvercroft is the field in Combe Batch where the council houses and Combe Batch Rise are now built.[23] A croft is an enclosed piece of land usually near a house. The name Culvercroft, which lay on the eastern edge of the ancient Borough, recalls the dovecote which stood within its own enclosure. Culverhays was another name I found for the same field, *hay* being the OE word for a hedged enclosure.[24] During the building of Combe Batch Rise some large stones were said to have been uncovered. Unfortunately this discovery was not reported and the stones were reburied. These stones might perhaps have been the base of the dovecote.

Culver Close, where 'close' is once again the old term for an enclosed or fenced area, is at West Stoughton.[25] Presumably another of the Wedmore dovecotes was sited there in medieval times.

Cut Down Bacon

Here is a very odd name! Cut Down Bacon, or Cutty Downe Bacon in 1698, is the name of a group of fields in Blackford, along the Poolbridge Road to the east of Overbrook Farm.[26] Is it referring to some event that happened there before 1698, preserved as a field name that is now a mystery to us? Or was it a piggery and slaughterhouse? Despite hours of research, the answer has not yet been found, so it must remain a tantalising puzzle for now.

Daddocks

Daddocks is a field which is in Mark parish, but which once belonged to the Manor of Blackford. Daddocks, as it is spelt in 1820,[27] could be dialect for 'dead wood', and this was the Revd S.H.A. Harvey's guess at the meaning of the name. However, earlier spellings show it to be Dodwicks (in 1772)[28] or Doddicks (in 1660).[29] This suggests that the last part of the name is -wick, from the OE *wic*, a very ancient name for a farm, usually a dairy farm.[30] It is a name that excites the historian because it could denote a very early farmstead. Dodd could well be a personal name, so Doddwicks in fact probably means Dodd's dairy farm.

Doles and Dolemead

Several fields in this parish, as in others in this area, are called Doles. These were fields allocated between tenants on a dole or share-drawing system. The actual system varied from village to village, and might be quite an elaborate ritual for drawing lots. We do not, unfortunately, have any details of how the Wedmore dole allocation was made. The Wedmore Doles were in Gooseham, where in 1554 Dole Mead was meadow land divided up between four tenants, Richard Manyman, John Bultinge, Joan Davye and Thomas Poole. Richard Manyman called his plot 'a Runnynge Acre' and every year the tenants changed places so that 'he that lyethe in this place this yere, is Removed to Another the nexte'.[31] This rotating system meant that, over four years, each of the tenants had a fair share of the best and the poorer meadowland and its hay, and that every fourth year Richard Manyman and his neighbours, or their successors as tenants, arrived back at the same plot. It would be fascinating to know more of how this system originated and operated, and why it was used on some fields and not others.

Dragfurlong

To the west of Townsend Lane are several fields called Dragfurlong.[32] These fields were ploughed in medieval times, and it must have been hard work for the ox team, as they are very steep. Drag- probably comes from the OE *draeg*, which means a steep hill where more than ordinary effort is needed to plough. The furlong was part of the medieval arable open field. The name sums up the medieval farmer's feelings about cultivating this difficult terrain. The same OE word *draeg* occurs in the name of Draycott, the cottage(s) on their equally steep hillside.

Dryalls

My house is one of two built in the field called Dryalls Orchard. The deeds show that the orchard belonged to James Dryall and his wife Mary, of Knowle in Bedminster, near Bristol, in 1741.[33] This, then, is another field called after someone who can be actually identified and dated, this time to the mid-1700s.

Elm Tining and Elm Hay

Several field names remind us how, until very recently, great elm trees were such a noticeable feature of our Wedmore landscape. Now we have to remind ourselves from old photographs of the impact massed elms had upon the appearance of the countryside. Medieval Wedmore farmers recall this lost landscape with their field names. Elm Tining at Theale,[34] and Elm Hay at Mudgley,[35] both identify enclosed (-tining) or hedged (-hay) fields by their elm trees.

Elynstubbe or Elenstubbe

Elynstubbe is a field in Panborough mentioned in 1516.[36] It means the field where there were stumps of elder trees, from OE *ellern*, elder and OE *stubb* - a stub or stump. Elder is so difficult to eradicate, this name perhaps reflects the attempts of a medieval farmer to cut down and kill the elder trees on his land. Alternatively, he may have been pollarding them deliberately, and the rows of sprouting stumps or stubs, like willow pollards, became a landmark that gave the field its name.

Flaxland

Flax was widely grown in England in the 1600s and 1700s, but then became less frequent as a crop by the late 1700s. Flaxland is an area of fields above Crickham. The name is recorded in 1700, a time when local flax growing was around its peak.[37]

Folly

A triangular piece of land in Crickham is called Folly in 1820.[38] This corner was originally part of Crickham open arable field, until a new road cut across to link two other roads. It cut off this small piece, making it a little 'island' of ground between the roads. The name does not appear at any earlier date, and is presumably a wry comment by local farmers of the early 1800s, on road developments that have left such a tiny and useless patch of ploughland.

Frogland

The name of this group of fields, near the golf course, is found in documents as early as 1609.[39] I assume it is the farmer's way of commenting on the soggy nature of the ground, even though it is on the top of the hill. It is interesting that Frogland is close by Snipefield, since snipe also favour damp pastureland. The names show the sharp eye of early farmers, on foot and not high up on a tractor, for the wildlife in their fields.

Garlick Hill

Garlick Hill is an area of steep fields north west of Bagley. The name occurs, as Garlycke Hill, in 1542.[40] It suggests that the fields were carved out of the extensive Bagley Wood in medieval times, and that the pungent wild garlic plant (ramsons), characteristic of woodland and very difficult to eradicate, continued to sprout in the newly ploughed land, and to contaminate the crops of grain grown there. Here is a field name recording a smell! Garlic was, however, also grown as a herb and for use in the treatment of leprosy.

Garston

Garston or Garston Orchard is only found in our parish at Clewer. There the name goes back to 1365, when it seemed to have been written as Carston.[41] This, however, does not make sense and may be a medieval clerk's error. Garston is OE *gaers-tun*, a grass enclosure or paddock, usually close by a farmstead.

Gogsham

Gogsham at Sand in 1559 contains a tricky OE word, either *-ham* or *-hamm*, and it is not now possible to be certain which was originally intended.[42] OE *ham* is a village or homestead; and OE *hamm* is a lush meadow, bordering on a river, stream or moor and used for early grazing and hay. What Gogs or Gogges means is a mystery; it may be a personal name, in which case it certainly sounds very old. Does the field name, however, mean Gog's homestead, or Gog's hay meadow? It is on the outskirts of Sand village, and beside the upper reaches of the Wedmore Brook, so either would be applicable, and we cannot now tell which. Gogsham has no connection that I have been able to find with Gogs House (and nearby Gogs Orchard) at West End, Wedmore. Gogsham is very much the older name, and, if anything, Gogs House is perhaps called after the Sand field, and not the other way round; but proper evidence is lacking.

Goldfinches

Just one field near Latcham is called Goldfinches in 1820 and it makes us think that it is named after the birds, often seen on the teasles growing along the rhynes.[43] However, the truth is probably more mundane: the field probably once belonged to a property over in Mudgley which was called Goldfinches, and simply took the name from there.[44] The Mudgley tenement, in turn, probably took its name from an earlier tenant; and why he was called John (or whatever) Goldfinch, we shall probably never know.

Gooseham

When I was a child my grandmother would often mention going to Gooseham Races. It was a mythical event as far as I know! Gooseham, below Latcham, was another early Old English (OE) *hamm* (see Gogsham). The land gently rising out of Wedmore Moor would have been good meadowland, and handy for medieval people to keep their geese. Gooseham is first recorded in documents in 1558, but by then the land is partly ploughed and partly meadow, and there are no references to geese being kept there.[45]

Gore or Goar

A gore or goar (OE *gara*) is a small corner or triangle of land left over when the rectangular pattern of ploughed furlongs has been laid out in the medieval open field. Gore occurs in our field names from the 1500s.[46] The strange thing about Gore in Wedmore, however, is that the name covers a very large area and many fields. It is certainly not one small triangular piece of land. Has the original name spread, or does it mean something entirely different?

Hawkers Wear

Hawkers Wear in 1820 is a field in Yeo Moor at Theale, on the bank of the river Axe.[47] The field name has changed over the centuries, and proves to be nothing to do with anyone called Hawker. It may be easier to start at the beginning, with its first recorded name, in Saxon times. In 956 there was a place called Tunsingwere.[48] This was the fish trap or weir of a Saxon called Tunsing, in the river Axe. It was a landmark on the estate boundary described in the Panborough Saxon charter, which can be located quite precisely on the ground, although there is no trace of any fish weir to see now; and it gave its name to the adjacent field. By 1516 the name of the Saxon owner of the fish trap had been forgotten, and the field was called Hakewere.[49] This describes the type of fish trap, a hatch-weir where the fish were encouraged to swim through one particular opening in a wattle barrier, into a wicker basket, and a 'hatch' or sliding door was dropped down behind them to trap them. Over the years the fish trap itself disappeared, and the name was mistakenly corrupted, into Hawkswear and later still to Hawkers Wear. The field name is a remarkable, if garbled, survival of a very ancient feature.

Honnieland

Honnieland (1605)[50] or Honey Land (1820)[51] is a single field on the edge of the village of Crickham. It is probably where the beehives were located, from OE *hunig*, honey.

Hope

Behind Theale Great House is a big field called Hope. It has two large hillocks in it, and it rises up towards Garlick Hill. The OE word *hop*, which means a small enclosed valley, or a blind valley, here presumably means the small valley between the two hillocks. 'The Hoppe' is first recorded in 1554.[52] It is an example of a modern-seeming word which in fact has an entirely different original meaning.

Hoverelulley

The name of this field on Mudgley Hill is first mentioned in the early 1200s, in a document dated some time between 1236 and 1242.[53] It means Over or Upper Lulley. It appears as Lulley or Lullie in 1554.[54] The -ley is from OE *leah*, a wood-clearing or the meadow or pasture in the clearing. In a field name as early as this one, the first part is probably Lull or Lulla, the name of an early tenant of the land, who sounds a real Saxon. We thus have Lull's wood-clearing, taking us back to the very early stages of our Mudgley farming landscape.

Hundred Acres

Hundred Acres is a joke name, for a very tiny field in Theale.[55] It seems to have been a small piece left over when the strips were laid out in the ploughed open field in medieval times.

Innick

A field in Stoughton is called Innick or Inhoke in 1609[56] and 1820,[57] and a small group of fields in Theale have the same name in 1516.[58] The name comes from a medieval or Middle English (ME) word *inhoke*, originally meaning land temporarily enclosed for cultivation while the remainder of the arable open field was left fallow. The name gives us a little detail of medieval farming practice.

Jacks Cross

On the west side of Lascot Hill, at the top, are two fields which in 1820 were called Jacks Cross.[59] We have other Jack names in the parish, such as Jackshay (1636)[60] and Jacks Lane (1559) at Heath House.[61] Jack in Jacks Cross is probably nothing to do with anyone called Jack. There is another meaning for 'Jacks': it was a medieval slang word for 'No Man's Land': vacant, unused or unclaimed land, often marginal and difficult to cultivate. This could well apply to the Jacks Cross fields. The 'cross' part of the field name refers to a crossroads made by former field tracks.

Kills Wall

This rather gruesome name of a field between Mudgley and Sand occurs only in the 1700s.[62] I have been able to pinpoint the site. It is on the boundary of the deer park of Mudgley Manor, which existed from the 1100s to the 1500s. The park was subsequently divided up into fields, and this one was up against the boundary wall where, presumably, deer were driven to be picked off for the manorial larder.

Knapp

Knapp is the name of some fields just below the former Wedmore School, on the Cheddar Road.[63] As the land slopes towards the moor, there is a slight rise or hillock. It is hardly visible to us, but shows up on the contour lines of a detailed map, and would have been obvious to the medieval ploughman on the ground as an area of drier land rising out of one of the wettest parts of the moor. Knapp means just that, from OE *cneapp*, a hillock.

Lampers Acre

On the bank of the River Axe below Panborough lies a small field. The Revd S.H.A. Hervey, in the 1880s, interpreted its name as meaning Lambs' Acre. Today, through studying early documents that were not available to Hervey, we now know it means something entirely different. In 1517 it is called Lampreys Acre.[64] Lampreys are an eel-like fish and were a medieval delicacy. The now derelict Marchey Farm stands on the other side of the river opposite this field. This is a very ancient farmstead, which in 1189 paid a yearly rent to Glastonbury Abbey.[65] This annual rent was seven thousand eels which could well have included the sought-after lampreys. Lampreys Acre must have been the site for the eel traps in the 1500s, and perhaps back in the 1100s.

Leppinge Stoone

This field name appears in a document just once, in 1544.[66] At the eastern end of Mudgley village the steep unmade lane called White Horse Lane runs up to link with Bagley. The field called Leppinge Stoone was on the west side of the lane. Years ago, I did find a large stone post, set in the hedge at the edge of the field on the west side of the lane - perhaps this was the actual 'leaping stone'? But what was it? The name conjures up all kinds of ideas. Sometimes boundary perambulations included special stones that youngsters had to jump over, so that the spot was imprinted on their memories; but this is not on an estate or parish boundary, though it is on the boundary of ancient Bagley Wood. Was it a ritual stone that villagers had to jump over for some rites of passage? Or perhaps, like Deerleap names which occur on the edge of ancient woodland, it refers to deer coming out of Bagley Wood into the fields.[67]

Lineage and Longhedge

Lineage Farm will be familiar to all Wedmore golf enthusiasts. The farm took its name from the earlier fields there called Lineage. In 1715 these fields are called Linidge.[68] This, however, seems to be a corruption or dialect version of another field name which spreads right across the hilltop. This is the field name Longhedge, which can be traced back to 1559.[69] The fields called Lineage and Longhedge may both mark the line of the very long ancient boundary hedge, the route of which can still be traced in parts, stretching east-west across the hilltop between Wedmore and Stoughton Cross. It could represent a division between the open fields of Wedmore and Stoughton - fields that were laid out in the 900s or 1000s. In times when many farming people could not write, the local dialect shows through in what are really two versions of the same name.

Lousey Bush

This is one of our most exciting field names, because it takes us directly back to the Saxon landscape of Wedmore. From Lousey Bush in the 1800s right back to Lowsie Boshe in 1554[70] the name is little altered. Lowsie (OE or Saxon *hlose*) means pigsty; and bush (OE *busc*) means, as you might expect, uncultivated land covered with scrub or bushes. Lousey Bush, on the hilly slopes near Townsend Lane was where our Saxon ancestors kept their pigs, in a landscape not yet cut up and cultivated in fields. The open fields were probably there by the 10-1100s, so the name must be older than that. It survived to be used down the centuries to identify the later fields in that same area.

Lords Furlong and Little Field

Lords Furlong, recorded in 1638, was in Blackford, and was a part of Little Field.[71] Little Field was an area of ploughland north of the Bishop's Palace, and was probably the very early, original arable ground for Blackford, which expanded to become Blackford North Field in the later middle ages, when the population grew. Lords Furlong was presumably that part of the arable which belonged to the Lord of the Manor, who from the 1060s to the 1500s was the Bishop of Bath and Wells.

Maltfield

A large stretch of the hilltop between Wedmore and Mudgley, and other fields at Blackford, are called Maltfield. Malt was the fermented barley grain, and so Maltfield was the land where barley was grown for malting, to make ale. People drank ale rather than water – so needed a lot of local barley. In 1558, Maltfield, Over Maltfield and Nether Maltfield all lie above Mudgley.[72]

Manships or Manchips

Manships (1778)[73] or Manchips (1820)[74] is the large field at the junction of Plud Street and Mad Womans Lane. There are two meanings to this name. It could mean land held by the community from the Old English (OE) *gemaenescip*, perhaps part of the earliest communal village in-field. Or it could mean land held by someone with the name Manship. As there is documentary evidence of a John and William Manshipe living in Wedmore in 1299 this seems the most probable explanation.[75] This surname is itself of interest, because it comes from the Latin for a 'freed serf'.

Meeting House Orchard

There is no mystery about this name. Meeting House Orchard, in 1820, was the name of the steep orchard in Grants Lane which now has bungalows on it, perched high above the road.[76] It is next to the Baptist Church or 'The Meeting House', as it used to be called. The present Baptist Church was built in 1857,[77] but this 1820 field name shows that there was an earlier chapel on the site. George Champeney of Theale who died in 1835 left his son Stephen, land called 'Melliars adjoining the Anna baptist Meeting House'. His will was made in 1829.[78]

Midemede

Midemede first appears in Theale in 956, when it is a landmark on the Saxon boundary.[79] It means the Middle Meadow, and lay just to the east of West Well Lane. The Mead part of the name has survived right through to the present day, with other attachments, such as Crook Mead.

Moor Door

Two fields on either side of Wedmore Moor Drove are called Moor Door in 1778.[80] The names mean exactly what they seem to be telling us, that they mark the entrance to the open moor, which begins beyond them. Wedmore Moor was not enclosed into fields until 1778.

Murielesham

This is another Theale field name, recorded in 1517.[81] It was on the ancient boundary between the Theale/Northload estate and Wedmore. It lies next to a field called plain Lesham[82] in 1517, and its name is obviously a development of the simpler one. Murielesham disappears from the records, but Lesham or Leaseham survives today. Leas-*hamm* means the enclosed hay meadows; but what does the distinctive Murie- mean? It could be just a corruption of OE *mor*, meaning moor or marsh: the moorside enclosed hay meadow. There is, however, another more exciting possibility. The ancient boundary between the two estates was marked, in the middle ages, by an earth bank, often called a mud wall, and the subject of much disputation between Wedmore and Theale in the 1400s. Could Murie- be derived from the Latin for wall, *murus*? Is Murielesham the enclosed hay meadow by the wall, as opposed to the plain Lesham next to it on the other side? When the boundary wall was demolished, the distinctive field name lost its significance and was forgotten.

Murveyland

Murveyland is recorded in 1747, in Blackford.[83] Earlier, in 1646 it appears as Murviland and Murviland Furlong.[84] By 1820, the name has gone, changed to plain Moor Furlong.[85] The 'land' element in the name, and the appearance of 'furlong' in association with it, indicate that it was an area of ploughland. While they have long been pasture, the name suggests that this sloping land above Blackford Moor was cultivated in the medieval period. There is no clue as to the meaning of Murvey/Murvi; it is probably a lost dialect word.

New Ham

There are many 'new' field names in the parish: New Ham, New Close, New Mead. The 'new' was often, however, 'new' when the farmers made the fields, 400 or more years ago - and the name has stuck ever since. New Ham at Latcham is first recorded in 1509,[86] when it was a block of twenty acres, part of the holding of the chantry of St Anne in Wedmore Church. In 1558 Newhams is still held by the Church and is divided into six closes of meadow, and the rent for each close was 20 shillings.[87] These Newhams are just above Wedmore Moor at Latcham, and had been taken out of the common moor, drained and enclosed, perhaps long before the name was first written down in 1509 - but how long before, is not known.

Nugginham

Nuggingham is a group of fields in Yeomoor. These hams or enclosed meadows were called Nuggereshame in 1517.[88] Nugg or Nugger may be the name of a previous owner or perhaps a dialect word for something which we do not now understand.

Old Wood

Old Wood near Sand recalls the time when this area was wooded. It was also called Old Park in 1558.[89] Both names refer to the Dean of Wells' deer park which lay between Sand and Mudgley in medieval times. Many 'Park' field names still survive in this area, now with personal or descriptive names attached: Pews [Pugh's] Park, Lyons Park, Cowslip Park, Briary Park.[90]

Oslakesleagh

This is another field name that existed in Bagley in 956.[91] Oslakesleagh was on the top of the hill, where old Bagley School stands. The - leagh (from OE *leah*) here means a clearing in the wood, and Oslak was probably the name of the Saxon who cleared and cultivated this patch of land. Whether Oslak was still alive in 956 is unknown; he may have lived many years earlier. There are, however, still fields called Leigh in the same area today.

Ovemestfurlong

This field name, the Topmost or Uppermost Furlong, is mentioned in a document of 1325.[92] It was part of an area of arable land lying between Combe Batch and Latcham, probably on the north side of the road. If it was the 'uppermost' or higher part, it was probably the part nearer the road. There were at this time no houses along the road, until Latcham Farm.

Paradice

Paradice in 1820,[93] or Pardis in 1617,[94] is the name of a field at Blackford. The field is right next to the site of the Bishop's moated country palace (demolished 1391)[95], and 'paradise' was the medieval name for a garden belonging to a great house - so here was the Bishop's garden, long vanished but still pinpointed by the name of the field.

Pennardes Bowshe

Pennardes Bowshe was a field somewhere along Mudgley hilltop in 1544.[96] It may, by then, have been a personal name: Mr Pennard's bushy scrubland. However, 'pennard' is from the Welsh *pen* (hill) and *ardd* (high), which became, in Old English, *pen-eard*: the high hill. The name survives intact, in its old form, at Pennard near Glastonbury. The position of this scrubland on the Mudgley hilltop would fit the meaning of the field name.

Pennyland

Fields can be called Pennyland as a term of derision: land that is useless, hardly worth a penny. The name could also mean that a rent of one penny was once paid for it. Pennyland in Wedmore was arable land in the 1700s, on the hilltop near Snipefield Lane.[97] Hyther Penny Lande and Furder Penny Lande are mentioned in 1554.[98]

Pepperhay

Pepperhay is at Blackford, at one end of the village.[99] There was once a medieval farm on the site, but this had gone by the 1660s. The name may come from a nominal 'peppercorn' rent paid for it - but why just one farm in Blackford should have this privilege is not known. Alternatively, it could be the enclosure where peppermint or pepperwort grew.

Picked Ham

A group of fields at Westham is called Picked Ham.[100] Picked comes from OE *piced* - land which comes to a point; and one of these hams or enclosed meadows is a distinctive triangular shape. It has given its name to the whole group.

Pile Stiles

This curious field name is last recorded in 1818.[101] A very strange mis-spelling of it in 1724, as Hilestitles, makes no sense and is perhaps a clerical error.[102] The 'pile' was from OE *pil*, a pointed stake, probably referring to the Park Pale or paling fence of Wedmore Deer Park in Sand Road; and 'stiles' was from OE *stigol*, which means, as today, a stile to get over this fence. The field name preserves the memory of a way into the manorial deer park, which ceased to exist in the 1500s and of which there are virtually no traces left on the ground today.

Popham's Grave, Popham's Batch

Right on the parish boundary between Wedmore and Allerton, on the further bank of the Washbrook, there used to be one small field with the odd name of Popham's Grave,[103] which belonged to Wedmore parish although all the rest of the land was in Allerton. At Blackford there is another field, called Popham's Batch.[104] The Popham family have lived in the area since at least the 1500s. Popham's Batch was a little area of rising ground where some member of the family perhaps lived, or farmed; but what of Popham's Grave? The boundary between two parishes was traditionally the place where criminals or suicides, excluded from the parish churchyard, were buried. Was one of the Pophams the black sheep of the family, and when? Or was the land so difficult to farm that it gained the rueful name of Popham's Grave from derisive fellow-farmers? And when?

Post

This field name at the junction of Snipefield Lane with the Wedmore/Stoughton road is probably referring to a direction post which once stood there, now long gone. While I have found it written down as a field name in 1820, the deeds of the field might show it (and the direction post) to be considerably older.[105]

Poundhay Orchard, Pound Close

Poundhay Orchard in Combe Batch,[106] Wedmore was the hedged enclosure by the small walled pound, where stray animals were penned until reclaimed. The pound is still in existence, one of the earliest medieval remains in the village. There are also several fields called Pound Close lying along the Washbrook stream, near Ashton Mill some distance from any settlement.[107] These field names may recall enclosures where sheep were herded and penned, to be dipped in the adjacent stream.

Quarry Ground

Scattered across the hill top of the parish are several 'Quarry' field names. These fields are where the shallow layers of local Wedmore stone were dug out. Because it was relatively easy to restore to farming use, many quarry sites still retain their original field names, and did not change to Quarry Ground or similar names. There were several quarries mentioned in Mudgley in 1554.[108] Quarry Ground at Heath House is where Roman skeletons were found when the stone was dug in the mid -1800s.[109]

Redhill

Fields in Wedmore and Cocklake are called Redhill in 1653,[110] and Redd hill in 1605;[111] and when they are, occasionally, ploughed today it is easy to see why. They take their name from the red colour of the soil, which is red marl from the Triassic period. There are also fields called Redeham near Northload Farm, Theale (1517)[112] Redland (1621),[113] and Redham (1820)[114] where the soil is noticeably red.

Revel Batch

Revel Batch occurs as a field name in 1820 at Clewer, and identifies the field where the annual village revel was held.[115] A revel was originally a celebration of a holy day, and a fund-raising occasion for the parish church; but by the early 1800s it had become a holiday with an unsavoury reputation for excessive drinking and gambling. I do not know when Clewer revels stopped being held, but there is no mention of them in the 1830s when the Revd William White was campaigning against the revels in Theale and Wedmore (see Chapter 13). The field adjoining Revel Batch in Clewer is called Bull Acre.[116] Perhaps this is the field where the bull was kept for the bull-baiting, or where it ended up as barbecued meat after the chase through the village.

Riding Stream

Riding Stream[117] is the name of a group of fields in what was, until the end of the medieval period, Bagley Wood. Riding is a corruption of 'ridding', clearing the ground of trees, so the name records the creation of these fields out of the woodland, by the stream, in the 1500s.

Rosey Pool

Some names can, on investigation, prove an illusion. This field in Panborough had such a romantic name in 1820.[118] Unfortunately, while searching through a document of 1517 I discovered that the original and much more mundane spelling was in fact Horsy pole or Horse Pool![119] It is a good example of how easily a name, passed down generations by word of mouth, can get twisted.

Rowditch

Several fields at Blackford are called Rowditch from 1820[120] back to 1636.[121] Row probably means rough, presumably referring to the quality of the ground; though why this should be is not clear, as it is part of one of the medieval arable fields closest to Blackford and has presumably been cultivated since earliest times. The ditch is a drainage ditch which ran along the edge of the field, against the lane from Stoughton. In 1641 it is recorded that the tenants of Blackford, to keep this watercourse open, 'shall cast upp the earthe at the headds of their landes whereby the water may pass in his right Course'.[122]

La Sarchynge

La Sarchynge was the name of fields in Yeo Moor at Theale in 1517.[123] Part of the common moor had by then been drained and enclosed. The name may have come from the medieval Middle English word *sart*, to assart or take a piece of land from waste or woodland in order to cultivate it. The ending -ynge could come from the OE word *inning*: land taken in and enclosed. By 1820 the name has become Sercham.[124]

Shutters Stile

Shutters Stile is on the hill slope at Long Hill, near Crickham, and is called Shute Stile in 1678.[125] *Shute* is the OE word for a steep hill, as in Shute Shelve near Axbridge. Stile comes from OE *stigol*, which originally meant a steep path, but soon came to mean what it does today: a barrier that has to be climbed over. Shutters Stile was the stile on the hill, the way uphill to Crickham Field, the ploughland of that village.[126]

Skuttells Barrough or Skuttelesbarrowgh

This is one of our strangest field names, and one of the most difficult to interpret with any certainty. It shows just how complicated a field name study can be! In 1559 Skuttells Barrough was an area of ploughland along Quab Lane, half way to Stoughton.[127] Barrow is probably from OE *beorg*, a hill or mound, and raised hopes of finding a prehistoric burial mound - but no trace of such a thing has been found there so far. Alternatively, it could perhaps be a corruption of OE *bearu*, a grove or wood. What is Skuttells? The OE word *scytel* means dung. Was the dung from the farmsteads piled here, in a mound, before being spread on the fields? That would neatly explain the non-existent 'barrow', which would come and go with the seasons. Names are, however, rarely so simple.

There is a very similar OE word, *scyt(t)el* or *scyt(t)le*, which means a bolt or a bar, while a Somerset dialect word 'skuttle' can mean the horizontal bar of a gate. Moreover, while the name is spelt Scuttels Barrows in 1711,[128] it is Scutlers Bars in 1747[129] and by 1820 it is Cutlers Bars.[130] Usually one puts most trust in the earliest spelling, but could it be that in this case the 'barrow' is an error, and the name simply means a barred gate here on Quab Lane, at the point where the fields of Wedmore ended and those of Stoughton began? But can we even trust the 'skuttle' of *scyt(t)el*? It is easy to assume that Cutlers is a later distortion of Skuttells - but there was a family called Cutler living in Wedmore from at least the 1600s until 1774.[131] Is the name just a coincidence, or was there some link with this Cutler family?

Yet another interpretation was told to Wedmore farmer David Banwell by an old farmer, who believed that the name came from 19th century farm workers who, objecting to the introduction of machinery, put metal spikes or bars in the field to damage the newfangled mowing machines. This idea could have developed from stories of machine-breaking elsewhere in England, and shows how fieldname traditions can spring up; but I suspect our Wedmore Cutlers Bars derives from the much older Skuttells Barrough. But was it the Cutler family's bar or gate - or a much older mound, or a dunghill? I will leave it to the reader to puzzle out!

Snailham Corner

Snailham Corner in 1820,[132] or Snaylehams Corner in 1554,[133] is a field at the bottom of Sand Drove. It was the corner of the *hamm* or enclosed meadows which ran along under Sand Hill at the edge of the moor. Clearly, an abundance of snails must have given it its name. The field name is in fact even older, because in 1299 Thomas de Snaylham lived in Sand and he presumably took his name from the meadow, of which he was probably one of the tenants.[134]

Stinking Acre

Somewhere in Theale is a lost field which was called Stinking Acre in 1740,[135] and Stinking Mears in 1809.[136] We do not know what happened, or what grew, in the field to merit this description, but presumably there was a very unpleasant smell, and the farmer's feelings have been preserved for posterity in its name!

Stooles Leg

Two fields between Sand and Heath House are called Stooles Leg in 1707.[137] In shape, they are clearly based on the furlongs of a medieval open arable field and do not resemble the leg of a milking stool at all. The name has probably become distorted over time and may be referring to coppiced 'stools' possibly of hazel trees, as this hill-top area was once ancient woodland, later cleared for arable farming.

Swinshurst, Swyneshurst

Swinehurst (1820)[138] at Westham can be traced back as a field name to Swineshurst (1772),[139] Swyneshurst (1657)[140] and Swinshurst (1612);[141] but it must be much older than that. Swine-hurst means the wooded hill (OE *hyrst*) where the pigs were turned out. Medieval (and Saxon) pigs were regularly herded into the woods in autumn, to fatten up on fallen nuts and acorns. The wood was Westhams Wood, and the last remnants of it had been cleared for fields by 1555:[142] so the Swinehurst field name is a memory of its use long before the 1550s.

Summerleaze

Summerleaze, recorded in 1820[143] and as Somerleaze in 1576,[144] is a very large field in a far corner of the parish, right on the parish boundary near Mark Moor. This was presumably the meadow used mainly in the summer, when it was drier. It is an area which is just a little higher than the adjacent flood-prone moor, and would have been lusher grassland than the surrounding rough moorland pasture.

Tadham

Many present-day fields below Sand are called Tadham because they were enclosed in 1778 from the common moor called Tadham Moor, and retained the old name.[145] *Tadde* is Old English for a toad. The *hamm* (enclosed meadow by a river or moor) in the name, however, is a name that implies not open moorland, but deliberately created fields on the edge of the moor. Tadham first appears in a document in 1322,[146] suggesting that somebody was making the first fields there a long time before the 1778 Enclosure Act. The adjacent moor took its name from these early fields, and gave its name in turn to the new fields of 1778.

Tealham

Tealham Moor, below Heath House, adjoins Tadham; and the name has a similar history. Tealham Moor was enclosed and divided into fields in 1785, so there are many fields now called Tealham.[147] Here, *teal* is Old English for the wild duck, as now. The name Tealham is one of our earliest field names, dating right back to 1139[148] and, once again, the *hamm* in the name implies that there were moorside meadows here in very early medieval times.

Tent Land

Tent Land, in 1820, is a field just above the village of Crickham.[149] The name probably means the land where cloth was stretched (on frames and 'tenterhooks') after fulling, to prevent it from shrinking. Often, it was a field where the cloth-stretching frames were left fixed, semi-permanently. It is a rare suggestion of local cloth-making, probably in late medieval times when sheep farming was at its height. Perhaps not just woollen cloth - is it a coincidence that the fields called Flaxland are close by?

Three-corner Cap

Three-corner Cap, a field at Bagley so named in 1820, is a small triangular field, so the name is very descriptive.[150]

Trendle

Fields near the parish boundary at Washbrook are called Trendle in 1715.[151] This, like Blackland, is a name which interests archaeologists because the word is OE *trendel*, a circle or ring - often indicating an Iron Age farmstead; these late prehistoric farms were usually enclosed within a circular bank. The tidy, squared-up fields of the time of the Enclosure Acts, and modern farming since have, however, removed any visible trace of a circular earthwork, if there was one, either on the ground or on air photographs: so it is impossible to be certain that this is the meaning of the field name. There was, however, a Walter Trendel (and others with a similar surname) living in Blackford in 1189.[152] Did he perhaps give his name to the fields, or did he take his name from an earthwork which was still to be seen there in the 1100s?

Tumbledown Dicks

Tumbledown Dicks is the name of the orchard behind the New Inn in Combe Batch. The Revd S.H.A. Hervey gives an explanation of this name in *The Wedmore Chronicles*, and I have no reason to disagree with it![153] Tumbledown Dick was the nickname of Richard Cromwell, the son of Oliver Cromwell. When Oliver Cromwell died in 1658, Richard succeeded him as Lord Protector of England; but, as so often happens, the son had not inherited his father's shrewd intelligence, drive or personality. Within eight months, he had retired in ignominy. His rapid downfall from the highest office in the country earned him the nickname of Tumbledown Dick. He died in 1712. Why this orchard was so called, neither Hervey nor I have been able to find out.

Urdelande

Here is a very ancient-sounding field name. It is recorded in 1558, and is spelt in various ways: Urdelande, Urdelond, Erlond.[154] In 1605 the same field is called Eareland.[155] This field was ploughland along the Latcham Road, and the name comes from Saxon or OE *erth*, meaning just that: ploughed land. Such a simple name suggests it is a very early field: perhaps what is called the 'in-field' of the early village, the first and nearest ploughed ground, dating from before the development of the medieval open fields - and they, probably, originated in the 1000s. So this name may be very ancient indeed. Ovemestfurlong (q.v.) of 1325[156] was probably part of Urdelande.

Very Bowshe

An unidentified field in Mudgley in 1559 is called Very Bowshe.[157] 'Bowshe' is bush or scrub (cf. Lousey Bush), but what is 'very'? It is possibly from *vair* which was a medieval word for a weasel, so Very Bush would be the scrub land where weasels abounded. It is interesting that the word comes from the Old French *vaire*, fur - obtained from squirrels or martens, and used in the middle ages to line and trim gowns. Cinderella's slippers were originally 'vaire' - fur - which became confused with the similar-sounding French word 'verre' - glass. 'Vair' is still the heraldic term for ermine fur when depicted on a coat of arms. An ermine is a weasel whose brown coat turns white in winter.

Wether Slade

Wether Slade is another Mudgley field of 1542,[158] probably not far from Ballardes Lyee, and is another field named from medieval sheep farming. 'Slad' or 'slade' is dialect for a valley, or the steep side of a valley, or, as at Mudgley, the steep hillside used as a grassy sheep-walk. A 'wether' is a sheep, older than a 'ballard' and usually a ram, especially a castrated ram. The 'bellwether' was the old sheep with a bell round its neck which was the leader of the flock.

Whore Meadow

This field lies between Clewer and Cocklake. In 1605 it is Whore Meare,[159] and in 1678 Hore Meare.[160] Its name does not refer to ladies of dubious reputation, but to something entirely different. Whore here means a 'hoary' or grey landmark, from OE *har*, hoary or grey. The term is often applied to an old stone or aged tree, covered in lichen, which marked the boundary of an estate in Saxon times. Significantly, Meare (in the 1605 and 1678 versions of the name) is the OE word for a boundary, from the OE word [ge]*maere*. So the older, truer versions of the fieldname mean, in Saxon, the old grey [landmark] on the boundary. The boundary is between the Clewer and Cocklake estates, and what the grey landmark was then, we cannot tell now. Nowadays there is just the slightest remaining trace of a medieval (or earlier) bank marking the boundary line, with a 19th century field hedge on top of it.

Whotley

A field called Whotley in 1820[161] is the last survivor of a whole block of land between West End and Sand which is called Wateligh in 1378.[162] This name means the clearing where wheat is grown, from OE *whaete*, and *leah*, and so indicates a cultivated field. The Saxon or early medieval farmers who grew their wheat there probably cleared woodland in this area for cultivation long before the more distant parts of the hilltop, suggesting it is another of the earliest fields to serve the village. In 1378 Wateligh had a sheepfold on it. The field may well still have been ploughed and sown with wheat, but after the grain was harvested, and the straw taken for bedding and thatch, sheep would be turned out on it to glean and manure the field before the next planting. They would have been 'folded', shut up in the sheepfold, at night.

Winniards Orchard

This orchard at Mudgley on the steep slope above the road is where the Dean of Wells in medieval times had his vineyard, facing south out over the Brue valley. By 1520 the name is Wynnardes or The Wynerde,[163] but by then the vineyard was probably already just a memory. That memory has been preserved as its name down the centuries since.

Wormes Close

Wormes Close, in 1711,[164] is a name which could mean a snake or even a dragon, from OE *wyrm*, a worm. However, before we get too excited by the vision of dragons inhabiting this field at West End in Saxon times, we must check other, earlier spellings. The Warman family were living in the parish in the 1500s and 1600s, and this field is called Warmans Close after them. Only later was it corrupted into 'Wormes' close or field, as the name spoken in the local dialect was first written down as it sounded.

X is for a Cross, as in Crosse Furlong

In 1517 Crosse Furlong was part of Theale's open field, on the north side of the road, extending out to Yeo Moor.[165] The 'cross' might be because this furlong or subdivision of the great ploughed field was laid out at right angles to the adjoining furlongs; or it might be a reference to the nearby crossroads where the lane to Northload and Snake Lane meet the main road.

Yellow Batches

Before the moors were enclosed into fields, the tenants of the various manors turned their cows out to pasture freely over the open ground. Yellow Batches is identified in 1781 as a milking place, out in Tealham Moor.[166] Apparently the cows were not always herded back to the hill at milking time; sometimes at least the village milkmaids would walk out to their cows, each recognising their own animals, milk them there, and carry the milk pails (probably using yokes) back to the farms. The 'batch' implies it was a slightly raised area, drier than the surrounding peat, where the milkmaids and their cows could congregate, and it was yellow presumably from the summer buttercups and dandelions there.

What about Z?

Many of our field names and place names in Somerset beginning with S often sound, when spoken in our dialect, as though they start with Z - and when they first came to be written down, they were often spelt as they sounded! So, in the 1490s, a legal clerk trying to take down the evidence given in court by a man living at Sand could not understand the name of the witness's village. After several attempts, he decided it was **ZOND**.[167]

Zillingway

Zillingway was a large area of ploughland north of Blackford, linked to the village by an ancient lane; and the name is recorded thus in 1609.[168] It was later written as Sullingway, but the version beginning with Z shows how it would have sounded when our local farmers of the 1600s said where they were going to plough. The name Sullingway or Zillingway comes from the Saxon word for a plough, OE *sulh*; it is the lane along which the ploughs went out to the great open arable field in medieval times. About 150 years ago, farmers told the Revd S.H.A. Hervey that they were ploughing with their 'zulls', showing just how these ancient names, and their local pronunciations, have lasted.

Chapter 17
Lost and Found

The Wedmore coin hoard

Underneath one of the yew trees bordering the path in the north-east corner of Wedmore Churchyard stands a stone commemorating the marriage of the Duke of York and Princess May of Teck on 6th July 1893. Of more local interest, the stone also commemorates the finding in 1853 of a hoard of over 200 silver coins from the late Saxon period.

In March 1853 Tucker Coles was widening the churchyard path, when he discovered, buried just below the surface, an earthenware pot containing the coins.[1] The Vicar, the Revd John Kempthorne, reported this discovery to the Treasury. An inquest was held by the coroner, at which the jury decided that the hoard was treasure trove, and belonged to the Crown and not to the finder. Gold and silver objects found buried are treasure trove if the court is satisfied that the unknown owner buried them with every intention of recovering them later. The finder, however, normally receives a reward to the value of the treasure itself.

In June 1853 the British Museum bought from the Treasury 148 Anglo Saxon coins from this hoard. These coins were added to the national collection they already had and not kept as a separate exhibit, although such a hoard of Anglo Saxon coins was 'a very exceptional incident'.[2] Many of the coins were new to the British Museum's collection, and added greatly to their knowledge. It is a matter of regret to Wedmore that the hoard was not kept together as one unit at the time, so that we cannot now go to London and see our treasure.

Who buried the coins, and why were they buried? We can never be certain, as whoever did it forgot to pop their name and address into the pot! We may deduce that whoever it was, they were living in fear. Perhaps those were troubled times in the village, and they thought a dark corner of the church-yard was the safest place to hide their

Actual size

Silver penny of Cnut (1016-35), minted in Lincoln by Lifinc, found in Wedmore Churchyard 1853

fortune. They never came back to retrieve their treasure, but they were proved right: the churchyard was a safe hiding place until that day in 1853.

We know more about when the coins were buried. The latest coins were of the time of Harthacnut, son of Cnut (Canute). Harthacnut reigned from 1040 to 1042, when Edward the Confessor succeeded him. As there were no coins of Edward the Confessor included, it seems the hoard was probably buried in 1041 or 1042.

The coins range from the time of Ethelred the Unready (1014-1016) and Cnut (1016-1035) to his sons Harold Harefoot (1035-1040) and Harthacnut (1040-1042). Most of them are from the time of Cnut. Coins at that time were made not just in London but in royal licensed mints in important towns all over the kingdom. These coins came from mints as far apart as York, Lincoln, London, Southampton, Oxford, Dover and Exeter. Fourteen came from Somerset mints at Bath, Bruton, Crewkerne, Ilchester, Langport, Taunton and Watchet.

The only Anglo Saxon coin in use was the silver penny. The coins were made of very pure silver. On the front was the king's head; on the back usually a cross-shape with the name of the moneyer who made the coin, and the place where he worked. One of the Wedmore Cnut coins was made by AELFRIC ON BADA, Aelfric at Bath; another by EDRIC ON TANTU, Edric at Taunton.[3] Two of the coins had been cut in half to make halfpennies. The cross design on the reverse made it easier to cut halves (for halfpennies) and quarters (for farthings) accurately. Round halfpennies and farthings were not made until the late 1200s. It is difficult to know what the value of one silver penny was at that time. Most dealings for small everyday items would probably have been by barter. To the person who buried the hoard, therefore, his 200 or more silver coins must have represented a considerable fortune.

So what of Tucker Coles the finder? His full name was John Tucker Coles, illegitimate son of Sarah Coles, called Tucker after his presumed father.[4] The 1851 Wedmore census lists John T. Coles, aged 43, labourer, living in Quab Lane with his wife Elizabeth, 43, stay maker. They had five children at home: Ann (12), John nicknamed Tucker (10), Robert (9), Thomas (6), and Elizabeth (1). With the reward Tucker received for finding the hoard, he decided to seek a better life for his family in America. Unfortunately it was reported later that Tucker was killed there in the Civil War.[5] His family survived, and descendants have since visited Wedmore to search for their ancestral home.

What happened to the fifty or so coins not now in the British Museum? These seem to have been sold off to local residents, probably before the inquest took place. In 1853 Somerset Archaeological Society was given twelve Saxon pennies, all of Cnut, by Mr RP Edwards of Sand Hall.[6] These coins were later claimed by the Treasury as part of the original hoard; but seven of them were eventually returned to the Society at Taunton Castle, and the other five kept by the British Museum in exchange for 'others of equal rarity and value'. About 1925, Mr Edward's grand-daughter Mrs Saunders gave Taunton Museum six more Cnut coins. These later additions are the only six firmly identified as being from the original Wedmore hoard. We do not know what happened to the remaining thirty or so coins; perhaps they are still tucked at the back of someone's drawer, somewhere in Wedmore.

Stray finds

The Saxon hoard is not the only 'treasure' that has been found in the parish. Single coins have turned up in various places, including another silver Saxon penny in the churchyard.[7] This one, however, was of much earlier date than the hoard, being of the time of King Ethelbert (860-866), an older brother of King Alfred; it is a reminder of the royal Saxon hall or house nearby.

Earlier coins from Roman times have also been discovered, scattered all over the parish in Wedmore, Theale, Heath House and even out in Tealham Moor. Most of these coins are in private hands, and were not accurately identified at the time of finding. One large brass Roman coin found at Blackford was of the time of the Emperor Augustus (27 BC - 14 AD).[8] Another coin hoard was discovered at Combe Batch in the 1940s. These might have been Roman - Roman pottery was found nearby - but could have been as late as Georgian. Sadly, this hoard has since disappeared, so it is impossible to know what date the coins were.[9]

Most coins are dropped at random; but sometimes they can give us a clue for dating a part of a building or earthwork. It is important to tell the archaeologists or the local historian exactly where a coin is found, to help their researches. Any finds of gold and silver must be reported to the County Archaeologist as they could be treasure trove . It may be great fun to use a metal detector to find 'buried treasure', but there are laws concerning metal detecting. The landowner must always give permission first, and come to some arrangement about any finds that may be made. It is illegal to use a metal detector on archaeological sites. Anywhere, random digging destroys for ever vital but slight traces (was the object in a cloth bag? or inside a wooden building?) that often only a trained archaeological eye can detect from stains in the soil. On certain types of site, enthusiasts using metal detectors have worked together with archaeologists to produce very useful results.

Coins have been found at two of our medieval archaeological sites. A silver penny of King Edward I (1272-1307) minted at Canterbury was discovered during the dig in the 1950s at the Bishop's Palace site at Blackford.[10] This coin must have been dropped when the palace was in its hey-day. Other coins were found at the Dean of Wells' medieval house at Mudgley when it was excavated in 1878. These included a penny and a groat (a fourpenny piece) of Edward III (1327-1377), and a penny of Richard II (1377-1399).[11] Sometime in the mid-1800s, a small silver coin was found on this site at Mudgley, in the field called Court Garden. The coin was said to have 'sails like a florin'.[12] The Victorian florin or 2s piece had a cross-shape on the back. Perhaps the farm worker who found the coin thought that the cross resembled the 'sails' of the windmills which still then dotted the Wedmore landscape. His description certainly suggests his find was medieval in date. It is not known what has happened to the coin since.

The Mudgley site produced another interesting find in 1843.[13] This was a beautiful medieval spoon, which was bought from the finder by the then Vicar of Theale, the Revd J Williamson. He eventually presented it to the Ashmolean Museum at Oxford, in 1873. This spoon is nearly 6 inches (14.5 cms) long, with a pear-shaped bowl. Its straight, six-sided stem has a cone-shaped knob or diamond point at the end. It must have been a great loss to the owner, perhaps the Dean himself.

Lost and Found

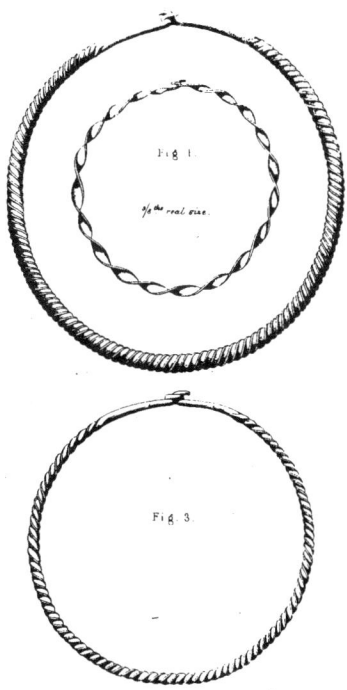

Bronze Age torcs found at Heath House 1846. Journal of the British Archaeological Association vol XXI (1865) facing page 232

Several Bronze Age weapons have been found out in the moors when rhines were being dug, presumably dropped by Bronze Age hunters after prey. In 1846 a labourer digging near Heath House discovered something buried about 6 feet below the surface.[14] The find turned out to be three Bronze Age torcs, a few amber beads strung on a wire, and two celts (axe heads). The torcs were made of 'yellow bronze', beautifully hammered and twisted into two solid necklets and an armlet. These objects probably belonged to a Bronze Age chieftain who might have lived at Heath House. The torcs eventually ended up at Badgworth Court, at that time the home of Colonel Luttrell, a relative of Robert Phippen on whose land they were found. Despite endless enquiries the torcs have since vanished. There is no trace of them in any museum. Sadly, a unique and important piece of Wedmore's earliest history has disappeared.

An unexpected stray find was made in 1988, which shows the Saxons were in Wedmore long before King Alfred. While working in a garden just on the outskirts of the village, the owner found 'a bit of old wire' which turned out to be an early Saxon finger-ring. It is dated to the 500s or 600s AD. This intricate ring is made from two lengths of fine bronze (copper alloy) wire twisted into an elaborate decorative knot.[15]

Saxon ring found in Wedmore

In complete contrast was a public house token or check I was shown: it was made for use in the George Hotel during the 19th century. These checks were a form of exchange or local currency and usually made of brass or copper. Most checks are circular, but a few, like this one, are oval. They were usually made in Birmingham and stamped with the name of the pub or hotel, the place, and their value. This ranged from one penny to one shilling, the most common values being 1½d and 3d.

Millions of checks were in use throughout England and Wales in the mid-1800s, but strangely very little is known of their actual function. No-one is quite sure how Somerset checks were used. In some parts of England, certainly, they were used in pub games such as skittles. The two teams decided on a stake, perhaps a pint of beer. When the game finished the losing captain collected the price of two pints of beer from each player. This was exchanged for checks of equivalent value. One check was handed to each skittler, and when he wanted his drink he handed it over the bar. The check could be kept to use later. It was a way of making sure the landlord kept his customer and the stake was not spent elsewhere. Such checks may also have proved useful in the pub when there was a shortage of small change.

The George Hotel and the Swan Hotel both produced 3d brass checks; their reverse sides were blank.

Although of little intrinsic value, these checks are as historically interesting as the other much older and perhaps more valuable objects. Such unexpected finds, if properly reported and recorded, can make a real contribution to Wedmore history.

Wedmore public house tokens, 19th century. Actual size

The lost letter

It is exciting to make a new find when studying the history of the village. It is just as exciting when something which has been lost is unexpectedly rediscovered.

Several years ago the late Mr Geoffrey Pavey of Wedmore was visiting Prebendary H.T.C. Morgan, who had been Vicar of Wedmore from 1936 to 1970. Prebendary Morgan, then retired, had been sorting through some old papers, and had found a very old letter. He knew nothing about it, but realised its historic interest, and gave it to Mr Pavey who kindly passed it on to me. This came as a remarkable and welcome surprise, for I had known of the existence of this letter. It had been described in 1920, in *Notes & Queries for Somerset and Dorset*, by the Revd S.H.A. Hervey.[16] He had by then been long retired and was living in Sussex; and presumably had the letter with him. He had also made a note about it in the margin of his own copy of the *Wedmore Chronicle*. It had, however, apparently disappeared and not been heard of since. It now seems probable that it passed from the Revd S.H.A. Hervey to Mrs Connelly of Wedmore with other documents about the parish, and that she may have returned it to Prebendary Morgan, then vicar. It was very thrilling to have the original letter in front of me.

At the same time Mr Pavey gave me a cutting from the *Weston-super-Mare Gazette* of 30th August 1902 which he, by coincidence, happened to have. This printed snippet gave the background story of the finding of the letter itself in 1902, by Mr John Larder of Wedmore, builder, while he was pulling down a wall in a house in Church Street.

> 'WEDMORE: DISCOVERY - *Mr John Larder having recently purchased an old dwelling-house in front of the church, was on Friday morning last pulling down a wall, when he noticed a bottle deposited in a stone in the middle of the wall with a letter inside, of which the following is a copy, dated 101 years ago. The writer of the paper was a curate at Wedmore in the time of Hannah More, and is spoken of by her as her 'fast friend'.*'

The letter is in two parts:

> *1801*
> *April 15th*
> *My dear fellow mortal,*
>
> *If any of my family I mean my children should settle here - shew them this paper - Be*

good - Be good my dear children - In goodness is happiness. How oft has my heart bled for your little wants and misfortunes? Pray God grant you grace & gratitude to think of me - & how I have toild for you - <u>I am dead and rotten</u> - tho' now only 38 years. My children are registerd in this parish.

Wm. Eyre.

1801
April 15th

This wall was built at the expence of the Revd. William Eyre by the Tillys (masons of Allerton) - The great scarcity of bread is likely to bring on troubles - The quartern loaf sells for one shilling and ten pence - peas at 6s 6d per peck & every thing in proportion - potatoes even exceed this ratio - They have sold at from one guinea to thirty shillings per sack - I write this in full strength of Body - and perhaps it may fall into hands yet unborn -

O think! think!! think!!! of <u>eternity</u>.

Adieu Adieu Adieu

Wm Eyre

The letter was found 'in the back wall of the old house'[17] which is next to the Vicarage in Church Street (now the Old Vicarage). The letter is written on a sheet of paper, folded in half. William Eyre's touching plea is on the front, and his note about the wall and food prices is on the back. Although the paper is much creased, rubbed and spotted after its time in the bottle buried in the wall, the writing is still perfectly clear.

William Eyre was the curate in charge of the whole of Wedmore parish between 1793 and 1803.[18] The Vicar, the Revd William Bishop, never lived in the village; he preferred to live in Bath, and only visited very rarely. William Eyre did all the work, looking after 4,000 souls in the big parish. William Eyre and his wife Charlotte had six children: Charlotte, born 1791; Christian, b. 1792; Richard Cocks, b. 1793; Thomas Dowling, b. 1795; and William, b. 1798, who were all baptised together in 1798. Their youngest child, Charles Cocks, was born in Wedmore in January 1803.[19]

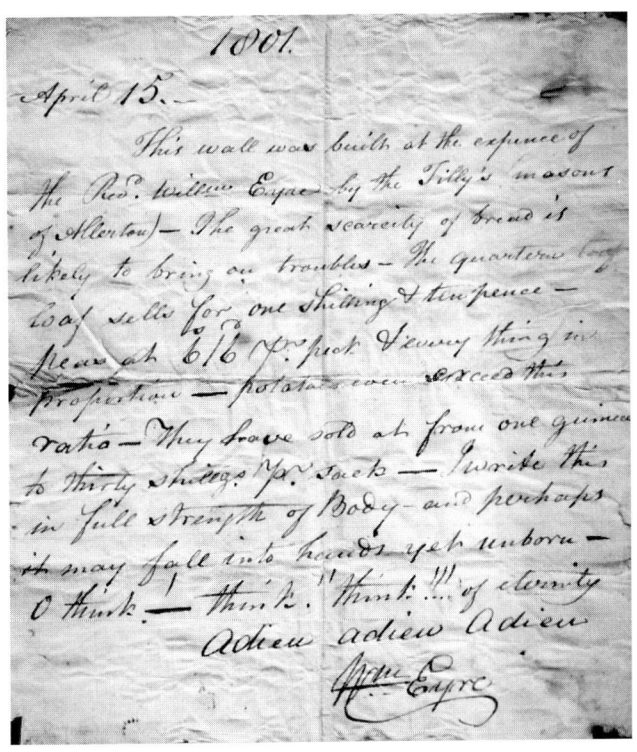

William Eyre's letter, 1801

William Eyre wrote and hid his letter to the future at a time of great troubles in England. The country had been expensively at war with France since 1793. Harvests had been very bad for two years running. Terrible storms occurred in the summer and during the harvest. Hailstones eleven inches in circumference fell in Bedfordshire, killing hares and partridges. Wheat almost doubled in price.[20] Food became very scarce, and there were food riots. The average daily wage of a farm labourer in 1796 was 1s with cider in winter time. Men could work more hours during summer time so the wages went up to 1s 4d. A woman could earn 6d a day, again with cider provided, and 8d in summer time. The wages did increase by a third in 1797. The average rent of a two-roomed cottage was 30s-50s a year.[21]

The quartern loaf mentioned by William Eyre was double the size of our large loaf. A farm labourer, therefore, had to work for almost two days to earn enough money to buy one loaf of bread - and this at a time when large families were the norm! Fortunately the harvest of 1801, after William Eyre's desperate letter had been buried in the wall, was very good and prices fell rapidly.[22] In 1803 William Eyre and his family left Wedmore, and we know nothing of where they went or what happened to them afterwards. Life, however, was clearly very, very hard for the villagers in 1801, and William Eyre's letter vividly conveys that hardship to us across the years.

Another lost letter

While searching the newspapers of 1878 I read of another bottle buried in a wall in Wedmore, but this one has yet to be found. This 1878 bottle contained a letter and was buried just two houses away from the earlier one. The person who hid it knew nothing of the 1801 bottle because that was not discovered until 1902.

Weston-super-Mare Gazette, December 14th, 1878.

'WEDMORE: A New Building.

Adjoining the premises where once stood the Bell Inn and almost close to the spot where not many years since, the Wedmore Revel was held, there is now in the course of erection under the direction of Mr JJ Spencer, architect of Wedmore, a very substantial villa. The materials in the walls are principally of freestone, Draycott Stone and Wedmore Stone. Its style of architecture is of a character that is somewhat peculiar and novel. In the north wall is deposited a bottle carefully cemented with a cork, containing a manuscript bearing the following record.

'This house is built by Mr Solomon Wall, the proprietor, of this parish, in the year of our Lord 1878, in which was commemorated here, the millennium of the signing of the Peace of Wedmore, between the Danish Prince Guthrum and King Alfred the Great in A.D. 878.

From here should in a thousand years
This house be standing here,
For aught we know it then may be
The great sabbatic year,
If not - 'twill not be far away,
Then hail! O! hail the millennial day.

Oh! what a jubilee's begun,
When Christ does to his kingdom come,
Then may the inmates loud proclaim -
And laud the great Messiah's reign.'

Solomon Wall at Stonesteps, c1930

The bottle was buried in the front wall of Stonesteps, east of the Post Office in Church Street. Stonesteps was built by Solomon Wall (1844-1936), a local builder. Solomon's house was specially designed to show off his workmanship and the latest styles. It was a 'pattern book' for his clients. Today we can still see the three different chimney stacks, and the varied tile patterns on the roof. The front of the house is built of Draycott pudding stone or conglomerate; the rest is built of local Wedmore stone. It seems that in 1878 the house which we now think of as a pretty Victorian villa, was 'peculiar and novel'. Solomon Wall constructed several Victorian houses and farms in the parish, and his handiwork can be recognised around the village. Among the larger houses he built were the (Victorian) Vicarage (1879), Cross Farm (1880) and Townsend Farm, Sand (1900) which cost £500.

The 1878 newspaper report refers to the former Bell Inn, next door to Stonesteps. This house now the Post Office, has its own interesting history. It was the Bell Inn during the late 1700s and early 1800s. In 1785 a distress warrant was served on John Morgan who was living at The Bell. The owner, Edward Taverner, was owed 10 shillings rent. The money was not forthcoming, so the following goods were seized: 'one feather bed and bolster, one bolster cloth, one sheet, one blanket, one old Rugge, two bedsteads, two Matts and cords, one frying pan, one tea kettle, one arm chair'.[23]

In 1786 the parish paid 3 shillings to the Bell Inn when Jeremy Fisher was held there under guard. Jeremy had been arrested for not complying with a bastardy order.[24] A few years before, in 1781, the Overseers of the Poor had paid 8s 4d for two officers and a guard to hold Jeremy Parfitt at the Bell Inn.[25] The Bell Inn must have had some small secure room used as a lockup on these occasions since Wedmore, unlike Axbridge, Wrington or Pensford, had no lockup of its own. The officers and guard could presumably refresh themselves before taking the offender away for trial. No other Wedmore inns are mentioned as offering such a facility.

The Bell may have been an inn for many years before the first written record of it. It was still an inn in 1814 when the landlord Joseph Hill was in gaol for debt. The church vestry meeting decided that, as his family were in distress and therefore being looked after by the parish, they would pay for his licence and settle his debts, on the condition that Joseph 'conducts himself in a decent and proper manner.'[26] There is no record of whether he did. The Bell Inn later became a shop and by 1861 it was already the village Post Office.

Solomon Wall's letter, besides dating his house so precisely, gives a clue to the mood of the village in the year 1878. Wedmore celebrated the thousandth anniversary of the Peace of Wedmore, between Saxon Alfred the Great and Guthrum the Dane, in style. On August 8th a service was held in St Mary's Church, the preacher being the Bishop of Bath and Wells, father of the Vicar the Revd S.H.A. Hervey. At 12.15 pm a meeting was held in the Assembly Rooms (now the Masonic building in Church Street) followed by a public luncheon at 2 pm and a tea at 6 pm.[27] Later in the year the Revd S.H.A. Hervey started his excavations of the reputed site of 'King Alfred's Palace' at Mudgley, which turned out to be the country house of the medieval Deans of Wells (see Chapter 7).[28] It was presumably the junketings of August that encouraged Solomon Wall to bury his commemorative letter and poem while building his house. He must, clearly, have supplied a copy to the newspaper at the time, as the original has remained hidden ever since. His house still stands safe and sound, and it may be many years before the bottle with its letter and poem is found again. The Wedmore of that era will no doubt be very different from the Wedmore of 1878.

Chapter 18
The Vicar and the Dinosaurs

Local history is full of surprises. We have looked at road names, school histories, some houses, holy wells, mills and other local industries, people, curious incidents, folk tales - and still have not run out of subjects. Things worth investigating can turn up, unexpectedly, at any time; and the local history trail in pursuit of elusive evidence is never ending.

The Revd S.H.A. Hervey was involved in an astonishing discovery which was made in Wedmore in 1893 - one which takes us back millions of years, to the time when dinosaurs roamed the area, and which even today fires our imaginations about the most dim and distant past of the place where we now live. He did not however publish details of it, perhaps because his historical interests did not go back further than the medieval history of Wedmore; or perhaps because after the publication of Darwin's *Origin of the Species*, it might have been a source of awkwardness among his clerical colleagues and the teaching of the established church.

In 1893 some workmen were quarrying for stone on the hilltop along the Mudgley Road. As they cleared away the soil and dug down they discovered 'bones'. Hervey heard about the discovery, and contacted his brother-in-law William Ayshford Sanford of Nynehead Court near Wellington, who had married Hervey's younger sister Sarah. Sanford was a palaeontologist (one who studies fossils).

At the first opportunity, Sanford visited Wedmore - but he 'was with a party of ladies, and therefore had but a short time for examination'. It is a reflection of our changed times that today the ladies would probably be just as enthusiastic about dinosaur-hunting in Wedmore as the gentlemen. Hervey went into the quarry and came out 'with a large fragment of bone on his shoulder' which Sanford 'instantly recognised as the lower part of the large bone of the leg of a very large saurian' - in short, a large dinosaur leg!

Together they collected a few other smaller fragments. They then went to the cottage of one of the workmen, who had saved other bones, and collected together 'a nearly complete femur or thigh bone, a number of large portions of vertebrae or backbone joints, and some other fragments'. Later Hervey obtained from the workmen some other bones including a perfect claw bone and other portions of a foot, the lower ends of two small bones of a hind leg, and fragments of ribs, some of which fitted together. Hervey and Sanford subsequently made further excavations in the quarry, finding teeth and other bone fragments.

William Sanford wrote up the discovery of these dinosaur fossils in 1894, in the Somerset Archaeological & Natural History Society *Proceedings* vol.40.[1] Our Wedmore dinosaur, he claimed, was the first large dinosaur to be found in England. The fossilised bones were buried in rocks laid down in the Triassic period, 215 million years ago. This was a lower and earlier geological level than those in which large dinosaurs had hitherto been found. Wedmore at that time had been part of a land mass lying just north of the equator.

The fossils were donated to the Natural History Museum in London, where they were examined by H.G. Seeley, FRS, Professor of Geology at King's College, London. In a long article in the *Geological Magazine* for 1898 Professor Seeley concluded that the fossil remains were actually parts of not one, but two dinosaurs.[2] He decided that there were no other bones quite like them in the national collection, and so the two dinosaurs were given new names: one was called *Avalonia sanfordi*, after our Avalon (Glastonbury) and Mr Sanford; the other was named *Picrodon herveyi*, after the Revd S.H.A. Hervey. *Avalonia sanfordi* was described as a large lizard-like dinosaur of a new genus, which was carniverous. *Picrodon herveyi* was a slightly smaller animal, and the few bones found suggested it belonged to the genus *Picrodon*, examples of which had already been found.

So how large was *Avalonia sanfordi*? The upper legbone or femur was about a metre long, that is almost three times the length of a human femur. One of its pointed teeth was described as being 12mm wide. *Avalonia sanfordi* was clearly a formidable beast, about 9 metres long. The remains have since been reassessed, and it has been decided that *Avalonia sanfordi* in fact belongs to the family *Melanorosauridae*, meaning 'black lizard'. It name has been changed to *Camelotia borealis*: *Camelotia* after King Arthur's Camelot, and *borealis* ('northern') as it is the only recorded example of this family from the northern hemisphere - which explains why Sanford thought it was a new genus. Dennis Parsons of Somerset County Museum, drew my attention to the Seeley article with its illustrations. PM Galton in 1998 published a scientific paper on Saurischian dinosaurs from the Upper Triassic of England, including *Camelotia* and *Avalonianus*.[3] He describes the fossils remains as vertebrae, pubis, ischium, femur, tibia, and phalanges.

In 1985 *Camelotia* was described as a herbivore, although the Natural History Museum still classifies it as Sanford did, as a carnivore; but in 1961 one expert didn't classify it as a dinosaur at all! Clearly, the arguments between the experts continue!

This drawing, on a glass lantern slide, was made about 1910 by Dr Bracey for one of his lectures on Wedmore history, given in the Wedmore Assembly Rooms (see *Wedmore Past*, 22-23). It is titled 'Saurian Reptile - fossilised remains found at Wedmore', and probably marked the start of his lecture, describing the Isle of Wedmore set among primeval swamps. While the picture may not bear much resemblance to either of the Wedmore dinosaurs, Dr Bracey has drawn a fearsome 'black lizard' for his audience.

A Wedmore dinosaur as visualised by Dr Bracey for a lantern slide show, c1910

Our two dinosaurs are still in the Natural History Museum - not on show, but safely packed in boxes in its store. Through the kindness of Dr Angela Milner, Curator in Palaeontology, I had the privilege of studying them there in July 1997. They still seem to be the only ones of their kind so far discovered in Great Britain. It has always been hoped that the bones, or casts of them, could be on display in the Somerset County Museum at Taunton, but that has not happened yet, and our own Wedmore dinosaurs remain comparatively unknown locally. It seems a pity that a fictitious Arthurian association has been superimposed upon the larger of our very real dinosaurs, when it was renamed *Camelotia borealis*. *Picrodon herveyi*, however, retains its original name. It must be the ultimate accolade for a local historian - even one more interested in medieval and later history - to have a dinosaur called after them!

I only discovered the reports of Hervey's and Sanford's find in the course of investigating, in documents and on the ground, the evidence of quarrying in Wedmore. Having identified several characteristic shallow scrapes of in-filled quarries on the Mudgley Road, I was able to match one exactly with Sanford's description. It is certainly a dramatic example of just where an interest in local history, following clues and information back from the 19th-20th century, to the middle ages and beyond, can lead.

Postscript

Work continues on the next hundred articles in the *Isle of Wedmore News*. Many aspects of the history and archaeology of the parish still remain to be recorded. The fascination of research in an area as rich in local history as Wedmore, is that it is never finished. There will always be much more to do. One enquiry solved may well lead on to two or three others to be investigated - especially if people continue to bring me documents, photographs or garden finds, which can provide such important additions to our common knowledge of our past. Who knows, I might even find another dinosaur!

Hazel Hudson
2002

References

Introduction
1 Manuscript in family ownership

Chapter 1: Villages Old and New
Place names in the Parish
1. PH Sawyer, *Anglo-Saxon Charters* (1968) p456 no 1167: lost charter of Centwine dated 676x685: Adam de Domerham, *Historia de…Glaston*, ed T Hearne (1727) I, 53, 'Dedit Wilfredus episcopus insulam de Wethmore XX hides'
2. R McDonnell 'The Upper Axe Valley, an interim statement' *Somerset Archaeology* vol 123 (1979)
3. E Ekwall. *The Concise Oxford Dictionary of English Place Names* (1959)
4. D Whitelock, ed, and others, *Anglo-Saxon Chronicle* ed (1961) 49-50
5. Sawyer no 1668. Adam de Domerham…'a rege Kentwino sibi datas, & villam de Cliwere 1 hidam'
6. SRO DD/S/HY30
7. Sawyer no 562
8. H Hudson & F Neale 'Panborough Saxon Charter, AD 956', *Somerset Archaeology* 127 (1983) 55-69
9. SRO DD/SAS C/212
10. HS 2
11. HMC *Wells* i 208
12. ibid
13. SRO DD/SAS PR 462 f28
14. SRO DD/SAS PR 462 f23
15. WR
16. SRO T/PH/vch II
17. HMC *Wells* i 534
18. ibid, i 285
19. SRO D/P/wed 13/10/17
20. SRO DD/SAS PR 462 f39v
21. SRO Q/AG il4/3
22. *Western Flying Post* Aug 25th 1827
23. SRO D/P/ilch 2/1/6
24. WR
25. HS 2
26. HMC *Wells* i 534
27. ibid, i 226
28. WR
29. SRO DD/SE 65
30. WR
31. SRS vol 3, 60
32. H Hudson & F Neale 'Panborough Saxon Charter 956 A D', *Somerset Archaeology* 127 (1983) 55-69
33. BL Egerton Mss 3034 f98
34. HMC *Wells* i 75
35. ibid, 133
36. WC I, 17-33
37. *Somerset Archaeology* vol 132 (1988) 212
38. B & J Coles *Sweet Track to Glastonbury* (1986) 19, 30-1

New villages
39. WC I, 213
40. SRO D/P/wed 13/10/17
41. SRO Wedmore & Northload Tithe Map (1838)
42. SRO D/P/the 2/1/1
43. SRO Wedmore census 1841
44. SRO D/P/wed 2/1/1

Lost settlements
45. SRS vol 76
46. OS 25inch Map 1st edition 1885/1886
47. SRO DD/SAS PR 462 f46v
48. HMC *Wells* i 50

Two vanished Tudor villages
49. Wells Cathedral: Almshouse Archives AH 435A
50. Wells Cathedral: Almshouse Archives ADD/1304
51. SRO Q/SR 128/20
52. SRO Q/SR 128/21
53. SRO Q/SR 130/32

References

Chapter 2: Parish Road Names

Wedmore

1. M Aston & R Leech, *Historic Towns in Somerset* (1977) 104
2. *Calendar of Charter Rolls Henry III* vol 1, 446
3. HMC *Wells* i 210
4. WC I, 130
5. SRO D/P/wed 13/10/17
6. WC II, 130
7. WR
8. WC II, 110
9. SRO DD/THD
10. ibid
11. SRO DD/SAS PR 462 f48
12. SRO D/P/wed 2/1/17
13. SRO DD/X/CR
14. R Atthill *Old Mendip* (1964) 106, 118-9
15. SRO D/P/wed 13/10/1, 2, 3
16. Kate Stickland, personal recollection
17. WC II, 146
18. WR
19. ibid
20. WC II, 96
21. SRO D/P/wed 14/7/1
22. SRO T/PH/vch 11, 7
23. SRO DD/SAS PR 462 f29
24. WC II, 268-9
25. *Calendar of the Patent Rolls Henry VI* vol V 1446-1452 (1971) 263-4
26. SRO E/4 box 74
27. SRO D/P/wed 14/7/1; *Somerset Archaeology* 131 (1987) 223
28. SRO DD/SAS PR 462 f8
29. Geoffrey Pavey, personal recollection
30. *West of England Advertiser* 20 May 1909
31. SRO DD/SAS PR 462 f62
32. WC I, 286
33. SRO DD/HS box 4
34. SRO Q/AP 88/1
35. ibid
36. SRO Q/AGs 14/1; Q/SCs 171-220
37. SRO DD/SAS PR 462 f26
38. SRS vol 56, 13
39. BL Add Ch 6550
40. SRO DD/CC 114091/2
41. WC I, 373
42. *Somerset Archaeology* 137 (1993) 136; C & N Hollinrake *The Close, Wedmore, An Archaeological Evaluation* (1993) (unpublished typescript)
43. SRO D/P/wed 13/10/1
44. SRO D/P/wed 14/7/1
45. SRO D/P/wed 13/10/1
46. SRO Q/REI 4/8
47. SRO D/D/Ct

Road names around the Parish

48. SRO DD/SE 59 box 13
49. WR
50. SRO DD/SE 64
51. HS 81
52. R Atthill *Old Mendip* (1964) 106,118-9
53. SRO DD/SAS PR 462 Perambulation
54. SRO DD/X IBL
55. SRO D/P/wed 13/10/17
56. SRO DD/X/HMD box 129
57. SRO DD/SE 63
58. SRO DD/X/HMD box 129
59. *Oxford English Dictionary*
60. SRO DD/SE 65
61. ibid
62. SRO DD/SE 63
63. SRO DD/SE 64
64. SRO T/PH/vch 11
65. SRO DD/BV 13
66. SRO DD/SAS PR 462 f15v
67. SRO DD/SE 63
68. SRO DD/SE 64
69. SRO DD/SAS PR 462 f8
70. SRO DD/SE 64
71. ibid
72. SRO DD/SE 63
73. SRO DD/SAS PR 462 f8
74. SRO DD/SAS PR 462 f24
75. SRO DD/WY box 84
76. SRO DD/SAS PR 462 f21
77. ibid, f11
78. WC I, 38
79. WC II, 75
80. SRO DD/SAS PR 462 Perambulation
81. SRO Q/RVi 9
82. SRO DD/SAS PR 462 f20
83. SRO DD/SAS PR 462 Perambulation
84. SRO DD/SAS PR 462 f37
85. R Atthill *Old Mendip* (1964) 106

86 SRO DD/SAS PR 462 f43
87 ibid f18
88 ibid f24
89 SRO DD/SAS C/212
90 B & J Coles *Sweet Track to Glastonbury* (1986) 19
91 ibid 30-1
92 SRO DD/SAS PR 462 f56
93 H Hudson & F Neale 'Panborough Saxon Charter AD 965' *Somerset Archaeology* 127 (1983) 55-69
94 PRO STAC 1/1 no36
95 BL Egerton Mss 3034 f96
96 H Hudson & F Neale 'Panborough Saxon Charter AD 956' *Somerset Archaeology* 127 (1983) 55-69
97 SRO DD/SAS PR 462 f39
98 BL Egerton Mss 3034 f30b
99 SRO DD/SAS C/212
100 WC I, 212-3
101 SRO DD/SAS PR 462 f18v
102 SRO Q/RDe 125
103 BL Egerton Mss 3034 f102
104 R Atthill *Old Mendip* (1964) 106,118-9
105 SRO DD/GS 20
106 R Atthill *Old Mendip* (1964) 106,118-9
107 SRO D/P/wed 13/10/1
108 SRO DD/FS box12
109 ibid
110 SRO D/P/wed 14/2/24
111 SRO DD/FS box12
112 ibid
113 SRO DD/GS 20
114 WR
115 R Atthill *Old Mendip* (1964) 106,118-9
116 *Proc SANHS* vol 62 (1916) Memoirs of St Dunstan 22
117 WR
118 SRO DD/BV no12
119 SRO D/P/wed 14/7/1
120 SRO DD/SE 63
121 SRO DD/SAS PR 462 f14v
122 SRO DD/BV no 11

Chapter 3: Wedmore Manor and its Manor House

1 P Rahtz *The Saxon and Medieval Palaces at Cheddar BAR British Series* 65 (1979); and 'The Saxon and Medieval Palaces at Cheddar, Somerset' Interim report *Proc SAHNS* 108 (1964) 99-112
2 D Whitelock, DC Douglas and SI Tucker *The Anglo Saxon Chronicle* (1961) 49-50
3 S Keynes & M Lapidge *Alfred The Great* (1983) 85
4 HMC *Wells* i 16
5 ibid, i 33
6 ibid, i 235
7 ibid, i 284-5
8 ibid, i 455
9 ibid, ii 208
10 ibid
11 E Green 'Had King Alfred a residence in Wedmore?' *Bath Field Club* (1881) 11-12
12 PRO E 310/23/124 fol 14
13 PRO Patent I Eliz Roll 94 mem11
14 SRO DD/SH box 16
15 WR
16 SRO T/PH/vch 11
17 SRO D/P/shep.b. 2/1/1
18 WR
19 SRO D/P/shep.b. 2/1/1
20 WR
21 ibid
22 Brown *Somerset Wills* vol I (1887) 83-4
23 WC I, 251
24 J Foster *Alumni Oxonienses 1500-1712* (1891)
25 M McGarvie *The Antiquities of Mells, Elm and Buckland in 1730* (1983)
26 Elizabeth: SRO DD/SH 79/3; Jane SRO DD/SH Box 16 (will 1671)
27 SRO DD/SH 33
28 J Billingsley *General View of the Agriculture of the County of Somerset* (1797) 259
29 B Strachey *The Strachey Line* (1985)
30 SRO DD/SH 79/12
31 A Roberts *Mendip Annals* (1859) 207
32 W Marston Acres *A Brief History of Wedmore* (1953) 51
33 ibid, 62-3
34 ibid, 63

References

Chapter 4: St. Mary's Parish Church, Wedmore

1. Information from a *Guide* to St Mary's Church, Wedmore, by Hazel Hudson & Frances Neale (1996)
2. *SDNQ* vol VIII (1902-3) 266 item 222
3. ibid, vol IX (1905) 39 item 15
4. SRS vol 19 43
5. ibid, vol 21 178-9

A busy day in Wedmore Church, 1350

6. *Calendar of Inquisitions Post Mortem 1370-1373* (1954) 208-9
7. HMC *Wells* i 229
8. ibid, 50, 67
9. A fuller version of this item has appeared in *SDNQ* vol xxxiii item 336 (September 1992) 171-3, H Hudson & F Neale 'A Busy Day in Wedmore Church 1350'

In Wedmore churchyard

10. *Weston-super-Mare Gazette* Oct 1917
11. WR
12. SRO D/P/wed 13/10/17

Chapter 5: Wedmore Borough

Markets and Fairs

1. *Calendar of Charter Rolls Henry III* vol I 446
2. Lambeth Palace Library ED 266: ED 1093
3. In the parish records still in Wedmore church (2002); SRO DD/X/SOM 41-5
4. WC II, 331
5. *Weston-super-Mare Gazette* July 26 1879
6. *Weston-super-Mare Mercury & Somersetshire Herald* July 25 1896
7. *Weston-super-Mare Gazette* August 6 1898

Chapter 6: Wedmore Houses

People and houses in The Borough

1. SRO D/P/wed 13/10/17
2. Dr Bracey lantern slide privately owned
3. SRO Q/RDe 136
4. Lambeth Palace Library ED 266, ED 1093
5. Private deeds
6. In the parish records still in Wedmore church (2002)
7. Lambeth Palace Library ED 266, ED 1093
8. ibid

Two house plots in The Borough: Jobs and Drakeshay

9. Dr Bracey lantern slide privately owned
10. SRO DD/SAS C/127 bundle 2 no 1
11. SRS vol 2, 69
12. SRS vol 77, 98-9
13. SRS vol 2, 250-4
14. Lambeth Palace Library ED 266, ED 1093
15. SRO DD/SAS C/127 bundle 2 no 2
16. SRO DD/SH 108
17. SRO DD/BV no12
18. SRO DD/S/WH 209
19. SRO DD/SG 4
20. SRO D/P/wed 13/10/1
21. Dr Bracey lantern slide privately owned
22. In the parish records still in Wedmore church (2002)

Minstrels Gallery and Lloyds Chemist

23. Private deeds
24. Wedmore census 1851
25. SRO D/D/RM vol 1
26. SRO Q/RCc2
27. ibid

The Old Vicarage and Buoys Cottage, Wedmore

28. WC I, 273-5
29. WC I, 274
30. M Ponsford 'A Bearded Face Jug from Wedmore, Somerset and Anthropomorphic Medieval Vessels from Bristol' *Rescue Archaeology in the Bristol Area: 1* (City of Bristol Museum & Art Gallery Monograph no. 2, 1977), 49-55
31. Wells Museum: jug ref no 545, 546; cresset lamp ref no 1415
32. Wells Museum ref no 1412
33. London Museum, *Medieval Catalogue* (reprint 1957) 274-276 & Plate LXXVIII no 3

34	HMC *Wells* vol ii 126		*Rev John Richards A.M.* published privately [c1826]
35	WR		
36	SRO D/D/Rg 91	40	SRO D/D/Bbm 229
37	SRO DD/v AXr 27; personal communication Commander Williams	41	SRO D/D/Bbm 293
		42	SRO DD/SAS C/120/12
38	WC I, 256, 263	43	WC I, 200
39	[anon.] *A Brief Memoir & Sermons of the*	44	ibid, 210

Chapter 7: Ancient Landscapes

The search for King Alfred's Palace at Mudgley

1. WC I, 17-33
2. H Hudson & F Neale Wedmore, 'Court Garden, Mudgley' *Somerset Archaeology* 126 (1982) 80-1
3. HMC *Wells* i 534
4. HMC *Wells* i 235
5. HMC *Wells* i 284-5
6. Private papers
7. J Blezzard 'The Wells Musical Slates' from *Musical Times*, cxx, no.1631. Jan 1979, 26-30
8. *Weston-super-Mare Gazette* 13th Sept 1879
9. *Weston-super-Mare Gazette* reports: 1878 Nov 2nd, 16th, 30th; 1879 25th Jan, 1st Feb, 5th July, 9th Aug, 13th Sept; 1880 Jan 10th, Nov 13th
10. SRO D/P wed 13/10/17
11. OS 1st edition 25" 1885-6
12. SRO DD/BV no12

Alexander of Mudgley's farm, 1220

13. HMC *Wells* i 50
14. HMC *Wells* i 284-5

Theale Landscape: The Battle of Kyppmerwalle

15. PRO STAC 1/1 no36
16. SRS vol 27, 56-62
17. PRO STAC 1/1 no36, & 2/26/86
18. PRO STAC 2/19/282

Chapter 8: Ancient Landmarks

Ancient stone crosses

1. *Calendar of Charter Rolls Hen III* vol I 446
2. SRO DD/X/MRD
3. SRO DD/THG
4. SRO D/P/wed 13/10/17
5. C Pooley *Old Crosses of Somerset* (1877) 114-5
6. BL ADD 33653 f.205 8452708 Revd John Skinner 1819
7. SRO D/P/wed 4/1/2
8. C Pooley *Old Crosses of Somerset* (1877) 111
9. Courtauld Institue neg. 762/44 (22) John Buckler 1844
10. C Pooley *Old Crosses of Somerset* (1877) 111-2

The manorial pounds

11. *Somerset Archaeology* vol 130 (1986) 155
12. SRO DD/THG Box 8
13. SRO D/P/wed 13/10/17
14. SRO DD/SAS PR 462 Customs
15. SRO DD/S/HY 30
16. SRS vol 11 249
17. SRO DD/SE 64 Box 18
18. SRO DD/X/HMD Box 129
19. SRO DD/SE 64 Box 18
20. ibid
21. SRO DD/S/WH 209

Holy wells and other springs

22. WC I, 338
23. SRO DD/CC 8598
24. *Somerset Folk Series* no 12 (1923) 23
25. SRS vol 27 60
26. BL Egerton Mss 3034 ff3-8
27. J Collinson *History & Antiquities of Somerset* (1791)i 187

References

28 SRO DD/SE 64
89 J Collinson *History & Antiquities of Somerset* (1791)i 187
30 WC I, 24
31 SRO DD/SAS PR 462 f34
32 J Carley *Glastonbury Abbey* (1988) 181
33 SRO DD/SAS C/212
34 SRO T/PH/vch 11
35 SRO DD/FS Box 12
36 SRO DD/SAS PR 462 f45v
37 SRO T/PH/vch 11
38 SRO DD/SAS PR 462 f45v
39 SRO DD/FS Box 12
40 SRO DD/SAS PR 424
41 SRO T/PH/vch 11
42 J Collinson *History & Antiquities of Somerset* (1791) i 189

Crossroad elms and boundary trees

43 SRO DD/BV 12
44 SRO DD/SAS PR 462 f31
45 SRO DD/SAS PR 462 Perambulation
46 SRO DD/SAS PR 462 f45v
47 ibid, f39v
48 SRO DD/GS 20
49 SRO DD/SAS PR 462 f10
50 SRO DD/SE 64
51 SRO DD/SE 65
52 SRO D/P/ched 24/2
53 SRO DD/SE 42
54 SRO DD/SAS PR 462 f24v
55 ibid, f7v
56 SRO DD/SAS C/127

Chapter 9: The Mills of Wedmore Parish

Watermills

2 PRO Patent Rolls 1 Eliz Roll 94 mem 11
2 HMC *Wells* i 226
3 *Somerset Archaeology* vol 130 (1986) 156
4 BL Egerton Mss 3034 f96
5 WC I, 292
6 SRO D/P/wed 13/2/7
7 WC II, 137; SRO DD/X/HKN 1&2
8 BL Add Ch 6550
9 SRO D/P/wed 13/10/17
10 SRO D/P/wed 13/2/7
11 WC II, 226
12 *Somerset Archaeology* vol 136 (1992) 176 & vol 137 (1993) 136; C & N Hollinrake *The Close, Wedmore, An Archaeological Evaluation* (1993) (unpublished typescript)

Windmills

13 SRS vol 8 (1894) 150
14 BL Egerton Mss 3034 f90,96,96v
15 SRO DD/SAS PR 462 f26
16 Emanuel Bowen, Map of Somerset c1760
17 SRO Q/Rde 83
18 SRO D/P/wed 14/2/4
19 ibid
20 SRO D/P wed 13/10/1
21 Coulthard & Watts *Windmills of Somerset* (1978) 63
22 *Somerset Archaeology* vol 131 (1987) 228
23 SRO DD/SAS PR 462 f26
24 SRO D/P/wed 13/10/1
25 SRO DD/SAS C/127 bundle 2 no1
26 SRO DD/SAS C/120/12
27 SRO THG 8
28 SRO D/P/wed 13/10/1
29 SRO DD/SAS C/127 bundle 2 no1
30 SRS vol 79 (1985) 63
31 SRS vol 51 (1936) 155
32 SRO T/PH/vch 11
33 SRS vol 23 (1907) 17-8
34 WC II, 157-8
35 WC II, 139
36 The original journal is now in SRO ref DD/X/HKN, extracts are quoted from WC as indicated
37 WC II, 140
38 WC II, 158
39 Coulthard & Watts *Windmills of Somerset* (1978) 44
40 SRO D/P/w.st.c 17/1/10
41 SRO DD/SAS PR 462 f41v
42 PRO Patent I Eliz Roll 94 mem 11
43 SRO DD/SAS PR 462 f41v
44 SRO D/P/w.st.c 17/1/2
45 SRO DD/SAS 20/54
46 SRO D/P/w.st.c 17/1/1
47 SRO D/P/wed 13/10/1
48 SRO DD/FS Box 12
49 SRO DD/SX 67/3

50	SRO Q/REI 4/8	56	Coulthard & Watts *Windmills of Somerset* (1978) 63-4
51	SRO DD/X/MRD		
52	SRO DD/SE 85	57	WR
53	Coulthard & Watts *Windmills of Somerset* (1978) 65		

A miller's diary

58 Extracts from the diary reproduced with the permission of William Tucker's granddaughter, Miss Ruth Tucker

54 SRO DD/SE 64 Box 18
55 WR

Chapter 10: Local Industries and Transport

The Wedmore Gas Company Ltd.
1. Private papers
2. Hazel Hudson *More Wedmore Past* (1995) 54
3. *Wells Journal* 29th May 1936
4. *Wells Journal* 1st Feb 1952
5. *Mendip Gazette* 28th Feb 1947

Wedmore Electric Light and Power Company
6. *Wells Journal* 15th Aug 1911
7. *Weston-super-Mare Gazette* 16th Sept 1911
8. SRO C/E/69/225/1
9. Hazel Hudson *Wedmore Past* (1993) 64
10. Bramwell Freckingham, son of Wedmore Gas works manager J Freckingham
11. Thanks to Peter Lamb, Chairman of the South Western Electrical Historical Society

Wedmore Brick and Tile Works
12. Kelly's *Directory of Somersetshire* (1875)
13. *Weston-super-Mare Mercury & Somersetshire Herald* 21st July 1900
14. Private deeds
15. Report & Plans of the barn at Brickyard Farm, prior to conversion: Nealon Tanner Architects (1988), with contribution from Brian J Murless of Somerset Industrial Archaeological Society.

A Wedmore Tannery
16. SRO Q/REI 4/8 (1792)
17. ibid, (1814)
18. SRO D/P/wed 14/2/4
19. SRO D/P/wed 13/10/17
20. SRO D/P/wed 13/10/1
21. SRO D/P/wed 13/2/7
22. SRO Q/RDe 82
23. SRO Q/REI 4/8 (1766)
24. Hazel Hudson *Wedmore Past* (1993) 11
25. SRO D/D/ct (will & inventory)
26. WR
27. A formal report on the identification and history of the tannery in Glanville Road was published in *Somerset and Dorset Notes & Queries* vol. xxxii pt 330 (September 1989) 790: 'Wedmore Tan-Houses' by H Hudson and F Neale

The Highbridge, Wedmore & Cheddar Light Railway
28. SRO D/RA 2/10/1
29. SRO D/P/Wed 13/2/12
30. SRO D/SE 72
31. SRO D/RA 2/10/1

Wedmore's first bus service
32. For a different picture of the bus see Hazel Hudson *Wedmore Past* (1993) 66

The Wedmore Cheddar Cheese School
33. *Journal of the Bath & West of England Society* vol xiv p184, vol xvi 108-10
34. SRO DD/S/FRD S/1891
35. ibid
36. AW Coysh, EJ Mason & V Waite *The Mendips* (1954) 109
37. ibid

Chapter 11: Schools

Early Schools in Wedmore
1. SRO D/D/OL no 39
2. WC II, 343
3. ibid
4. WC I, 86

References

5 ibid, 175
6 ibid, 176
7 SRO *Somerset Charity Commissioners Report* 1819-37
8 WC II, 192
9 SRO D/P/wed 13/2/7
10 ibid
11 SRO D/P/wed 13/2/7
12 WC II, 182
13 ibid 184
14 ibid 196
15 SRO D/P/wed 13/2/9

Hannah More at Wedmore

16 MA Hopkins *Hannah More and Her Circle* (1947); J & M Collingwood *Hannah More* (1990)
17 A Roberts *Mendip Annals* 207-228
18 SRO D/P/wed 13/2/9
19 MG Jones *Hannah More* (1952) 182
20 A Roberts *Mendip Annals* (1859) 228
21 W Roberts *Memoirs of the Life and Correspondence of Hannah More* (1834) vol III 146
22 A Roberts *Mendip Annals* (1859) 220
23 W Roberts *Memoirs of the Life and Correspondence of Hannah More* (1834) vol III 51
24 SRO D/P/wed 13/2/9
25 Private notes of Revd S.H.A. Hervey in his own copy of *Wedmore Chronicles* now in Wells Museum
26 [Revd W White] *Life of the Revd William White* (1860) 20-21
27 SRO C/C box 7
28 Wedmore Census 1851
29 Private notes of Revd S.H.A. Hervey in his own copy of *Wedmore Chronicles* now in Wells Museum

Early schools in Blackford and Theale

30 SRO DD/PLE box 41
31 SRO D/P/the 9/1/1
32 Bagley Close Board School Log Books in private hands

Wedmore Board School

33 SRO D/P/w.st.c 17/1/45
34 SRO E/4 box 74

Theale and Bagley Close Board School

35 Bagley Close Board School Log Books in private hands

Blackford Board School

36 SRO Q/RU 167
37 SRO C/E 76
38 SRO DD/X/IBL 2

Hugh Sexey and Sexey's School, Blackford

39 For a fuller account see Hazel Hudson *Hugh Sexey Church of England Middle School 1899-1999* (1999)
40 J Henderson *Hugh Sexey and Bruton* (1992)
41 *Proc SANHS* vol 24 (1908) 33
42 SRO DD/SE 39
43 ibid 38
44 ibid 39
45 SRO DD/SE 46 1 of 4
46 SRO DD/SE 39
47 SRO DD/X IBL 1
48 SRO C/E 73
49 A Swallow A *History of Sexey's Blackford School* (1957)

Chapter 12: Chapels

Wedmore Methodist Chapel

1 SRO D/D/Rm 1
2 A Roberts *Mendip Annals* (1859) 213
3 MC Jones *Hannah More* (1952) 182
4 ibid, 175
5 Private notes of Revd S.H.A. Hervey in his own copy of *Wedmore Chronicle* now in Wells Museum
6 SRO D/D/Rm 5
7 BRO 36266/CV11/F/1(a)
8 ibid
9 *Weston-super-Mare Mercury & Somersetshire Herald* March 28th; April 18th 1896
10 BRO 36266/CV11/F/1(a)
11 *Weston-super-Mare Mercury & Somersetshire Herald* Oct 26th 1901
12 BRO 3622/CV11/F/1(a)
13 Unnamed newspaper cutting with photographs in the church
14 Personal contribution Revd Leslie Craze retired Methodist Minister & former Missionary in India

The Mission Chapels of Wedmore
15 Personal communication from his granddaughter Muriel Welch
16 *Bagley Baptist Church History 25 Years.* Private Publication [1991]

Chapter 13: People

Jeremy Horler and Ann Hodges: a Civil War love story?
1 WC I, 252
2 J Foster *Alumni Oxonienses 1500-1714* vol I (1891) 745
3 SRO DD/SH Box 33; Boxes 77/11; 77/12; 79/3
4 *Marriage Allegations in the Diocese of Gloucester vol II 1681-1700* ed B Frith. Bristol & Gloucester Archaeological Society Record Section vol 9 (1970) 52
5 GRO GDR WILLS 1686/176
6 J Foster *Alumni Oxonienses 1500-1714* vol I (1891) 745

Wedmore and the Monmouth Rebellion, 1685
7 SRS vol 179, iii
8 ibid 169
9 PRO E178/6676
10 SRO DD/X/HKN 1&2
11 WC I, 314-6
12 WC II, 141-2
13 SRS vol 179, 222
14 SRO Q/RCc2 no 15

John Tucker of Blackford, 1700–1779
15 WR
16 SRO DD/SE 65
17 WR
18 SRO D/P/bla 17/1/1
19 WC II, 333

Church v Chapel, 1891
17 *Weston-super-Mare Gazette* Oct-Dec 1891; *Wells Journal* Oct-Dec 1891; *Bridgwater Mercury* Dec 1891

The story of Mary Hardwick, 1752-1813
20 SRO D/P/wed: Poor Book 9/1/2; Examination before JP 1787, 13/3/1; Letters from Edward & Mary Hardwick to Wedmore Overseers 13/7/1; Notebook, Inventory & Papers 13/10/8; WR
21 J Billingsley *General view of the Agriculture of the County of Somerset* (1797) 259

Joseph Stickland, 1773-1824: an apprentice and his descendants
22 SRO DD/SE 46
23 *Charity Commissioners Report* 393-5
24 ibid
25 SRO D/P/brut 2/1/4
26 SRO DD/SE 46
27 WR & Wedmore Methodist Church Records
28 BRO 36266/CV11/F/1(a); Daily Workbook of Edward & George Stickland (1895-1900) privately owned
29 SRO C/E 70
30 SRO C/E 69

The Reverend William White, 1793-1867
31 WR
32 WC II, 326

Richard Lyde Stott, 1816-1899: the Bard of Wedmore
33 *Wells Journal* 1st July 1886

Chapter 14: The wrong side of the Law

The Wedmore Riot, 1885
4 *The Western Gazette* Dec 11th, 18th 1885; Jan 15th, 22nd, 29th 1886; June 4th 1886; *Wells Journal* Dec 5th, 10th 1885; *Weston-super-Mare Gazette* Dec 12th, 19th 1885; Jan 9th 1886; *Somerset County Gazette* Jan 23rd, 30th 1886

A village burglary in 1909
2 *Weston Mercury & Somersetshire Herald* Jan 29th 1909; *Wells Journal* Jan 28th 1909; various newspaper cuttings from scrapbooks

The Tin-Pot Band
3 *Weston-super-Mare Mercury* Jan 27th 1900

4 ibid, Feb 17th 1900
5 ibid, Feb & March issues
6 RL Tongue *Somerset Folklore* (1995) 181
7 SRS vol 86, 303

Chapter 15: Wedmore in wartime, 1939-1945

5 SRO D/P/wed 23/2 part 2 of 2
2 SRO E/4 Box 74
3 *Cheddar Valley Gazette* 11th Sept 1986
4 *The Women of Wedmore WVS Civil Defence 1939-1945* Booklet published privately
5 ibid
6 ibid
7 ibid
8 ibid

Chapter 16: A field name alphabet: A-Z

1 WC I, 115-29; 176-218, 283-335, 370-83
2 SRO D/P/wed 13/10/17, 13/10/1, 2, & 3; DD/X/MRD, Tithe maps Blackford, Northload & Wedmore
3 SRO DD/SS 6:5
4 SRO DD/SE 26
5 SRO DD/SAS PR 462 f16
6 BL Egerton Mss 3034 f95b
7 HS 2
8 *Calendar of Patent Rolls 2 Hen V pt III* 269
9 SRO DD/SE 59 box 13
10 SRO DD/SAS PR 462 f31
11 ibid, ff14v,41v
12 SRO D/P/wed 13/2/4-7
13 SRO D/P/w.st.c 17/1/1
14 WC I, 130
15 SRO DD/SAS PR 462 f7
16 HS 83
17 HMC *Wells* i 229
18 *Calendar of Patent Rolls Ed I 1292-1301* 472
19 SRO DD/SS 6:4
20 H Hudson & F Neale 'Panborough Saxon Charter, AD 956' *Somerset Archaeology* 127 (1983) 55-69
21 JP Carley *John of Glastonbury: Cronica* (1978) 17
22 PRO Patent Roll I Eliz 94 mem11
23 SRO DD/THG
24 SRO DD/BV 12
25 SROD/P/wed 13/10/1
26 SRO DD/SE 64
27 SRO D/P/wed 13/10/1
28 SRO DD/SE 65
29 ibid, 42
30 *Somerset Archaeology* vol 130 (1986) 154
31 SRO DD/SAS PR 462 f47v
32 SRO D/P/wed 13/10/1
33 SRO DD/BR 1ch 13
34 SRO D/P/wed 13/10/1
35 SRO Q/RDe 83
36 BL Egerton Mss 3034 f 96v
37 SRO DD/FS box12
38 SRO D/P/wed 13/10/1
39 SRO T/PH/vch 11
40 SRO DD/SAS PR 462 f12
41 SRO DD/SS 6:5
42 SRO DD/SAS PR 462 f7v
43 SRO D/P/wed 13/10/1
44 SRO Q/RDe 136
45 SRO DD/SAS PR 462 f7
46 WR: SRO DD/SAS PR 462 f6: SRO T/PH/vch 11
47 SRO D/P/wed 13/10/1
48 H Hudson & F Neale 'Panborough Saxon Charter AD 956' *Somerset Archaeology* 127 (1983) 55-69
49 JG(H) 304
50 SRO DD/GS 20
51 SRO D/P/wed 13/10/1
52 SRO DD/SAS PR 462 f24
53 HMC *Wells* i 50
54 SRO DD/SAS PR 462 f41v
55 SRO D/P/wed 13/10/1
56 SRO T/PH/vch 11
57 SRO D/P/wed 13/10/1
58 BL Egerton Mss 3034 f90
59 SRO D/P/wed 13/10/1
60 SRO WY 84
61 SRO DD/SAS PR 462 f21
62 SRO DD/BV 12
63 SRO DD/GS 20
64 BL Egerton Mss 3034 f97
65 HS 9
66 SRO DD/SAS PR 462 f18v

67 *Somerset Archaeology* vol 142 (1998) 210
68 SRO DD/OB Bd85
69 SRO DD/SAS PR 462 f7v
70 ibid, f9
71 SRO DD/SE 64
72 SRO DD/SAS PR 462 f7v
73 SRO Q/RDe 82
74 SRO D/P/wed 13/10/1
75 *Calendar of Patent Rolls Ed I 1292-1301* 472
76 SRO D/P/wed 13/10/1
77 Wedmore Baptist Church records
78 SRO DD/ED box 139 f189
79 H Hudson & F Neale 'Panborough Saxon Charter AD 956' *Somerset Archaeology* 127 (1983) 55-69
80 SRO Q/RDe 82
81 BL Egerton Mss 3034 f101
82 ibid, f98
83 SRO DD/SE 65
84 ibid, 63
85 SRO D/P/wed 13/10/1
86 HMC *Wells* ii 218
87 SRO DD/SAS PR 462 f28
88 BL Egerton Mss 3034 f98b
89 SRO DD/SAS PR 462 Perambulation
90 SRO D/P/wed 13/10/1
91 H Hudson & F Neale 'Panborough Saxon Charter AD 956' *Somerset Archaeology* 127 (1983) 55-69
92 HMC *Wells* i 210
93 SRO D/P/wed 13/10/1
94 WR
95 HMC *Wells* i 303
96 SRO DD/SAS PR 462 f18v
97 SRO D/P/ched 24/2
98 SRO DD/SAS PR 462 f48
99 SRO DD/SE 42
100 ibid, 59
101 SRO D/P/wed 14/2/1
102 SRO DD/SAS C/171
103 SRO D/P/w.st.c 17/1/36
104 SRO D/P/w.st.c 17/1/1
105 SRO D/P/wed 13/10/1
106 ibid
107 SRO D/P/ched 24
108 SRO DD/SAS PR 462 f9
109 WC I, 138
110 Wells Cathedral Chapter Archives ADD/1204
111 SRO DD/GS 20
112 BL Egerton Mss 3034 f98
113 SRO D/P/w.st.c 17/1/1
114 SRO D/P/wed 13/10/1
115 ibid
116 ibid
117 ibid
118 ibid
119 BL Egerton Mss 3034 f90b
120 SRO D/P/wed 13/10/1
121 SRO DD/SE 64
122 ibid
123 BL Egerton Mss 3034 f95b
124 SRO D/P/wed 13/10/1
125 SRO DD/FS box 12
126 SRO D/P/wed 13/10/1
127 SRO DD/SAS PR 462 f7v
128 SRO DD/BV no12
129 SRO DD/SE 65
130 SRO D/P/wed 13/10/1
131 WR
132 SRO D/P/wed 13/10/1
133 SRO DD/SAS PR 462 f14
134 *Calendar of Patent Rolls Edward I 1292-1301* 472
135 SRO DD/NW 4
136 SRO THG box 8
137 SRO DD/SAS C/127/1
138 SRO D/P/wed 13/10/1
139 SRO DD/SE 65
140 ibid, 63
141 ibid, 26
142 SRO DD/SAS PR 462 f23
143 SRO D/P/wed 13/10/1
144 SRO DD/SH 16
145 SRO Q/RDe 82
146 HMC *Wells* i 200
147 SRO Q/RDe 136
148 HS 84
149 SRO D/P/wed 13/10/1
150 ibid
151 SRO DD/OB bd 85
152 HS 83
153 WC I, 215
154 SRO DD/SAS PR 462 ff21,38,35
155 SRO DD/GS 20
156 HMC *Wells* i 210
157 SRO DD/SAS PR 462 f21
158 ibid f44v

159 SRO DD/GS 20
160 SRO DD/FS box 12
161 SRO D/P/wed 13/10/1
162 HMC *Wells* i 284-5
163 SRO DD/SAS PR 462 f32
164 SRO DD/BV no 12
165 BL Egerton Mss 3034 f96
166 SRO DD/SE 69
167 PRO STAC 2/26/86
168 SRO T/PH/vch 11

Chapter 17: Lost and Found

The Wedmore coin hoard
1   WC II, 306
2   H Symonds, 'Anglo Saxon Coins found at Wedmore in 1853' *Proc SANHS* vol 69 (1923) 30-7
3   ibid
4   WR
5   WC II, 306
6   *Proc SANHS* vol 69 (1923) 34

Stray finds
7   WC II, 306
8   WC I, 378
9   *Somerset Archaeology* vol 132 (1988) 213
10 *Proc SANHS* vol 107 (1963) 72-8
11 WC I, 38
12 Private notes of Revd S.H.A. Hervey in his own copy of *Wedmore Chronicles* now in Wells Museum
13 H Hudson & F Neale Wedmore, 'Court Garden, Mudgley' *Somerset Archaeology* 126 (1983) 80-1
14 *Archaeological Journal* vol vi (1847) 81; *Journal of British Archaeological Association* (1st Series) vol xxi (1865) 232; DP Dobson *The Archaeology of Somerset* (1931) 89-90;
15 H Hudson & F Neale 'A Saxon Ring from Wedmore' *Somerset Archaeology* 133 (1989) 188-191

The lost letter
16 SDNQ vol 124 255-256
17 ibid
18 WC I, 270
19 WR
20 JM Stratton *Agricultural Records AD 220-1977* (2nd edition 1978) 92-4
21 J Billingsley *General view of the Agriculture of the County of Somerset* (1797) 259,33
22 JM Stratton Agricultural Records AD 220-1977 (2nd edition 1978) 94

Another lost letter
23 SRO D/P/wed 13/2/8
24 ibid
25 SRO D/P/wed 13/2/7
26 WC II p205
27 *Weston–super-Mare Gazette* August 8th 1878
28 WC I, 17-33

Chapter 18: The Vicar and the Dinosaurs

1   *Proc SANHS* vol 40 (1894) pt II 227-35
2   *The Geological Magazine* Decade IV vol V no 403 (January 1898) 1-6 & Plate I
3   PM Galton 'Saurischian dinosaurs from the Upper Triassic of England' *Palaeontographica* A250 (4-6) 671-6

Abbreviations

BGAS	*Bristol & Gloucestershire Archaeological Society*
BL	British Library
BRO	Bristol Record Office
GRO	Gloucestershire Record Office
HMC *Wells*	Historic Manuscripts Commission *Calendar of the Manuscripts of the Dean and Chapter of Wells* vols. i, ii (1907, 1914)
HS	JE Jackson, ed, *Liber Henrici de Soliaco: An Inquistion of the Manors of Glastonbury Abbey, 1189* (Roxburghe Club, 1882)
SDNQ	Somerset and Dorset Notes & Queries
Proc SANHS	Somerset Archaeological & Natural History Society *Proceedings* up to and including vol 111 (1967)
Somerset Archaeology	*Somerset Archaeology & Natural History:* Proceedings of the Somerset Archaeological & Natural History Society from vol 112 (1968) onwards
SRO	Somerset Record Office
SRS	*Somerset Record Society*
WC	SHA Hervey, *Wedmore Chronicle* vol I 1881-1887 (1887), vol II 1888-1898 (1898)
WR	SHA Hervey, *Wedmore Parish Registers:* Baptisms 1561-1812, (1890) Marriages 1561-1839, (1888) Burials 1561-1860 (1890)

Footnote references to Wedmore Parish Registers (WR) are not given where they are already mentioned as a source in the text. It will also be clear from the text whether the reference is to the Baptisms, Marriages or Burials volume.

Selected Bibliography

Acres W Marston *A Brief History of Wedmore* (1953)
Atthill R *Old Mendip* (1964)
Carley J *Glastonbury Abbey* (1988)
Coles B & J *Sweet Track to Glastonbury* (1986)
Collingwood J & M *Hannah More* (1990)
Collinson J *History & Antiquities of Somerset* (1791)
Coultard AJ & Watts M *Windmills of Somerset* (1978)
Coysh AW & Mason EJ *The Mendips* (1954)
Ekwall E *The Concise Dictionary of English Place-Names* (1960)
Elworthy FT *The Dialect of West Somerset* (1875-6)
Field J *A History of English Field Names* (1993)
Hearne T *Historia de…Glaston* (1727)
Henderson J *Hugh Sexey & Bruton* (1992)
Hervey SHA *Wedmore Chronicle I* (1887) & II (1898);
Hervey SHA *Wedmore Parish Registers: Baptisms 1561-1812* (1890), *Marriages 1561-1839* (1888), *Burials 1561-1860* (1890)
Historic Manuscripts Commission *Calendar of the Manuscripts of the Dean and Chapte of Wells i & ii* (1907, 1914)
Hopkins MA *Hannah More & Her Circle* (1947)
Hudson H *Wedmore Past* (1993), *More Wedmore Past* (1995)
Hudson H *Hugh Sexey Church of England Middle School 1899-1999* (1999)
Jackson JE *Liber Henrici de Soliaco: An Inquistion of the Manors of Glastonbury Abbey 1189*, Roxburghe Club (1882)
Jones MC *Hannah More* (1952)
Keynes S & Lapidge M *Alfred the Great* (1983)
McGarvie M *The Antiquities of Mells, Elm & Buckland in 1730* (1983)
Pooley C *Old Crosses of Somerset* (1877)
Somerset Archaeological & Natural History Society Proceedings, later *Somerset Archaeology*
Rahtz P *The Saxon & Medieval Palaces at Cheddar* BAR British Series 65 (1979)
Richards, *A Brief Memoir & Sermons of the Revd John* [anon.] published privately [c1826]
Roberts A *Mendip Annals* (1859)
Roberts W *Memoirs of the Life & Correspondence of Mrs Hannah More* vol III (1834)
Sawyer PH *Anglo-Saxon Charters* (1968)
Somerset and Dorset Notes & Queries
Somerset Folk Series
Somerset Record Society publications
Strachey B *The Strachey Line* (1985)
Stratton JM *Agricultural Records AD 220-1977* (1978)
Swallow A *A History of Sexey's Blackford School* (1957)
[White W] *Life of the Revd William White* (1860)
Whitelock D, Douglas DC, Tucker SI *The Anglo Saxon Chronicle* (1961)
Williams M *Draining of the Somerset Levels* (1970)

Measures

Area

1 acre	= 4840 square yards		= 0.40 hectares
1 furlong	= 48.400 square yards	= 10 acres	= 4 hectares
1 rood	= 1210 square yards	= 0.25 acre	= 1012 square metres
1 perch	= 30.25 square yards		= 25.3 square metres

A yard is a very small area.

Linear

1 mile	= 1760 yards	= 1.6 kilometres
1 rod, pole or perch	= 5.5 yards	= 5 metres
1 furlong	= 220 yards	= 201 metres
1 yard	= 3 feet	= 0.91 metres
1 foot	= 12 inches	= 0.30 metres
1 inch		= 25 millimetres
A rope	= 20 feet	= 6 metres

A stitch is a very small strip of land.

Weights

1 hundredweight (cwt)	= 51 kilograms
1 pound	= 0.454 kilograms

Money

£1 (pound)	= 20 shillings (s) or 240 pennies (d, old pence)
1 mark	= 13s 4d
½ mark	= 6s 8d

Index

All places are in Wedmore Parish or the Isle of Wedmore unless stated otherwise, and incidental references to Wedmore and the Isle of Wedmore have not been included in the Index.

A

Adams, John 69
Addams, Richard 55
Air Raid Precaution Wardens 219, 222
alder groves 94, 95
Alexander of Mudgley 18, 93, 94, 95
Alfred, King 16, 22, 37, 47, 57, 68, 81, 88, 90–92, 252, 256, 258
Algar/Algare, John 96, 98, 99
Algare/Alger, William 63, 65, 96
Aller 47
Aller Moor/Allermoor 24, 42
Allermoor Farm 25
Allerton 49, 114, 223, 243
Allington House 74, 81, 211
Allington House Dress Shop 67
Alves, Alexander 209, 210
Amesbury, Henry 161
Andrews 71, 73
Andrews, George 148
Andrews, Henry 31
Andrews, Samuel 188
Andrews, Thomas 29
Andus [Andrews], John 30
Antwerp, seige of 49
Arnold, Edward 163
Ashton Mill 114, 115
Assembly Rooms/Masonic building 136, 258
Athelard, William 58, 59
Athelard, William the younger 59
Athelney 47
Auxiliary Fire Service 219, 222
Axe *see* River Axe

B

Badgworth Court 253
Bagg, Charlie 119, 122
Bagg family 22
Bagg, George and Maria 25
Bagley 22, 27, 153, 154, 159, 162, 220, 233, 236, 239, 247
    roads of 43–45
Bagley Baptist Church 177
Bagley Close [Board] School 22, 161–163, 241

Bagley Green 27
Bagley Wood 22, 27, 44, 236, 239, 244
Bailey family 55
Bailey, John Frederick 66
Baker, John 80
Banckes, Thomas and Anne 167, 168
Bancroft, Miss 160
Banwell *see also* Benwell
Banwell, Alan 219, 224
Banwell, Benjamin 150
Banwell, David 245
Banwell, Ernest 219, 224
Banwell, Francis 221
Banwell, Henry 73
Banwell, J. 124
Banwell, John 148
Banwell, Richard 139
Baptist Church 240
Barghe [or Barrow], John 111
Barnard, John 71
Barnards 29, 69, 71, 72, 73, 207
Barnes, Mary 188
Barnett, John 148
Barnett, Mr 162, 163
Barnstaple, Mrs 68
Barrell, Robert 186
Barrett, Henry 83
Barrett, Robert 186
Barrot 147
Barrow family 55, 58
Barrow Hill 16, 108
Barrow House Farm 58
Barrow, John 55, 56, 66, 111, 148, 150, 152, 198
Barrow, Mrs 148
Barrow/Barwe, Ralph 58
Barrows 73
Bartholomew of the Borough 29
Basset, John 98
Bath and Wells *(see* Bishops of*)*
Batt, Mr 198, 199
Batten, Edward 131
Batten, James (Jimmy) 126, 128
Batten, Mary 126

Baylie, John, J.P. 27
Belgian refugees 135, 158
Bench House 151, 211
Benet/Bennet, John 65
Benwell, John 75
Bethel, Percy 135, 136
Betty, Mrs 68
Beveridge, Jim 133
Billing, John 32
Binning, Hannah 187
Binning, James 207, 210
Bisgrove 148
Bishop Giso 57
Bishop of Exeter 57
Bishop, Revd William 255
Bishops of Bath and Wells
    13, 27, 47, 48, 57, 150, 199, 211, 258
Blackford 15, 17, 18, 45, 46, 61, 106, 109, 131,
    133, 135, 136, 140, 141, 165, 169, 170, 188,
    196, 216, 218, 230, 231, 232, 234, 239, 240,
    241, 242, 243, 244, 247, 249, 252
    Bishop's Palace 40, 239, 242, 252
    Chapel *see* Holy Trinity Church
    early schools 152, 153
    fete 123
    Holy Trinity Church 39, 199
    Hugh Sexey Middle School
        39, 163, 165, 167–170
        see also Sexey's School
    Manor of
        18, 21, 41, 109, 116, 167–169, 232, 234
    manorial court 116
    pound 104
    road names 39–41
    Sexey's Farm School 170
    Sexey's School
        131, 135, 143, 165, 166, 170, 196
    Sexey's Technical School 167
    Village Hall 153
Blackford [Board] School
    39, 40, 143, 156–158, 163
Blackford Brook 17, 35, 106
Blackford Moor 36, 241
Blakeway 19, 20, 25, 162, 223, 231
    see also Roads
Bleadney 20
Bletchly, Mary 70
Boake, Mr 149
Bodman 148
Boer War 156, 161
Boley, Bill 219
Bond, Ernest 131, 134, 135, 136

Borde, Thomas 65
Borough House 74
Borough Mall 70, 73, 74, 76, 231
Borough, The 29, 63, 69, 70, 75, 76, 77, 78
    see also Roads
Borough Venture, The 28, 74
Borough, WG *see* Burrough, William George
Boulgin/Bulgin, Gabriel 26
Boundary trees 107–108
Bowler, Police Sergeant 36
Bowyer, FW 136
Boys family 84
Boys, Richard and Elizabeth 85
Bracey, Dr William Edelsten
    25, 60, 69, 126, 134, 260
Bracey, Victor Charles Edelsten 60
Bracher 112
Bradreney, Beatrice 58
Breche, Adam atte 29
Brice, Robert 210
bricks, Tonkin 78
brickyard 137–138
Brickyard Farm 78, 137
Bridges, Harry 67
Bridgwood 224
Bright, Thomas 75
Brinscombe 108
Brockley 149
Bronze Age 37, 253
    rubbish tip 37
    torcs 253
    weapons 253
brooch, medieval 82
Brown, James 102, 184
Brown, William 187
Brownyng, John 111
Brue, River *see* River Brue
Bruton 167, 169
Bulgen *see* Boulgin
Bull family 73
Bull, Henry 77
Bulls 73, 77
Bultinge, John 234
Bunn families 24
Bunn, John 148
Bunn, Robert 70, 71, 75
Bunn, Solomon 148
Bunn, William 69
Bunns 73
Buoys Cottage 84–87
burgages and burgage plots *see* Wedmore
Burnett 147

Burnett, Jeffery 148
Burnham 142
Burnt Mill 115
Burrough, Charles 130
Burrough, William George 129–131, 134, 136, 140, 143, 144, 162, 172, 217
Burrows, John 116
Bussell, Francis 186
Bussell, John 186
Buxton, Edward 186
Buxton, John 194, 195
Byrchmore, Reverend Joseph 58, 84

C

Cannon, Miss Edith J 145
Cannon, Miss Emma 145
Carrol, Mrs 150, 151
Carsley, John 148
Carter, William 186
Castle Farm 106, 220
Catley, Charles and Mary Ann 24
Cattle, Mr 198
Cavil, James 174
Cedars, The 152, 169
Centwine, King 15, 16
Chalcroft, Marjorie 113
Chalcroft, Robert 96
Chalcroft, William 98, 99
Chambers, Mary 31
Champeney, Charles 164
Champeney, George 240
Champeney, Mr 154
Champeny, C. 121
Champeny, Clifford 169
Champeny/Champney, Ethel 169
Champion, Stephen 80
Chandler, Sarah 188
Chandos, Duke of 85, 86
Chapel Allerton 217
Chapel Farm 162
Chapman, Joseph 148
Charell, John 186
Charlewell/Charwell 39, 106
Cheddar 21, 140, 142, 148, 222
Cheddar Station 141, 142
cheese making 144–146
Chestnut Farm 95
Chiplegh, Joan de 58
Chudderlegh, John de 59, 233
Church Villas 134
Churchland, Manor of 18, 85, 104, 109, 115
Churchouse, John 53

cider 55, 164
Clap, Hannah 195
Clapp's Windmill 115
Clarke, Bessie 156
Claxton, Nicholas 113
Clewer 16, 45, 46, 109, 115, 141, 206, 230, 233, 236, 243, 248
    Manor 109
    pound 104
    revels 244
Close, The 33, 111, 226
Close Watermill, The 110
Club, George 37
Cobbe, Walter 104
Cock, Herman 169
Cock, Samuel 214
Cock, SN 162
Cocklake 19, 21, 46, 96, 106, 115, 131, 141, 142, 152, 156, 243, 248
    roads of 45
Coke, John 63
Coker, James 58
Cole, Edward 148
Cole, Robert 83
Cole, Thomas 27
Coleman, James 58
Coles 71
Coles, Henry 213
Coles, John 70, 71
Coles, John Tucker 250, 251
Coles, Robert 80
Coles, Sarah 251
Collard, CH 143
Collerigge, John 96
Collins, Samuel 137
Colne, William 58
Colston, Richard 79
Combe Batch 107
    coin hoard 252
Combe, Edith 80
Combe, Edward 80
Combe family 79, 80
Combe Sydenham 77
Combe, William 80
Comer family 71
Comer, C 169
Comer, Joseph 192
Connelly, Joan 13, 38, 254
Cook, C 121
Cook, Edward 157
Cook, Leslie 36, 219, 222, 223
Cook, Mrs 162

Cook, Sid 219
Cooper, E. 120, 122
Cope, Arthur 157
Corell, Thomas 65, 75
Cornish, Goody 55
Cotland, William 157
Counsell family 107, 152
Counsell, James 147
Counsell, John 186
Counsell, Robert 96
Counsell/Councell, William 80, 97, 104
Court, Benjamen 148
Court Cottage 81
Court Farm 26, 43
Court, John 148
Court, Sydney 24
Courteys, John 65
Cousin's Garage 70
Cousins, Worthington 177
Couzens/Cozens, Samuel 66, 67, 72
Coward, William 70, 71
Cowards 71, 73, 77
Cox, Robert 186
Coysgarne, John 70, 75
Crannell Windmill 115
Cras, Thomas 58
Crease, Alice 214
Crease, Emma 40
Crease, Frederick 143, 213, 215
Creese 148
Cresswell, Joan 131, 133
Crickham
    18, 33, 37, 45, 115, 220, 232, 235, 237, 244, 246
    pound 104
Crickham Elm 107, 108
Cridland, Jane 152
Crispina 29
Crookers/crooking 53, 54
Cross Farm
    29, 69, 73, 100, 151, 184, 196, 257
Crosses 100–103
    Churchyard 100, 101
    Stoughton 100, 102
    Wedmore Market 100, 101
Culbury, Thomas 63
Cullen, William 189
Curtin, Frederick 134, 135
Curtis, John 70
Curtis or Lemons 73
Cutler family 245
Cutler, Francis 53

D

Dagg, John and Alice 44
dame schools 151, 152, 198
Dando family 32
Danes 16, 37, 47, 57, 68, 88
David, a peasant 18, 93–95
Davis, Harold 134
Davis, Police Constable Edwin, 208, 210
Davye, Joan 234
Dawson, Elizabeth 202
Day, George 112
Day, John 112, 176
Deane, William 53, 70, 71, 80
Dean's 71
Deans of Wells 19, 21, 48, 53, 54, 59, 93, 94, 95,
    97, 99, 104, 105, 115, 150
deer park 26, 42, 92–95, 238, 241, 242
Delly Cross Elm 107
Dinham, Herbert 216
dinosaurs 259–261
Dodd, Helen 166
Domesday Book 16, 17, 41, 47, 109
Dommetts 73
Doolan, Francis Taylor 85, 86
Doolan, Maria 85
dovecotes 49, 109, 233, 234
Downton, Richard 86
Dr Barnado's Home 156, 160, 165
Drake, John 77
Drake, Richard 174
Drake, Sir Francis 77
Drakeshay 73, 74, 76, 77
Draycott 206
Drew, Richard 148
Drew, William 191
Drewitt, Mr 149
Dryall, James and Mary 235
Duckett, Arthur 221
Duckett, Eliza 125
Duckett family 124, 166
Duckett, John 79, 150
Duckett, Margaret 169
Duckett, Mary 169
Duckett, Michael 124
Duckett, William 117, 134
Dungate, Tomline 154, 155, 160
Dunnicks Mead Garage 19, 36
Dwale, Richard 97, 98
Dyer, Abraham 77, 79, 80, 171

Index

E

Eadwig, King 16
East Elms Windmill 112, 113
East Mark 104
East Mill *see* East Windmill
East Theale *see* Theale
East Windmill 36, 111–113
Edginton, Reverend Edwin 211
Edington 47
Edney, Mary 225
Edney, Thomas 216
Edward the Confessor, King 47
Edwardes, Richard 107
Edwards, Hester 26
Edwards, John 67
Edwards, Mr 199
Edwards, Richard 26, 27
Edwards, RP 251
Egan, WJ 222
Eglantine House 152
Electric/Electricity House/Station, The 129, 134, 136
Electric Light and Power Company 128–136
Elm and Buckland, Frome 52
Elmsett Hall
    30, 38, 111, 135, 195, 224, 225, 228
Elyott, John 49
Emery, Richard 116
Enclosure Acts 24, 25, 43, 71, 75, 96, 231, 246
Ethandune 47
Ethelbert, King 252
Evans, Philip 103
Eyre family 255
Eyre, Revd. William 149, 150, 255, 256

F

face jugs 82
fairs *see* Wedmore
Fear, Frederick 124
Fear, Nicholas 186
Fenny Castle 96
Feoffer, Katerine 75
Fernhall Farm 81, 90, 106
Fernside 151
field, stitch in medieval open 42
Fields
    Abovedoores 230
    Aeroplane Field/Ground, The 224, 231
    Allermoor 231
    Alwoshulleisballe 230

Fields cont'd
    Amerell 231
    Ballardes Lyee 231
    Barley/Berleye 231
    Benpool 110, 231
    Blackford East Field 115
    Blackford North Field 239
    Blackland 18, 232
    Blackpitt 232
    Breach 232
    Brewers Hay 232
    Briary Park 241
    Bull Acre 244
    Burnt Mill Field 115
    Calvecroft 232
    Castle 42
    Chitterley 42, 59, 233
    Clyfforlange 233
    Coudenesham 233
    Court Garden 88, 89, 91, 252
    Cowslip Park 241
    Crannell Field 115
    Crickham Field 244
    Crook Mead 240
    Crosse Furlong 249
    Culver Close 233
    Culvercroft 233
    Culvershays 233
    Cut Down Bacon 234
    Cutlers Bars 245
    Daddocks 234
    Damseland 40
    Davidges Ham 233
    Dolemead 234
    Doles 234
    Dragfurlong/Drag Furlong 113, 234
    Dryalls 235
    Elm Hay 235
    Elm Tining 235
    Elms Millfield 113
    Elynstubbe/Elenstubbe 235
    Erlond 247
    Fishers Ham 233
    Flaxland 235, 247
    Folly 235
    Frogland 235
    Garlick Hill 236, 237
    Garston 236
    Gogsham 37, 236
    Goldfinches 236
    Gooseham 25, 234, 236
    Gore/Goar 237

Fields cont'd
    Hangacre 185
    Hawkers Wear 237
    Hely Thorn Furlong 106
    Honnieland 237
    Hope 237
    Hore Meare 248
    Horse Pool 244
    Hoverelulleg/Hoverelulley 93, 94, 237
    Hozzard 41
    Hundred Acres 238
    Innick 238
    Jacks Cross 238
    Kills Wall 92, 238
    Knapp 238
    La Sarchynge/Sercham 244
    Ladie Mede 43
    Lampers Acre 238
    Lascot Hill Copse 55
    Laver Hill 112
    Leigh 22, 241
    Leppinge Stoone 239
    Lesham 240
    Lineage/Longhedge 239
    Little Field 239
    Longhedge 239
    Lords Furlong 239
    Lousey Bush 239
    Lowgrounds, The 37
    Lygh 22
    Lyons Park 241
    Madwomans Lane *see also* Roads
    Maltfield 32, 107, 112, 220, 240
    Manships/Manchips 240
    Meeting House Orchard 240
    Melliars 240
    Midemede 240
    Mill Batch 113, 115
    Moor Door 240
    Mudgley Field 113
    Murielesham 240
    Murveyland 241
    Mylmote 111
    New Close 241
    New Ham 241
    New Mead 241
    Nugginham 241
    Old Wood 241
    Oslakesleagh/Oslakeslegh 22, 241
    Ovemestfurlong 242
    Paradice 242
    Pennardes Bowshe 242

Fields cont'd
    Pennyland 242
    Pepperhay 242
    Pews/Pugh's Park 241
    Picked Ham 242
    Pile Stiles 242
    Pillmead 36
    Popham's Batch 243
    Popham's Grave 243
    Post 243
    Pound Close 243
    Poundhay Orchard 243
    Quarry Ground 243
    Redhill 243
    Revel Batch 243
    Riding Stream 244
    Rosey Pool 244
    Rowditch 244
    Sercham 244
    Shutters Stile 244
    Skuttells Barrough/Skuttelesbarrowgh 245
    Snailham Corner 245
    Snipefield 40, 115, 220, 236
    South Mead 45
    Speke Close 65
    Spekehegge 65
    Stanilond 93, 94
    Stenning Bridge 19
    Stinking Acre 245
    Stinking Mears 245
    Stooles Leg 246
    Sullingway 249
    Summerleaze 246
    Swinshurst/Swyneshurst 246
    Tadham 246
    Tealham 246
    Tent Land 246
    Three-corner Cap 247
    Trendle 247
    Tumbledown Dicks 247
    Twelve Acres 37, 38
    Urdelande 247
    Very Bowshe 247
    Warmans Close 249
    Wateligh 248
    Wedmore East Field/Eastfield
        32, 36, 40, 85, 112, 113, 231
    Wedmore North Field 114
    Wedmore West Field 114, 116
    Westovers Mill Tyning 113
    Wether Slade 248
    Whore Meadow/Meare 248

Fields cont'd
    Whotley 248
    Winniards Orchard 248
    Wormes Close 249
    Wymyllmote 111
    Yellow Batches 249
    Zillingway 249
First Aid Unit 219, 222
First World War 68, 131, 135, 158, 162, 167
Fisher, Charles 186
Fisher, Jeremy 257
Fisher, Richard 34
Fisher, T 124
Ford, Dr 210
Francis, Benjamin 163
Franks, Mr 216
Freckingham, Bramwell 133
Freckingham, Ivy 162
Freckingham, J 128
Frempton, Robert 65
Fritz, Wolfgang 223
Frost, Charles 73
Frost, Edgar 156
Frost, Mrs 214
Fry, Mr 148
Fudge, Francis 113, 186, 187
Fudge, Henry 113

G

Gardiner, John 38, 139, 140
Gardiners tan house 139
Gas Works 73, 126–129
Gibbs, William 66, 67, 71
Giles, Mr 198
Gillibanks/Gilbanks, Sergeant/Superintendent
    124, 210
Gilson, Police Constable 210
Giso, Bishop of Wells 47, 57
Glanville, Dr William 30
Glanville family 30
Glanville Road Watermill 110
Glastonbury Abbey/Abbot of 16, 17, 20, 21, 47,
    95, 97, 99, 105, 238
Glendale 196
Glendale Farm 143, 144
Goathland, HMS 226
Godelee, John de, Dean of Wells 48
Godfrey 93, 94, 95
Godney Moor 99
Gogs House 37, 236
Gogs Orchard 236
Golledge family 40

Goodridge, Alfred E 131, 136
Goodridge, Charles 131
Gooseham 25
Goudie, Revd James 175, 177–180
Grant, Ann 29
Grant family 29
Grantchester 201
Gray, John 102, 184
Green, Harry 66, 67
Green, John 150
Green, Mr 199
Green, Sergeant 210
Gresham, Sir Thomas 49, 109, 114
Grove Cottage 188
Guildhall Lane Watermill 110
Guthrum, King of the Danes 47, 57, 256, 258
Guylbert, John 97

H

Hall, The 34, 36, 81, 150, 193, 198, 223
Hancock, Miss 73
Hankinson, John 130, 131, 134
Hansford, Police Constable 134, 158
Harbett, John 170
Harding, George 219, 222
Harding, Hannah 25
Harding, Leslie 36
Hardwich, Hugh 97, 98
Hardwick, Edward 189, 191, 193
Hardwick family 194
Hardwick, Mary 189–194
    household goods of 189–191
Hardy, Richard 55
Harptre, Thomas de 82
Harris, George 137
Harris/Harys, Richard 65
Harvey, Ann 153
Harvey family 112
Harvey, Henry 120, 137, 148, 211
Harvey, Mary 151
Harvey, William junior 211
Harvey, William senior 211
Harvon, Mr 149, 150, 171
Hathaway, Mr 133
Hawkins, Edward 134
Hawkins, T 143
Haynes, John and Sarah 153
Heath House
    18, 33, 41, 46, 93, 94, 106, 108, 116, 119,
    124, 177, 220, 222, 223, 238, 243, 246, 253
    mill house 117
    Windmill 108–116, 118

Heath House cont'd
    Windmill, diary re 119–125
Heath, The 24, 25, 93, 94, 159, 164
Heathcross Elm 107, 108
Heggs, William 148
Hellier, Amy 161
Hellier, Stephen 161
Hembry, Isaac 66, 67
Hembry, William 209
Hembury 148
Hembury, Roger 134
Henderson, Edwin 67
Henry de Mudesleg/Mudgley 95
Henson, Dr 135
Hervey, Revd S.H.A. 13, 14, 22, 31, 32, 34, 35, 37, 38, 44, 66, 81, 83, 84, 88, 90, 92, 105, 110, 151, 165, 172, 176, 177–180, 182, 184, 185, 188, 201, 211, 229, 234, 238, 247, 249, 254, 258–260
Hesse, Colonel 210
Hickie, Dr Maurice 214
Highbridge 140, 142
Highbridge Station 140
Highbridge, Wedmore & Cheddar Light Railway 140–142
Highbury Barn 169
Hill, Freddy 223
Hill House 129, 140, 172
Hill, Joseph 257
Hill, Sidney 176
Hill, Thomas 54, 110
Hillside 31
Hitches, George James and Mrs 159, 160
Hobbs, Ida 219, 225
Hodges, Agatha, née Rodney 49, 50
Hodges, Ann née Mansell 51, 181–183
Hodges, Eleanor née Rosse 50, 51
Hodges family 54
Hodges, George 50, 51, 181
    tomb of 55
Hodges, George II 51
Hodges, Hannibal 50
Hodges, Jane 51, 182 *see also* Strachey
Hodges, Margaret 49, 50
Hodges, Mary 50, 51, 52, 53, 54, 182
Hodges, Suzanna 50
Hodges, Thomas, I 49, 50
Hodges, Thomas II 49, 50
Hodges, Thomas III 51
Hodges, William 52, 53, 54, 55
Holbrook, David de 233
Holbrook, William de 233

Holdenhurst 70, 71, 73, 76, 77
Hole, Edmund 72, 210
Hole, Emmie 225
Hole, Mrs Tom 228
Hole, Tom 226
Holes, Mr 121
Homan/Honan, Richard 186
Home Guard 219, 222
Home Guard Auxiliary Unit 219, 221
Homfray, Charles Augustus 55, 66
Homfray family 60
Homfray, Francis 60
Honan *see* Homan
Honeybourne 31
Honeysuckle Cottage 69, 71, 73
Hooper, Elizabeth Ann 214
Hooper, Florence 145
Hooper, Mary 153
Hopper, Edward 113
Horler, Ann, formerly Hodges 51, 183
Horler, Jeremy 51, 181–183, 182
Horler, Jeremy, junior 183
Horley, Paul 87
Horner, Thomas 168
Horsepool Farm 81
Hospital of Hugh Sexey 141, 169, 194
House, Martha 217
House, Poundhay 72
Hove College 224, 225, 228
Howell, Hugh 67
Hoyland, William de 22
Hoyle, Mr 158
Hubbard, Sergeant 213
Hudson, Joan 195
Hudson, Kate 165
Hugyn, John 59
Hurst, Revd 90

I

Ilchester Gaol 19
Inns
    Alma Inn 24
    Bell Inn 86, 256, 257–258
    George Hotel/Inn 28, 63, 66, 67, 68, 143, 144, 209, 211, 226, 228, 253, 254
    Grouse & Pheasant Inn 119
    New Inn 207, 247
    Panborough Inn 201
    Sexey's Arms 152, 163
    Swan Hotel/Inn 70, 73, 211, 219, 220, 222, 225, 228, 254
    The Sportsman's Arms 25

Index

Inns cont'd
    The Traveller's Rest 25
Innys, Andrew 80
Invasion Committee 222, 226
Iron Age 37, 92
    farm 37
Isgar, Henry 216
Isobel, daughter of Josce 22
Ivy House, The 46
Ivyleafe family 61
Ivyleafe, Gabriel, senior and junior 60

J

Jannys, Roger 82
Jeffreys, Judge 184, 185
Jenkins, William 186
Jernegan, Sir Henry 48
Jobs 73–75
John, sergeant of Blackford 104

K

Kastur, India 173
Kelson, Elinor 33
Kelson family 46
Kelson, John 33
Kelson, Nicholas 33
Kelson, William 33
Kelsons Farm 33
Kemm, Doctor 225
Kempthorne, Revd John 102, 152, 250
Kills Wall bank 92
Kingsbury, Albert 216
Kirkeby/Kyrkeby/Kerby, Richard 65, 75
Kitmore 99
Knyfton, Thomas 199
Kynge, Roger 65
Kyppmerwalle 95, 96, 97, 99
    battle of, 95–100

L

La Hethe 93, 94
Lacham *see also* Latcham
Lacham, John 53
Lacham, William 97, 98
Lader *see also* Larder
Lader 148
Lader, William 186
Landcourse Rhyne 96
Lansdowne, John 69
Larder *see also* Lader
Larder, John 173, 196, 254
Larder, Joseph 35

Larder, Walter 157
Larder, William 186
Lascot 142
Lascot/Lascotts Hill 32, 37, 140, 198, 220, 221, 223, 225
Latcham *see also* Lacham
    18, 19, 21, 44, 108, 236, 241, 242
Latcham, Augustus 216
Latcham, Betsy 152
Latcham, Charles 31
Latcham Elms 107, 108
Latcham Farm 19, 108, 242
Latcham, Francis 169
Latcham Garage 36
Latcham, George 104
Latcham, Hannah 20, 188
Latcham, Hester 187, 188
Latcham, John 152
Latcham, Philip and Hannah 19
Latcham, Priscilla 151, 198
Latcham/Latchem, Richard 80, 186
Latcham, William 19, 20, 188
Laurel Bank 87, 173
Laurels, The 134
Law, Mathew 82
Law, Bishop George Henry 199
Lawrence, John 67
Lea, A 211
Leakey, Grace 86
Leaping Stone 45
Leigh family 185
Leigh, George and Sarah 25
Leigh, John 35
Leigh, Sally 185
Leigh, Sarah 36
Leigh, William 36
Lerburne House 69, 73, 138, 211
Lerburne, The 31, 37, 100
Lineage Farm 239
Little Ireland 23
Lloyds Chemist 77, 134, 137, 171, 224
Locke, John 52
Locke, Matthew 80
Locke, Robert 80
London, William 75
Long, Frank 216
Long, Henry 216
Long, Richard 216
Longe, Alice 75
Lower Farm 104
Lukin, Dean George W 149
Lukins, Bill 227

Lukins, Mercen 158
Lussher, Joan 77
Lydiat *see also* Lytheat
Lydiat, John 113
Lydiat/Lythiat family 113
Lye, George 54, 186
Lye, William 186
Lytheat *see also* Lydiat
Lytheat, William 113

M

Malger 93, 94, 95
Malherbe, Robert 93, 94, 95
Mannyman, John 69, 71
Manor Farm 46
Manor House 47–56, 60, 75, 134, 140, 148, 161, 188, 198, 222, 226
Manorial pounds 103–105
    Blackford 104
    Clewer 104
    Crickham 104
    Mudgley 104
    Northload Manor 104
    Sand 104
    Stoughton 104
    Theale 104
    Wedmore 103
Manshipe, John 240
Manshipe, William 240
Manyman, Richard 234
Mapson, Henry 69
Mapson/Mapstone, Henry 71
Mapstones 71
Marchey *see also* Martsey
Marchey Farm 204, 238
Mareys, John 63, 65
Mark 39, 52, 76, 77, 140, 142, 174, 234
Mark Moor 246
Mark School 143
Martin 148
Martin, Frederick 31, 66, 67
Martin, Isaac 148
Martsey, John of 96
Masonic Hall 136, 225
Matilda, Queen 57
Mave, Richard 98, 99
May, Revd Robert Augustus 84, 157, 215
Mayne, Elizabeth 187
Mayne, Grace 187
Meare 16
Medlam, Ann 187
Melliar, Ann 188

Melliar, William 187
Mendip Cottage 138, 195
Mendip View 156
Menymen, Richard 71
Merevill, John 27
Merriman, James 157, 158, 166, 167
Merritt, Miss 158, 163
Methodism in Wedmore 79, 80, 152
Methodist Chapel 128, 152, 171–173, 196
Methodist Church Schoolroom/Sunday School 171, 173, 196, 225
Miceter, Stephen 53
Michell, Simon 58
Middle Stoughton *see* Stoughton
Milk Factory 75, 222
Millard family 173
Millard, George 72, 86, 87, 171
Millard, George Henry 87
Millard, JC 173
Millard, John 86
Millard, John Burrel 87, 143, 173
Millard, Mr 211
Millard, Mrs JB 173
Millard, Robert 73
Millard, William 72, 112, 208
Millard/Taylor, George 86, 87
miller, diary of 118–125
mills 49, 109–125
Minstrels Gallery 77, 80, 137, 171
Mitchell, Thomas Henry 157, 158, 164, 165, 166
Mitchell, William 104
Modeslee, William de 59
Modesley *see also* Mudgley
Modesley, Alice 59
Modesley, Joan 58
Modesley, John of 58
Modesley, William 58, 59, 60
Monmouth Rebellion 113, 183–187
Moon, Elthelred W 178
Moore, Ruth née Stickland 196, 197
Moore, Thomas 104
More, Agnes 97
More, Hannah 55, 148–149, 171, 254
    see also Schools *and* Wedmore
More, John 96
More, Martha 55, 148, 150, 151
Morgan 148
Morgan, Frederick 138
Morgan, John 257
Morgan, Mrs 227
Morgan, Prebendary H.T.C. 254
Morgan, Richard 73

Morgan, William 70
Morgans 73
Morris, Reverend Daven 227
Mudgley 22, 32, 41, 46, 58, 88, 90, 92, 93, 95, 106, 107, 111, 113, 153, 220, 231, 232, 235, 236, 240, 241, 242, 243, 247, 248, 252, 258
    chapel 88, 90
    Dean of Wells' house
        13, 22, 43, 48, 88, 92–94, 252
        excavations of 88–91, 93, 258
    deer park 26, 238, 241
    fishponds 88, 91, 92, 106
    garden 88
    King Alfred's Palace 88
    Manor of
        18, 21, 44, 59, 93, 107, 109, 112–114
    manorial court 88
    music slates 88, 89
    pound 104
    road names 42, 43
    Roman buildings 23, 90
    spoon, medieval 88, 252
    vineyard 248
        see also Alexander of Mudgley, Henry of Mudgley
Mudgley Elm 107
Mudgley Hill 237
Mudgley Hill Farm 43, 90–92, 95, 111
Mulberry House 60
Mylborne, John 110
Myrtles, The 134

N

New Town 23, 24
Newcomb, William 59
Newton, Mr 152
Nicholls, Joseph 66, 67
Nicholls, William 148
Nonconformist Chapels 173–180
nonconformity 79, 80, 152, 171–180, 186
Norman, Mary Jane 73
Norman, Stuart 206
Norris, Clifford 165
Norris, Victor 165
North, Tom 219, 220
Northload 20, 21, 43, 44, 95, 96, 97, 249
    Manor 20, 104, 105, 109, 111, 231
    Watermill 109, 110
Northload Farm 20, 44, 81, 109, 243
Northload, John of 109
Nyland View 138, 195

O

Old Bakery 69, 72
Old Cottage, The 139, 195
Old Park 241
Old Rhyne 45
Old Sexeys Farm 106, 187
Old Vicarage, The see Vicarage
Old Wood/Oldwood 26, 27, 42, 93, 221
omnibuses, first 142–144
open fields 92, 94, 108, 115, 239
Overbrook Farm 234
Overseers of the Poor 189, 257
Owen, Grace 169
Owen, Mrs W 173
Owen, William 79, 134, 172, 173, 224

P

Page, F 120
Paget, Colonel Richard H 207
Palmere, John 59
Panborough 16, 20, 43, 45, 58, 95, 96, 108, 111, 153, 160, 235, 238, 244
    Saxon charter 22, 233
    Windmill 111
Panborough Drain 45
Panborough Friendly Society 201
Panborough Gap 99
Panborough Moor 96, 97
Pareys, Henry 59
Parfitt, Horace 163
Parfitt, Jeremy 257
Parfitt, Mr 135
Parker, Annie 208
Parker, George 208, 209, 210
Parker, John 148
Parker, William John 214
Parsonage House, Theale 200
Parsons, Jeremiah Dewdney 37
Patterson, Mr 222
Pavey, Charles 222
Pavey, Geoffrey 68, 206, 219, 224, 254
Payn, John 59
Peace of Wedmore
    16, 37, 47, 57, 68, 88, 160, 258
Pearce, Joseph 153
peat digging 174
Pelham, Jane 80
Pelham, Sir Nicholas 80
Perrow 108
Perrow Farm 46
Perry, Thomas 137

Petheram, John 182
Petheram, Widow 54
Petherham, John 83
Petherham, Nicholas 63, 65
Phillips, Ernest H 167
Phippen, Arthur 73
Phippen, Robert 253
Pickford, James 71
Pickfords 73
Pilham Farm 81
Pillmead 36
Pillmead Moor 36, 110
Pillmead Watermill 110, 115
Pitcairn, Mrs 55
place names 15–27
plague 83
Pola, Norman de 39
Pola, Richard de 39
police station 213, 219
Poolbridge 39
Poole, Thomas 234
Popham, John 96
Poplar Farm 41
Poplars, The 60
Pople, Lilian 162
Pople, Mrs W 173
Pople, William 137, 162, 172, 211
Porch House 110, 113, 114, 185
Porter, Mr 124
Porter, W 144
Porter, William 58
portreeves 29, 65, 66, 71, 101
Post Office 86, 257, 258
pounds 103–105
Poundhay House 73, 103
Poundhay Orchard 103
Price, Edith 157
Price, Samuel 134, 155, 157, 172, 215
Pridy, Margery 26
Prior, Thomas 98
Providence House 28, 70, 73
public house tokens/checks 253–254
Puddy, Albert E 155
Puddy, Amy 163
Puddy, Cecil 128, 222, 224
Puddy, Edith 157
Puddy, Keith 223, 226
Puddy, Tom 222
Puddy, W. 121

Q

quarry sites 243
Quick, John 53

R

Ragwood Farm 46
railway 140–142
Rakesworth, John 59
Ralli, Pandeli 207
Ralph of Northilade 20
Ratcliffe Bros Garage 19, 36
Rauns, Thomas 174
Redhill 211
Redhill Farm 211
Redhill Villas 204, 206, 211
Redman, Ann 188
Redman family 39
Redman, George 66, 67, 152
Redman, Joseph 191
Redman, Laura 164
Redman, Robert 66, 67, 71, 72, 207, 209
Redman, Sidney 211
Redman, Walter 207, 211
Redwood, John 188
Reeve the younger, William 36
Retford, John 58, 82
Revette, William 75
Richards, John 65, 84
Richards, Reverend Joseph 199
Richardson, Alfred 156
Rickard, John 148
Rickard, William 148, 151
Rickards, Ann 153
Ridge, Thomas 66, 67
riding Skimmetty 217
River Axe 19–21, 31, 36, 44, 46, 95, 96, 99, 109, 142, 157, 221, 237, 238
River Brue 39, 99, 221
River Yeo 142
Roads, Lanes and Streets
    Allermoor Lane 42
    Bagley Green 44
    Bagley Road 44
    Batch, The 46
    Battens Lane 42
    Billings Hill 32
    Blackford Road 37, 147
    Blakeway 23, 24, 43, 175
    Blakeway backway 43
    Borough Mall 110, 222

Index

Roads, Lanes and Streets cont'd
    Borough, The 28, 29, 31, 63, 80, 100, 101, 110, 126, 137, 138, 151, 204, 207, 209, 211, 224
    Browns Lane 44
    Castle Lane 42
    Cheddar Road 28, 37, 45, 63, 65, 66, 76, 77, 147, 154, 204, 211, 238
    Chitterleys Lane 42
    Cholwell/Charlewell Lane 39
    Church Lane 39
    Church Street, Blackford 39
    Church Street, Wedmore 28, 29, 63, 66, 75, 77, 78, 80, 81, 83, 134, 137, 172, 193, 225, 227, 254, 255, 257, 258
    Church Way, The 46
    Clewer Lane 46
    Club Lane 37
    Coldnose 44
    Combe Batch 28, 29, 31, 63, 66, 67, 103, 151, 185, 207, 211, 219, 233, 242, 243, 247
    Combe Batch Rise 233
    Connelly Drive 38
    Cooks Lane 32
    Coronation Road 35
    Cotton Street 40
    Counsells Crosse 107
    Court Lane 43
    Courte Weye 43
    Crib House/Cribhouse Lane 45, 104, 108
    Crickham Lane 108
    Daggs Lane 44, 233
    Damsells/Damses Lane 40
    Dandos Lane 32, 33, 112
    Danes Lea 37
    Delly Cross Way 107
    Drang, The 31
    Droveway 188
    Dungeon, The 21, 45
    Dunns Close 38
    Eastfield Lane 40
    Exeter Lane 46
    Flood Street 33
    Foss Lane 41
    Gallingale Way 40
    Gardiners Orchard 38, 139
    Gasworks Lane 31
    Glanville Road 28, 30, 31, 33, 38, 84, 110, 111, 135, 138, 139, 152, 156, 158, 189, 195

Roads, Lanes and Streets cont'd
    Goatway 45
    Gogs Orchard 37
    Golledge Way 40
    Gooseham Lane 25
    Grants Lane 28, 29, 30, 32, 60, 74, 129, 134, 173, 224, 240
    Green Way 40, 41
    Guildhall Lane/Street *alias* Guilo 33, 34, 105, 111
    Guilo *see* Guildhall
    Haines Lane 32
    Hangary Lane 43
    Hervey Close 38
    High Street 39, 40
    Hozzard Lane 41
    Jacks Drove 25, 41
    Jacks/Jackes Lane 42, 238
    Kelsons Lane 33, 35, 46, 221
    Keyton Hill 41
    King Alfreds Way 37
    Kitmore Drove 43
    Lady Mead/Ladie Mede Lane 43
    Lascot/Lascots Hill 32, 35, 147, 213, 238
    Latcham Road 247
    Leighs Lane 36
    Lerburne, The/Lane 31, 38, 110, 126, 137, 177, 221
    Long Hill 45, 244
    Madwomans Lane 18, 35, 42, 46, 240
    Manor Lane 37
    Martin's Drang 31
    Mead Lane 46
    Mill Lane 36, 111
    Moor Lane 126
    Mudgley Hill 42, 107
    Mudgley Road 112, 259
    Mutton Lane 28, 31, 35–36, 63
    New Blake Way 43
    New Lane 45
    New Road 39
    Northload Lane 44
    Nuport, La 29
    Old Blake Way 43
    Old Farm Court 39
    Old Parke Lane 42
    Oldwood Lane 42, 92
    Orchard, The 37, 111
    Parsons Twelve Acres 37
    Perrow Lane 46
    Perry Lane 40, 41
    Pig Lane 42

Roads, Lanes and Streets cont'd
   Pilcorn Street
      34, 37, 151, 189, 201, 213, 214, 215
   Pillmead Lane 36–37, 110
   Plud Street 32, 134, 213, 214, 240
   Poolbridge Road 39, 41, 234
   Quab Lane 34, 35, 40, 113, 114, 115, 151, 220, 221, 245, 251
   Redmans Hill 39
   Rogers Lane 40
   Rookery, The 31
   Rughill 45, 106
   Rush Hill/Rush Well Lane 41, 45, 106
   Sand Drove 25, 42, 106, 245
   Sand Hill 42
   Sand Road 32, 35, 37, 79, 87, 91, 92, 112, 134, 152, 171, 172, 173, 193, 223, 225, 242
   Saxon Way 37
   Shortland Lane 32
   Shutters/Shooters Hill 35, 36
   Silver Street 30, 31
   Skitmore Drove 43, 99
   Snake Lane 44, 249
   Snipefield Lane 40, 242, 243
   South Horse Wey 45
   South Mead Lane 45
   Springfield Drive 37
   Square, The 44
   St Marys Close 38
   St Medard Road 38
   Stitching Lane/Stychen Weye 42
   Sullingway 40
   Theale Road 134
   Tollgate trackway 43
   Towne Weye 42, 43
   Townsend Lane 36, 44, 107, 234, 239
   Trinity Close 39
   Tuckers Lane 46
   turnpikes 32, 39, 43, 45, 88, 163
   Victoria Street 30
   Walls Lane 46
   Wedmore Moor Drove 78, 137, 231, 240
   Wedmore Road, Blackford 41
   Wells Road, Wedmore 28, 31
   Wells Road, Theale 43, 105
   Wells Way, Blackford 40, 41, 170
   West End 33, 35, 60, 213, 219, 226, 232, 236, 248, 249
   West Well Lane 21, 43, 95, 97, 105, 240
   White Horse Lane 44, 45, 239
   Whites Lane 46

Roads, Lanes and Streets cont'd
   Worthington Close 38, 110
Robert, Bishop of Wells 57
Rodney, George 49, 113
Rodney Stoke 49, 113
Roe, Lot 121
Rogers family 40
Rogers, Lionel 133
Rogers, Mary 210
Rogers, Robert 210
Romano-British, 21, 22, 23, 31, 37, 41, 81, 90, 92, 243, 252
   buildings 23, 90
Romano-British, cont'd
   coins 252
   fields 21
   pottery 22, 31, 81
   salt-works 41
   settlement sites 31, 37, 92
   skeletons 243
Roper, Joseph 25
Roper, Mr 211
Roper, William and Hannah 116
Roscoe, Sir Henry 170
Rosse, John and Mary 50
Rothwell, John 58
rough music 217
Rowley, William 114
Rugwell 45
Rush Well 41
Russells Hill 45, 111
Rylbury, John 111
Ryman, Mr 160

S

Sally's 211
Sammes, Sir Gerard 169
Sand 18, 26, 35, 37, 41, 42, 44, 46, 58, 59, 80, 93, 94, 97, 104, 192, 221, 231, 233, 236, 241, 245, 246, 248, 249
   road names 42
Sand Drove Farm 25
Sand Hall 42, 106, 134, 192, 199, 251
Sand Hill 245
Sand House 61, 134, 150, 152, 197, 198, 200, 202
Sanford, William Ayshford 259, 260
Saunders, Elizabeth 187
Saunders, Mrs 251
Savage, Charles 137
Savage family 137
Savidge, Mary 152
Savidge, Welthian 26

Index

Savidge, William 152
Savidge/Savage family 61, 62
Sawley, Moses 211
Saxon 37, 44, 47, 57, 81, 250, 252, 253
    boundary line 44
    Church 47, 57, 81
    coins 250, 252
    ring 253
    settlement 37
Scarth, Prebendary H.M. 90
Schink, Heinrich 223
School Board 154
Schools
    Bagley
        Bagley Close [Board] School
            22, 161–163, 241
        see also Theale School
    Blackford
        Blackford [Board] School
            39, 40, 143, 156–158, 163
        early village schools 152, 153
        Hugh Sexey Middle School
            39, 163, 165, 167–170
        Sexey's Farm School 170
        Sexey's School
            131, 135, 143, 165, 166, 170, 196
        Sexey's Technical School 167
    Theale
        Theale [and Bagley Close Board] School
            156, 159, 160
        Theale National School 153, 159
    Wedmore
        Buoys, school at 87
        Church or Free School 152
        Church Schoolroom 136, 157, 158,
            171, 172, 207, 220, 227
        diocesan school 151
        early village schools 133, 134, 147–152
        Free School 171
        Hannah More's School 148–152
        Wedmore [Board] School 34, 133,
            154–158, 172, 223
Scourse, John and Peggy 224
Second World War 219–228
Sedgemoor, battle of 184, 186
Sexey, Dorothy née Uttley 167
Sexey, Hugh 167, 168, 169
Sexey, Ursula née Campernoun 168
Sexey's Farm 187
Sexey's Farm School 170
Sexey's School
    131, 135, 143, 165, 166, 170, 196

Sexey's Technical School 167
    see also Blackford: Hugh Sexey Middle
        School
Shapwick 77
Sheppard, Wm. 147
Shepton Beauchamp 50
Shipham Rhine 39
Short, Police Constable Edward 210
single-stick fighting 201, 202
skeletons 42, 243
Skimmington/Skimmerton riding 217, 218
Smart, William 169
Smith, Edith Mary 134
Smith, EH 143, 169
Smith family 55
Smith, JC 140, 142, 161
Smith, John 186
Smith, Mr 136
Smith, Mrs 135
Smith, Mrs EH 169
Smith, Thomas 186
Snaylham, Thomas de 245
Somers 210
Somerset, Duke of 48
South Bank 32, 129, 173
South Brent/Brent Knoll 52
South View Farm 46
Spearing, John 116
Special Constables 219, 222
Speke Close 84
Spencer, JJ 256
Spencer, Martha 152
Sperring, Mr 122
Sprake, Mrs 151
Springs and Wells 105–107
    Butterwell 106
    Caswell 106
    Charlewell/Charlwell 39, 106
    Church Well 106
    Coldwell 107
    Combe Batch well 107
    Crayswell 107
    Dunnicks Well 105
    Grayswell 107
    Helie Well 106
    Latcham 105
    Mudgley, petrifying spring at 106
    Rowshe Well 106
    Rugwell 106
    Sand, petrifying spring at 106
    Stoughton Cross well 105, 106
    Sunset Well 105

Springs and Wells cont'd
    Theale Well 97, 105
    Vicars/Vykerys Well 107
    Weights Well 107
    West Well 21, 43, 105
St John Ambulance Brigade 222
St Mary, parish church *see* Wedmore
St Mary's House 75
Standen, Constable 216
Stanfield, William 187
Stanton House 112
Star Chamber 95
Starr, Widow 69
Stars 72
Stert, George 186
Stevens, Robert 80
Stevens, Widow 113
Stickland, Albert Edward 195
Stickland, Dorothy 196
Stickland, Edward 139, 173, 195, 196, 197
Stickland, Elizabeth 152
Stickland, George 173, 196
Stickland, George Chilcott 195
Stickland, Hannah 195
Stickland, John 195
Stickland, Joseph 139, 140, 171, 194–197
Stickland, Kate 139, 156, 196
Stickland, Matthew 195
    see also Stickler/Sticklin
Stickler/Sticklin, Joseph the elder and Judith 195
Stock, Ernest 222
Stone Allerton 152, 220
Stone, Benjamin 31
Stone, Edward 53, 114
Stone family 147
Stone, Farmer 171
Stone, John 98
stone quarries 94
Stone, Thomas 114, 147
Stone, William 65, 98, 193
Stonecroft 224
Stones 29
Stone's Bakery 70, 71, 73, 126
Stone's Mill 113, 114
Stonesteps 257
Stott, Richard Lyle 72, 203–206
Stott, Thomas 208

Stoughton 21, 35, 40, 115, 165, 169, 186, 196, 238, 244, 245
    Cross 21, 108, 239
    cross, wayside 100, 102
    Middle 21, 40
    pound 104
    well at Stoughton Cross 102, 105
    West 21, 40, 107, 196, 234
    Windmill 115
Stoughton Cross 21, 108, 239
Stoughton/Stofftens Elm 107, 108
Strachey, Elizabeth 52
Strachey family 55
Strachey, Jane, née Hodges 51–55, 75, 182, 183
Strachey, Jane the younger 52
Strachey, John 52, 75, 182
Strachey, John the younger 52, 55
Stribling, Mr and Mrs 79
Summers, Sarah 153
Summers, Selina 216, 217, 218
Sunnydale 39
Sunnyside 213
Sutton Court 52, 53, 54, 55, 182
Sweet, John 55
Sweet, Mervyn 224
Sweet, Sellick 151
Sweet, Sherah 151
Sydenham, Elizabeth 77
Sydenham family 76, 77
Sydenham, Henry 76, 77
Sydenham, Richard 98
Sydenham, Sir George 77
Syms, Edward 53, 54

T

Tadham Moor 24, 223, 246
Taillour, Phillip 59
tannery/tanhouse 38, 111, 138
Taverner, Edward 257
Taviner, Grace 139, 140
Taylor, Ann 153
Taylor, Grace 86
Taylor, John 86
Taylor, Revd Francis 84, 85, 86
Taylor, Robert 153
Taylor, William 186
Tealham Chapel 162
Tealham Moor/Heath 174, 175, 177, 246, 249
Thatcher, Alice 185
Thatcher family 185
Thatcher, John 110, 139, 140

Thatcher, Mary 110, 140
Thatcher, Robert 185, 186
Thatcher, Samuel 140
Thatchers 139
Theale 15, 20, 21, 95, 96, 104, 105, 109, 131, 133, 135, 136, 154, 160, 231, 232, 237, 238, 240, 243, 244, 245, 249
    Chapel *see* Christ Church
    Christ Church 24, 61, 136, 151, 153, 159, 197, 199, 200
    Church Hall 153
    East 21
    mud wall at 95–99
    revels 201, 244
    Roads names 43–45
    West 21, 44
Theale and Bagley Close [Board] School 156, 159, 160
Theale Great House 183, 237
Theale National School 153, 159
Theale Well 21, 43
    see also West Well
Theyre, Thomas 96
Thompson, William 79
Thorn, Simon 55
Thurston, John junior 46
Thurston, William 98
Tin-Pot Band 216–218
Tincknell, Bert 219, 222
Tincknell, Henry 34
Tincknell, Mr 212
Tincknell/Tyntenhull, William 96, 97
Tincknells 74
Tomas, John 73
Tomson, Stanley 157
Tonkin, Elizabeth 78, 79
Tonkin, John 77–80, 137, 171
Tonkin, John junior 137
Tonkin, Sarah 79
Tonkin, William 79
Toogood, George junior 193
Toogood, George senior 193
Toogood, Mrs 134
Toomer, Miss 152
Totney 48
Tournour, Nicholas 59
Townsend Farm 42, 44, 257
Trendel, Walter 247
Tucker, Albert 134
Tucker, Catherine 87
Tucker, Charles 216

Tucker Coles family 251
Tucker, Edward 116
Tucker, Eliza, née Duckett 125
Tucker, Elizabeth 188
Tucker family 117
Tucker, Frank 212
Tucker, Henry and Grace 187
Tucker, James 189, 191
Tucker, John and Abigail 197
Tucker, John, of Blackford 187
Tucker, Mary 83, 187, 195
Tucker, Miss 211
Tucker, Mr 116, 121
Tucker, Robert 187
Tucker, Stanley 223
Tucker, Walter 216
Tucker, William 36, 116, 117, 118, 118–125
Tucker, William White 198
Tuckers 73
Tunsingwere. fish trap 237
Turner, Robert 152
turnpikes *see* Roads
Tutton, Edward 116
Tutton, George 192, 207, 210
Tutton, Joseph 53
Tutton's 71
Tyley, Benjamin 211
Tyley, Dr 84, 137, 156, 209
Tyley, Edward 148
Tyley, Frederick 73, 74
Tyley, Jane 199
Tyley, Phoebe 71, 73
Tyley, Thomas 79, 115
Tyntenhull *see* Tincknell

U

Uplands, The 60, 134
Urch, Herb 228
Urch, Mary 40
Urch, Mr 27

V

van der Meulen, Judith 229
Venne, Diana 26
Vicarage [now the Old Vicarage] 13, 31, 81–85, 211, 225, 255
Vicarage, Victorian 65, 257
Vicars Choral of Wells 22
Vigor, Samuel 147
Vowles 73, 148
Vowles, Elsie 169

Vowles, Francis 135
Vowles, George 136
Vowles, John 160, 161, 162, 163
Vowles, Mrs 162
Vowles, William 148

W

Walch, William 186
Wall 73
Wall, Arthur 13, 216
Wall, Benjamin 216
Wall, Edward 173
Wall, George 123, 160
Wall, Jeremiah 73, 116, 171
Wall, Joan 38
Wall, John 32, 211
Wall, Leonard 223
Wall, Mark 121, 207, 210
Wall, Mr 170
Wall, Richard 32
Wall, Robert 216
Wall, Solomon 84, 196, 256, 257, 258
Wall, William 54, 165
Wall, William Stone 201
Walnut House 214
Wanstrow, Manor of 168
Warman family 249
Warman, George 53
Warr, Ann 24
Wars *see* First, Second World War
Washbrook 243, 247
waste cottages 23
Waterdale House 81
Watermills 109–111
    Close, The 110
    Glanville Road 110
    Guildhall Lane 110
    Northload 110
    Pillmead 110, 231
Watts, Charles 179
Watts, Edward 164
Watts, George 73
Weare 52
Webb, Brigett 26
Webb, Charles Ernest 127
Webb, Judyth 26
Webb, Thomas 26
Webb, William 127, 128
Webb, William Cecil 127

Wedmore 15, 16, 29, 46, 109
  bricks 138
  Buoys, school at 87
  burgages and burgage plots
    29, 65, 69–71, 73, 75–77
  burglary in 213
  Choir Festival 123
  church, churchyard
    see St Mary's Parish Church
  churchyard cross
    see St Mary's Parish Church
  church house 48
  Church or Free School 152
  Church Schoolroom
    136, 157, 158, 171, 172, 207, 220, 227
    see also Village Hall
  coin hoard 250
  Court Leet 65–67, 69
  crosses 63, 76, 100, 101, 184
  deer park and park pale 242
  diocesan school 151
  dovecotes 109
    see also Fields, Culver Close etc.
  early village schools 133, 134, 147–152
  Election Riot, rioters 121, 207–213
  entertainments etc. in 120, 122–124, 156, 160, 161, 164, 165, 198
  fairs 54, 58, 63, 64, 66, 67, 100, 101, 122, 124, 139, 156, 161
  Free School 171
  Hannah More's School 148–152
  Isle of 15
  lockup 257
  Manor of 21, 63, 76, 85, 109, 110, 112, 114, 116, 182
    estate accounts of 52–54
    tithes of 53–54
  Manor House 47–56, 60, 75, 134, 140, 148, 161, 188, 198, 222, 226
    garden 53
    reconstruction and repairs 53, 55
  manorial court
    59, 63, 65, 66, 71, 73, 75, 102
  market cross 63, 76, 100, 101, 184
  markets 28, 29, 63–69, 74, 100, 101
  Methodism in 79, 80, 152
  Peace of 16, 37, 47, 57, 68, 88, 160, 258
  poorhouses 87, 139, 151, 193
  pound 67, 103
  revels 200, 202, 244, 256
  Saxon church 47, 57, 81

Wedmore cont'd
    Saxon royal estate 16, 21, 47, 57
    Saxon hall/*villa regia* 47, 252
    School Board 154
    schools, early village 133, 134, 147–152
    St Mary's Parish Church
        28, 31, 38, 57–62, 97, 181, 199, 258
        baptism in 58–60
        bells 187
        chandeliers 187, 188
        chantry 75
        chantry lands 114, 241
        churchyard 60–62, 193, 250
        churchyard cross 100, 101, 184
        dedication of 58
        Guild of St Mary in 34
        monuments in 49–51, 55, 60–62, 181, 203
        restoration of 13
    street lighting 128, 130, 131
    Village Hall 136, 158, 171
        see also Church Schoolroom
    Wesleyan Chapel
        see Wedmore Methodist Chapel
Wedmore Baptist Chapel 120, 177
Wedmore [Board] School
    34, 133, 154–158, 172, 223
Wedmore Bowls Club 221
Wedmore Brick and Tile Works 121, 137, 138
Wedmore Brook 33, 35, 37, 81, 84, 105, 110,
    111, 138, 139, 140, 236
Wedmore Cheddar Cheese School 144–146
Wedmore Chronicles 13
Wedmore Electric Light and Power Company
    128, 129, 131–139
Wedmore Free School 171
Wedmore Gas Company Ltd 73, 126–129
Wedmore Golf Course 220
Wedmore Methodist Chapel
    79, 128, 152, 171–173, 196
Wedmore Moor
    36, 96–99, 110, 137, 236, 240, 241
Welch, James 112
Wells *see* Springs and Wells
Wells Cathedral 18, 22, 57
    Dean of 28, 149
Wells Old Almshouses 26
Welsh, William 186
Wely, Richard 58
Wensley, James 154, 163
West Pennard 19
West Stoughton *see* Stoughton

West Theale *see* Theale
Weste Mill 114
Westfield Mill 116
Westham 18, 39, 41, 242, 246
Westham Farm 18
Westham Wood 232, 246
Westhay 43
Westholme Farm 219, 220
Westminster Bank 225
Westover, Dr John junior 29, 30, 33, 110, 114, 185
Westover, Dr John senior 113, 114
Westover family 115
Westover, Henry 113, 114
Westover House 32
Westover, Mistress 55
Westover, Mrs senior 113
Westover, William 114
Westovers 114
Westover's Mill, alias Stone's Mill 113, 114
Wheatley, Mr 129
White, Mrs Ann 152, 197
White, Clara 134
White family 61, 164, 202
White, Fred 156
White, Jane 200
White, Revd William 61, 62, 151, 197–202, 244
White, William 16, 61, 62, 150, 152, 197, 198, 199
Whitegates 135, 158
Whitfield House 65, 84, 196
Wichfilde, William 58
Wilberforce, William 150
Wilfred, Bishop 15, 16
Wilkins family 116
Wilkins, George 116, 120
Wilkins, Jane 116
Wilkins, John 116
Wilkins' Mill 116
Wilkins, Sarah 40
Wilkinson, Mr 135
Willet, Thomas 75
William of Northlode 231
William the Conqueror 48, 57
Williams, Amelia 196
Williams, Peter 75
Williams/Willyampus, Peter 64
Williams, Walter 208
Williamson, Revd J 252
Wilmot, Mary 195
Wilson, Mr 79
Windmills 111–125
    Ashton 114

Windmills cont'd
    Ashton Mill 115
    Clapp's Windmill 115
    Crannell Windmill 115
    East Elms 112, 113
    East Mill 113
    East Windmill 111
    Heath House Windmill 116
    Panborough 111
    Stone's Mill 113, 114
    Stoughton Windmill 115, 116
    Weste Mill 114
    Westover's 113, 114
Withers, WR 134
Wollen, Joseph 36, 150, 191, 193, 198
Women's Voluntary Service 219, 225, 226, 227
Woodward, Ralph 211
Woolcott, Mrs 214
Woolcott, Police Constable Robert 213
Worten, Ann 51
Wride, Eric 40
Wright, George 162

Y

Yate 51, 182
Yeo *see* River Yeo
Yeo Moor/Yeomoor 96, 97, 237, 241, 244, 249
Yeomoor 241
Young, John 67
Young, Sir George 50

Z

Zond 249